The Complete Wor

Washington Irving

Life and Voyages of Columbus

THE KELMSCOTT SOCIETY

PUBLISHERS : : NEW YORK

BOOK X.

CHAPTER 1.

DEPARTURE OF COLUMBUS FROM SPAIN ON HIS THIRD VOYAGE — DISCOVERY OF TRINIDAD.

[1498.]

On the 30th of May, 1498, Columbus set sail from the port of San Lucar de Barrameda, with his squadron of six vessels, on his third voyage of discovery. The route he proposed to take was different from that pursued in his former voyages He intended to depart from the Cape de Verde Islands, sailing to the south-west, until he should come under the equinoctial line, then to steer directly westward, with the favor of the trade-winds, until he should arrive at land, or find himself in the longitude of Hispaniola. Various considerations induced him to adopt this course. In his preceding voyage, when he coasted the southern side of Cuba, under the belief that it was the continent of Asia, he had observed that it swept off toward the south. From this circumstance, and from information gathered among the natives of the Caribbee Islands, he was induced to believe that a great tract of the main-land lay to the south of the countries he had already discovered. King John II. of Portugal appears to have entertained a similar idea: as Herrera records an opinion expressed by that monarch, that there was a continent in the southern ocean.[2] If this were the case, it was supposed by Columbus that, in proportion as he approached the equator, and extended his discoveries to climates more and more under the torrid influence of the sun, he should find the productions of nature sublimated by its rays to more perfect and precious qualities. He was strengthened in this belief by a letter written to him at the command of the queen, by one Jayne Ferrer, an eminent and learned lapidary, who, in the

---

[1] Herrera, Hist. Ind., decad. 1. lib. iii. cap. 9.

course of his trading for precious stones and metals, had been in the Levant and in various parts of the East; had conversed with the merchants of the remote parts of Asia and Africa, and the natives of India, Arabia, and Ethiopia, and was considered deeply versed in geography generally, but especially in the natural histories of those countries whence the valuable merchandise in which he dealt was procured. In this letter Ferrer assured Columbus that, according to his experience, the rarest objects of commerce, such as gold, precious stones, drugs, and spices, were chiefly to be found in the regions about the equinoctial line, where the inhabitants were black, or darkly colored; and that until the admiral should arrive among people of such complexions he did not think he would find those articles in great abundance.[1]

Columbus expected to find such people more to the south. He recollected that the natives of Hispaniola had spoken of black men who had once come to their island from the south and south-east, the heads of whose javelins were of a sort of metal which they called Guanin. They had given the admiral specimens of this metal, which, on being assayed in Spain, proved to be a mixture of eighteen parts gold, six silver, and eight copper, a proof of valuable mines in the country whence they came. Charlevoix conjectures that these black people may have come from the Canaries, or the western coast of Africa, and been driven by tempest to the shores of Hispaniola.[2] It is probable, however, that Columbus had been misinformed as to their color, or had misunderstood his informants. It is difficult to believe that the natives of Africa, or the Canaries, could have performed a voyage of such magnitude, in the frail and scantily provided barks they were accustomed to use.

It was to ascertain the truth of all these suppositions, and if correct, to arrive at the favored and opulent countries about the equator, inhabited by people of similar complexions with those of the Africans under the line, that Columbus in his present voyage to the New World took a course much farther to the south than that which he had hitherto pursued.

Having heard that a French squadron was cruising off Cape St. Vincent, he stood to the south-west after leaving St. Lucar, touching at the islands of Porto Santo and Madeira, where he remained a few days taking in wood and water and other supplies, and then continued his course to the Canary Islands. On the 19th of June he arrived at Gomara, where there lay at anchor

[1] Navarrete, Colec., tom. ii. doc. 68
[2] Charlevoix, Hist. St. Domingo, lib. iii. p. 162.

a French cruiser with two Spanish prizes. On seeing the squadron of Columbus standing into the harbor, the captain of the privateer put to sea in all haste, followed by his prizes; one of which, in the hurry of the moment, left part of her crew on shore, making sail with only four of her armament and six Spanish prisoners. The admiral at first mistook them for merchant ships alarmed by his warlike appearance: when informed of the truth, however, he sent three of his vessels in pursuit, but they were too distant to be overtaken. The six Spaniards, however, on board of one of the prizes, seeing assistance at hand, rose on their captors, and the admiral's vessel coming up, the prize was retaken, and brought back in triumph to the port. The admiral relinquished the ship to the captain, and gave up the prisoners to the governor of the island, to be exchanged for six Spaniards carried off by the cruiser [1]

Leaving Gomara on the 21st of June, Columbus divided his squadron off the island of Ferro: three of the ships he despatched direct for Hispaniola, to carry supplies to the colony. One of these ships was commanded by Alonzo Sanchez de Caravajal, native of Baeza, a man of much worth and integrity; the second by Pedro de Arana of Cordova, brother of Doña Beatrix Henriquez, the mother of the admiral's second son, Fernando. He was cousin also of the unfortunate officer who commanded the fortress of La Navidad at the time of the massacre. The third was commanded by Juan Antonio Columbus (or Colombo), a Genoese, related to the admiral, a man of much judgment and capacity. These captains were alternately to have the command, and bear the signal light a week at a time. The admiral carefully pointed out their course. When they came in sight of Hispaniola they were to steer for the south side, for the new port and town, which he supposed to be by this time established in the mouth of the Ozema, according to royal orders sent out by Coronel. With the three remaining vessels the admiral prosecuted his voyage toward the Cape de Verde Islands. The ship in which he sailed was decked, the other two were merchant caravels.[2] As he advanced within the tropics the change of climate and the close and sultry weather brought on a severe attack of the gout, followed by a violent fever. Notwithstanding his painful illness, he enjoyed the full possession of his faculties, and continued to keep his reckoning and make his observations with his usual vigilance and minuteness.

[1] Hist. del Almirante, cap. 66.　　[2] P. Martyr, decad. 1. lib. vi.

On the 27th of June he arrived among the Cape de Verde Islands, which, instead of the freshness and verdure which their name would betoken, presented an aspect of the most cheerless sterility. He remained among these islands but a very few days, being disappointed in his expectation of obtaining goats' flesh for ships' provisions, and cattle for stock for the island of Hispaniola. To procure them would require some delay; in the mean time the health of himself and of his people suffered under the influence of the weather. The atmosphere was loaded with clouds and vapors; neither sun nor star was to be seen; a sultry, depressing temperature prevailed; and the livid looks of the inhabitants bore witness to the insalubrity of the climate.[1]

Leaving the island of Buena Vista on the 5th of July, Columbus stood to the south-west, intending to continue on until he found himself under the equinoctial line. The currents, however, which ran to the north and north-west among these islands impeded his progress. and kept him for two days in sight of the Island del Fuego. The volcanic summit of this island, which, seen at a distance, resembled a church with a lofty steeple, and which was said at times to emit smoke and flames, was the last point discerned of the Old World.

Continuing to the south-west about one hundred and twenty leagues, he found himself, on the 13th of July, according to his observations, in the fifth degree of north latitude. He had entered that region which extends for eight or ten degrees on each side of the line, and is known among seamen by the name of the calm latitudes The trade-winds from the south-east and north-east, meeting in the neighborhood of the equator, neutralize each other, and a steady calmness of the elements is produced. The whole sea is like a mirror, and vessels remain almost motionless, with flapping sails; the crews panting under the heat of a vertical sun, unmitigated by any refreshing breeze. Weeks are sometimes employed in crossing this torpid tract of the ocean.

The weather for some time past had been cloudy and oppressive; but on the 13th there was a bright and burning sun. The wind suddenly fell, and a dead sultry calm commenced, which lasted for eight days. The air was like a furnace; the tar melted, the seams of the ships yawned, the salt meat became putrid; the wheat was parched as if with fire; the hoops shrank from the wine and water casks, some of which leaked, and

---

[1] Hist. del Almirante, cap. 65.

others burst, while the heat in the holds of the vessels was so suffocating that no one could remain below a sufficient time to prevent the damage that was taking place. The mariners lost all strength and spirits, and sank under the oppressive heat. It seemed as if the old fable of the torrid zone was about to be realized ; and that they were approaching a fiery region, where it would be impossible to exist. It is true the heavens were, for a great part of the time, overcast, and there were drizzling showers ; but the atmosphere was close and stifling, and there was that combination of heat and moisture which relaxes all the energies of the human frame.

During this time the admiral suffered extremely from the gout, but, as usual, the activity of his mind. heightened by his anxiety, allowed him no indulgence nor repose. He was in an unknown part of the ocean, where every thing depended upon his vigilance and sagacity ; and was continually watching the phenomena of the elements, and looking out for signs of land. Finding the heat so intolerable, he altered his course, and steered to the south-west. hoping to find a milder temperature farther on, even under the same parallel. He had observed, in his previous voyages. that after sailing westward a hundred leagues from the Azores, a wonderful change took place in the sea and sky, both becoming serene and bland, and the air temperate and refreshing. He imagined that a peculiar mildness and suavity prevailed over a great tract of ocean extending from north to south, into which the navigator, sailing from east to west, would suddenly enter, as if crossing a line. The event seemed to justify his theory, for after making their way slowly for some time to the westward, through an ordeal of heats and calms, with a murky, stifling atmosphere, the ships all at once emerged into a genial region, a pleasant, cooling breeze played over the surface of the sea, and gently filled their sails, the close and drizzling clouds broke away, the sky became serene and clear, and the sun shone forth with all its splendor. but no longer with a burning heat.

Columbus had intended on reaching this temperate tract. to have stood once more to the south and then westward ; but the late parching weather had opened the seams of his ships. and caused them to leak excessively, so that it was necessary to seek a harbor as soon as possible. where they might be refitted. Much of the provisions also was spoiled, and the water nearly exhausted. He kept on therefore directly to the west. trusting, from the flights of birds and other favorable indications, he should soon arrive at land. Day after day passed **away** without his expectations being realized. The distresses of his men became continually more urgent, wherefore, supposing himself in the longitude of the Caribbee Islands, he bore away toward the northward in search of them.[1]

On the 31st of July there was not above one cask of water remaining in each ship, when, about midday, a mariner at the masthead beheld the summits of three mountains rising above the horizon, and gave the joyful cry of land. As the ships drew nearer it was seen that these mountains were united at the base. Columbus had determined to give the first land he should behold the name of the Trinity. The appearance of these three mountains united into one struck him as a singular coincidence; and, with a solemn feeling of devotion, he gave the island the name of La Trinidad, which it bears at the present day.[2]

CHAPTER II.

VOYAGE THROUGH THE GULF OF PARIA.

[1498.]

SHAPING his course for the island. Columbus approached its eastern extremity, to which he gave the name of Punta de la Galera, from a rock in the sea, which resembled a galley under sail. He was obliged to coast for five leagues along the southern shore before he could find safe anchorage. On the following day (August 1), he continued coasting westward, in search of water and a convenient harbor where the vessels might be careened. He was surprised at the verdure and fertility of the country, having expected to find it more parched and sterile as he approached the equator; whereas he beheld groves of palm-trees and luxuriant forests, sweeping down to the seaside, with fountains and running streams. The shores were low and uninhabited, but the country rose in the interior, was cultivated in many places, and enlivened by hamlets and scattered habitations. In a word, the softness and purity of the climate, and the verdure, freshness, and sweetness of the country, appeared to him to equal the delights of early spring in the beautiful province of Valencia.[3]

Anchoring at a point to which he gave the name of Punta de

---

[1] Hist. del Almirante, cap. 67.   [2] Ibid., ubi sup
[3] Letter of Columbus to the Sovereigns from Hispaniola, Navarrete, Colec. tom. l.

la Playa, he sent the boats on shore for water. They found an abundant and limpid brook, at which they filled their casks, but there was no safe harbor for the vessels, nor could they meet with any of the islanders, though they found prints of footsteps, and various fishing implements, left behind in the hurry of flight. There were tracks also of animals, which they supposed to be goats, but which must have been deer, with which, as it was afterward ascertained, the island abounded.

While coasting the island Columbus beheld land to the south, stretching to the distance of more than twenty leagues. It was that low tract of coast intersected by the numerous branches of the Oronoco, but the admiral, supposing it to be an island, gave it the name of La Isla Santa : little imagining that he now for the first time beheld that continent, that Terra Firma, which had been the object of his earnest search.

On the 2d of August he continued on to the south-west point of Trinidad, which he called Point Arenal. It stretched toward a corresponding point of Terra Firma, making a narrow pass, with a high rock in the centre, to which he gave the name of El Gallo. Near this pass the ships cast anchor. As they were approaching this place, a large canoe with five and twenty Indians put off from the shore, but paused on coming within bow-shot, and hailed the ships in a language which no one on board understood. Columbus tried to allure the savages on board, by friendly signs, by the display of looking-glasses, basins of polished metal, and various glittering trinkets, but all in vain. They remained gazing in mute wonder for above two hours, with their paddles in their hands, ready to take to flight on the least attempt to approach them. They were all young men, well formed, and naked, excepting bands and fillets of cotton about their heads, and colored cloths of the same about their loins. They were armed with bows and arrows, the latter feathered and tipped with bone, and they had bucklers, an article of armor seen for the first time among the inhabitants of the New World.

Finding all other means to attract them ineffectual, Columbus now tried the power of music. He knew the fondness of the Indians for dances performed to the sound of their rude drums and the chant of their traditional ballads. He ordered something similar to be executed on the deck of his ship, where, while one man sang to the beat of the tabor, and the sound of other musical instruments, the ship-boys danced, after the popular Spanish fashion. No sooner, however, did this symphony strike up, than the Indians, mistaking it for a signal of hostilities, put their bucklers on their arms, seized their bows, and let fly a shower of arrows. This rude salutation was immediately answered by the discharge of a couple of cross-bows, which put the auditors to flight, and concluded this singular entertainment.

Though thus shy of the admiral's vessel, they approached one of the caravels without hesitation, and, running under the stern, had a parley with the pilot, who gave a cap and a mantle to the one who appeared to be the chieftain. He received the presents with great delight, inviting the pilot by signs to come to land, where he should be well entertained, and receive great presents in return. On his appearing to consent, they went to shore to wait for him. The pilot put off in the boat of the caravel to ask permission of the admiral, but the Indians, seeing him go on board of the hostile ship, suspected some treachery, and springing into their canoe, darted away, nor was any thing more seen of them.[1]

The complexion and other physical characteristics of these savages caused much surprise and speculation in the mind of Columbus. Supposing himself in the seventh degree of latitude, though actually in the tenth, he expected to find the inhabitants similar to the natives of Africa under the same parallel, who were black and ill-shaped, with crisped hair, or rather wool; whereas these were well formed, had long hair, and were even fairer than those more distant from the equator. The climate, also, instead of being hotter as he approached the equinoctial, appeared more temperate. He was now in the dog-days, yet the nights and mornings were so cool that it was necessary to use covering as in winter. This is the case in many parts of the torrid zone, especially in calm weather, when there is no wind, for nature, by heavy dews, in the long nights of those latitudes, cools and refreshes the earth after the great heats of the day. Columbus was at first greatly perplexed by these contradictions to the course of nature, as observed in the Old World; they were in opposition also to the expectations he had founded on the theory of Ferrer the lapidary, but they gradually contributed to the formation of a theory which was springing up in his active imagination, and which will be presently shown.

After anchoring at Point Arenal, the crews were permitted to land and refresh themselves. There were no runs of water, but by sinking pits in the sand they soon obtained sufficient to

---

[1] Hist. del Almirante, cap 88. P. Martyr, decad. i lib vi. Las Casas, Hist Ind., lib. cap. 138. MS. Letter of Columbus to the Castilian Sovereigns. Navarrete Colec., tom i.

fill the casks. The anchorage, at this place, however, was extremely insecure. A rapid current set from the eastward through the strait formed by the main-land and the island of Trinidad, flowing, as Columbus observed, night and day, with as much fury as the Guadalquiver when swollen by floods. In the pass between Point Arenal and its corresponding point, the confined current boiled and raged to such a degree that he thought it was crossed by a reef of rocks and shoals, preventing all entrance. with others extending beyond, over which the waters roared like breakers on a rocky shore. To this pass, from its angry and dangerous appearance, he gave the name of Boca del Sierpe (the Mouth of the Serpent). He thus found himself placed between two difficulties. The continual current from the east seemed to prevent all return, while the rocks which appeared to beset the pass threatened destruction if he should proceed. Being on board of his ship, late at night, kept awake by painful illness and an anxious and watchful spirit, he heard a terrible roaring from the south, and beheld the sea heaped up, as it were, into a great ridge or hill, the height of the ship, covered with foam, and rolling toward him with a tremendous uproar. As this furious surge approached, rendered more terrible in appearance by the obscurity of night, he trembled for the safety of his vessels. His own ship was suddenly lifted up to such a height that he dreaded lest it should be overturned or cast upon the rocks, while another of the ships was torn violently from her anchorage. The crews were for a time in great consternation, fearing they should be swallowed up; but the mountainous surge passed on. and gradually subsided, after a violent contest with the counter-current of the strait.[1] This sudden rush of water, it is supposed, was caused by the swelling of one of the rivers which flow into the Gulf of Paria, and which were as yet unknown to Columbus.

Anxious to extricate himself from this dangerous neighborhood, he sent the boats on the following morning to sound the depth of water at the Boca del Sierpe, and to ascertain whether it was possible for ships to pass through to the northward To his great joy, they returned with a report that there were several fathoms of water, and currents and eddies setting both ways, either to enter or return. A favorable breeze prevailing, he immediately made sail, and passing through the formidable strait in safety, found himself in a tranquil expanse beyond.

He was now on the inner side of Trinidad. To his left

---

[1] Letter of Columbus to the Castilian Sovereigns, Navarrete, Colec., tom 1. Herrera Hist. Ind., decad. i. lib. iii. cap. 10. Hist. del Almirante, cap. 69.

spread the broad gulf since known by the name of Paria, which
he supposed to be the open sea, but was surprised, on tasting
it, to find the water fresh. He continued northward, toward a
mountain at the north-west point of the island, about fourteen
leagues from Point Arenal. Here he beheld two lofty capes
opposite each other, one on the island of Trinidad, the other
to the west, on the long promontory of Paria, which stretches
from the main-land and forms the northern side of the gulf,
but which Columbus mistook for an island, and named Isla de
Gracia.

Between these capes there was another pass, which appeared
even more dangerous than the Boca del Sierpe, being beset with
rocks, among which the current forced its way with roaring
turbulence. To this pass Columbus gave the name of Boca del
Dragon. Not choosing to encounter its apparent dangers, he
turned northward, on Sunday, the 5th of August, and steered
along the inner side of the supposed island of Gracia, intending
to keep on until he came to the end of it, and then to strike
northward into the free and open ocean, and shape his course
for Hispaniola.

It was a fair and beautiful coast, indented with fine harbors
lying close to each other; the country cultivated in many
places, in others covered with fruit-trees and stately forests,
and watered by frequent streams. What greatly astonished
Columbus was still to find the water fresh, and that it grew
more and more so the farther he proceeded, it being that season of the year when the various rivers which empty themselves
into this gulf are swollen by rains, and pour forth such quantities of fresh water as to conquer the saltness of the ocean.
He was also surprised at the placidity of the sea, which appeared as tranquil and safe as one vast harbor, so that there
was no need of seeking a port to anchor in.

As yet he had not been able to hold any communication with
the people of this part of the New World. The shores which
he had visited, though occasionally cultivated, were silent and
deserted, and, excepting the fugitive party in the canoe at
Point Arenal, he had seen nothing of the natives. After sailing several leagues along the coast, he anchored, on Monday,
the 6th of August, at a place where there appeared signs of
cultivation, and sent the boats on shore. They found recent
traces of people, but not an individual was to be seen. The
coast was hilly, covered with beautiful and fruitful groves, and
abounding with monkeys. Continuing farther westward, to where
the country was more level, Columbus anchored in a river.

Immediately a canoe, with three or four Indians, came off to the caravel nearest to the shore, the captain of which, pretending a desire to accompany them to land, sprang into their canoe, overturned it, and, with the assistance of his seamen, secured the Indians as they were swimming. When brought to the admiral, he gave them beads, hawks' bells, and sugar, and sent them highly gratified on shore, where many of their countrymen were assembled. This kind treatment had the usual effect. Such of the natives as had canoes came off to the ships with the fullest confidence. They were tall of stature, finely formed, and free and graceful in their movements. Their hair was long and straight: some wore it cut short, but none of them braided it, as was the custom among the natives of Hispaniola. They were armed with bows, arrows, and targets; the men wore cotton cloths about their heads and loins, beautifully wrought with various colors, so as at a distance to look like silk; but the women were entirely naked. They brought bread, maize, and other eatables, with different kinds of beverage, some white, made from maize, and resembling beer, and others green, of a vinous flavor, and expressed from various fruits. They appeared to judge of every thing by the sense of smell, as others examine objects by the sight or touch. When they approached a boat, they smelt to it, and then to the people. In like manner every thing that was given them was tried. They set but little value upon beads, but were extravagantly delighted with hawks' bells. Brass was also held in high estimation: they appeared to find something extremely grateful in the smell of it, and called it Turey, signifying that it was from the skies.[1]

From these Indians, Columbus understood that the name of their country was Paria, and that farther to the west he would find it more populous. Taking several of them to serve as guides and mediators, he proceeded eight leagues westward to a point which he called Aguja or the Needle. Here he arrived at three o'clock in the morning. When the day dawned he was delighted with the beauty of the country. It was cultivated in many places, highly populous, and adorned with magnificent vegetation; habitations were interspersed among groves laden with fruits and flowers; grape-vines intwined themselves among the trees, and birds of brilliant plumage fluttered from branch to branch. The air was temperate and bland, and sweetened by the fragrance of flowers and blossoms

---

[1] Herrera, Hist Ind., decad. i. lib. iii. cap. 11.

and numerous fountains and limpid streams kept up a universal verdure and freshness. Columbus was so much charmed with the beauty and amenity of this part of the coast that he gave it the name of The Gardens.

The natives came off in great numbers, in canoes, of superior construction to those hitherto seen, being very large and light, with a cabin in the centre for the accommodation of the owner and his family. They invited Columbus, in the name of their king, to come to land. Many of them had collars and burnished plates about their necks, of that inferior kind of gold called by the Indians Guanin. They said that it came from a high land, which they pointed out, at no great distance, to the west, but intimated that it was dangerous to go there, either because the inhabitants were cannibals, or the place infested by venomous animals.[1] But what aroused the attention and awakened the cupidity of the Spaniards, was the sight of strings of pearls round the arms of some of the natives. These, they informed Columbus, were procured on the seacoast, on the northern side of Paria, which he still supposed to be an island; and they showed the mother-of-pearl shells whence they had been taken. Anxious for further information, and to procure specimens of these pearls to send to Spain, he despatched the boats to shore. A multitude of the natives came to the beach to receive them, headed by the chief cacique and his son. They treated the Spaniards with profound reverence, as beings descended from heaven, and conducted them to a spacious house, the residence of the cacique, where they were regaled with bread and various fruits of excellent flavor, and the different kinds of beverage already mentioned. While they were in the house, the men remained together at one end of it, and the women at the other. After they had finished their collation at the house of the cacique, they were taken to that of his son, where a like repast was set before them. These people were remarkably affable, though, at the same time, they possessed a more intrepid and martial air and spirit than the natives of Cuba and Hispaniola. They were fairer, Columbus observes, than any he had yet seen, though so near to the equinoctial line, where he had expected to find them of the color of Ethiopians. Many ornaments of gold were seen among them, but all of an inferior quality: one Indian had a piece of the size of an apple. They had various kinds of domesticated parrots, one of a light green color, with a yellow neck, and the

---

[1] Letter of Columbus to the Castilian Sovereigns, Navarrete, Colec., tom. i. p. 252.

tips of the wings of a bright red; others of the size of domestic fowls, and of a vivid scarlet, excepting some azure feathers in the wings. These they readily gave to the Spaniards; but what the latter most coveted were the pearls, of which they saw many necklaces and bracelets among the Indian women. The latter gladly gave them in exchange for hawks' bells or any article of brass, and several specimens of fine pearls were procured for the admiral to send to the sovereign.[1]

The kindness and amity of this people were heightened by an intelligent demeanor and a martial frankness. They seemed worthy of the beautiful country they inhabited. It was a cause of great concern both to them and the Spaniards, that they could not understand each other's language. They conversed, however, by signs: mutual good-will made their intercourse easy and pleasant; and at the hour of vespers the Spaniards returned on board of their ships, highly gratified with their entertainment.

CHAPTER III.

CONTINUATION OF THE VOYAGE THROUGH THE GULF OF PARIA — RETURN TO HISPANIOLA.

[1498.]

THE quantity of fine pearls found among the natives of Paria was sufficient to arouse the sanguine anticipations of Columbus. It appeared to corroborate the theory of Ferrer, the learned jeweller, that as he approached the equator he would find the most rare and precious productions of nature. His active imagination, with its intuitive rapidity, seized upon every circumstance in unison with his wishes, and, combining them, drew thence the most brilliant inferences. He had read in Pliny that pearls are generated from drops of dew which fall into the mouths of oysters; if so, what place could be more propitious to their growth and multiplication than the coast of Paria? The dew in those parts was heavy and abundant, and the oysters were so plentiful that they clustered about the roots and pendent branches of the mangrove trees, which grew within the margin of the tranquil sea. When a branch which had drooped for a time in the

---

[1] Letter of Columbus. Herrera, Hist. Ind., decad. 1. lib. iii. cap. 11. Hist. del Almirante, cap. 70.

water was drawn forth. it was found covered with oysters. Las Casas, noticing this sanguine conclusion of Columbus, observes, that the shell-fish here spoken of are not of the kind which produce pearl, for that those by a natural instinct, as if conscious of their precious charge, hide themselves in the deepest water.[1]

Still imagining the coast of Paria to be an island, and anxious to circumnavigate it, and arrive at the place where these pearls were said by the Indians to abound, Columbus left the Gardens on the 10th of August, and continued coasting westward within the gulf, in search of an outlet to the north. He observed portions of Terra Firma appearing toward the bottom of the gulf, which he supposed to be islands, and called them Isabeta and Tramontana, and fancied that the desired outlet to the sea must lie between them. As he advanced, however, he found the water continually growing shallower and fresher, until he did not dare to venture any farther with his ship. which. he observed. was of too great a size for expeditions of this kind, being of an hundred tons burden. and requiring three fathoms of water. He came to anchor, therefore, and sent a light caravel called the Correo, to ascertain whether there was an outlet to the ocean between the supposed islands. The caravel returned on the following day. reporting that at the western end of the gulf there was an opening of two leagues, which led into an inner and circular gulf. surrounded by four openings, apparently smaller gulfs, or rather mouths of rivers, from which flowed the great quantity of fresh water that sweetened the neighboring sea. In fact, from one of these mouths issued the great river the Cuparipari. or, as it is now called, the Paria. To this inner and circular gulf Columbus gave the name of the Gulf of Pearls, through a mistaken idea that they abounded in its waters, though none, in fact. are found there. He still imagined that the four openings of which the mariners spoke might be intervals between islands, though they affirmed that all the land he saw was connected.[2] As it was impossible to proceed farther westward with his ships. he had no alternative but to retrace his course, and seek an exit to the north by the Boca del Dragon. He would gladly have continued for some time to explore this coast, for he considered himself in one of those opulent regions described as the most favored upon earth, and which increase in riches toward the equator.

---

[1] Las Casas, Hist. Ind., cap. 136.   [2] Hist. del Almirante. cap 75.

Imperious considerations, however, compelled him to shorten his voyage, and hasten to San Domingo. The sea-stores of his ships were almost exhausted, and the various supplies for the colony, with which they were freighted, were in danger of spoiling. He was suffering, also, extremely in his health. Besides the gout, which had rendered him a cripple for the greater part of the voyage, he was afflicted by a complaint in his eyes, caused by fatigue and over-watching, which almost deprived him of sight. Even the voyage along the coast of Cuba, he observes, in which he was three and thirty days almost without sleep, had not so injured his eyes and disordered his frame, or caused him so much painful suffering as the present.[1]

On the 11th of August, therefore, he set sail eastward for the Boca del Dragon, and was borne along with great velocity by the currents, which, however, prevented him from landing again at his favorite spot, the Gardens. On Sunday, the 13th, he anchored near to the Boca, in a fine harbor, to which he gave the name of Puerto de Gatos, from a species of monkey called gato paulo, with which the neighborhood abounded. On the margin of the sea he perceived many trees which, as he thought, produced the mirabolane, a fruit only found in the countries of the East. There were great numbers also of mangroves growing within the water, with oysters clinging to their branches, their mouths open, as he supposed, to receive the dew, which was afterward to be transformed to pearls.[2]

On the following morning, the 14th of August, toward noon the ships approached the Boca del Dragon, and prepared to venture through that formidable pass. The distance from Cape Boto at the end of Paria, and Cape Lapa the extremity of Trinidad, is about five leagues; but in the interval there were two islands, which Columbus named Caracol and Delphin. The impetuous body of fresh water which flows through the gulf, particularly in the rainy months of July and August, is confined at the narrow outlets between these islands, where it causes a turbulent sea, foaming and roaring as if breaking over rocks, and rendering the entrance and exit of the gulf extremely dangerous. The horrors and perils of such places are always tenfold to discoverers, who have no chart, nor pilot, nor advice of previous voyager, to guide them. Columbus, at first, apprehended sunken rocks and shoals; but on attentively considering the commotion of the strait, he attributed it to the conflict be-

---

[1] Letter of Columbus to the Sovereigns, Navarrete, tom. i. p 252.
[2] Herrera, Hist. Ind., decad. i. lib. iii. cap. 10.

tween the prodigious body of fresh water setting through the gulf and struggling for an outlet, and the tide of salt water struggling to enter. The ships had scarcely ventured into the fearful channel when the wind died away, and they were in danger every moment of being thrown upon the rocks or sands. The current of fresh water, however, gained the victory, and carried them safely through. The admiral, when once more safe in the open sea, congratulated himself upon his escape from this perilous strait, which he observes, might well be called the mouth of the Dragon.[1]

He now stood to the westward. running along the outer coast of Paria, still supposing it an island, and intending to visit the Gulf of Pearls. which he imagined to be at the end of it, opening to the sea. He wished to ascertain whether this great body of fresh water proceeded from rivers, as the crew of the caravel Correo had affirmed; for it appeared to him impossible that the streams of mere islands. as he supposed the surrounding lands, could furnish such a prodigious volume of water.

On leaving the Boca del Dragon, he saw to the north-east, many leagues distant, two islands, which he called Assumption and Conception; probably those now known as Tobago and Granada. In his course along the northern coast of Paria he saw several other small islands and many fine harbors, to some of which he gave names, but they have ceased to be known by them. On the 15th he discovered the islands of Margarita and Cubagua, afterwards famous for their pearl fishery. The Island of Margarita, about fifteen leagues in length and six in breadth, was well peopled The little island of Cubagua, lying between it and the mainland. and only about four leagues from the latter, was dry and sterile, without either wood or fresh water, but possessing a good harbor. On approaching this island the admiral beheld a number of Indians fishing for pearls, who made for the land. A boat being sent to communicate with them, one of the sailors noticed many strings of pearls round the neck of a female. Having a plate of Valencia ware. a kind of porcelain painted and varnished with gaudy colors, he broke it, and presented the pieces to the Indian woman. who gave him in exchange a considerable number of her pearls. These he carried to the admiral, who immediately sent persons on shore, well provided with Valencian plates and hawks' bells, for which in a little time he procured about three pounds' weight

---

[1] Herrera, Hist. Ind., decad i. lib. iii. cap. 11.

of pearls, some of which were of a very large size, and were sent by him afterward to the sovereigns as specimens.[1]

There was great temptation to visit other spots, which the Indians mentioned as abounding in pearls. The coast of Paria also continued extending to the westward as far as the eye could reach, rising into a range of mountains, and provoking examination to ascertain whether, as he began to think, it was a part of the Asiatic continent. Columbus was compelled, however, though with the greatest reluctance, to forego this most interesting investigation.

The malady of his eyes had now grown so virulent that he could no longer take observations or keep a lookout, but had to trust to the reports of the pilots and mariners. He bore away, therefore, for Hispaniola, intending to repose there from the toils of his voyage, and to recruit his health, while he should send his brother, the Adelantado, to complete the discovery of this important country. After sailing for five days to the northwest, he made the island of Hispaniola on the 19th of August, fifty leagues to the westward of the river Ozema, the place of his destination, and anchored on the following morning under the little island of Beata.

He was astonished to find himself so mistaken in his calculations, and so far below his destined port; but he attributed it correctly to the force of the current setting out of the Boca del Dragon, which, while he had lain to at nights, to avoid running on rocks and shoals, had borne his ship insensibly to the west. This current which sets across the Caribbean Sea, and the continuation of which now bears the name of the Gulf Stream, was so rapid, that on the 15th, though the wind was but moderate, the ships had made seventy-five leagues in four and twenty hours. Columbus attributed to the violence of this current the formation of that pass called the Boca del Dragon, where he supposed it had forced its way through a narrow isthmus that formerly connected Trinidad with the extremity of Paria. He imagined, also, that its constant operation had worn away and inundated the borders of the mainland, gradually producing that fringe of islands which stretches from Trinidad to the Lucayos or Bahamas, and which, according to his idea, had originally been part of the solid continent. In corroboration of this opinion, he notices the form of those islands: narrow from north to south, and extending in length from east to west, in the direction of the current.[2]

---

[1] Charlevoix, Hist. St. Domingo. lib. iii p. 169.
[2] Letter to the King and Queen, Navarrete Colec., tom. i.

The island of Beata, where he had anchored, is about thirty leagues to the west of the river Ozema, where he expected to find the new seaport which his brother had been instructed to establish.   The strong and steady current from the east, however, and the prevalence of winds from that quarter, might detain him for a long time at the island, and render the remainder of his voyage slow and precarious.   He sent a boat on shore, therefore, to procure an Indian messenger to take a letter to his brother, the Adelantado.   Six of the natives came off to the ships, one of whom was armed with a Spanish cross-bow. The admiral was alarmed at seeing a weapon of the kind in the possession of an Indian.   It was not an article of traffic, and he feared could only have fallen into his hands by the death of some Spaniard.[1]   He apprehended that further evils had befallen the settlement, during his long absence, and that there had again been troubles with the natives.

Having despatched his messenger, he made sail, and arrived off the mouth of the river on the 30th of August   He was met on the way by a caravel, on board of which was the Adelantado, who, having received his letter, had hastened forth with affectionate ardor to welcome his arrival.   The meeting of the brothers was a cause of mutual joy; they were strongly attached to each other, each had had his trials and sufferings during their long separation, and each looked with confidence to the other for comfort and relief.   Don Bartholomew appears to have always had great deference for the brilliant genius, the enlarged mind, and the commanding reputation of his brother; while the latter placed great reliance in times of difficulty, on the worldly knowledge, the indefatigable activity, and the lionhearted courage of the Adelantado.

Columbus arrived almost the wreck of himself.   His voyages were always of a nature to wear out the human frame, having to navigate amid unknown dangers, and to keep anxious watch, at all hours, and in all weathers.   As age and infirmity increased upon him, these trials became the more severe.   His constitution must originally have been wonderfully vigorous: but constitutions of this powerful kind, if exposed to severe hardships at an advanced period of life, when the frame has become somewhat rigid and unaccommodating, are apt to be suddenly broken up, and to be a prey to violent aches and maladies.   In this last voyage Columbus had been parched and consumed by fever, racked by gout, and his whole system disordered by incessant

---

[1] Las Casas. Hist. Ind.. lib. 1. cap. 148.

watchfulness ; he came into port haggard. emaciated. and almost blind. His spirit, however, was, as usual, superior to all bodily affliction or decay, and he looked forward with magnificent anticipations to the result of his recent discoveries, which he intended should be immediately prosecuted by his hardy and enterprising brother.

CHAPTER IV.

SPECULATIONS OF COLUMBUS CONCERNING THE COAST OF PARIA.

[1498.]

THE natural phenomena of a great and striking nature presented to the ardent mind of Columbus in the course of this voyage, led to certain sound deductions and imaginative speculations The immense body of fresh water flowing into the Gulf of Paria, and thence rushing into the ocean, was too vast to be produced by an island or by islands. It must be the congregated streams of a great extent of country pouring forth in one mighty river, and the land necessary to furnish such a river must be a continent. He now supposed that most of the tracts of land which he had seen about the Gulf were connected ; that the coast of Paria extended westward far beyond a chain of mountains which he had beheld afar off from Margarita ; and that the land opposite to Trinidad, instead of being an island, continued to the south, far beyond the equator, into that hemisphere hitherto unknown to civilized man. He considered all this an extension of the Asiatic continent ; thus presuming that the greater part of the surface of the globe was firm land. In this last opinion he found himself supported by authors of the highest name both ancient and modern : among whom he cites Aristotle and Seneca, St. Augustine and Cardinal Pedro de Alliaco. He lays particular stress also on the assertion of the apocryphal Esdras, that of seven parts of the world, six are dry land, and one part only is covered with water.

The land, therefore, surrounding the Gulf of Paria, was but the border of an almost boundless continent, stretching far to the west and to the south, including the most precious regions of the earth, lying under the most auspicious stars and benignant skies, but as yet unknown and uncivilized, free to be discovered and appropriated by any Christian nation "May it please our Lord," he exclaims in his letter to the sovereigns, "to give long life and health to your highnesses, that you may prosecute this noble enterprise, in which, methinks, God will receive great service, Spain vast increase of grandeur, and all Christians much consolation and delight, since the name of our Saviour will be divulged throughout these lands."

Thus far the deductions of Columbus, though sanguine, admit of little cavil; but he carried them still farther, until they ended in what may appear to some mere chimerical reveries. In his letter to the sovereigns he stated that on his former voyages, when he steered westward from the Azores, he had observed, after sailing about a hundred leagues, a sudden and great change in the sky and the stars, the temperature of the air, and the calmness of the ocean. It seemed as if a line ran from north to south, beyond which every thing became different. The needle which had previously inclined toward the north-east, now varied a whole point to the north-west. The sea, hitherto clear, was covered with weeds so dense that in his first voyage he had expected to run aground upon shoals. A universal tranquillity reigned throughout the elements, and the climate was mild and genial whether in summer or winter. On taking his astronomical observations at night, after crossing that imaginary line, the north star appeared to him to describe a diurnal circle in the heavens, of five degrees in diameter.

On his present voyage he had varied his route, and had run southward from the Cape de Verde Islands for the equinoctial line. Before reaching it, however, the heat had become insupportable, and a wind springing up from the east, he had been induced to strike westward, when in the parallel of Sierra Leone in Guinea. For several days he had been almost consumed by scorching and stifling heat under a sultry yet clouded sky, and in a drizzling atmosphere, until he arrived at the ideal line already mentioned, extending from north to south. Here suddenly, to his great relief, he had emerged into serene weather, with a clear blue sky and a sweet and temperate atmosphere. The farther he had proceeded west, the more pure and genial he had found the climate; the sea tranquil, the breezes soft and balmy. All these phenomena coincided with those he had remarked at the same line, though farther north, in his former voyages, excepting that here there was no herbage in the sea, and the movements of stars were different. The polar star appeared to him here to describe a diurnal circle of ten degrees instead of five; an augmentation which struck him with astonishment, but which, he says, he ascertained by observations taken in different nights, with his quadrant. Its greatest altitude at the former place, in the parallel of the Azores, he had found to be ten degrees, and in the present place fifteen.

From these and other circumstances, he was inclined to doubt the received theory with respect to the form of the earth. Philosophers had described it as spherical; but they knew nothing of the part of the world which he had discovered. The ancient part, known to them, he had no doubt was spherical, but he now supposed the real form of the earth to be that of a pear, one part much more elevated than the rest, and tapering upward toward the skies. This part he supposed to be in the interior of this newly found continent, and immediately under the equator. All the phenomena which he had previously noticed, appeared to corroborate this theory. The variations which he had observed in passing the imaginary line running from north to south, he concluded to be caused by the ships having arrived at this supposed swelling of the earth, where they began gently to mount toward the skies into a purer and more celestial atmosphere.[1] The variation of the needle he ascribed to the same cause, being affected by the coolness and mildness of the climate; varying to the north-west in proportion as the ships continued onward in their ascent.[2] So also the altitude of the north star, and the circle it described in the heavens, appeared to be greater, in consequence of being regarded from a greater elevation, less obliquely, and through a purer medium of atmosphere; and these phenomena would be found to increase the more the navigator approached the equator, from the still increasing eminence of this part of the earth.

He noticed also the difference of climate, vegetation, and people of this part of the New World from those under the same parallel in Africa. There the heat was insupportable, the land parched and sterile, the inhabitants were black, with crisped wool, ill-shapen in their forms, and dull and brutal in their natures. Here, on the contrary, although the sun was in Leo, he found the noontide heat moderate, the mornings and evenings fresh and cool, the country green and fruitful, and covered with beautiful forests, the people fairer even than those in the lands he had discovered farther north, having long hair,

---

[1] Peter Martyr mentions that the admiral told him, that, from the climate of great heat and unwholesome air, he had ascended the back of the sea as it were ascending a high mountain toward heaven. Decad. i. lib. vi.

[2] Columbus, in his attempts to account for the variation of the needle, supposed that the north star possessed the quality of the four cardinal points, as did likewise the loadstone. That if the needle were touched with one part of the loadstone, it would point east, with another west, and so on. Wherefore, he adds, those who prepare or magnetize the needles, cover the loadstone with a cloth, so that the north part only remains out, that is to say, the part which possesses the virtue of causing the needle to point to the north. Hist. del Almirante, cap. 66.

with well-proportioned and graceful forms. lively minds. and courageous dispositions. All this in a latitude so near to the equator. he attributed to the superior altitude of this part of the world, by which it was raised into a more celestial region of the air. On turning northward. through the Gulf of Paria, he had found the circle described by the north star again to diminish. The current of the sea also increased in velocity, wearing away, as has already been remarked, the borders of the continent, and producing by its incessant operation the adjacent islands. This was a further confirmation of the idea that he ascended in going southward, and descended in returning northward.

Aristotle had imagined that the highest part of the earth, and the nearest to the skies, was under the antarctic pole. Other sages had maintained that it was under the arctic. Hence it was apparent that both conceived one part of the earth to be more elevated and noble. and nearer to the heavens than the rest. They did not think of this eminence being under the equinoctial line, observed Columbus, because they had no certain knowledge of this hemisphere. but only spoke of it theoretically and from conjecture.

As usual. he assisted his theory by Holy Writ. "The sun, when God created it," he observes, "was in the first point of the Orient, or the first light was there." That place, according to his idea, must be here, in the remotest part of the East, where the ocean and the extreme part of India meet under the equinoctial line, and where the highest point of the earth is situated.

He supposed this apex of the world, though of immense height, to be neither rugged nor precipitous, but that the land rose to it by gentle and imperceptible degrees. The beautiful and fertile shores of Paria were situated on its remote borders, abounding of course with those precious articles which are congenial with the most favored and excellent climates. As one penetrated the interior and gradually ascended. the land would be found to increase in beauty and luxuriance, and in the exquisite nature of its productions. until one arrived at the summit under the equator. This he imagined to be the noblest and most perfect place on earth, enjoying from its position an equality of nights and days and a uniformity of seasons; and being elevated into a serene and heavenly temperature, above the heats and colds, the clouds and vapors, the storms and tempests which deform and disturb the lower regions In a word, here he supposed to be situated the original abode of our first parents, the primitive seat of human innocence and bliss, the Garden of Eden, or terrestrial paradise!

He imagined this place, according to the opinion of the most eminent fathers of the church, to be still flourishing, possessed of all its blissful delights, but inaccessible to mortal feet, excepting by divine permission. From this height he presumed, though of course from a great distance, proceeded the mighty stream of fresh water which filled the Gulf of Paria, and sweetened the salt ocean in its vicinity, being supplied by the fountain mentioned in Genesis as springing from the tree of life in the Garden of Eden.

Such was the singular speculation of Columbus. which he details at full length in a letter to the Castilian sovereigns,[1] citing various authorities for his opinions, among which were St. Augustine, St. Isidor, and St. Ambrosius, and fortifying his theory with much of that curious and speculative erudition in which he was deeply versed.[2] It shows how his ardent mind was heated by the magnificence of his discoveries. Shrewd men, in the coolness and quietude of ordinary life, and in these modern days of cautious and sober fact, may smile at such a revery, but it was countenanced by the speculations of the most sage and learned of those times; and if this had not been the case, could we wonder at any sally of the imagination in a man placed in the situation of Columbus? He beheld a vast world, rising, as it were, into existence before him, its nature and extent unknown and undefined, as yet a mere region for conjecture. Every day displayed some new feature of beauty and sublimity; island after island, where the rocks, he was told. were veined with gold, the groves teemed with spices, or the shores abounded with pearls. Interminable ranges of coast. promontory beyond promontory. stretching as far as the eye could reach, luxuriant valleys sweeping away into a vast interior. whose distant mountains. he was told. concealed still happier lands, and realms of greater opulence. When he looked upon all this region of golden promise. it was with the glorious conviction that his genius had called it into existence; he regarded it with the triumphant eye of a discoverer. Had

---

[1] Navarrete, Colec de Viages, tom. i p 242.

[2] See Illustrations, article "Situation of the Terrestrial Paradise."

NOTE. — A great part of these speculations appear to have been founded on the treatise of the Cardinal Pedro de Aliaco, in which Columbus found a compendium of the opinions of various eminent authors on the subject; though it is very probable he consulted many of their works likewise. In the volume of Pedro de Aliaco, existing in the library of the Cathedral at Seville, I have traced the germs of these ideas in various passages of the text, opposite to which marginal notes have been made in the handwriting of Columbus.

not Columbus been capable of these enthusiastic soarings of the imagination, he might, with other sages, have reasoned calmly and coldly in his closet about the probability of a continent existing in the west; but he would never have had the daring enterprise to adventure in search of it into the unknown realms of ocean.

Still, in the midst of his fanciful speculations, we find that sagacity which formed the basis of his character. The conclusion which he drew from the great flow of the Oronoco, that it must be the outpouring of a continent, was acute and striking. A learned Spanish historian has also ingeniously excused other parts of his theory. " He suspected," observes he, " a certain elevation of the globe at one part of the equator; philosophers have since determined the world to be a spheroid, slightly elevated in its equatorial circumference. He suspected that the diversity of temperatures influenced the needle, not being able to penetrate the cause of its inconstant variations; the successive series of voyages and experiments have made this inconstancy more manifest, and have shown that extreme cold sometimes divests the needle of all its virtue. Perhaps new observations may justify the surmise of Columbus. Even his error concerning the circle described by the polar star, which he thought augmented by an optical illusion in proportion as the observer approached the equinox, manifests him a philosopher superior to the time in which he lived." [1]

---

[1] Muñoz, Hist. N Mundo, lib. vi § 32.

BOOK XI.

CHAPTER I.

ADMINISTRATION OF THE ADELANTADO — EXPEDITION TO THE PROVINCE OF XARAGUA.

[1498.]

COLUMBUS had anticipated repose from his toils on arriving at Hispaniola, but a new scene of trouble and anxiety opened upon him, destined to impede the prosecution of his enterprises, and to affect all his future fortunes. To explain this, it is necessary to relate the occurrences of the island during his long detention in Spain.

When he sailed for Europe in March, 1496, his brother, Don Bartholomew, who remained as Adelantado, took the earliest measures to execute his directions with respect to the mines recently discovered by Miguel Diaz on the south side of the island. Leaving Don Diego Columbus in command at Isabella, he repaired with a large force to the neighborhood of the mines, and, choosing a favorable situation in a place most abounding in ore, built a fortress, to which he gave the name of San Christoval. The workmen, however, finding grains of gold among the earth and stone employed in its construction, gave it the name of the Golden Tower.[1]

The Adelantado remained here three months, superintending the building of the fortress, and making the necessary preparations for working the mines and purifying the ore. The progress of the work, however, was greatly impeded by scarcity of provisions, having frequently to detach a part of the men about the country in quest of supplies. The former hospitality of the island was at an end. The Indians no longer gave their

---

[1] Peter Martyr, decad. i. lib. iv.

provisions freely; they had learned from the white men to profit by the necessities of the stranger, and to exact a price for bread. Their scanty stores, also, were soon exhausted, for their frugal habits, and their natural indolence and improvidence, seldom permitted them to have more provisions on hand than was requisite for present support.[1] The Adelantado found it difficult, therefore, to maintain so large a force in the neighborhood, until they should have time to cultivate the earth, and raise live-stock, or should receive supplies from Spain. Leaving ten men to guard the fortress, with a dog to assist them in catching utias, he marched with the rest of his men, about four hundred in number, to Fort Conception, in the abundant country of the Vega. He passed the whole month of June collecting the quarterly tribute, being supplied with food by Guarionex and his subordinate caciques. In the following month (July, 1496), the three caravels commanded by Niño arrived from Spain, bringing a re-enforcement of men, and, what was still more needed, a supply of provisions. The latter was quickly distributed among the hungry colonists, but unfortunately a great part had been injured during the voyage. This was a serious misfortune in a community where the least scarcity produced murmur and sedition.

By these ships the Adelantado received letters from his brother directing him to found a town and seaport at the mouth of the Ozema, near to the new mines. He requested him, also, to send prisoners to Spain such of the caciques and their subjects as had been concerned in the death of any of the colonists; that being considered as sufficient ground, by many of the ablest jurists and theologians of Spain, for selling them as slaves. On the return of the caravels, the Adelantado despatched three hundred Indian prisoners, and three caciques. These formed the ill-starred cargoes about which Niño had made such absurd vaunting, as though the ships were laden with treasure, and which had caused such mortification, disappointment, and delay to Columbus.

Having obtained by this arrival a supply of provisions, the Adelantado returned to the fortress of San Christoval, and thence proceeded to the Ozema, to choose a site for the proposed seaport. After a careful examination, he chose the eastern bank of a natural haven at the mouth of the river. It was easy of access, of sufficient depth, and good anchorage. The river ran through a beautiful and fertile country; its

---

[1] Peter Martyr, decad. i. lib. v.

waters were pure and salubrious, and well stocked with fish ; its banks were covered with trees bearing the fine fruits of the island, so that in sailing along, the fruits and flowers might be plucked with the hand from the branches which overhung the stream.[1] This delightful vicinity was the dwelling-place of the female cacique who had conceived an affection for the young Spaniard Miguel Diaz, and had induced him to entice his countrymen to that part of the island. The promise she had given of a friendly reception on the part of her tribe was faithfully performed.

On a commanding bank of the harbor Don Bartholomew erected a fortress, which at first was called Isabella, but afterward San Domingo, and was the origin of the city which still bears that name. The Adelantado was of an active and indefatigable spirit. No sooner was the fortress completed than he left in it a garrison of twenty men, and with the rest of his forces set out to visit the dominions of Behechio, one of the principal chieftains of the island. This cacique, as has already been mentioned, reigned over Xaragua. a province comprising almost the whole coast at the west end of the island, including Cape Tiburon, and extending along the south side as far as Point Aguida, or the small island of Beata. It was one of the most populous and fertile districts, with a delightful climate ; and its inhabitants were softer and more graceful in their manners than the rest of the islanders. Being so remote from all the fortresses, the cacique, although he had taken a part in the combination of the chieftains, had hitherto remained free from the incursions and exactions of the white men.

With this cacique resided Anacaona, widow of the late formidable Caonabo. She was sister to Behechio, and had taken refuge with her brother after the capture of her husband. She was one of the most beautiful females of the island ; her name in the Indian language signified "The Golden Flower." She possessed a genius superior to the generality of her race, and was said to excel in composing those little legendary ballads. or areytos, which the natives chanted as they performed their national dances. All the Spanish writers agree in describing her as possessing a natural dignity and grace hardly to be credited in her ignorant and savage condition. Notwithstanding the ruin with which her husband had been overwhelmed by the hostility of the white men, she appears to have entertained

---

[1] Peter Martyr, decad. i. lib. v.

no vindictive feeling toward them, knowing that he had provoked their vengeance by his own voluntary warfare. She regarded the Spaniards with admiration as almost superhuman beings, and her intelligent mind perceived the futility and impolicy of any attempt to resist their superiority in arts and arms. Having great influence over her brother Behechio, she counselled him to take warning by the fate of her husband, and to conciliate the friendship of the Spaniards; and it is supposed that a knowledge of the friendly sentiments and powerful influence of this princess, in a great measure prompted the Adelantado to his present expedition.[1]

In passing through those parts of the island which had hitherto been unvisited by Europeans, the Adelantado adopted the same imposing measures which the admiral had used on a former occasion; he put his cavalry in the advance, and entered all the Indian towns in martial array, with standards displayed, and the sound of drum and trumpet.

After proceeding about thirty leagues, he came to the river Neyva, which, issuing from the mountains of Cibao, divides the southern side of the island. Crossing this stream, he despatched two parties of ten men each along the seacoast in search of brazil-wood. They found great quantities, and felled many trees, which they stored in the Indian cabins, until they could be taken away by sea.

Inclining with his main force to the right, the Adelantado met, not far from the river, the cacique Behechio, with a great army of his subjects, armed with bows and arrows and lances. If he had come forth with the intention of opposing the inroad into his forest domains, he was probably daunted by the formidable appearance of the Spaniards. Laying aside his weapons, he advanced and accosted the Adelantado very amicably, professing that he was thus in arms for the purpose of subjecting certain villages along the river, and inquiring, at the same time, the object of this incursion of the Spaniards. The Adelantado assured him that he came on a peaceful visit, to pass a little time in friendly intercourse at Xaragua. He succeeded so well in allaying the apprehensions of the cacique, that the latter dismissed his army, and sent swift messengers to order preparations for the suitable reception of so distinguished a guest. As the Spaniards advanced into the territories of the chieftain, and passed through the districts of his inferior caciques, the latter brought forth cassava bread, hemp, cotton, and various other

[1] Charlevoix, Hist. St. Domingo, lib. ii. p. 147　Muñoz, Hist. N. Mundo, lib. vi. § 6

productions of the land. At length they drew near to the residence of Behechio, which was a large town situated in a beautiful part of the country near the coast, at the bottom of that deep bay, called at present the Bight of Leogan.

The Spaniards had heard many accounts of the soft and delightful region of Xaragua, in one part of which Indian traditions placed their Elysian fields. They had heard much, also, of the beauty and urbanity of the inhabitants: the mode of their reception was calculated to confirm their favorable prepossessions. As they approached the place, thirty females of the cacique's household came forth to meet them, singing their areytos, or traditionary ballads, and dancing and waving palm branches. The married females wore aprons of embroidered cotton, reaching half way to the knee: the young women were entirely naked, with merely a fillet round the forehead, their hair falling upon their shoulders. They were beautifully proportioned, their skin smooth and delicate, and their complexion of a clear, agreeable brown. According to old Peter Martyr, the Spaniards when they beheld them issuing forth from their green woods, almost imagined they beheld the fabled Dryads, or native nymphs and fairies of the fountains, sung by the ancient poets.[1] When they came before Don Bartholomew, they knelt and gracefully presented him the green branches. After these came the female cacique Anacaona, reclining on a kind of light litter borne by six Indians. Like the other females, she had no other covering than an apron of various-colored cotton. She wore round her head a fragrant garland of red and white flowers, and wreaths of the same round her neck and arms. She received the Adelantado and his followers with that natural grace and courtesy for which she was celebrated, manifesting no hostility toward them for the fate her husband had experienced at their hands.

The Adelantado and his officers were conducted to the house of Behechio, where a banquet was served up of utias, a great variety of sea and river fish, with roots and fruits of excellent quality. Here first the Spaniards conquered their repugnance to the guana, the favorite delicacy of the Indians, but which the former had regarded with disgust, as a species of serpent. The Adelantado, willing to accustom himself to the usages of the country, was the first to taste this animal, being kindly pressed thereto by Anacaona. His followers imitated his example; they found it to be highly palatable and delicate; and

---

[1] Peter Martyr. decad i. lib. v.

from that time forward the guana was held in repute among Spanish epicures.[1]

The banquet being over, Don Bartholomew with six of his principal cavaliers were lodged in the dwelling of Behechio; the rest were distributed in the houses of the inferior caciques where they slept in hammocks of matted cotton, the usual beds of the natives.

For two days they remained with the hospitable Behechio, entertained with various Indian games and festivities, among which the most remarkable was the representation of a battle. Two squadrons of naked Indians, armed with bows and arrows, sallied suddenly into the public square and began to skirmish in a manner similar to the Moorish play of canes, or tilting reeds. By degrees they became excited, and fought with such earnestness, that four were slain, and many wounded, which seemed to increase the interest and pleasure of the spectators. The contest would have continued longer, and might have been still more bloody. had not the Adelantado and the other cavaliers interfered and begged that the game might cease.[2]

When the festivities were over. and familiar intercourse had promoted mutual confidence, the Adelantado addressed the cacique and Anacaona on the real object of his visit. He informed him that his brother, the admiral, had been sent to this island by the sovereigns of Castile. who were great and mighty potentates, with many kingdoms under their sway. That the admiral had returned to apprise his sovereigns how many tributary caciques there were in the island, leaving him in command, and that he had come to receive Benechio under the protection of these mighty sovereigns, and to arrange a tribute to be paid by him, in such manner as should be most convenient and satisfactory to himself.[3]

The cacique was greatly embarrassed by this demand, knowing the sufferings inflicted on the other parts of the island by the avidity of the Spaniards for gold. He replied that he had been apprised that gold was the great object for which the white men had come to their island, and that a tribute was

---

[1] "These serpentes are lyke unto crocodiles, saving in bygness, they call them guanas Unto that day none of owre men durste adventure to taste of them, by reason of theyre horrible deformitie and lothsomnes. Yet the Adelantado being entysed by the pleasantnes of the king's sister, Anacaona, determined to taste the serpentes. But when he felte the flesh thereof to be so delycate to his tongue, he fel to amayne without al feare. The which thyng his companions perceiving, were not behynde hym in greedynesse: insomuche that they had now none other talke than of the sweetnesse of these serpentes, which they affirm to be of more pleasant taste than eyther our phesantes or partriches." Peter Martyr, decad i. book v Eden's Eng Trans.

[2] Las Casas, Hist. Ind., tom. i cap. 113.

[3] Ibid.. lib. i. cap. 114.

paid in it by some of his fellow-caciques; but that in no part of his territories was gold to be found; and his subjects hardly knew what it was. To this the Adelantado replied with great adroitness, that nothing was farther from the intention or wish of his sovereigns than to require a tribute in things not produced in his dominions, but that it might be paid in cotton, hemp, and cassava bread, with which the surrounding country appeared to abound. The countenance of the cacique brightened at this intimation; he promised cheerful compliance, and instantly sent orders to all his subordinate caciques to sow abundance of cotton for the first payment of the stipulated tribute. Having made all the requisite arrangements, the Adelantado took a most friendly leave of Behechio and his sister, and set out for Isabella.

Thus by amicable and sagacious management, one of the most extensive provinces of the island was brought into cheerful subjection, and had not the wise policy of the Adelantado been defeated by the excesses of worthless and turbulent men, a large revenue might have been collected, without any recourse to violence or oppression. In all instances these simple people appear to have been extremely tractable, and meekly and even cheerfully to have resigned their rights to the white men, when treated with gentleness and humanity.

CHAPTER II.

ESTABLISHMENT OF A CHAIN OF MILITARY POSTS — INSURRECTION OF GUARIONEX. THE CACIQUE OF THE VEGA.

[1496.]

On arriving at Isabella, Don Bartholomew found it, as usual, a scene of misery and repining. Many had died during his absence; most were ill. Those who were healthy complained of the scarcity of food, and those who were ill, of the want of medicines. The provisions distributed among them, from the supply brought out a few months before by Pedro Alonzo Niño, had been consumed. Partly from sickness, and partly from a repugnance to labor, they had neglected to cultivate the surrounding country, and the Indians, on whom they chiefly depended, outraged by their oppressions, had abandoned the vicinity, and fled to the mountains; choosing rather to subsist on roots and herbs, in their rugged retreats, than remain in the luxuriant plains, subject to the wrongs and cruelties of the white men. The history of this island presents continual pictures of the miseries, the actual want and poverty produced by the grasping avidity of gold. It had rendered the Spaniards heedless of all the less obvious, but more certain and salubrious sources of wealth. All labor seemed lost that was to produce profit by a circuitous process. Instead of cultivating the luxuriant soil around them, and deriving real treasures from its surface, they wasted their time in seeking for mines and golden streams, and were starving in the midst of fertility.

No sooner were the provisions exhausted which had been brought out by Niño than the colonists began to break forth in their accustomed murmurs. They represented themselves as neglected by Columbus, who, amid the blandishments and delights of a court, thought little of their sufferings. They considered themselves equally forgotten by government; while, having no vessel in the harbor, they were destitute of all means of sending home intelligence of their disastrous situation, and imploring relief.

To remove this last cause of discontent, and furnish some object for their hopes and thoughts to rally round, the Adelantado ordered that two caravels should be built at Isabella, for the use of the island. To relieve the settlement, also, from all useless and repining individuals, during this time of scarcity, he distributed such as were too ill to labor, or to bear arms, into the interior, where they would have the benefit of a better climate, and more abundant supply of Indian provisions. He at the same time completed and garrisoned the chain of military posts established by his brother in the preceding year, consisting of five fortified houses, each surrounded by its dependent hamlet. The first of these was about nine leagues from Isabella, and was called la Esperanza. Six leagues beyond was Santa Catalina. Four leagues and a half farther was Magdalena, where the first town of Santiago was afterward founded: and five leagues farther Fort Conception — which was fortified with great care, being in the vast and populous Vega, and within half a league from the residence of its cacique, Guarionex.[1] Having thus relieved Isabella of all its useless population, and left none but such as were too ill to be removed, or were required for the service and protection of the place, and the construction of the caravels, the Adelantado returned, with a

---

[1] P. Martyr, decad. i. lib. v. Of the residence of Guarionex, which must have been a considerable town, not the least vestige can be discovered at present.

large body of the most effective men, to the fortress of San Domingo.

The military posts thus established, succeeded for a time in overawing the natives; but fresh hostilities were soon manifested, excited by a different cause from the preceding. Among the missionaries who had accompanied Friar Boyle to the island, were two of far greater zeal than their superior. When he returned to Spain, they remained, earnestly bent upon the fulfilment of their mission. One was called Roman Pane, a poor hermit, as he styled himself, of the order of St. Geronimo, the other was Juan Borgoñon, a Franciscan. They resided for some time among the Indians of the Vega, strenuously endeavoring to make converts, and had succeeded with one family of sixteen persons, the chief of which, on being baptized, took the name of Juan Mateo. The conversion of the cacique Guarionex, however, was their main object. The extent of his possessions made his conversion of great importance to the interests of the colony, and was considered by the zealous fathers a means of bringing his numerous subjects under the dominion of the church. For some time he lent a willing ear; he learnt the Pater Noster, the Ave Maria, and the Creed, and made his whole family repeat them daily. The other caciques of the Vega and of the provinces of Cibao, however, scoffed at him for meanly conforming to the laws and customs of strangers, usurpers of his domains and oppressors of his nation. The friars complained that, in consequence of these evil communications, their convert suddenly relapsed into infidelity, but another and more grievous cause is assigned for his recantation. His favorite wife was seduced or treated with outrage by a Spaniard of authority; and the cacique renounced all faith in a religion, which, as he supposed, admitted of such atrocities. Losing all hope of effecting his conversion, the mission removed to the territories of another cacique, taking with them Juan Mateo, their Indian convert. Before their departure they erected a small chapel, and furnished it with an altar, crucifix, and images, for the use of the family of Mateo

Scarcely had they departed, when several Indians entered the chapel, broke the images in pieces, trampled them under foot, and buried them in a neighboring field. This, it is said, was done by order of Guarionex, in contempt of the religion from which he had apostatized. A complaint of this enormity was carried to the Adelantado, who ordered a suit to be immediately instituted, and those who were found culpable, to be punished according to law. It was a period of great rigor in ecclesiastical law, especially among the Spaniards. In Spain all heresies in religion, all recantations from the faith, and all acts of sacrilege, either by Moor or Jew, were punished with fire and fagot. Such was the fate of the poor ignorant Indians, convicted of this outrage on the church. It is questionable whether Guarionex had any hand in this offence, and it is probable that the whole affair was exaggerated. A proof of the credit due to the evidence brought forward, may be judged by one of the facts recorded by Roman Pane, " the poor hermit." The field in which the holy images were buried was planted, he says, with certain roots shaped like a turnip, or radish, several of which, coming up in the neighborhood of the images, were found to have grown most miraculously in the form of a cross.[1]

The cruel punishment inflicted on these Indians, instead of daunting their countrymen, filled them with horror and indignation. Unaccustomed to such stern rule and vindictive justice, and having no clear ideas nor powerful sentiments with respect to religion of any kind, they could not comprehend the nature nor extent of the crime committed. Even Guarionex, a man naturally moderate and pacific, was highly incensed with the assumption of power within his territories, and the inhuman death inflicted on his subjects. The other caciques perceived his irritation, and endeavored to induce him to unite in a sudden insurrection, that by one vigorous and general effort, they might break the yoke of their oppressors. Guarionex wavered for some time. He knew the martial skill and prowess of the Spaniards; he stood in awe of their cavalry; and he had before him the disastrous fate of Caonabo: but he was rendered bold by despair, and he beheld in the domination of these strangers the assured ruin of his race. The early writers speak of a tradition current among the inhabitants of the island, respecting this Guarionex. He was of an ancient line of hereditary caciques. His father, in times long preceding the discovery, having fasted for five days, according to their superstitious observances, applied to his zemi, or household deity, for information of things to come. He received for answer that within a few years there should come to the island a nation covered with clothing, which should destroy all their customs and ceremonies, and slay their children or reduce them to painful servitude.[2] The tradition was probably invented by the Butios, or priests, after the Spaniards had begun to exercise

---

[1] Escritura de Fr. Roman, Hist. del Almirante.   [2] Peter Martyr, decad. 1. lib. ix.

their severities. Whether their prediction had an effect in disposing the mind of Guarionex to hostilities is uncertain. Some have asserted that he was compelled to take up arms by his subjects, who threatened, in case of his refusal, to choose some other chieftain, others have alleged the outrage committed upon his favorite wife, as the principal cause of his irritation.[1] It was probably these things combined, which at length induced him to enter into the conspiracy. A secret consultation was held among the caciques, wherein it was concerted that on the day of payment of their quarterly tribute, when a great number could assemble without causing suspicion, they should suddenly rise upon the Spaniards and massacre them.[2]

By some means the garrison at Fort Conception received intimation of this conspiracy. Being but a handful of men, and surrounded by hostile tribes, they wrote a letter to the Adelantado, at San Domingo, imploring immediate aid. As this letter might be taken from their Indian messenger, the natives having discovered that these letters had a wonderful power of communicating intelligence, and fancying they could talk, it was enclosed in a reed, to be used as a staff. The messenger was, in fact, intercepted: but, affecting to be dumb and lame, and intimating by signs that he was returning home, was permitted to limp forward on his journey. When out of sight he resumed his speed, and bore the letter safely and expeditiously to San Domingo.[3]

The Adelantado, with his characteristic promptness and activity, set out immediately with a body of troops for the fortress; and though his men were much enfeebled by scanty fare, hard service, and long marches, hurried them rapidly forward. Never did aid arrive more opportunely. The Indians were assembled on the plain, to the amount of many thousands, armed after their manner, and waiting for the appointed time to strike the blow. After consulting with the commander of the fortress and his officers, the Adelantado concerted a mode of proceeding. Ascertaining the places in which the various caciques had distributed their forces, he appointed an officer with a body of men to each cacique, with orders, at an appointed hour of the night, to rush into the villages, surprise them asleep and unarmed, bind the caciques, and bring them off prisoners. As Guarionex was the most important personage, and his capture would probably be attended with most

[1] Las Casas, Hist. Ind., lib. i. cap. 121.
[2] Herrera. decad. 1 lib iii. cap. 65. Peter Martyr. decad. vi. lib. v.
[3] Herrera, Hist. Ind., decad. 1. lib. iii cap. 7.

difficulty and danger, the Adelantado took the charge of it upon nimself, at the head of one hundred men.

This stratagem, founded upon a knowledge of the attachment of the Indians to their chieftains, and calculated to spare a great effusion of blood, was completely successful. The villages having no walls nor other defences, were quietly entered at midnight, and the Spaniards, rushing suddenly into the houses where the caciques were quartered. seized and bound them, to the number of fourteen, and hurried them off to the fortress, before any effort could be made for their defence or rescue. The Indians, struck with terror, made no resistance, nor any show of hostility ; surrounding the fortress in great multitudes, but without weapons, they filled the air with doleful howlings and lamentations, imploring the release of their chieftains. The Adelantado completed his enterprise with the spirit. sagacity, and moderation with which he had hitherto conducted it. He obtained information of the causes of this conspiracy. and the individuals most culpable. Two caciques, the principal movers of the insurrection. and who had most wrought upon the easy nature of Guarionex, were put to death. As to that unfortunate cacique, the Adelantado. considering the deep wrongs he had suffered, and the slowness with which he had been provoked to revenge, magnanimously pardoned him ; nay, according to Las Casas, he proceeded with stern justice against the Spaniard whose outrage on his wife had sunk so deeply in his heart. He extended his lenity also to the remaining chieftains of the conspiracy ; promising great favors and rewards, if they should continue firm in their loyalty ; but terrible punishments snould they again be found in rebellion. The heart of Guarionex was subdued by this unexpected clemency. He made a speech to his people setting forth the irresistible might and valor of the Spaniards ; their great lenity to offenders. and their generosity to such as were faithful ; and he earnestly exhorted them henceforth to cultivate their friendship. The Indians listened to him with attention ; his praises of the white men were confirmed by their treatment of himself ; when he had concluded, they took him upon their shoulders, bore him to his habitation with songs and shouts of joy. and for some time the tranquillity of the Vega was restored.[1]

---

[1] Peter Martyr. decad. 1. lib. v Herrera. Hist. Ind., decad. 1. lib. iii. cap. 6.

CHAPTER III.

THE ADELANTADO REPAIRS TO XARAGUA TO RECEIVE TRIBUTE.

[1497.]

WITH all his energy and discretion, the Adelantado found it difficult to manage the proud and turbulent spirit of the colonists. They could ill brook the sway of a foreigner, who, when they were restive, curbed them with an iron hand. Don Bartholomew had not the same legitimate authority in their eyes as his brother. The admiral was the discoverer of the country, and the authorized representative of the sovereigns; yet even him they with difficulty brought themselves to obey. The Adelantado, on the contrary, was regarded by many as a mere intruder, assuming high command without authority from the crown, and shouldering himself into power on the merits and services of his brother. They spoke with impatience and indignation, also, of the long absence of the admiral, and his fancied inattention to their wants, little aware of the incessant anxieties he was suffering on their account, during his detention in Spain. The sagacious measure of the Adelantado in building the caravels, for some time diverted their attention. They watched their progress with solicitude, looking upon them as a means either of obtaining relief or of abandoning the island. Aware that repining and discontented men should never be left in idleness, Don Bartholomew kept them continually in movement, and indeed a state of constant activity was congenial to his own vigorous spirit. About this time messengers arrived from Behechio, cacique of Xaragua, informing him that he had large quantities of cotton, and other articles, in which his tribute was to be paid, ready for delivery. The Adelantado immediately set forth with a numerous train, to revisit this fruitful and happy region. He was again received with songs and dances, and all the national demonstrations of respect and amity by Behechio and his sister Anacaona. The latter appeared to be highly popular among the natives, and to have almost as much sway in Xaragua as her brother. Her natural ease, and the graceful dignity of her manners, more and more won the admiration of the Spaniards.

The Adelantado found thirty-two inferior caciques assembled in the house of Behechio, awaiting his arrival with their respective tributes. The cotton they had brought was enough to fill one of their houses. Having delivered this, they gratuitously offered the Adelantado as much cassava bread as he desired. The offer was most acceptable in the present necessitous state of the colony; and Don Bartholomew sent to Isabella for one of the caravels, which was nearly finished, to be despatched as soon as possible to Xaragua, to be freighted with bread and cotton.

In the mean time the natives brought from all quarters large supplies of provisions, and entertained their guests with continual festivity and banqueting. The early Spanish writers, whose imaginations, heated by the accounts of the voyagers, could not form an idea of the simplicity of savage life, especially in these newly discovered countries which were supposed to border upon Asia, often speak in terms of Oriental magnificence of the entertainments of the natives, the palaces of the caciques, and the lords and ladies of their courts, as if they were describing the abodes of Asiatic potentates. The accounts given of Xaragua, however, have a different character; and give a picture of savage life, in its perfection of idle and ignorant enjoyment. The troubles which distracted the other parts of devoted Hayti had not reached the inhabitants of this pleasant region. Living among beautiful and fruitful groves, on the borders of a sea, apparently forever tranquil and unvexed by storms; having few wants, and those readily supplied, they appeared emancipated from the common lot of labor, and to pass their lives in one uninterrupted holiday. When the Spaniards regarded the fertility and sweetness of this country, the gentleness of its people, and the beauty of its women, they pronounced it a perfect paradise.

At length the caravel arrived which was to be freighted with the articles of tribute. It anchored about six miles from the residence of Behechio, and Anacaona proposed to her brother that they should go together to behold what she called the great canoe of the white man. On their way to the coast, the Adelantado was lodged one night in a village, in a house where Anacaona treasured up those articles which she esteemed most rare and precious. They consisted of various manufactures of cotton, ingeniously wrought, of vessels of clay, moulded into different forms; of chairs, tables, and like articles of furniture formed of ebony and other kinds of wood, and carved with various devices — all evincing great skill and ingenuity in a people who had no iron tools to work with. Such were the simple treasures of this Indian princess, of which she made numerous presents to her guest.

Nothing could exceed the wonder and delight of this intelligent woman when she first beheld the ship. Her brother, who treated her with a fraternal fondness and respectful attention, worthy of civilized life, had prepared two canoes, gayly painted and decorated, one to convey her and her attendants, and the other for himself and his chieftains. Anacaona, however, preferred to embark with her attendants in the ship's boat with the Adelantado. As they approached the caravel, a salute was fired. At the report of the cannon, and the sight of the smoke, Anacaona, overcome with dismay, fell into the arms of the Adelantado, and her attendants would have leaped overboard, but the laughter and the cheerful words of Don Bartholomew speedily reassured them. As they drew nearer to the vessel, several instruments of martial music struck up, with which they were greatly delighted. Their admiration increased on entering on board. Accustomed only to their simple and slight canoes, every thing here appeared wonderfully vast and complicated But when the anchor was weighed, the sails were spread, and, aided by a gentle breeze, they beheld this vast mass, moving apparently by its own volition, veering from side to side, and playing like a huge monster in the deep, the brother and sister remained gazing at each other in mute astonishment.[1] Nothing seems to have filled the mind of the most stoical savage with more wonder than that sublime and beautiful triumph of genius, a ship under sail.

Having freighted and despatched the caravel, the Adelantado made many presents to Behechio, his sister, and their attendants, and took leave of them, to return by land with his troops to Isabella. Anacaona showed great affliction at their parting, entreating him to remain some time longer with them, and appearing fearful that they had failed in their humble attempt to please him. She even offered to follow him to the settlement, nor would she be consoled until he had promised to return again to Xaragua.[2]

We cannot but remark the ability shown by the Adelantado in the course of his transient government of the island. Wonderfully alert and active, he made repeated marches of great extent, from one remote province to another, and was always at the post of danger at the critical moment. By skilful management, with a handful of men he defeated a formidable insurrection without any effusion of blood. He conciliated the most inveterate enemies among the natives by great moderation,

[1] Peter Martyr, decad. i. lib. v.   Herrera, decad. i. lib. iii. cap. 6.
[2] Ramusio vol. iii. p. 9.

while he deterred all wanton hostilities by the infliction of signal punishments. He had made firm friends of the most important chieftains, brought their dominions under cheerful tribute, opened new sources of supplies for the colony, and procured relief from its immediate wants. Had his judicious measures been seconded by those under his command, the whole country would have been a scene of tranquil prosperity, and would have produced great revenues to the crown, without cruelty to the natives; but, like his brother the admiral, his good intentions and judicious arrangements were constantly thwarted by the vile passions and perverse conduct of others. While he was absent from Isabella, new mischiefs had been fomented there, which were soon to throw the whole island into confusion.

CHAPTER IV.

CONSPIRACY OF ROLDAN.

[1497.]

THE prime mover of the present mischief was one Francisco Roldan, a man under the deepest obligations to the admiral. Raised by him from poverty and obscurity, he had been employed at first in menial capacities; but, showing strong natural talents and great assiduity, he had been made ordinary alcalde, equivalent to justice of the peace. The able manner in which he acquitted himself in this situation, and the persuasion of his great fidelity and gratitude, induced Columbus, on departing for Spain, to appoint him alcalde mayor, or chief judge of the island. It is true he was an uneducated man, but, as there were as yet no intricacies of law in the colony, the office required little else than shrewd good sense and upright principles for its discharge.[1]

Roldan was one of those base spirits which grow venomous in the sunshine of prosperity. His benefactor had returned to Spain apparently under a cloud of disgrace; a long interval had elapsed without tidings from him; he considered him a fallen man, and began to devise how he might profit by his downfall. He was intrusted with an office inferior only to that of the Adelantado; the brothers of Columbus were highly unpopular; he

---

[1] Herrera, decad. i. lib iii. cap. 1.

imagined it possible to ruin them, both with the colonists and with the government at home, and by dexterous cunning and bustling activity, to work his way into the command of the colony. The vigorous and somewhat austere character of the Adelantado for some time kept him in awe; but when he was absent from the settlement, Roldan was able to carry on his machinations with confidence. Don Diego, who then commanded at Isabella, was an upright and worthy man, but deficient in energy. Roldan felt himself his superior in talent and spirit, and his self-conceit was wounded at being inferior to him in authority. He soon made a party among the daring and dissolute of the community, and secretly loosened the ties of order and good government by listening to and encouraging the discontents of the common people, and directing them against the character and conduct of Columbus and his brothers. He had heretofore been employed as superintendent of various public works; this brought him into familiar communication with workmen, sailors, and others of the lower order. His originally vulgar character enabled him to adapt himself to their intellects and manners, while his present station gave him consequence in their eyes. Finding them full of murmurs about hard treatment, severe toil, and the long absence of the admiral, he affected to be moved by their distresses. He threw out suggestions that the admiral might never return, being disgraced and ruined in consequence of the representations of Aguado. He sympathized with the hard treatment they experienced from the Adelantado and his brother Don Diego, who, being foreigners, could take no interest in their welfare, nor feel a proper respect for the pride of a Spaniard; but who used them merely as slaves, to build houses and fortresses for them, or to swell their state and secure their power, as they marched about the island enriching themselves with the spoils of the caciques. By these suggestions he exasperated their feelings to such a height, that they had at one time formed a conspiracy to take away the life of the Adelantado, as the only means of delivering themselves from an odious tyrant. The time and place for the perpetration of the act were concerted. The Adelantado had condemned to death a Spaniard of the name of Berahona, a friend of Roldan, and of several of the conspirators. What was his offence is not positively stated, but from a passage in Las Casas,[1] there is reason to believe that he was the very Spaniard who had violated the favorite wife of Guarionex, the cacique of the Vega.

---

[1] Las Casas, Hist. Ind., lib. 1 cap. 118.

The Adelantado would be present at the execution. It was arranged therefore that when the populace had assembled, a tumult should be made as if by accident, and in the confusion of the moment Don Bartholomew should be despatched with a poniard. Fortunately for the Adelantado, he pardoned the criminal, the assemblage did not take place, and the plan of the conspirators was disconcerted.[1]

When Don Bartholomew was absent collecting the tribute in Xaragua, Roldan thought it was a favorable time to bring affairs to a crisis. He had sounded the feelings of the colonists, and ascertained that there was a large party disposed for open sedition. His plan was to create a popular tumult, to interpose in his official character of alcalde mayor, to throw the blame upon the oppression and injustice of Don Diego and his brother, and, while he usurped the reins of authority, to appear as if actuated only by zeal for the peace and prosperity of the island, and the interests of the sovereigns.

A pretext soon presented itself for the proposed tumult. When the caravel returned from Xaragua laden with the Indian tributes, and the cargo was discharged, Don Diego had the vessel drawn up on the land, to protect it from accidents, or from any sinister designs of the disaffected colonists. Roldan immediately pointed this circumstance out to his partisans. He secretly inveighed against the hardship of having this vessel drawn on shore instead of being left afloat for the benefit of the colony, or sent to Spain to make known their distresses. He hinted that the true reason was the fear of the Adelantado and his brother, lest accounts should be carried to Spain of their misconduct, and he affirmed that they wished to remain undisturbed masters of the island, and keep the Spaniards there as subjects, or rather as slaves. The people took fire at these suggestions. They had long looked forward to the completion of the caravels as their only chance for relief; they now insisted that the vessel should be launched and sent to Spain for supplies. Don Diego endeavored to convince them of the folly of their demand, the vessel not being rigged and equipped for such a voyage; but the more he attempted to pacify them, the more unreasonable and turbulent they became. Roldan, also became more bold and explicit in his instigations. He advised them to launch and take possession of the caravel, as the only mode of regaining their independence. They might then throw off the tyranny of these upstart strangers, enemies in their

---

[1] Hist. del Almirante, cap. 73.

hearts to Spaniards, and might lead a life of ease and pleasure; sharing equally all that they might gain by barter in the island, employing the Indians as slaves to work for them, and enjoying unrestrained indulgence with respect to the Indian women.[1]

Don Diego received information of what was fermenting among the people, yet feared to come to an open rupture with Roldan in the present mutinous state of the colony. He suddenly detached him, therefore, with forty men, to the Vega, under pretext of overawing certain of the natives who had refused to pay their tribute, and had shown a disposition to revolt. Roldan made use of this opportunity to strengthen his faction. He made friends and partisans among the discontented caciques, secretly justifying them in their resistance to the imposition of tribute. and promising them redress. He secured the devotion of his own soldiers by great acts of indulgence, disarming and dismissing such as refused full participation in his plans, and returned with his little band to Isabella, where he felt secure of a strong party among the common people.

The Adelantado had by this time returned from Xaragua; but Roldan. feeling himself at the head of a strong faction. and arrogating to himself great authority from his official station, now openly demanded that the caravel should be launched. or permission given to himself and his followers to launch it. The Adelantado peremptorily refused. observing that neither he nor his companions were mariners, nor was the caravel furnished and equipped for sea. and that neither the safety of the vessel nor of the people should be endangered by their attempt to navigate her.

Roldan perceived that his motives were suspected, and felt that the Adelantado was too formidable an adversary to contend with in any open sedition at Isabella. He determined, therefore, to carry his plans into operation in some more favorable part of the island, always trusting to excuse any open rebellion against the authority of Don Bartholomew, by representing it as a patriotic opposition to his tyranny over Spaniards. He had seventy well-armed and determined men under his command. and he trusted, on erecting his standard, to be joined by all the disaffected throughout the island. He set off suddenly, therefore, for the Vega, intending to surprise the fortress of Conception, and by getting command of that post and the rich country adjacent. to set the Adelantado at defiance.

He stopped on his way at various Indian villages in which

---

[1] Hist. del Almirante, cap. 73.

the Spaniards were distributed, endeavoring to enlist the latter in his party, by holding out promises of great gain and free living. He attempted also to seduce the natives from their allegiance, by promising them freedom from all tribute. Those caciques with whom he had maintained a previous understanding, received him with open arms, particularly one who had taken the name of Diego Marque, whose village he made his headquarters, being about two leagues from Fort Conception. He was disappointed in his hopes of surprising the fortress. Its commander, Miguel Ballester, was an old and staunch soldier, both resolute and wary. He drew himself into his stronghold on the approach of Roldan, and closed his gates. His garrison was small, but the fortification, situated on the side of a hill, with a river running at its foot, was proof against any assault. Roldan had still some hopes that Ballester might be disaffected to government, and might be gradually brought into his plans, or that the garrison would be disposed to desert, tempted by the licentious life which he permitted among his followers. In the neighborhood was the town inhabited by Guarionex. Here were quartered thirty soldiers, under the command of Captain Garcia de Barrantes. Roldan repaired thither with his armed force, hoping to enlist Barrantes and his party; but the captain shut himself up with his men in a fortified house, refusing to permit them to hold any communication with Roldan. The latter threatened to set fire to the house but after a little consideration, contented himself with seizing their store of provisions, and then marched toward Fort Conception, which was not quite half a league distant.[1]

---

[1] Herrera, decad. i lib iii. cap. 7   Hist del Almirante, cap. 74.

Extract of a letter from T. S. Heneken, Esq., 1847.

Fort Conception is situated at the foot of a hill now called Santo Cerro. It is constructed of bricks, and is almost as entire at the present day as when just finished It stands in the gloom of an exuberant forest which has invaded the scene of former bustle and activity a spot once considered of great importance, and surrounded by swarms of intelligent beings.

What has become of the countless multitudes this fortress was intended to awe? Not a trace of them remains excepting in the records of history The silence of the tomb prevails where their habitations responded to their songs and dances. A few indigent Spaniards, living in miserable hovels, scattered widely apart in the bosom of the forest, are now the sole occupants of this once fruitful and beautiful region.

A Spanish town gradually grew up round the fortress, the ruins of which extend to a considerable distance. It was destroyed by an earthquake, at nine o'clock of the morning of Saturday, 20th April, 1564, during the celebration of mass. Part of the massive walls of a handsome church still remain, as well as those of a very large convent or hospital, supposed to have been constructed in pursuance of the testamentary dispositions of Columbus The inhabitants who survived the catastrophe retired to a small chapel, on the banks of a river, about a league distant, where the new town of La Vega was afterward built.

CHAPTER V.

THE ADELANTADO REPAIRS TO THE VEGA IN RELIEF OF FORT
CONCEPTION — HIS INTERVIEW WITH ROLDAN.

[1497.]

THE Adelantado had received intelligence of the flagitious
proceedings of Roldan, yet hesitated for a time to set out in
pursuit of him. He had lost all confidence in the loyalty of
the people around him, and knew not how far the conspiracy
extended, nor on whom he could rely. Diego de Escobar,
alcayde of the fortress of La Madelena, together with Adrian
de Moxica and Pedro de Valdivieso, all principal men, were in
league with Roldan. He feared that the commander of Fort
Conception might likewise be in the plot, and the whole island
in arms against him. He was re-assured, however, by tidings
from Miguel Ballester. That loyal veteran wrote to him pressing letters for succor, representing the weakness of his garrison,
and the increasing forces of the rebels.

Don Bartholomew hastened to his assistance with his accustomed promptness, and threw himself with a re-enforcement into
the fortress. Being ignorant of the force of the rebels, and
doubtful of the loyalty of his own followers, he determined to
adopt mild measures. Understanding that Roldan was quartered at a village but half a league distant, he sent a message to
him, remonstrating on the flagrant irregularity of his conduct,
the injury it was calculated to produce in the island, and the
certain ruin it must bring upon himself, and summoning him to
appear at the fortress, pledging his word for his personal safety.
Roldan repaired accordingly to Fort Conception, where the
Adelantado held a parley with him from a window, demanding
the reason of his appearing in arms, in opposition to royal
authority. Roldan replied boldly, that he was in the service of
his sovereigns, defending their subjects from the oppression
of men who sought their destruction. The Adelantado ordered
him to surrender his staff of office, as alcalde mayor, and to
submit peaceably to superior authority. Roldan refused to
resign his office, or to put himself in the power of Don Bartholomew, whom he charged with seeking his life. He refused also
to submit to any trial, unless commanded by the king. Pretending, however, to make no resistance to the peaceable exercise

of authority, he offered to go with his followers, and reside at any place the Adelantado might appoint. The latter immediately designated the village of the cacique Diego Colon, the same native of the Lucayos Islands who had been baptized in Spain, and had since married a daughter of Guarionex. Roldan objected, pretending there were not sufficient provisions to be had there for the subsistence of his men, and departed, declaring that he would seek a more eligible residence elsewhere.[1]

He now proposed to his followers to take possession of the remote province of Xaragua. The Spaniards who had returned thence gave enticing accounts of the life they had led there: of the fertility of the soil, the sweetness of the climate, the hospitality and gentleness of the people, their feasts, dances, and various amusements, and, above all, the beauty of the women; for they had been captivated by the naked charms of the dancing nymphs of Xaragua. In this delightful region, emancipated from the iron rule of the Adelantado, and relieved from the necessity of irksome labor, they might lead a life of perfect freedom and indulgence, and have a world of beauty at their command. In short, Roldan drew a picture of loose sensual enjoyment such as he knew to be irresistible with men of idle and dissolute habits. His followers acceded with joy to his proposition. Some preparations, however, were necessary to carry it into effect. Taking advantage of the absence of the Adelantado, he suddenly marched with his band to Isabella, and entering it in a manner by surprise, endeavored to launch the caravel, with which they might sail to Xaragua. Don Diego Columbus, hearing the tumult, issued forth with several cavaliers; but such was the force of the mutineers and their menacing conduct, that he was obliged to withdraw, with his adherents, into the fortress. Roldan held several parleys with him, and offered to submit to his command, provided he would set himself up in opposition to his brother the Adelantado. His proposition was treated with scorn. The fortress was too strong to be assailed with success; he found it impossible to launch the caravel, and feared the Adelantado might return, and he be enclosed between two forces. He proceeded, therefore, in all haste to make provisions for the proposed expedition to Xaragua. Still pretending to act in his official capacity, and to do every thing from loyal motives, for the protection and support of the oppressed subjects of the crown, he broke open the royal warehouse, with shouts of " Long live the king!"

---

[1] Herrera, decad 1. lib. iii cap. 7. Hist. del Almirante, cap 74.

supplied his followers with arms, ammunition, clothing, and whatever they desired from the public stores , proceeded to the enclosure where the cattle and other European animals were kept to breed, took such as he thought necessary for his intended establishment, and permitted his followers to kill such of the remainder as they might want for present supply. Having committed this wasteful ravage, he marched in triumph out of Isabella.[1] Reflecting, however, on the prompt and vigorous character of the Adelantado, he felt that his situation would be but little secure with such an active enemy behind him ; who, on extricating himself from present perplexities, would not fail to pursue him to his proposed paradise of Xaragua. He determined, therefore, to march again to the Vega, and endeavor either to get possession of the person of the Adelantado, or to strike some blow, in his present crippled state, that should disable him from offering further molestation. Returning, therefore, to the vicinity of Fort Conception, he endeavored in every way, by the means of subtle emissaries, to seduce the garrison to desertion, or to excite it to revolt.

The Adelantado dared not take the field with his forces, having no confidence in their fidelity. He knew that they listened wistfully to the emissaries of Roldan, and contrasted the meagre fare and stern discipline of the garrison, with the abundant cheer and easy misrule that prevailed among the rebels. To counteract these seductions, he relaxed from his usual strictness, treating his men with great indulgence, and promising them large rewards. By these means he was enabled to maintain some degree of loyalty amongst his forces, his service having the advantage over that of Roldan, of being on the side of government and law.

Finding his attempts to corrupt the garrison unsuccessful, and fearing some sudden sally from the vigorous Adelantado, Roldan drew off to a distance, and sought by insidious means to strengthen his own power and weaken that of the government. He asserted equal right to manage the affairs of the island with the Adelantado, and pretended to have separated from him on account of his being passionate and vindictive in the exercise of his authority. He represented him as the tyrant of the Spaniards, the oppressor of the Indians. For himself, he assumed the character of a redresser of grievances and champion of the injured. He pretended to feel a patriotic indignation at the affronts heaped upon Spaniards by a family

---

[1] Hist. del Almirante, cap. 74. Herrera, decad. 1. lib. III. cap. 7.

of obscure and arrogant foreigners; and professed to free the natives from tributes wrung from them by these rapacious men for their own enrichment, and contrary to the beneficent intentions of the Spanish monarchs. He connected himself closely with the Carib cacique Manicaotex, brother of the late Caonabo, whose son and nephew were in his possession as hostages for payment of tributes. This warlike chieftain he conciliated by presents and caresses, bestowing on him the appellation of brother.[1] The unhappy natives, deceived by his professions, and overjoyed at the idea of having a protector in arms for their defence, submitted cheerfully to a thousand impositions, supplying his followers with provisions in abundance, and bringing to Roldan all the gold they could collect; voluntarily yielding him heavier tributes than those from which he pretended to free them.

The affairs of the island were now in a lamentable situation. The Indians, perceiving the dissensions among the white men, and encouraged by the protection of Roldan. began to throw off all allegiance to the government. The caciques at a distance ceased to send in their tributes. and those who were in the vicinity were excused by the Adelantado, that by indulgence he might retain their friendship in this time of danger. Roldan's faction daily gained strength; they ranged insolently and at large in the open country, and were supported by the misguided natives; while the Spaniards who remained loyal, fearing conspiracies among the natives, had to keep under shelter of the fort, or in the strong houses which they had erected in the villages. The commanders were obliged to palliate all kinds of slights and indignities, both from their soldiers and from the Indians, fearful of driving them to sedition by any severity. The clothing and munitions of all kinds, either for maintenance or defence, were rapidly wasting away, and the want of all supplies or tidings from Spain was sinking the spirits of the well-affected into despondency. The Adelantado was shut up in Fort Conception, in daily expectation of being openly besieged by Roldan, and was secretly informed that means were taken to destroy him, should he issue from the walls of the fortress.[2]

Such was the desperate state to which the colony was reduced. in consequence of the long detention of Columbus in Spain, and the impediments thrown in the way of all his measures for the benefit of the island by the delays of cabinets and the chi-

---

[1] Las Casas. Hist. Ind., lib. 1. cap. 118.   [2] Las Casas. Hist. Ind., lib. 1. cap. 119.

canery of Fonseca and his satellites. At this critical juncture, when faction reigned triumphant, and the colony was on the brink of ruin, tidings were brought to the Vega that Pedro Fernandez Coronal had arrived at the port of San Domingo, with two ships, bringing supplies of all kinds, and a strong re-enforcement.[1]

CHAPTER VI.

SECOND INSURRECTION OF GUARIONEX, AND HIS FLIGHT TO THE MOUNTAINS OF CIGUAY.

[1498.]

THE arrival of Coronal, which took place on the third of February, was the salvation of the colony. The re-enforcements of troops, and of supplies of all kinds, strengthened the hands of Don Bartholomew. The royal confirmation of his title and authority as Adelantado at once dispelled all doubts as to the legitimacy of his power : and the tidings that the admiral was in high favor at court, and would soon arrive with a powerful squadron, struck consternation into those who had entered into the rebellion on the presumption of his having fallen into disgrace.

The Adelantado no longer remained mewed up in his fortress, but set out immediately for San Domingo with a part of his troops, although a much superior rebel force was at the village of the cacique Guarionex, at a very short distance. Roldan followed slowly and gloomily with his party, anxious to ascertain the truth of these tidings, to make partisans, if possible, among those who had newly arrived, and to take advantage of every circumstance that might befriend his rash and hazardous projects. The Adelantado left strong guards on the passes of the roads to prevent his near approach to San Domingo, but Roldan paused within a few leagues of the place.

When the Adelantado found himself secure in San Domingo with this augmentation of force, and the prospect of a still greater re-enforcement at hand, his magnanimity prevailed over his indignation, and he sought by gentle means to allay the popular seditions that the island might be restored to tranquillity before his brother's arrival. He considered that the colo-

---

[1] **Las Casas. Herrera, Hist del Almirante.**

nists had suffered greatly from the want of supplies; that their discontents had been heightened by the severities he had been compelled to inflict; and that many had been led to rebellion by doubts of the legitimacy of his authority. While therefore he proclaimed the royal act sanctioning his title and powers, he promised amnesty for all past offences. on condition of immediate return to allegiance. Hearing that Roldan was within five leagues of San Domingo with his band, he sent Pedro Fernandez Coronal, who had been appointed by the sovereigns alguazil mayor of the island. to exhort him to obedience. promising him oblivion of the past. He trusted that the representations of a discreet and honorable man like Coronal, who had been witness of the favor in which his brother stood in Spain, would convince the rebels of the hopelessness of their course

Roldan. however, conscious of his guilt, and doubtful of the clemency of Don Bartholomew, feared to venture within his power; he determined also to prevent his followers from communicating with Coronal, lest they should be seduced from him by the promise of pardon. When that emissary, therefore, approached the encampment of the rebels, he was opposed in a narrow pass by a body of archers, with their cross-bows levelled. "Halt there! traitor!" cried Roldan; "had you arrived eight days later. we should all have been united as one man." [1]

In vain Coronal endeavored by fair reasoning and earnest entreaty to win this perverse and turbulent man from his career. Roldan answered with hardihood and defiance, professing to oppose only the tyranny and misrule of the Adelantado, but to be ready to submit to the admiral on his arrival. He and several of his principal confederates wrote letters to the same effect to their friends in San Domingo, urging them to plead their cause with the admiral when he should arrive, and to assure him of their disposition to acknowledge his authority

When Coronal returned with accounts of Roldan's contumacy, the Adelantado proclaimed him and his followers traitors. That shrewd rebel, however, did not suffer his men to remain within either the seduction of promise or the terror of menace; he immediately set out on his march for his promised land of Xaragua, trusting to impair every honest principle and virtuous tie of his misguided followers by a life of indolence and libertinage.

In the mean time the mischievous effects of his intrigues

---

[1] Herrera, decad. i lib iii. cap. 8

among the caciques became more and more apparent. No sooner had the Adelantado left Fort Conception than a conspiracy was formed among the natives to surprise it. Guarionex was at the head of this conspiracy, moved by the instigations of Roldan, who had promised him protection and assistance, and led on by the forlorn hope, in this distracted state of the Spanish forces, of relieving his paternal domains from the intolerable domination of usurping strangers. Holding secret communications with his tributary caciques, it was concerted that they should all rise simultaneously and massacre the soldiery quartered in small parties in their villages : while he, with a chosen force, should surprise the fortress of Conception. The night of the full moon was fixed upon for the insurrection.

One of the principal caciques, however, not being a correct observer of the heavenly bodies, took up arms before the appointed night, and was repulsed by the soldiers quartered in his village. The alarm was given, and the Spaniards were all put on the alert. The cacique fled to Guarionex for protection, but the chieftain, enraged at his fatal blunder, put him to death upon the spot.

No sooner did the Adelantado hear of this fresh conspiracy than he put himself on the march for the Vega with a strong body of men. Guarionex did not await his coming. He saw that every attempt was fruitless to shake off these strangers, who had settled like a curse upon his territories. He had found their very friendship withering and destructive, and he now dreaded their vengeance. Abandoning, therefore, his rightful domain, the once happy Vega, he fled with his family and a small band of faithful followers to the mountains of Ciguay. This is a lofty chain, extending along the north side of the island, between the Vega and the sea. The inhabitants were the most robust and hardy tribe of the island, and far more formidable than the mild inhabitants of the plains. It was a part of this tribe which displayed hostility to the Spaniards in the course of the first voyage of Columbus, and in a skirmish with them in the Gulf of Samana the first drop of native blood had been shed in the New World. The reader may remember the frank and confiding conduct of these people the day after the skirmish, and the intrepid faith with which their cacique trusted himself on board of the caravel of the admiral, and in the power of the Spaniards. It was to this same cacique, named Mayohanex, that the fugitive chieftain of the Vega now applied for refuge. He came to his residence at an Indian town near Cape Cabron, about forty leagues east of Isabella, and implored shelter for his wife and children, and his handful of loyal followers. The noble-minded cacique of the mountains received him with open arms. He not only gave an asylum to his family, but engaged to stand by him in his distress, to defend his cause, and share his desperate fortunes.[1] Men in civilized life learn magnanimity from precept, but their most generous actions are often rivalled by the deeds of untutored savages, who act only from natural impulse.

CHAPTER VII.

CAMPAIGN OF THE ADELANTADO IN THE MOUNTAINS OF CIGUAY.

[1498.]

AIDED by his mountain ally, and by bands of hardy Ciguayans, Guarionex made several descents into the plain, cutting off straggling parties of the Spaniards, laying waste the villages of the natives which continued in allegiance to them, and destroying the fruits of the earth. The Adelantado put a speedy stop to these molestations; but he determined to root out so formidable an adversary from the neighborhood. Shrinking from no danger nor fatigue, and leaving nothing to be done by others which he could do himself, he set forth in the spring with a band of ninety men, a few cavalry, and a body of Indians, to penetrate the Ciguay mountains

After passing a steep defile, rendered almost impracticable for troops by rugged rocks and exuberant vegetation, he descended into a beautiful valley or plain, extending along the coast, and embraced by arms of the mountains which approached the sea. His advance into the country was watched by the keen eyes of Indian scouts, who lurked among rocks and thickets. As the Spaniards were seeking the ford of a river at the entrance of the plain, two of these spies darted from among the bushes on its bank. One flung himself headlong into the water, and swimming across the mouth of the river escaped; the other being taken, gave information that six thousand Indians lay in ambush on the opposite shore, waiting to attack them as they crossed.

The Adelantado advanced with caution, and finding a shallow

---

[1] Las Casas, Hist. Ind., cap. 121, MS. Peter Martyr, decad. 1. cap. 5.

place, entered the river with his troops. They were scarcely midway in the stream when the savages, hideously painted, and looking more like fiends than men, burst from their concealment. The forests rang with their yells and howlings. They discharged a shower of arrows and lances, by which, notwithstanding the protection of their targets, many of the Spaniards were wounded. The Adelantado, however, forced his way across the river, and the Indians took to flight. Some were killed, but their swiftness of foot, their knowledge of the forest, and their dexterity in winding through the most tangled thickets, enabled the greater number to elude the pursuit of the Spaniards, who were encumbered with armor, targets, crossbows, and lances.

By the advice of one of his Indian guides, the Adelantado pressed forward along the valley to reach the residence of Mayobanex, at Cabron. In the way he had several skirmishes with the natives, who would suddenly rush forth with furious war-cries from ambuscades among the bushes, discharge their weapons, and take refuge again in the fastness of their rocks and forests, inaccessible to the Spaniards.

Having taken several prisoners, the Adelantado sent one accompanied by an Indian of a friendly tribe, as a messenger to Mayobanex, demanding the surrender of Guarionex; promising friendship and protection in case of compliance, but threatening, in case of refusal, to lay waste his territory with fire and sword. The cacique listened attentively to the messenger: "Tell the Spaniards," said he in reply, "that they are bad men, cruel and tyrannical, usurpers of the territories of others, and shedders of innocent blood. I desire not the friendship of such men; Guarionex is a good man, he is my friend, he is my guest, he has fled to me for refuge. I have promised to protect him, and I will keep my word."

This magnanimous reply, or rather defiance, convinced the Adelantado that nothing was to be gained by friendly overtures. When severity was required, he could be a stern soldier. He immediately ordered the village in which he had been quartered, and several others in the neighborhood, to be set on fire. He then sent further messengers to Mayobanex warning him that, unless he delivered up the fugitive cacique, his whole dominions should be laid waste in like manner; and he would see nothing in every direction but the smoke and flames of burning villages. Alarmed at this impending destruction, the Ciguayans surrounded their chieftain with clamorous lamentations, cursing the day that Guarionex had taken refuge among

them, and urging that he should be given up for the salvation
of the country. The generous cacique was inflexible. He
reminded them of the many virtues of Guarionex and the sacred
claims he had on their hospitality, and declared he would abide
all evils rather than it should ever be said Mayobanex had
betrayed his guest.

The people retired with sorrowful hearts, and the chieftain,
summoning Guarionex into his presence, again pledged his
word to protect him, though it should cost him his dominions.
He sent no reply to the Adelantado, and lest further messages
might tempt the fidelity of his subjects, he placed men in ambush, with orders to slay any messenger who might approach.
They had not lain in wait long before they beheld two men
advancing through the forest, one of whom was a captive
Ciguayan, and the other an Indian ally of the Spaniards.
They were both instantly slain. The Adelantado was following
at no great distance, with only ten foot soldiers and four horsemen. When he found his messengers lying dead in the forest
path, transfixed with arrows, he was greatly exasperated, and
resolved to deal rigorously with this obstinate tribe He
advanced, therefore, with all his force to Cabron, where Mayobanex and his army were quartered At his approach the
inferior caciques and their adherents fled, overcome by terror of
the Spaniards. Finding himself thus deserted, Mayobanex
took refuge with his family in a secret part of the mountains.
Several of the Ciguayans sought for Guarionex, to kill him or
deliver him up as a propitiatory offering, but he fled to the
heights, where he wandered about alone, in the most savage
and desolate places.

The density of the forests and the ruggedness of the mountains rendered this expedition excessively painful and laborious,
and protracted it far beyond the time that the Adelantado had
contemplated. His men suffered, not merely from fatigue,
but hunger. The natives had all fled to the mountains; their
villages remained empty and desolate : all the provisions of the
Spaniards consisted of cassava bread, and such roots and herbs
as their Indian allies could gather for them, with now and then
a few utias, taken with the assistance of their dogs. They slept
almost always on the ground, in the open air, under the trees,
exposed to the heavy dew which falls in this climate. For three
months they were thus ranging the mountains : until almost
worn out with toil and hard fare. Many of them had farms in
the neighborhood of Fort Conception, which required their
attention ; they, therefore, entreated permission, since the

Indians were terrified and dispersed, to return to their abodes in the Vega.

The Adelantado granted many of them passports, and an allowance out of the scanty stock of bread which remained. Retaining only thirty men, he resolved with these to search every den and cavern of the mountains until he should find the two caciques. It was difficult, however, to trace them in such a wilderness. There was no one to give a clew to their retreat, for the whole country was abandoned. There were the habitations of men, but not a human being to be seen, or if, by chance, they caught some wretched Indian stealing forth from the mountains in quest of food, he always professed utter ignorance of the hiding-place of the caciques.

It happened, one day, however, that several Spaniards, while hunting utias, captured two of the followers of Mayobanex who were on their way to a distant village in search of bread. They were taken to the Adelantado, who compelled them to betray the place of concealment of their chieftain, and to act as guides. Twelve Spaniards volunteered to go in quest of him. Stripping themselves naked, staining and painting their bodies so as to look like Indians, and covering their swords with palm-leaves, they were conducted by the guides to the retreat of the unfortunate Mayobanex. They came secretly upon him, and found him surrounded by his wife and children and a few of his household, totally unsuspicious of danger. Drawing their swords, the Spaniards rushed upon them and made them all prisoners. When they were brought to the Adelantado, he gave up all further search after Guarionex, and returned to Fort Conception.

Among the prisoners thus taken was the sister of Mayobanex. She was the wife of another cacique of the mountains, whose territories had never yet been visited by the Spaniards; and she was reputed to be one of the most beautiful women of the island. Tenderly attached to her brother, she had abandoned the security of her own dominions, and had followed him among rocks and precipices, participating in all his hardships, and comforting him with a woman's sympathy and kindness. When her husband heard of her captivity, he hastened to the Adelantado and offered to submit himself and all his possessions to his sway, if his wife might be restored to him. The Adelantado accepted his offer of allegiance, and released his wife and several of his subjects who had been captured. The cacique, faithful to his word, became a firm and valuable ally of the Spaniards, cultivating large tracts of land, and supplying them with great quantities of bread and other provisions.

Kindness appears never to have been lost upon the people of this island. When this act of clemency reached the Ciguayans, they came in multitudes to the fortress, bringing presents of various kinds, promising allegiance, and imploring the release of Mayobanex and his family. The Adelantado granted their prayers in part, releasing the wife and household of the cacique, but still detaining him prisoner to insure the fidelity of his subjects.

In the mean time, the unfortunate Guarionex, who had been hiding in the wildest parts of the mountains, was driven by hunger to venture down occasionally into the plain in quest of food. The Ciguayans looking upon him as the cause of their misfortunes, and perhaps hoping by his sacrifice to procure the release of their chieftain, betrayed his haunts to the Adelantado. A party was despatched to secure him. They lay in wait in the path by which he usually returned to the mountains. As the unhappy cacique, after one of his famished excursions, was returning to his den among the cliffs, he was surprised by the lurking Spaniards, and brought in chains to Fort Conception. After his repeated insurrections, and the extraordinary zeal and perseverance displayed in his pursuit, Guarionex expected nothing less than death from the vengeance of the Adelantado. Don Bartholomew, however, though stern in his policy, was neither vindictive nor cruel in his nature. He considered the tranquillity of the Vega sufficiently secured by the captivity of the cacique; and ordered him to be detained a prisoner and hostage in the fortress. The Indian hostilities in this important part of the island being thus brought to a conclusion, and precautions taken to prevent their recurrence, Don Bartholomew returned to the city of San Domingo, where, shortly after his arrival, he had the happiness of receiving his brother, the admiral, after nearly two years and six months' absence.[1]

Such was the active, intrepid, and sagacious, but turbulent and disastrous administration of the Adelantado, in which we find evidences of the great capacity, the mental and bodily vigor of this self-formed and almost self-taught man. He united, in a singular degree, the sailor, the soldier, and the legislator. Like his brother, the admiral, his mind and manners rose immediately to the level of his situation, showing no arrogance nor ostentation, and exercising the sway of sudden

---

[1] The particulars of this chapter are chiefly from P. Martyr, decad. i. lib vi.; the manuscript history of Las Casas, lib. i. cap. 121, and Herrera, Hist. Ind., decad. i. lib. iii. cap. 8, 9.

and extraordinary power, with the sobriety and moderation of one who had been born to rule. He has been accused of severity in his government, but no instance appears of a cruel or wanton abuse of authority. If he was stern toward the factious Spaniards, he was just; the disasters of his administration were not produced by his own rigor, but by the perverse passions of others, which called for its exercise; and the admiral, who had more suavity of manner and benevolence of heart, was not more fortunate in conciliating the good-will and insuring the obedience of the colonists. The merits of Don Bartholomew do not appear to have been sufficiently appreciated by the world. His portrait has been suffered to remain too much in the shade; it is worthy of being brought into the light, as a companion to that of his illustrious brother. Less amiable and engaging, perhaps, in its lineaments, and less characterized by magnanimity, its traits are nevertheless bold, generous, and heroic, and stamped with iron firmness.

BOOK· XII.

CHAPTER I.

[August 30, 1498.]

COLUMBUS arrived at San Domingo. wearied by a long and arduous voyage, and worn down by infirmities; both mind and body craved repose, but from the time he first entered into public life he had been doomed never again to taste the sweets of tranquillity. The island of Hispaniola, the favorite child, as it were, of his hopes, was destined to involve him in perpetual troubles, to fetter his fortunes, impede his enterprises, and imbitter the conclusion of his life. What a scene of poverty and suffering had this opulent and lovely island been rendered by the bad passions of a few despicable men! The wars with the natives and the seditions among the colonists had put a stop to the labors of the mines, and all hopes of wealth were at an end. The horrors of famine had succeeded to those of war. The cultivation of the earth had been generally neglected; several of the provinces had been desolated during the late troubles; a great part of the Indians had fled to the mountains, and those who remained had lost all heart to labor, seeing the produce of their toils liable to be wrested from them by ruthless strangers. It is true, the Vega was once more tranquil, but it was a desolate tranquillity. That beautiful region, which the Spaniards but four years before had found so populous and happy, seeming to enclose in its luxuriant bosom all the sweets of nature, and to exclude all the cares and sorrows of the world. was now a scene of wretchedness and repining. Many of those Indian towns, where the Spaniards had been detained by genial hospitality. and almost worshipped as beneficent deities, were now silent and deserted.

Some of their late inhabitants were lurking among rocks and caverns: some were reduced to slavery: many had perished with hunger, and many had fallen by the sword. It seems almost incredible, that so small a number of men, restrained too by well-meaning governors, could in so short a space of time have produced such wide-spreading miseries. But the principles of evil have a fatal activity. With every exertion, the best of men can do but a moderate amount of good; but it seems in the power of the most contemptible individual to do incalculable mischief.

The evil passions of the white men which had inflicted such calamities upon this innocent people, had insured likewise a merited return of suffering to themselves. In no part was this more truly exemplified than among the inhabitants of Isabella, the most idle, factious, and dissolute of the island. The public works were unfinished; the gardens and fields they had begun to cultivate lay neglected: they had driven the natives from their vicinity by extortion and cruelty, and had rendered the country around them a solitary wilderness. Too idle to labor, and destitute of any resources with which to occupy their indolence, they quarrelled among themselves, mutinied against their rulers, and wasted their time in alternate riot and despondency. Many of the soldiery quartered about the island had suffered from ill health during the late troubles, being shut up in Indian villages where they could take no exercise, and obliged to subsist on food to which they could not accustom themselves. Those actively employed had been worn down by hard service, long marches, and scanty food. Many of them were broken in constitution, and many had perished by disease. There was a universal desire to leave the island, and escape from miseries created by themselves. Yet this was the favored and fruitful land to which the eyes of philosophers and poets in Europe were fondly turned, as realizing the pictures of the golden age. So true it is that the fairest Elysium fancy ever devised would be turned into a purgatory by the passions of bad men!

One of the first measures of Columbus on his arrival was to issue a proclamation approving of all the measures of the Adelantado, and denouncing Roldan and his associates. That turbulent man had taken possession of Xaragua, and been kindly received by the natives. He had permitted his followers to lead an idle and licentious life among its beautiful scenes, making the surrounding country and its inhabitants subservient to their pleasures and their passions. An event happened previous to their knowledge of the arrival of Columbus, which threw supplies into their hands and strengthened their power. As they were one day loitering on the sea-shore, they beheld three caravels at a distance, the sight of which, in this unfrequented part of the ocean, filled them with wonder and alarm. The ships approached the land and came to anchor The rebels apprehended at first they were vessels despatched in pursuit of them. Roldan, however, who was sagacious as he was bold, surmised them to be ships which had wandered from their course, and been borne to the westward by the currents, and that they must be ignorant of the recent occurrences of the island Enjoining secrecy on his men he went on board, pretending to be stationed in that neighborhood for the purpose of keeping the natives in obedience, and collecting tribute. His conjectures as to the vessels were correct. They were, in fact, the three caravels detached by Columbus from his squadron at the Canary Islands, to bring supplies to the colonies. The captains, ignorant of the strength of the currents, which set through the Caribbean Sea, had been carried west far beyond their reckoning until they had wandered to the coast of Xaragua.

Roldan kept his secret closely for three days. Being considered a man in important trust and authority, the captains did not hesitate to grant all his requests for supplies. He procured swords, lances, cross-bows, and various military stores : while his men dispersed through the three vessels, were busy among the crews, secretly making partisans, representing the hard life of the colonists at San Domingo, and the ease and revelry in which they passed their time at Xaragua. Many of the crews had been shipped in compliance with the admiral's ill-judged proposition, to commute criminal punishments into transportation to the colony. They were vagabonds, the refuse of Spanish towns, and culprits from Spanish dungeons ; the very men, therefore, to be wrought upon by such representations, and they promised to desert on the first opportunity and join the rebels.

It was not until the third day that Alonzo Sanchez de Carvajal, the most intelligent of the three captains, discovered the real character of the guests he had admitted so freely on board of his vessels. It was then too late ; the mischief was effected. He and his fellow-captains had many earnest conversations with Roldan, endeavoring to persuade him from his dangerous opposition to the regular authority. The certainty that Columbus was actually on his way to the island, with additional forces and augmented authority, had operated strongly on his mind. He had, as has already been intimated, prepared his friends at San Domingo to plead his cause with the admiral, assuring him that he only acted in opposition to the injustice and oppression of the Adelantado, but was ready to submit to Columbus on his arrival. Carvajal perceived that the resolution of Roldan and of several of his principal confederates was shaken, and flattered himself that, if he were to remain some little time among the rebels, he might succeed in drawing them back to their duty. Contrary winds rendered it impossible for the ships to work up against the currents to San Domingo. It was arranged among the captains, therefore, that a large number of the people on board, artificers and others most important to the service of the colony, should proceed to the settlement by land. They were to be conducted by Juan Antonio Colombo, captain of one of the caravels, a relative of the admiral, and zealously devoted to his interests. Arana was to proceed with the ships, when the wind would permit, and Carvajal volunteered to remain on shore to endeavor to bring the rebels to their allegiance.

On the following morning Juan Antonio Colombo landed with forty men well armed with cross-bows, swords, and lances, but was astonished to find himself suddenly deserted by all his party excepting eight. The deserters went off to the rebels, who received with exultation this important re-enforcement of kindred spirits. Juan Antonio endeavored in vain by remonstrances and threats to bring them back to their duty. They were most of them convicted culprits, accustomed to detest order, and to set law at defiance. It was equally in vain that he appealed to Roldan, and reminded him of his professions of loyalty to the government. The latter replied that he had no means of enforcing obedience; his was a mere "Monastery of Observation," where every one was at liberty to adopt the habit of the order. Such was the first of a long train of evils, which sprang from this most ill-judged expedient of peopling a colony with criminals, and thus mingling vice and villany with the fountain-head of its population.

Juan Antonio, grieved and disconcerted, returned on board with the few who remained faithful. Fearing further desertions, the two captains immediately put to sea, leaving Carvajal on shore to prosecute his attempt at reforming the rebels. It was not without great difficulty and delay that the vessels reached San Domingo; the ship of Carvajal having struck on a sand-bank, and sustained great injury. By the time of their arrival, the greater part of the provisions with which they had been freighted was either exhausted or damaged. Alonzo Sanchez de Carvajal arrived shortly afterward by land, having been escorted to within six leagues of the place by several of the insurgents, to protect him from the Indians. He failed in his attempt to persuade the band to immediate submission; but Roldan had promised that the moment he heard of the arrival of Columbus he would repair to the neighborhood of San Domingo, to be at hand to state his grievances, and the reasons of his past conduct, and to enter into a negotiation for the adjustment of all differences. Carvajal brought a letter from him to the admiral to the same purport, and expressed a confident opinion, from all that he observed of the rebels, that they might easily be brought back to their allegiance by an assurance of amnesty.[1]

CHAPTER II.

NEGOTIATION OF THE ADMIRAL WITH THE REBELS — DEPARTURE OF SHIPS FOR SPAIN.

[1498.]

NOTWITHSTANDING the favorable representations of Carvajal, Columbus was greatly troubled by the late event at Xaragua He saw that the insolence of the rebels and their confidence in their strength must be greatly increased by the accession of such a large number of well-armed and desperate confederates. The proposition of Roldan to approach to the neighborhood of San Domingo startled him. He doubted the sincerity of his professions, and apprehended great evils and dangers from so artful, daring, and turbulent a leader, with a rash and devoted crew at his command. The example of this lawless horde, roving at large about the island, and living in loose revel and open prodigacy, could not but have a dangerous effect upon the colonists newly arrived; and when they were close at hand, to carry on secret intrigues, and to hold out a camp of refuge to all malcontents, the loyalty of the whole colony might be sapped and undermined.

Some measures were immediately necessary to fortify the fidelity of the people against such seductions. He was aware

---

[1] Las Casas, lib. i cap. 149, 150. Herrera, decad. i. lib. iii cap. 12. Hist del Almirante, cap. 77.

of a vehement desire among many to return to Spain; and of an assertion industriously propagated by the seditious, that he and his brothers wished to detain the colonists on the island through motives of self-interest. On the 12th of September, therefore, he issued a proclamation, offering free passage and provisions for the voyage to all who wished to return to Spain. in five vessels nearly ready to put to sea. He hoped by this means to relieve the colony from the idle and disaffected: to weaken the party of Roldan, and to retain none about him but such as were sound-hearted and well-disposed.

He wrote at the same time to Miguel Ballester, the stanch and well-tried veteran who commanded the fortress of Conception, advising him to be upon his guard, as the rebels were coming into his neighborhood. He empowered him also to have an interview with Roldan; to offer him pardon and oblivion of the past, on condition of his immediate return to duty; and to invite him to repair to San Domingo to have an interview with the admiral under a solemn, and, if required, a written assurance from the latter, of personal safety. Columbus was sincere in his intentions. He was of a benevolent and placable disposition, and singularly free from all vindictive feeling toward the many worthless and wicked men who heaped sorrow on his head.

Ballester had scarcely received this letter when the rebels began to arrive at the village of Bonao. This was situated in a beautiful valley, or Vega, bearing the same name, about ten leagues from Fort Conception, and about twenty from San Domingo, in a well-peopled and abundant country. Here Pedro Requelme, one of the ringleaders of the sedition, had large possessions, and his residence became the headquarters of the rebels. Adrian de Moxica, a man of turbulent and mischievous character, brought his detachment of dissolute ruffians to this place of rendezvous. Roldan and others of the conspirators drew together there by different routes.

No sooner did the veteran Miguel Ballester hear of the arrival of Roldan than he set forth to meet him. Ballester was a venerable man, gray-headed, and of a soldier-like demeanor. Loyal, frank, and virtuous, of a serious disposition, and great simplicity of heart. he was well chosen as a mediator with rash and profligate men; being calculated to calm their passions by his sobriety; to disarm their petulance by his age: to win their confidence by his artless probity; and to awe their licentiousness by his spotless virtue.[1]

---

[1] Las Casas, Hist. Ind., lib. 1 cap. 153.

Ballester found Roldan in company with Pedro Requelme, Pedro de Gamez, and Adrian de Moxica, three of his principal confederates. Flushed with a confidence of his present strength, Roldan treated the proffered pardon with contempt, declaring that he did not come there to treat of peace, but to demand the release of certain Indians captured unjustifiably, and about to be shipped to Spain as slaves, notwithstanding that he, in his capacity of alcalde mayor, had pledged his word for their protection. He declared that, until these Indians were given up, he would listen to no terms of compact, throwing out an insolent intimation at the same time, that he held the admiral and his fortunes in his hand, to make and mar them as he pleased.

The Indians here alluded to were certain subjects of Guarionex, who had been incited by Roldan to resist the exaction of tribute, and who, under the sanction of his supposed authority, had engaged in the insurrections of the Vega. Roldan knew that the enslavement of the Indians was an unpopular feature in the government of the island, especially with the queen; and the artful character of this man is evinced in his giving his opposition to Columbus the appearance of a vindication of the rights of the suffering islanders. Other demands were made of a highly insolent nature, and the rebels declared that, in all further negotiations, they would treat with no other intermediate agent than Carvajal, having had proofs of his fairness and impartiality in the course of their late communications with him at Xaragua

This arrogant reply to his proffer of pardon was totally different from what the admiral had been led to expect, and placed him in an embarrassing situation. He seemed surrounded by treachery and falsehood. He knew that Roldan had friends and secret partisans even among those who professed to remain faithful; and he knew not how far the ramifications of the conspiracy might extend. A circumstance soon occurred to show the justice of his apprehensions. He ordered the men of San Domingo to appear under arms, that he might ascertain the force with which he could take the field in case of necessity. A report was immediately circulated that they were to be led to Bonao against the rebels. Not above seventy men appeared under arms, and of these not forty were to be relied upon. One affected to be lame, another ill: some had relations, and others had friends among the followers of Roldan; almost all were disaffected to the service.[1]

---

[1] Hist. del Almirante, cap. 78.

Columbus saw that a resort to arms would betray his own weakness and the power of the rebels, and completely prostrate the dignity and authority of government. It was necessary to temporize, therefore, however humiliating such conduct might be deemed. He had detained the five ships for eighteen days in port, hoping in some way to have put an end to this rebellion, so as to send home favorable accounts of the island to the sovereigns. The provisions of the ships, however, were wasting. The Indian prisoners on board were suffering and perishing; several of them threw themselves overboard, or were suffocated with heat in the holds of the vessels. He was anxious also that as many of the discontented colonists as possible should make sail for Spain before any commotion should take place.

On the 18th of October, therefore, the ships put to sea.[1] Columbus wrote to the sovereigns an account of the rebellion, and of his proffered pardon being refused. As Roldan pretended that it was a mere quarrel between him and the Adelantado, of which the admiral was not an impartial judge, the latter entreated that Roldan might be summoned to Spain, where the sovereigns might be his judges; or that an investigation might take place in presence of Alonzo Sanchez de Carvajal, who was friendly to Roldan, and of Miguel Ballester, as witness on the part of the Adelantado. He attributed, in a great measure, the troubles of this island to his own long detention in Spain, and the delays thrown in his way by those appointed to assist him, who had retarded the departure of the ships with supplies, until the colony had been reduced to the greatest scarcity. Hence had arisen discontent, murmuring, and finally rebellion. He entreated the sovereigns, in the most pressing manner, that the affairs of the colony might not be neglected, and those at Seville, who had charge of its concerns, might be instructed at least not to devise impediments instead of assistance. He alluded to his chastisement of the contemptible Ximeno Breviesca, the insolent minion of Fonseca, and entreated that neither that nor any other circumstance might be allowed to prejudice him in the royal favor, through the misrepresentations of designing men. He assured them that the natural resources of the island required nothing but good management to supply all the wants of the colonists; but that the latter were indolent and profligate. He proposed to send home by every ship, as in the present instance, a number of the discontented and worthless, to be replaced by sober and industrious men. He begged also that

---

[1] In one of these ships sailed the father of the venerable historian, Las Casas, from whom he derived many of the facts of his history Las Casas, lib. i. cap 153.

ecclesiastics might be sent out for the instruction and conversion of the Indians; and, what was equally necessary, for the reformation of the dissolute Spaniards. He required also a man learned in the law to officiate as judge over the island, together with several officers of the royal revenue. Nothing could surpass the soundness and policy of these suggestions; but unfortunately one clause marred the moral beauty of this excellent letter. He requested that for two years longer the Spaniards might be permitted to employ the Indians as slaves; only making use of such, however, as were captured in wars and insurrections. Columbus had the usage of the age in excuse for this suggestion; but it is at variance with his usual benignity of feeling, and his paternal conduct toward these unfortunate people.

At the same time he wrote another letter, giving an account of his recent voyage, accompanied by a chart, and by specimens of the gold, and particularly of the pearls found in the Gulf of Paria. He called especial attention to the latter as being the first specimens of pearls found in the New World. It was in this letter that he described the newly discovered continent in such enthusiastic terms as the most favored part of the East, the source of inexhaustible treasures, the supposed seat of the terrestrial paradise : and he promised to prosecute the discovery of its glorious realms with the three remaining ships as soon as the affairs of the island should permit.

By this opportunity Roldan and his friends likewise sent letters to Spain, endeavoring to justify their rebellion by charging Columbus and his brothers with oppression and injustice, and painting their whole conduct in the blackest colors. It would naturally be supposed that the representations of such men would have little weight in the balance against the tried merits and exalted services of Columbus; but they had numerous friends and relatives in Spain; they had the popular prejudice on their side, and there were designing persons in the confidence of the sovereigns ready to advocate their cause. Columbus, to use his own simple but affecting words, was " absent, envied, and a stranger." [1]

---

[1] Las Casas, Hist. Ind., lib. 1 cap. 157.

CHAPTER III.

NEGOTIATIONS AND ARRANGEMENTS WITH THE REBELS.

[1498.]

THE ships being despatched, Columbus resumed his negotiation with the rebels, determined at any sacrifice to put an end to a sedition which distracted the island and interrupted all his plans of discovery His three remaining ships lay idle in the harbor, though a region of apparently boundless wealth was to be explored. He had intended to send his brother on the discovery, but the active and military spirit of the Adelantado rendered his presence indispensable, in case the rebels should come to violence. Such were the difficulties encountered at every step of his generous and magnanimous enterprises ; impeded at one time by the insidious intrigues of crafty men in place, and checked at another by the insolent turbulence of a handful of ruffians.

In his consultations with the most important persons about him, Columbus found that much of the popular discontent was attributed to the strict rule of his brother, who was accused of dealing out justice with a rigorous hand. Las Casas. however, who saw the whole of the testimony collected from various sources with respect to the conduct of the Adelantado. acquits him of all charges of the kind, and affirms that, with respect to Roldan in particular. he had exerted great forbearance. Be this as it may, Columbus now, by the advice of his counsellors, resolved to try the alternative of extreme lenity. He wrote a letter to Roldan, dated the 20th of October, couched in the most conciliating terms, calling to mind past kindnesses, and expressing deep concern for the feud existing between him and the Adelantado. He entreated him, for the common good, and for the sake of his own reputation, which stood well with the sovereigns, not to persist in his present insubordination, and repeated the assurance that he and his companions might come to him, under the faith of his word for the inviolability of their persons.

There was a difficulty as to who should be the bearer of this letter. The rebels had declared that they would receive no one as mediator but Alonzo Sanchez de Carvajal. Strong doubts, however, existed in the minds of those about Columbus as to the integrity of that officer. They observed that he had suffered Roldan to remain two days on board of his caravel at Xaragua; had furnished him with weapons and stores, had neglected to detain him on board, when he knew him to be a rebel; had not exerted himself to retake the deserters; had been escorted on his way to San Domingo by the rebels, and had sent refreshments to them at Bonao. It was alleged, moreover, that he had given himself out as a colleague of Columbus, appointed by government to have a watch and control over his conduct. It was suggested, that, in advising the rebels to approach San Domingo, he had intended, in case the admiral did not arrive, to unite his pretended authority as colleague, to that of Roldan, as chief judge, and to seize upon the reins of government. Finally, the desire of the rebels to have him sent to them as an agent, was cited as proof that he was to join them as a leader, and that the standard of rebellion was to be hoisted at Bonao.[1] These circumstances, for some time, perplexed Columbus: but he reflected that Carvajal, as far as he had observed his conduct, had behaved like a man of integrity; most of the circumstances alleged against him admitted of a construction in his favor, the rest were mere rumors, and he had unfortunately experienced in his own case, how easily the fairest actions and the fairest characters may be falsified by rumor He discarded, therefore, all suspicion, and determined to confide implicitly in Carvajal, nor had he ever any reason to repent of his confidence.

The admiral had scarcely despatched this letter, when he received one from the leaders of the rebels, written several days previously. In this they not merely vindicated themselves from the charge of rebellion, but claimed great merit, as having dissuaded their followers from a resolution to kill the Adelantado, in revenge of his oppressions, prevailing upon them to wait patiently for redress from the admiral. A month had elapsed since his arrival, during which they had awaited anxiously for his orders, but he had manifested nothing but irritation against them. Considerations of honor and safety, therefore, obliged them to withdraw from his service, and they accordingly demanded their discharge. This letter was dated from Bonao, the 17th of October, and signed by Francisco Roldan, Adrian de Moxica, Pedro de Gamez, and Diego de Escobar.[2]

---

[1] Hist. del Almirante, cap. 78.
[2] Hist. del Almirante, cap. 79. Herrera, decad. 1. lib. iii cap. 15.

In the mean time Carvajal arrived at Bonao, accompanied by Miguel Ballester. They found the rebels full of arrogance and presumption. The conciliating letter of the admiral however, enforced by the earnest persuasions of Carvajal and the admonitions of the veteran Ballester, had a favorable effect on several of the leaders, who had more intellect than their brutal followers. Roldan, Gamez, Escobar, and two or three others, actually mounted their horses to repair to the admiral, but were detained by the clamorous opposition of their men; too infatuated with their idle, licentious mode of life, to relish the idea of a return to labor and discipline. These insisted that it was a matter which concerned them all; whatever arrangement was to be made, therefore, should be made in public, in writing, and subject to their approbation or dissent. A day or two elapsed before this clamor could be appeased. Roldan then wrote to the admiral, that his followers objected to his coming, unless a written assurance, or passport, was sent, protecting the persons of himself and such as should accompany him. Miguel Ballester wrote, at the same time, to the admiral, urging him to agree to whatever terms the rebels might demand. He represented their forces as continually augmenting, the soldiers of his garrison daily deserting to them; unless, therefore, some compromise were speedily effected, and the rebels shipped off to Spain, he feared that, not merely the authority, but even the person of the admiral would be in danger; for though the Hidalgos and the officers and servants immediately about him would, doubtless, die in his service, the common people were but little to be depended upon.[1]

Columbus felt the increasing urgency of the case, and sent the required passport. Roldan came to San Domingo; but, from his conduct, it appeared as if his object was to make partisans, and gain deserters, rather than to effect a reconciliation. He had several conversations with the admiral, and several letters passed between them. He made many complaints, and numerous demands; Columbus made large concessions, but some of the pretensions were too arrogant to be admitted.[2] Nothing definite was arranged. Roldan departed under the pretext of conferring with his people, promising to send his terms in writing. The admiral sent his mayordomo, Diego de Salamanca, to treat in his behalf.[3]

On the 6th of November Roldan wrote a letter from Bonao,

---

[1] Las Casas, Hist. Ind., lib. 1 cap. 153   [2] Ibid., cap. 158.
[3] Hist. del Almirante, cap 79.

containing his terms, and requesting that a reply might be sent to him to Conception, as scarcity of provisions obliged him to leave Bonao. He added that he should wait for a reply until the following Monday (the 11th). There was an insolent menace implied in this note, accompanied as it was by insolent demands. The admiral found it impossible to comply with the latter; but to manifest his lenient disposition, and to take from the rebels all plea of rigor, he had a proclamation affixed for thirty days at the gate of the fortress, promising full indulgence and complete oblivion of the past to Roldan and his followers, on condition of their presenting themselves before him and returning to their allegiance to the crown within a month; together with free conveyance for all such as wished to return to Spain; but threatening to execute rigorous justice upon those who should not appear within the limited time. A copy of this paper he sent to Roldan by Carvajal, with a letter, stating the impossibility of compliance with his terms, but offering to agree to any compact drawn up with the approbation of Carvajal and Salamanca.

When Carvajal arrived, he found the veteran Ballester actually besieged in his fortress of Conception by Roldan, under pretext of claiming, in his official character of alcalde mayor, a culprit who had taken refuge there from justice. He had cut off the supply of water from the fort, by way of distressing it into a surrender. When Carvajal posted up the proclamation of the admiral on the gate of the fortress, the rebels scoffed at the proffered amnesty, saying that, in a little while, they would oblige the admiral to ask the same at their hands. The earnest intercessions of Carvajal, however, brought the leaders at length to reflection, and through his mediation articles of capitulation were drawn up. By these it was agreed that Roldan and his followers should embark for Spain from the port of Xaragua in two ships, to be fitted out and victualled within fifty days. That they should each receive from the admiral a certificate of good conduct, and an order for the amount of their pay, up to the actual date. That slaves should be given to them, as had been given to others, in consideration of services performed, and as several of their company had wives, natives of the island, who were pregnant, or had lately been delivered, they might take them with them, if willing to go, in place of the slaves. That satisfaction should be made for property of some of the company which had been sequestrated, and for live stock which had belonged to Francisco Roldan. There were other conditions, providing for the security of their per sons, and it was stipulated that, if no reply were received to these terms within eight days, the whole should be void.[1]

This agreement was signed by Roldan and his companions at Fort Conception on the 16th of November, and by the admiral at San Domingo on the 21st. At the same time, he proclaimed a further act of grace, permitting such as chose to remain in the island either to come to San Domingo, and enter into the royal service, or to hold lands in any part of the island. They preferred, however, to follow the fortunes of Roldan, who departed with his band for Xaragua. to await the arrival of the ships, accompanied by Miguel Ballester, sent by the admiral to superintend the preparations for their embarkation.

Columbus was deeply grieved to have his projected enterprise to Terra Firma impeded by such contemptible obstacles, and the ships which should have borne his brother to explore that newly-found continent devoted to the use of this turbulent and worthless rabble. He consoled himself, however, with the reflection, that all the mischief which had so long been lurking in the island, would thus be at once shipped off, and thenceforth every thing restored to order and tranquillity. He ordered every exertion to be made, therefore, to get the ships in readiness to be sent round to Xaragua; but the scarcity of sea-stores, and the difficulty of completing the arrangements for such a voyage in the disordered state of the colony, delayed their departure far beyond the stipulated time. Feeling that he had been compelled to a kind of deception toward the sovereigns, in the certificate of good conduct given to Roldan and his followers, he wrote a letter to them, stating the circumstances under which that certificate had been in a manner wrung from him to save the island from utter confusion and ruin. He represented the real character and conduct of those men; how they had rebelled against his authority; prevented the Indians from paying tribute: pillaged the island: possessed themselves of large quantities of gold, and carried off the daughters of several of the caciques. He advised, therefore, that they should be seized, and their slaves and treasure taken from them, until their conduct could be properly investigated. This letter he intrusted to a confidential person, who was to go in one of the ships.[2]

The rebels having left the neighborhood, and the affairs of San Domingo being in a state of security, Columbus put his brother Don Diego in temporary command, and departed with

---

[1] Hist. del Almirante, cap. 80.   [2] Herrera Hist. Ind.. decad i. lib. iii cap. 16.

the Adelantado on a tour of several months to visit the various stations, and restore the island to order.

The two caravels destined for the use of the rebels sailed from San Domingo for Xaragua about the end of February; but, encountering a violent storm, were obliged to put into one of the harbors of the island, where they were detained until the end of March. One was so disabled as to be compelled to return to San Domingo. Another vessel was despatched to supply its place, in which the indefatigable Carvajal set sail, to expedite the embarkation of the rebels. He was eleven days in making the voyage, and found the other caravel at Xaragua.

The followers of Roldan had in the mean time changed their minds, and now refused to embark; as usual, they threw all the blame on Columbus, affirming that he had purposely delayed the ships far beyond the stipulated time, that he had sent them in a state not seaworthy, and short of provisions, with many other charges, artfully founded on circumstances over which they knew he could have no control. Carvajal made a formal protest before a notary who had accompanied him, and finding that the ships were suffering great injury from the teredo or worm, and their provisions failing, he sent them back to San Domingo, and set out on his return by land. Roldan accompanied him a little distance on horseback, evidently disturbed in mind. He feared to return to Spain, yet was shrewd enough to know the insecurity of his present situation at the head of a band of dissolute men, acting in defiance of authority. What tie had he upon their fidelity stronger than the sacred obligations which they had violated? After riding thoughtfully for some distance, he paused, and requested some private conversation with Carvajal, before they parted. They alighted under the shade of a tree. Here Roldan made further professions of the loyalty of his intentions, and finally declared, that if the admiral would once more send him a written security for his person, with the guaranty also of the principal persons about him, he would come to treat with him, and trusted that the whole matter would be arranged on terms satisfactory to both parties. This offer, however, he added, must be kept secret from his followers.

Carvajal, overjoyed at this prospect of a final arrangement, lost no time in conveying the proposition of Roldan to the admiral. The latter immediately forwarded the required passport or security, sealed with the royal seal, accompanied by a letter written in amicable terms, exhorting his quiet obedience to the authority of the sovereigns. Several of the principal persons also, who were with the admiral, wrote, at his request, a letter of security to Roldan, pledging themselves for the safety of himself and his followers during the negotiation, provided they did nothing hostile to the royal authority or its representative.

While Columbus was thus, with unwearied assiduity and loyal zeal, endeavoring to bring the island back to its obedience, he received a reply from Spain, to the earnest representations made by him, in the preceding autumn, of the distracted state of the colony and the outrages of these lawless men, and his prayers for royal countenance and support. The letter was written by his invidious enemy, the Bishop Fonseca, superintendent of Indian affairs. It acknowledged the receipt of his statement of the alleged insurrection of Roldan, but observed that this matter must be suffered to remain in suspense, as the sovereigns would investigate and remedy it presently.[1]

This cold reply had a disheartening effect upon Columbus. He saw that his complaints had little weight with the government : he feared that his enemies were prejudicing him with the sovereigns, and he anticipated redoubled insolence on the part of the rebels, when they should discover how little influence he possessed in Spain. Full of zeal, however, for the success of his undertaking, and of fidelity to the interests of the sovereigns, he resolved to spare no personal sacrifice of comfort or dignity in appeasing the troubles of the island. Eager to expedite the negotiation with Roldan, therefore, he sailed in the latter part of August with two caravels to the port of Azua, west of San Domingo, and much nearer to Xaragua. He was accompanied by several of the most important personages of the colony. Roldan repaired thither likewise, with the turbulent Adrian de Moxica, and a number of his band. The concessions already obtained had increased his presumption : and he had, doubtless, received intelligence of the cold manner in which the complaints of the admiral had been received in Spain. He conducted himself more like a conqueror, exacting triumphant terms, than a delinquent seeking to procure pardon by atonement. He came on board of the caravel, and with his usual effrontery, propounded the preliminaries upon which he and his companions were disposed to negotiate.

First, that he should be permitted to send several of his company, to the number of fifteen, to Spain, in the vessels which were at San Domingo. Secondly, that those who remained

---

[1] Herrara, decad. i. lib. iii. cap. 16.

should have lands granted them, in place of royal pay.   Thirdly, that it should be proclaimed that every thing charged against him and his party had been grounded upon false testimony, and the machinations of persons disaffected to the royal service. Fourthly, that he should be reinstated in his office of alcalde mayor, or chief judge.[1]

These were hard and insolent conditions to commence with, but they were granted.   Roldan then went on shore, and communicated them to his companions.   At the end of two days the insurgents sent their capitulations, drawn up in form, and couched in arrogant language, including all the stipulations granted at Fort Conception, with those recently demanded by Roldan, and concluding with one, more insolent than all the rest, namely, that if the admiral should fail in the fulfilment of any of these articles, they should have a right to assemble together, and compel his performance of them by force, or by any other means they might think proper.[2]   The conspirators thus sought not merely exculpation of the past, but a pretext for future rebellion.

The mind grows wearied and impatient with recording, and the heart of the generous reader must burn with indignation at perusing, this protracted and ineffectual struggle of a man of the exalted merits and matchless services of Columbus, in the toils of such miscreants.   Surrounded by doubt and danger ; a foreigner among a jealous people ; an unpopular commander in a mutinous island, distrusted and slighted by the government he was seeking to serve ; and creating suspicion by his very services, he knew not where to look for faithful advice, efficient aid, or candid judgment.   The very ground on which he stood seemed giving way under him, for he was told of seditious symptoms among his own people.   Seeing the impunity with which the rebels rioted in the possession of one of the finest parts of the island, they began to talk among themselves of following their example, of abandoning the standard of the admiral, and seizing upon the province of Higuey, at the eastern extremity of the island, which was said to contain valuable mines of gold

Thus critically situated, disregarding every consideration of personal pride and dignity, and determined, at any individual sacrifice, to secure the interests of an ungrateful sovereign, Columbus forced himself to sign this most humiliating capitulation.   He trusted that afterward, when he could gain quiet

---

[1] Herrera, decad. i lib iii. cap. 16   [2] Ibid.   Hist. del Almirante, cap. 38.

access to the royal ear, he should be able to convince the king and queen that it had been compulsory. and forced from him by the extraordinary difficulties in which he had been placed, and the imminent perils of the colony. Before signing it, however, he inserted a stipulation, that the commands of the sov reigns, of himself, and of the justices appointed by him, should be punctually obeyed.[1]

CHAPTER IV.

GRANTS MADE TO ROLDAN AND HIS FOLLOWERS — DEPARTURE OF SEVERAL OF THE REBELS FOR SPAIN.

[1499.]

WHEN Roldan resumed his office of alcalde mayor, or chie judge, he displayed all the arrogance to be expected from one who had intruded himself into power by profligate means. At the city of San Domingo he was always surrounded by his faction; communed only with the dissolute and disaffected; and, having all the turbulent and desperate men of the community at his beck, was enabled to intimidate the quiet and loyal by his frowns. He bore an impudent front against the authority even of Columbus himself, discharging from office one Rodrigo Perez, a lieutenant of the admiral, declaring that none but such as he appointed should bear a staff of office in the island.[1] Columbus had a difficult and painful task in bearing with the insolence of this man, and of the shameless rabble which had returned, under his auspices, to the settlements. He tacitly permitted many abuses; endeavoring by mildness and indulgence to allay the jealousies and prejudices awakened against him, and by various concessions to lure the factious to the performance of their duty. To such of the colonists generally as preferred to remain in the island, he offered a choice of either royal pay or portions of lands. with a number of Indians. some free, others as slaves, to assist in the cultivation. The latter was generally preferred: and grants were made out. in which he endeavored as much as possible to combine the benefit of the individual with the interests of the colony.

Roldan presented a memorial signed by upward of one hundred of his late followers. demanding grants of lands and

---

[1] Herrera, Hist. Ind., decad. I. lib. iii. cap. 16.   [2] Ibid.

licenses to settle, and choosing Xaragua for their place of abode. The admiral feared to trust such a numerous body of factious partisans in so remote a province, he contrived, therefore, to distribute them in various parts of the island, some at Bonao, where their settlement gave origin to the town of that name; others on the bank of the Rio Verde, or Green River, in the Vega; others about six leagues thence, at St. Jago. He assigned to them liberal portions of land, and numerous Indian slaves, taken in the wars. He made an arrangement, also, by which the caciques in their vicinity, instead of paying tribute, should furnish parties of their subjects, free Indians, to assist the colonists in the cultivation of their lands; a kind of feudal service, which was the origin of the repartimientos, or distributions of free Indians among the colonists, afterward generally adopted, and shamefully abused, throughout the Spanish colonies; a source of intolerable hardships and oppressions to the unhappy natives, and which greatly contributed to exterminate them from the island of Hispaniola.[1] Columbus considered the island in the light of a conquered country, and arrogated to himself all the rights of a conqueror, in the name of the sovereigns for whom he fought. Of course all his companions in the enterprise were entitled to take part in the acquired territory, and to establish themselves there as feudal lords reducing the natives to the condition of villains or vassals.[2] This was an arrangement widely different from his original intention of treating the natives with kindness, as peaceful subjects of the crown. But all his plans had been subverted, and his present measures forced upon him by the exigency of the times and the violence of lawless men. He appointed a captain with an armed band, as a kind of police, with orders to range the provinces; oblige the Indians to pay their tributes; watch over the conduct of the colonists; and check the least appearance of mutiny or insurrection.[3]

Having sought and obtained such ample provisions for his followers, Roldan was not more modest in making demands for himself. He claimed certain lands in the vicinity of Isabella, as having belonged to him before his rebellion, also a royal farm, called La Esperanza, situated on the Vega, and devoted to the rearing of poultry. These the admiral granted him with permission to employ, in the cultivation of the farm, the subjects of the cacique whose ears had been cut off by Alonzo de Ojeda in his first military expedition into the Vega. Roldan

---

[1] Herrera, decad. 1. lib. iii. cap 16.   [2] Munoz, Hist. N Mundo, lib. vi. § 50.
[3] Hist. del Almirante, cap. 84

received also grants of land in Xaragua, and a variety of live-stock from the cattle and other animals belonging to the crown. These grants were made to him provisionally, until the pleasure of the sovereigns should be known;[1] for Columbus yet trusted that when they should understand the manner in which these concessions had been extorted from him, the ringleaders of the rebels would not merely be stripped of their ill-gotten posses-sions, but receive well-merited punishment.

Roldan having now enriched himself beyond his hopes, requested permission of Columbus to visit his lands. This was granted with great reluctance. He immediately departed for the Vega, and stopping at Bonao, his late headquarters, made Pedro Requelme one of his most active confederates, alcalde, or judge of the place, with the power of arresting all delin-quents, and sending them prisoners to the fortress of Concep-tion, where he reserved to himself the right of sentencing them. This was an assumption of powers not vested in his office, and gave great offence to Columbus. Other circumstances created apprehensions of further troubles from the late insurgents. Pedro Requelme, under pretext of erecting farming buildings for his cattle, began to construct a strong edifice on a hill, capable of being converted into a formidable fortress. This, it was whispered, was done in concert with Roldan, by way of securing a stronghold in case of need. Being in the neighbor-hood of the Vega, where so many of their late partisans were settled, it would form a dangerous rallying place for any new sedition. The designs of Requelme were suspected and his proceedings opposed by Pedro de Arana, a loyal and honorable man, who was on the spot. Representations were made by both parties to the admiral, who prohibited Requelme from proceeding with the construction of his edifice.[2]

Columbus had prepared to return, with his brother, Don Bartholomew, to Spain, where he felt that his presence was of the utmost importance to place the late events of the island in a proper light; having found that his letters of explanation were liable to be counteracted by the misrepresentations of malevo-lent enemies. The island, however, was still in a feverish state. He was not well assured of the fidelity of the late rebels, though so dearly purchased, there was a rumor of a threatened descent into the Vega, by the mountain tribes of Ciguay, to attempt the rescue of their captive cacique Mayobanex, still detained a pris-oner in the fortress of Conception. Tidings were brought about the

---

[1] Herrera, decad. i. lib. iii. cap. 16.   [2] Ibid. Hist. del Almirante, cap 83, 84.

same time from the western parts of the island, that four strange ships had arrived at the coast, under suspicious appearances. These circumstances obliged him to postpone his departure, and held him involved in the affairs of this favorite but fatal island.

The two caravels were despatched for Spain in the beginning of October, taking such of the colonists as chose to return, and among them a number of Roldan's partisans. Some of these took with them slaves, others carried away the daughters of caciques, whom they had beguiled from their families and homes. At these iniquities, no less than at many others which equally grieved his spirit, the admiral was obliged to connive. He was conscious, at the same time, that he was sending home a re-enforcement of enemies and false witnesses, to defame his character and traduce his conduct, but he had no alternative. To counteract, as much as possible, their misrepresentations, he sent by the same caravel the loyal and upright veteran Miguel Ballester, together with Garcia de Barrantes, empowered to attend to his affairs at court, and furnished with the depositions taken relative to the conduct of Roldan and his accomplices.

In his letters to the sovereigns he entreated them to inquire into the truth of the late transactions. He stated his opinion that his capitulations with the rebels were null and void, for various reasons — viz., they had been extorted from him by violence, and at sea, where he did not exercise the office of viceroy : there had been two trials relative to the insurrection and the insurgents having been condemned as traitors, it was not in the power of the admiral to absolve them from their criminality ; the capitulations treated of matters touching the royal revenue, over which he had no control, without the intervention of the proper officers , lastly, Francisco Roldan and his companions, on leaving Spain, had taken an oath to be faithful to the sovereigns, and to the admiral in their name, which oath they had violated. For these and similar reasons, some just, others rather sophistical, he urged the sovereigns not to consider themselves bound to ratify the compulsory terms ceded to these profligate men, but to inquire into their offences, and treat them accordingly.[1]

He repeated the request made in the former letter, that a learned judge might be sent out to administer the laws in the island, since he himself had been charged with rigor, although conscious of having always observed a guarded clemency. He

---

[1] Herrera, decad. i. lib. iii. cap. 16.

requested also that discreet persons should be sent out to form a council, and others for certain fiscal employments, entreating. however. that their powers should be so limited and defined, as not to interfere with his dignity and privileges. He bore strongly on this point: as his prerogatives on former occasions had been grievously invaded. It appeared to him, he said. that princes ought to show much confidence in their governors; for without the royal favor to give them strength and consequence, every thing went to ruin under their command; a sound maxim, forced from the admiral by his recent experience, in which much of his own perplexities, and the triumph of the rebels. had been caused by the distrust of the crown. and its inattention to his remonstrances.

Finding age and infirmity creeping upon him. and his health much impaired by his last voyage, he began to think of his son Diego. as an active coadjutor: who, being destined as his successor, might gain experience under his eye, for the future discharge of his high duties. Diego. though still serving as a page at the court, was grown to man's estate, and capable of entering into the important concerns of life. Columbus entreated, therefore, that he might be sent out to assist him, as he felt himself infirm in health and broken in constitution, and less capable of exertion than formerly.[1]

CHAPTER V.

ARRIVAL OF OJEDA WITH A SQUADRON AT THE WESTERN PART OF THE ISLAND — ROLDAN SENT TO MEET HIM.

[1499.]

AMONG the causes which induced Columbus to postpone his departure for Spain. has been mentioned the arrival of four ships at the western part of the island. These had anchored on the 5th of September in a harbor a little below Jacquemel, apparently with the design of cutting dyewoods, which abound in that neighborhood. and of carrying off the natives for slaves. Further reports informed him that they were commanded by Alonzo de Ojeda, the same hot-headed and bold-hearted cavalier who had distinguished himself on various occasions in the

---

[1] Herrera, decad. 1. lib. iii. cap. 16.

previous voyages of discovery, and particularly in the capture of the cacique Caonabo. Knowing the daring and adventurous spirit of this man, Columbus felt much disturbed at his visiting the island in this clandestine manner, on what appeared to be little better than a freebooting expedition. To call him to account, and oppose his aggressions, required an agent of spirit and address. No one seemed better fitted for the purpose than Roldan. He was as daring as Ojeda, and of a more crafty character. An expedition of the kind would occupy the attention of himself and his partisans, and divert them from any schemes of mischief. The large concessions recently made to them would, he trusted, secure their present fidelity, rendering it more profitable for them to be loyal than rebellious.

Roldan readily undertook the enterprise. He had nothing further to gain by sedition, and was anxious to secure his ill-gotten possessions and atone for past offences by public services. He was vain as well as active, and took a pride in acquitting himself well in an expedition which called for both courage and shrewdness. Departing from San Domingo with two caravels, he arrived on the 29th of September within two leagues of the harbor where the ships of Ojeda were anchored. Here he landed with five and twenty resolute followers, well armed, and accustomed to range the forests. He sent five scouts to reconnoitre. They brought word that Ojeda was several leagues distant from his ships, with only fifteen men, employed in making cassava bread in an Indian village. Roldan threw himself between them and the ships, thinking to take them by surprise. They were apprised, however, of his approach by the Indians, with whom the very name of Roldan inspired terror, from his late excesses in Xaragua. Ojeda saw his danger: he supposed Roldan had been sent in pursuit of him, and he found himself cut off from his ships. With his usual intrepidity he immediately presented himself before Roldan, attended merely by half a dozen followers. The latter craftily began by conversing on general topics. He then inquired into his motives for landing on the island, particularly on that remote and lonely part, without first reporting his arrival to the admiral. Ojeda replied that he had been on a voyage of discovery, and had put in there in distress, to repair his ships and procure provisions. Roldan then demanded, in the name of the government, a sight of the license under which he sailed. Ojeda, who knew the resolute character of the man he had to deal with, restrained his natural impetuosity, and replied that his papers were on board of his ship. He declared his intention, on departing thence, to go to

San Domingo, and pay his homage to the admiral, having many things to tell him which were for his private ear alone. He intimated to Roldan that the admiral was in complete disgrace at court; that there was a talk of taking from him his command, and that the queen, his patroness, was ill beyond all hopes of recovery. This intimation, it is presumed, was referred to by Roldan in his despatches to the admiral, wherein he mentioned that certain things had been communicated to him by Ojeda, which he did not think it safe to confide to a letter.

Roldan now repaired to the ships. He found several persons on board with whom he was acquainted, and who had already been in Hispaniola. They confirmed the truth of what Ojeda had said, and showed a license signed by the Bishop of Fonseca, as superintendent of the affairs of the Indias. authorizing him to sail on a voyage of discovery.[1]

It appeared, from the report of Ojeda and his followers, that the glowing accounts sent home by Columbus of his late discoveries on the coast of Paria, his magnificent speculations with respect to the riches of the newly-found country, and the specimen of pearls transmitted to the sovereigns, had inflamed the cupidity of various adventurers. Ojeda happened to be at that time in Spain. He was a favorite of the Bishop of Fonseca, and obtained a sight of the letter written by the admiral to the sovereigns, and the charts and maps of his route by which it was accompanied. Ojeda knew Columbus to be embarrassed by the seditions of Hispaniola ; he found, by his conversations with Fonseca and other of the admiral's enemies, that strong doubts and jealousies existed in the mind of the king with respect to his conduct. and that his approaching downfall was confidently predicted. The idea of taking advantage of these circumstances struck Ojeda. and. by a private enterprise. he hoped to be the first in gathering the wealth of these newly-discovered regions. He communicated his project to his patron. Fonseca. The latter was but too ready for any thing that might defeat the plans and obscure the glory of Columbus : and it may be added that he always showed himself more disposed to patronize mercenary adventurers than upright and high-minded men. He granted Ojeda every facility ; furnishing him with copies of the papers and charts of Columbus, by which to direct himself in his course, and a letter of license signed with his own name, though not with that of the sovereigns. In this, it was stipulated that he should not touch at any land belonging

---

[1] Herrera. decad. 1. lib. iv. cap. 3.

to the King of Portugal, nor any that had been discovered by Columbus prior to 1495 The last provision shows the perfidious artifice of Fonseca, as it left Paria and the Pearl Islands free to the visits of Ojeda, they having been discovered by Columbus subsequent to the designated year. The ships were to be fitted out at the charges of the adventurers, and a certain proportion of the products of the voyage were to be rendered to the crown.

Under this license Ojeda fitted out four ships at Seville, assisted by many eager and wealthy speculators. Among the number was the celebrated Amerigo Vespucci, a Florentine merchant, well acquainted with geography and navigation. The principal pilot of the expedition was Juan de la Cosa, a mariner of great repute, a disciple of the admiral, whom he had accompanied in his first voyage of discovery, and in that along the southern coast of Cuba, and round the island of Jamaica. There were several also of the mariners, and Bartholomew Roldan, a distinguished pilot, who had been with Columbus in his voyage to Paria.[1] Such was the expedition which, by a singular train of circumstances, eventually gave the name of this Florentine merchant Amerigo Vespucci, to the whole of the New World.

This expedition had sailed in May, 1499. The adventurers had arrived on the southern continent, and ranged along its coast, from two hundred leagues east of the Oronoco, to the Gulf of Paria. Guided by the charts of Columbus, they had passed through this gulf, and through the Boca del Dragon, and had kept along westward to Cape de la Vela, visiting the island of Margarita and the adjacent continent, and discovering the gulf of Venezuela. They had subsequently touched at the Caribbee Islands, where they had fought with the fierce natives, and made many captives, with the intention of selling them in the slave-markets of Spain. Thence, being in need of supplies, they had sailed to Hispaniola, having performed the most extensive voyage hitherto made along the shores of the New World.[2]

Having collected all the information that he could obtain concerning these voyagers, their adventures and designs, and trusting to the declaration of Ojeda, that he should proceed forthwith to present himself to the admiral, Roldan returned to San Domingo to render a report of his mission.

---

[1] Las Casas.
[2] Herrera. Hist. Ind., decad. i. lib. iv. cap. 4. Muñoz, Hist. N. Mundo, part in MS unpublished.

CHAPTER VI.

MANŒUVRES OF ROLDAN AND OJEDA.

[1500.]

WHEN intelligence was brought to Columbus of the nature of the expedition of Ojeda, and the license under which he sailed, he considered himself deeply aggrieved, it being a direct infraction of his most important prerogatives, and sanctioned by authority which ought to have held them sacred. He awaited patiently, however, the promised visit of Alonzo de Ojeda to obtain further explanations. Nothing was farther from the intention of that roving commander than to keep such promise: he had made it merely to elude the vigilance of Roldan. As soon as he had refitted his vessels and obtained a supply of provisions, he sailed round to the coast of Xaragua, where he arrived in February. Here he was well received by the Spaniards resident in that province, who supplied all his wants. Among them were many of the late comrades of Roldan; loose, random characters, impatient of order and restraint, and burning with animosity against the admiral, for having again brought them under the wholesome authority of the laws.

Knowing the rash and fearless character of Ojeda, and finding that there were jealousies between him and the admiral, they hailed him as a new leader, come to redress their fancied grievances, in place of Roldan, whom they considered as having deserted them. They made clamorous complaints to Ojeda of the injustice of the admiral, whom they charged with withholding from them the arrears of their pay.

Ojeda was a hot-headed man, with somewhat of a vaunting spirit, and immediately set himself up for a redresser of grievances. It is said also that he gave himself out as authorized by government, in conjunction with Carvajal, to act as counsellors, or rather supervisors of the admiral; and that one of the first measures they were to take, was to enforce the payment of all salaries due to the servants of the crown.[1] It is questionable, however, whether Ojeda made any pretension of the kind, which could so readily be disproved, and would have tended to disgrace him with the government. It is probable that he was

---

[1] Hist. del Almirante, cap. 84.

encouraged in his intermeddling, chiefly by his knowledge of
the tottering state of the admiral's favor at court, and of his
own security in the powerful protection of Fonseca. He may
have imbibed also the opinion diligently fostered by those with
whom he had chiefly communicated in Spain, just before his
departure, that these people had been driven to extremities by
the oppression of the admiral and his brothers. Some feeling
of generosity, therefore, may have mingled with his usual love
of action and enterprise, when he proposed to redress all their
wrongs, put himself at their head, march at once to San
Domingo, and oblige the admiral to pay them on the spot,
or expel him from the island.

The proposition of Ojeda was received with acclamations of
transport by some of the rebels; others made objections.
Quarrels arose; a ruffianly scene of violence and brawl ensued,
in which several were killed and wounded on both sides; but
the party for the expedition to San Domingo remained triumphant.

Fortunately for the peace and safety of the admiral, Roldan
arrived in the neighborhood just at this critical juncture, attended by a crew of resolute fellows. He had been despatched
by Columbus to watch the movements of Ojeda, on hearing of
his arrival on the coast of Xaragua. Apprised of the violent
scenes which were taking place, Roldan, when on the way, sent
to his old confederate, Diego de Escobar, to follow him with all
the trusty force he could collect. They reached Xaragua within
a day of each other. An instance of the bad faith usual between
bad men was now evinced. The former partisans of Roldan,
finding him earnest in his intention of serving the government,
and that there was no hope of engaging him in their new sedition, sought to waylay and destroy him on his march, but his
vigilance and celerity prevented them.[1]

Ojeda, when he heard of the approach of Roldan and Escobar,
retired on board of his ships. Though of a daring spirit, he
had no inclination, in the present instance, to come to blows,
where there was a certainty of desperate fighting, and no gain;
and where he must raise his arm against government. Roldan
now issued such remonstrances as had often been ineffectually
addressed to himself. He wrote to Ojeda, reasoning with him
on his conduct, and the confusion he was producing in the
island, and inviting him on shore to an amicable arrangement
of all alleged grievances. Ojeda, knowing the crafty, vio-

---

[1] Hist. del Almirante, ubi sup.

lent character of Roldan, disregarded his repeated messages, and refused to venture within his power. He even seized one of his messengers, Diego de Truxillo, and landing suddenly at Xaragua, carried off another of his followers, named Toribio de Lenares, both of whom he detained in irons, on board of his vessel, as hostages for a certain Juan Pintor, a one-armed sailor, who had deserted, threatening to hang them if the deserter was not given up.[1]

Various manœuvres took place between these two well-matched opponents; each wary of the address and prowess of the other. Ojeda made sail, and stood twelve leagues to the northward, to the province of Cahay, one of the most beautiful and fertile parts of the country, and inhabited by a kind and gentle people. Here he landed with forty men, seizing upon whatever he could find of the provisions of the natives. Roldan and Escobar followed along shore, and were soon at his heels. Roldan then despatched Escobar in a light canoe, paddled swiftly by Indians, who approaching within hail of the ship, informed Ojeda that, since he would not trust himself on shore, Roldan would come and confer with him on board, if he would send a boat for him.

Ojeda now thought himself secure of his enemy; he immediately despatched a boat within a short distance of the shore, where the crew lay on their oars, requiring Roldan to come to them. "How many may accompany me?" demanded the latter. "Only five or six," was the reply. Upon this Diego de Escobar and four others waded to the boat. The crew refused to admit more. Roldan then ordered one man to carry him to the barge, and another to walk by his side and assist him. By this stratagem, his party was eight strong. The instant he entered the boat he ordered the oarsmen to row to shore. On their refusing, he and his companions attacked them sword in hand, wounded several, and made all prisoners, excepting an Indian archer, who, plunging under the water, escaped by swimming.

This was an important triumph for Roldan. Ojeda, anxious for the recovery of his boat, which was indispensable for the service of the ship, now made overtures of peace. He approached the shore in his remaining boat of small size, taking with him his principal pilot, an arquebusier, and four oarsmen. Roldan entered the boat he had just captured, with seven rowers and fifteen fighting men, causing fifteen others to be ready

---

[1] Las Casas, Hist. Ind., lib. i. cap. 169, MS.

on shore to embark in a large canoe, in case of need. A characteristic interview took place between these doughty antago-
nists, each keeping warily on his guard. Their conference was
carried on at a distance. Ojeda justified his hostile movements
by alleging that Roldan had come with an armed force to seize
him. This the latter positively denied, promising him the most
amicable reception from the admiral, in case he would repair
to San Domingo. An arrangement was at length effected; the
boat was restored, and mutual restitution of the men took
place, with the exception of Juan Pintor, the one-armed deserter,
who had absconded; and on the following day Ojeda, according to agreement, set sail to leave the island, threatening however, to return at a future time with more ships and men.[1]

Roldan waited in the neighborhood, doubting the truth of
his departure. In the course of a few days word was brought
that Ojeda had landed on a distant part of the coast. He immediately pursued him with eighty men, in canoes, sending
scouts by land. Before he arrived at the place Ojeda had again
made sail, and Roldan saw and heard no more of him. Las
Casas asserts, however, that Ojeda departed either to some remote district of Hispaniola, or to the island of Porto Rico,
where he made up what he called his *cavalgada*, or drove of
slaves. carrying off numbers of the unhappy natives, whom he
sold in the slave-market of Cadiz.[2]

CHAPTER VII.

CONSPIRACY OF GUEVARA AND MOXICA.

[1500.]

WHEN men have been accustomed to act falsely, they take
great merit to themselves for an exertion of common honesty.
The followers of Roldan were loud in trumpeting forth their
unwonted loyalty, and the great service they had rendered to
government in driving Ojeda from the island. Like all reformed knaves, they expected that their good conduct would
be amply rewarded. Looking upon their leader as having
every thing in his gift, and being well pleased with the delightful province of Cahay. they requested him to share the land

---

[1] Letter of Columbus to the Nurse of Prince Juan   [2] Las Casas, lib. i. cap 169.

among them, that they might settle there. Roldan would have had no hesitation in granting their request had it been made during his freebooting career; but he was now anxious to establish a character for adherence to the laws. He declined, therefore, acceding to their wishes, until sanctioned by the admiral. Knowing, however, that he had fostered a spirit among these men which it was dangerous to contradict, and that their rapacity, by long indulgence, did not admit of delay, he shared among them certain lands of his own, in the territory of his ancient host Behechio, cacique of Xaragua. He then wrote to the admiral for permission to return to San Domingo, and received a letter in reply, giving him many thanks and commendations for the diligence and address which he had manifested, but requesting him to remain for a time in Xaragua, lest Ojeda should be yet hovering about the coast, and disposed to make another descent in that province.

The troubles of the island were not yet at an end, but were destined again to break forth, and from somewhat of a romantic cause. There arrived about this time, at Xaragua, a young cavalier of noble family, named Don Hernando de Guevara. He possessed an agreeable person and winning manners, but was headstrong in his passions and dissolute in his principles. He was cousin to Adrian de Moxica, one of the most active ringleaders in the late rebellion of Roldan, and had conducted himself with such licentiousness at San Domingo that Columbus had banished him from the island. There being no other opportunity of embarking, he had been sent to Xaragua, to return to Spain in one of the ships of Ojeda, but arrived after their departure. Roldan received him favorably, on account of his old comrade, Adrian de Moxica, and permitted him to choose some place of residence until further orders concerning him should arrive from the admiral. He chose the province of Cahay, at the place where Roldan had captured the boat of Ojeda. It was a delightful part of that beautiful coast ; but the reason why Guevara chose it, was its vicinity to Xaragua. While at the latter place, in consequence of the indulgence of Roldan, he was favorably received at the house of Anacaona, the widow of Caonabo, and sister of the cacique Behechio. That remarkable woman still retained her partiality to the Spaniards, notwithstanding the disgraceful scenes which had passed before her eyes ; and the native dignity of her character had commanded the respect even of the dissolute rabble which infested her province. By her late husband, the cacique Caonabo, she had a daughter named Higuenamota, just grown up, and greatly admired for her beauty. Guevara, being often in company with her, a mutual attachment ensued. It was to be near her that he chose Cahay as a residence, at a place where his cousin Adrian de Moxica kept a number of dogs and hawks, to be employed in the chase. Guevara delayed his departure. Roldan discovered the reason, and warned him to desist from his pretensions and leave the province. Las Casas intimates that Roldan was himself attached to the young Indian beauty, and jealous of her preference of his rival. Anacaona, the mother, pleased with the gallant appearance and ingratiating manners of the youthful cavalier, favored his attachment. especially as he sought her daughter in marriage. Notwithstanding the orders of Roldan, Guevara still lingered in Xaragua, in the house of Anacaona; and sending for a priest, desired him to baptize his intended bride.

Hearing of this, Roldan sent for Guevara, and rebuked him sharply for remaining at Xaragua. and attempting to deceive a person of the importance of Anacaona, by insnaring the affections of her daughter. Guevara avowed the strength of his passion, and his correct intentions, and entreated permission to remain. Roldan was inflexible. He alleged that some evil construction might be put on his conduct by the admiral; but it is probable his true motive was a desire to send away a rival, who interfered with his own amorous designs. Guevara obeyed; but had scarce been three days at Cahay, when unable to remain longer absent from the object of his passion, he returned to Xaragua, accompanied by four or five friends, and concealed himself in the dwelling of Anacaona. Roldan, who was at that time confined by a malady in his eyes, being apprised of his return, sent orders for him to depart instantly to Cahay. The young cavalier assumed a tone of defiance. He warned Roldan not to make foes when he had such great need of friends; for to his certain knowledge, the admiral intended to behead him. Upon this. Roldan commanded him to quit that part of the island, and repair to San Domingo, to present himself before the admiral. The thoughts of being banished entirely from the vicinity of his Indian beauty checked the vehemence of the youth. He changed his tone of haughty defiance into one of humble supplication; and Roldan, appeased by this submission. permitted him to remain for the present in the neighborhood.

Roldan had instilled wilfulness and violence into the hearts of his late followers, and now was doomed to experience the effects. Guevara, incensed at his opposition to his passion,

meditated revenge. He soon made a party among the old comrades of Roldan, who detested, as a magistrate, the man they
had idolized as a leader. It was concerted to rise suddenly
upon him, and either to kill him or put out his eyes. Roldan
was apprised of the plot, and proceeded with his usual promptness. Guevara was seized in the dwelling of Anacaona, in the
presence of his intended bride; seven of his accomplices were
likewise arrested. Roldan immediately sent an account of the
affair to the admiral, professing, at present, to do nothing
without his authority, and declaring himself not competent to
judge impartially in the case. Columbus, who was at that
time at Fort Conception, in the Vega, ordered the prisoner to
be conducted to the fortress of San Domingo.

The vigorous measures of Roldan against his old comrades
produced commotions in the island. When Adrian de Moxica
heard that his cousin Guevara was a prisoner, and that, too,
by command of his former confederate, he was highly exasperated, and resolved on vengeance. Hastening to Bonao, the
old haunt of rebellion, he obtained the co-operation of Pedro
Requelme, the recently appointed alcalde. They went round
among their late companions in rebellion, who had received
lands and settled in various parts of the Vega, working upon
their ready passions, and enlisting their feelings in the cause
of an old comrade. These men seemed to have had an irresistible propensity to sedition. Guevara was a favorite with them
all; the charms of the Indian beauty had probably their
influence; and the conduct of Roldan was pronounced a tyrannical interference, to prevent a marriage agreeable to all parties, and beneficial to the colony. There is no being so odious
to his former associates as a reformed robber, or a rebel,
enlisted in the service of justice. The old scenes of faction were
renewed; the weapons which had scarce been hung up from
the recent rebellions, were again snatched down from the
walls, and rash preparations were made for action. Moxica
soon saw a body of daring and reckless men ready, with horse
and weapon, to follow him on any desperate enterprise. Blinded
by the impunity which had attended their former outrages, he
now threatened acts of greater atrocity, meditating, not merely
the rescue of his cousin, but the death of Roldan and the
admiral.

Columbus was at Fort Conception, with an inconsiderable
force, when this dangerous plot was concerted in his very
neighborhood. Not dreaming of any further hostilities from
men on whom he had lavished favors, he would doubtless have

fallen into their power, had not intelligence been brought him of the plot by a deserter from the conspirators. He saw at a glance the perils by which he was surrounded, and the storm about to burst upon the island. It was no longer a time for lenient measures; he determined to strike a blow which should crush the very head of the rebellion.

Taking with him but six or seven trusty servants, and three esquires, all well-armed, he set out in the night for the place where the ringleaders were quartered. Confiding probably in the secrecy of their plot, and the late passiveness of the admiral, they appeared to have been perfectly unguarded. Columbus came upon them by surprise, seized Moxica and several of his principal confederates, and bore them off to Fort Conception. The moment was critical: the Vega was ripe for a revolt; he had the fomenter of the conspiracy in his power, and an example was called for, that should strike terror into the factious He ordered Moxica to be hanged on the top of the fortress. The latter entreated to be allowed to confess himself previous to execution. A priest was summoned. The miserable Moxica, who had been so arrogant in rebellion, lost all courage at the near approach of death. He delayed to confess, beginning and pausing, and recommencing, and again hesitating, as if he hoped, by whiling away time, to give a chance for rescue. Instead of confessing his own sins, he accused others of criminality, who were known to be innocent; until Columbus, incensed at this falsehood and treachery, and losing all patience, in his mingled indignation and scorn, ordered the dastard wretch to be swung off from the battlements.[1]

This sudden act of severity was promptly followed up. Several of the accomplices of Moxica were condemned to death and thrown in irons to await their fate. Before the conspirators had time to recover from their astonishment, Pedro Requelme was taken, with several of his compeers, in his ruffian den at Bonao, and conveyed to the fortress of San Domingo, where was also confined the original mover of this second rebellion, Hernando de Guevara, the lover of the young Indian princess. These unexpected acts of rigor, proceeding from a quarter which had been long so lenient, had the desired effect. The conspirators fled for the most part to Xaragua, their old and favorite retreat. They were not suffered to congregate there again, and concert new seditions The Adelantado, seconded by Roldan, pursued them with his characteristic

---

[1] Herrera. decad. 1. lib iv. cap 5.

rapidity of movement and vigor of arm. It has been said that he carried a priest with him, in order that, as he arrested delinquents, they might be confessed and hanged upon the spot: but the more probable account is that he transmitted them prisoners to San Domingo. He had seventeen of them at one time confined in one common dungeon, awaiting their trial, while he continued in indefatigable pursuit of the remainder.[1]

These were prompt and severe measures; but when we consider how long Columbus had borne with these men; how much he had ceded and sacrificed to them: how he had been interrupted in all his great undertakings, and the welfare of the colony destroyed by their contemptible and seditious brawls; how they had abused his lenity, defied his authority, and at length attempted his life — we cannot wonder that he should at last let fall the sword of justice, which he had hitherto held suspended.

The power of faction was now completely subdued, and the good effects of the various measures taken by Columbus, since his last arrival, for the benefit of the island, began to appear. The Indians, seeing the inefficacy of resistance, submitted to the yoke. Many gave signs of civilization, having, in some instances, adopted clothing and embraced Christianity. Assisted by their labors the Spaniards now cultivated their lands diligently, and there was every appearance of settled and regular prosperity.

Columbus considered all this happy change as brought about by the especial intervention of Heaven. In a letter to Doña Juana de la Torre, a lady of distinction, aya or nurse of Prince Juan, he gives an instance of those visionary fancies to which he was subject in times of illness and anxiety. In the preceding winter, he says, about the festival of Christmas, when menaced by Indian war and domestic rebellion, when distrustful of those around him and apprehensive of disgrace at court, he sank for a time into complete despondency. In this hour of gloom, when abandoned to despair, he heard in the night a voice addressing him in words of comfort. "Oh man of little faith! why art thou cast down? Fear nothing, I will provide for thee. The seven years of the term of gold are not expired; in that, and in all other things, I will take care of thee."

The seven years term of gold here mentioned alludes to a vow made by Columbus on discovering the New World, and recorded by him in a letter to the sovereigns, that within seven

---

[1] Las Casas, Hist Ind., lib. i. cap. 170, MS. Herrera, decad i. lib. iv cap. 7.

years he would furnish, from the profits of his discoveries, fifty thousand foot and five thousand horse, for the deliverance of the holy sepulchre, and an additional force of like amount, within five years afterward.

The comforting assurance given him by the voice was corroborated, he says, that very day, by intelligence received of the discovery of a large tract of country rich in mines.[1] This imaginary promise of divine aid thus mysteriously given, appeared to him at present in still greater progress of fulfilment. The troubles and dangers of the island had been succeeded by tranquillity. He now anticipated the prosperous prosecution of his favorite enterprise, so long interrupted — the exploring of the regions of Paria, and the establishment of a fishery in the Gulf of Pearls. How illusive were his hopes! At this moment events were maturing which were to overwhelm him with distress, strip him of his honors, and render him comparatively a wreck for the remainder of his days!

---

[1] Letter of Columbus to the Nurse of Prince Juan. Hist. del Almirante, cap 84.

BOOK XIII.

CHAPTER 1.

[1500.]

WHILE Columbus was involved in a series of difficulties in the factious island of Hispaniola, his enemies were but too successful in undermining his reputation in the court of Spain. The report brought by Ojeda of his anticipated disgrace was not entirely unfounded; the event was considered near at hand, and every perfidious exertion was made to accelerate it. Every vessel from the New World came freighted with complaints, representing Columbus and his brothers as new men, unaccustomed to command. inflated by their sudden rise from obscurity; arrogant and insulting toward men of birth and lofty spirit; oppressive of the common people, and cruel in their treatment of the natives. The insidious and illiberal insinuation was continually urged, that they were foreigners, who could have no interest in the glory of Spain, or the prosperity of Spaniards; and contemptible as this plea may seem, it had a powerful effect. Columbus was even accused of a design to cast off all allegiance to Spain, and either make himself sovereign of the countries he had discovered, or yield them into the hands of some other power; a slander, which, however extravagant, was calculated to startle the jealous mind of Ferdinand.

It is true that by every ship Columbus likewise sent home statements, written with the frankness and energy of truth, setting forth the real cause and nature of the distractions of the island, and pointing out and imploring remedies, which. if properly applied, might have been efficacious. His letters, however, arriving at distant intervals, made but single and transient impressions on the royal mind, which were speedily

441

effaced by the influence of daily and active misrepresentation. His enemies at court, having continual access to the sovereigns, were enabled to place every thing urged against him in the strongest point of view, while they secretly neutralized the force of his vindications. They used a plausible logic to prove either bad management or bad faith on his part. There was an incessant drain upon the mother country for the support of the colony. Was this compatible with the extravagant pictures he had drawn of the wealth of the island, and its golden mountains, in which he had pretended to find the Ophir of ancient days, the source of all the riches of Solomon? They inferred that he had either deceived the sovereigns by designing exaggerations, or grossly wronged them by malpractices, or was totally incapable of the duties of government.

The disappointment of Ferdinand, in finding his newly-discovered possessions a source of expense instead of profit, was known to press sorely on his mind. The wars, dictated by his ambition, had straitened his resources, and involved him in perplexities. He had looked with confidence to the New World for relief, and for ample means to pursue his triumphs; and grew impatient at the repeated demands which it occasioned on his scanty treasury. For the purpose of irritating his feelings and heightening his resentment, every disappointed and repining man who returned from the colony was encouraged by the hostile faction, to put in claims for pay withheld by Columbus, or losses sustained in his service. This was especially the case with the disorderly ruffians shipped off to free the island from sedition. Finding their way to the court at Granada, they followed the king when he rode out, filling the air with their complaints, and clamoring for their pay. At one time about fifty of these vagabonds found their way into the inner court of the Alhambra, under the royal apartments: holding up bunches of grapes as the meagre diet left them by their poverty, and railing aloud at the deceits of Columbus and the cruel neglect of government. The two sons of Columbus, who were pages to the queen, happening to pass by, they followed them with imprecations, exclaiming, "There go the sons of the admiral, the whelps of him who discovered the land of vanity and delusion, the grave of Spanish hidalgos." [1]

The incessant repetition of falsehood will gradually wear its way into the most candid mind. Isabella herself began to entertain doubts respecting the conduct of Columbus   Where there

---

[1] Hist. del Almirante, cap. 85.

was such universal and incessant complaint, it seemed reasonable to conclude that there must exist some fault. If Columbus and his brothers were upright, they might be injudicious ;
and. in government. mischief is oftener produced through error
of judgment than iniquity of design. The letters written by
Columbus himself presented a lamentable picture of the confusion of the island. Might not this arise from the weakness
and incapacity of the rulers ? Even granting that the prevalent
abuses arose in a great measure from the enmity of the people
to the admiral and his brothers, and their prejudices against
them as foreigners, was it safe to intrust so important and distant a command to persons so unpopular with the community ?

These considerations had much weight in the candid mind of
Isabella, but they were all-powerful with the cautious and jealous Ferdinand. He had never regarded Columbus with real
cordiality ; and ever since he had ascertained the importance of
his discoveries. had regretted the extensive powers vested in
his hands. The excessive clamors which had arisen during the
brief administration of the Adelantado and the breaking out of
the faction of Roldan at length determined the king to send out
some person of consequence and ability to investigate the affairs
of the colony, and if necessary for its safety, to take upon himself the command This important and critical measure it
appears had been decided upon, and the papers and powers
actually drawn out, in the spring of 1499. It was not carried
into effect, however, until the following year. Various reasons
have been assigned for this delay The important services
rendered by Columbus in the discovery of Paria and the Pearl
Islands may have had some effect on the royal mind. The
necessity of fitting out an armament just at that moment, to
co-operate with the Venetians against the Turks ; the menacing
movements of the new king of France, Louis XII. ; the rebellion
of the Moors of the Alpuxarra mountains, in the lately conquered kingdom of Granada — all these have been alleged as
reasons for postponing a measure which called for much consideration, and might have important effects upon the newly
discovered possessions.[1] The most probable reason, however,
was the strong disinclination of Isabella to take so harsh a step
against a man for whom she entertained such ardent gratitude
and high admiration.

At length the arrival of the ships with the late followers of
Roldan, according to their capitulation. brought matters to a

---

[1] Muñoz, Hist N. Mundo, part unpublished.

crisis. It is true that Ballester and Barrantes came in these ships, to place the affairs of the island in a proper light, but they brought out a host of witnesses in favor of Roldan and letters written by himself and his confederates, attributing all their late conduct to the tyranny of Columbus and his brothers. Unfortunately the testimony of the rebels had the greatest weight with Ferdinand; and there was a circumstance in the case which suspended for a time the friendship of Isabella, hitherto the greatest dependence of Columbus.

Having a maternal interest in the welfare of the natives, the queen had been repeatedly offended by what appeared to her pertinacity on the part of Columbus, in continuing to make slaves of those taken in warfare, in contradiction to her known wishes. The same ships which brought home the companions of Roldan, brought likewise a great number of slaves. Some, Columbus had been obliged to grant to these men by the articles of capitulation; others they had brought away clandestinely. Among them were several daughters of caciques, seduced away from their families and their native island by these profligates. Some of these were in a state of pregnancy, others had newborn infants. The gifts and transfers of these unhappy beings were all ascribed to the will of Columbus, and represented to Isabella in the darkest colors. Her sensibility as a woman, and her dignity as a queen. were instantly in arms. "What power," exclaimed she indignantly, "has the admiral to give away my vassals?"[1] Determined, by one decided and peremptory act, to show her abhorrence of these outrages upon humanity, she ordered all the Indians to be restored to their country and friends. Nay, more; her measure was retrospective. She commanded that those formerly sent to Spain by the admiral should be sought out and sent back to Hispaniola. Unfortunately for Columbus, at this very juncture, in one of his letters he advised the continuance of Indian slavery for some time longer, as a measure important for the welfare of the colony This contributed to heighten the indignation of Isabella, and induced her no longer to oppose the sending out of a commission to investigate his conduct. and, if necessary, to supersede him in command.

Ferdinand was exceedingly embarrassed in appointing this commission, between his sense of what was due to the character and services of Columbus, and his anxiety to retract with delicacy the powers vested in him. A pretext at length was

---

[1] Las Casas, lib. 1.

furnished by the recent request of the admiral that a person of
talents and probity, learned in the law, might be sent out to
act as chief judge; and that an impartial umpire might be
appointed, to decide in the affair between himself and Roldan.
Ferdinand proposed to consult his wishes, but to unite those
two offices in one; and as the person he appointed would have
to decide in matters touching the highest functions of the
admiral and his brothers, he was empowered, should he find
them culpable. to supersede them in the government: a singular mode of insuring partiality.

The person chosen for this momentous and delicate office was
Don Francisco de Bobadilla, an officer of the royal household,
and a commander of the military and religious order of Cala-
trava. Oviedo pronounces him a very honest and religious
man;[1] but he is represented by others, and his actions corroborate the description, as needy, passionate, and ambitious —
three powerful objections to his exercising the rights of judica-
ture in a case requiring the utmost patience. candor, and cir-
cumspection, and where the judge was to derive wealth and
power from the conviction of one of the parties.

The authority vested in Bobadilla is defined in letters from
the sovereigns still extant. and which deserve to be noticed
chronologically; for the royal intentions appear to have varied
with times and circumstances. The first was dated on the 21st
of March, 1499, and mentions the complaint of the admiral that
an alcalde. and certain other persons had risen in rebellion
against him. "Wherefore," adds the letter, "we order you to
inform yourself of the truth of the foregoing: to ascertain who
and what persons they were who rose against the said admiral
and our magistracy, and for what cause: and what robberies
and other injuries they have committed; and furthermore, to
extend your inquiries to all other matters relating to the premises; and the information obtained, and the truth known,
whomsoever you find culpable, *arrest their persons, and
sequestrate their effects*, and thus taken, proceed against them
and the absent, both civilly and criminally, and impose and
inflict such fines and punishments as you may think fit." To
carry this into effect, Bobadilla was authorized, in case of
necessity, to call in the assistance of the admiral, and of all
other persons in authority

The powers here given are manifestly directed merely
against the rebels, and in consequence of the complaints of Co-

---

[1] Oviedo. Cronica. lib. III. cap 6.

lumbus Another letter, dated on the 21st of May, two months subsequently, is of quite different purport. It makes no mention of Columbus, but is addressed to the various functionaries and men of property of the islands and Terra Firma, informing them of the appointment of Bobadilla to the government, with full civil and criminal jurisdiction. Among the powers specified, is the following: "It is our will, that if the said commander, Francisco de Bobadilla, should think it necessary for our service, and the purposes of justice, that any cavaliers, or other persons who are at present in those islands, or may arrive there, should leave them, and not return and reside in them, and that they should come and present themselves before us, he may command it in our name, and oblige them to depart; and whomsoever he thus commands, we hereby order, that immediately, without waiting to inquire or consult us, or to receive from us any other letter or command, and without interposing appeal or supplication, they obey whatever he shall say and order, under the penalties which he shall impose on our part," etc., etc.

Another letter, dated likewise on the 21st of May, in which Columbus is styled simply " admiral of the ocean sea," orders him and his brothers to surrender the fortress, ships, houses, arms, ammunition, cattle, and all other royal property, into the hands of Bobadilla, as governor, under penalty of incurring the punishments to which those subject themselves who refuse to surrender fortresses and other trusts, when commanded by their sovereigns.

A fourth letter, dated on the 26th of May, and addressed to Columbus, simply by the title of admiral, is a mere letter of credence, ordering him to give faith and obedience to whatever Bobadilla should impart.

The second and third of these letters were evidently provisional, and only to be produced, if, on examination, there should appear such delinquency on the part of Columbus and his brothers as to warrant their being divested of command.

This heavy blow, as has been shown, remained suspended for a year: yet, that it was whispered about, and triumphantly anticipated by the enemies of Columbus, is evident from the assertions of Ojeda, who sailed from Spain about the time of the signature of those letters, and had intimate communications with Bishop Fonseca, who was considered instrumental in producing this measure. The very license granted by the bishop to Ojeda to sail on a voyage of discovery in contravention of the prerogatives of the admiral, has the air of being given on a presumption of his speedy downfall; and the same presumption, as has already been observed, must have encouraged Ojeda in his turbulent conduct at Xaragua.

At length the long projected measure was carried into effect. Bobadilla set sail for San Domingo about the middle of July, 1500, with two caravels, in which were twenty-five men, enlisted for a year, to serve as a kind of guard. There were six friars likewise, who had charge of a number of Indians sent back to their country. Besides the letters patent, Bobadilla was authorized, by royal order, to ascertain and discharge all arrears of pay due to persons in the service of the crown, and to oblige the admiral to pay what was due on his part, " so that those people might receive what was owing to them, and there might be no more complaints." In addition to all these powers, Bobadilla was furnished with many blank letters signed by the sovereigns, to be filled up by him in such manner, and directed to such persons, as he might think advisable, in relation to the mission with which he was intrusted.[1]

CHAPTER II.

ARRIVAL OF BOBADILLA AT SAN DOMINGO — HIS VIOLENT ASSUMPTION OF THE COMMAND.

[1500.]

COLUMBUS was still at Fort Conception, regulating the affairs of the Vega, after the catastrophe of the sedition of Moxica: his brother, the Adelantado, accompanied by Roldan, was pursuing and arresting the fugitive rebels in Xaragua; and Don Diego Columbus remained in temporary command at San Domingo. Faction had worn itself out: the insurgents had brought down ruin upon themselves; and the island appeared delivered from the domination of violent and lawless men.

Such was the state of public affairs, when, on the morning of the 23d of August, two caravels were descried off the harbor of San Domingo, about a league at sea. They were standing off and on, waiting until the sea breeze, which generally prevails about ten o'clock, should carry them into port. Don Diego Columbus supposed them to be ships sent from Spain

---

* Herrera, decad. i. lib. iv. cap. 7.

with supplies, and hoped to find on board his nephew Diego, whom the admiral had requested might be sent out to assist him in his various concerns. A canoe was immediately despatched to obtain information, which, approaching the caravels, inquired what news they brought, and whether Diego, the son of the admiral, was on board. Bobadilla himself replied from the principal vessel, announcing himself as a commissioner sent out to investigate the late rebellion. The master of the caravel then inquired about the news of the island, and was informed of the recent transactions. Seven of the rebels, he was told, had been hanged that week, and five more were in the fortress of San Domingo, condemned to suffer the same fate. Among these were Pedro Requelme and Fernando de Guevara, the young cavalier whose passion for the daughter of Anacaona had been the original cause of the rebellion. Further conversation passed, in the course of which Bobadilla ascertained that the admiral and the Adelantado were absent, and Don Diego Columbus in command.

When the canoe returned to the city with the news that a commissioner had arrived to make inquisition into the late troubles, there was a great stir and agitation throughout the community. Knots of whisperers gathered at every corner; those who were conscious of malpractices were filled with consternation; while those who had grievances, real or imaginary, to complain of, especially those whose pay was in arrear, appeared with joyful countenances.[1]

As the vessels entered the river, Bobadilla beheld on either bank a gibbet with a body of a Spaniard hanging on it, apparently but lately executed. He considered these as conclusive proofs of the alleged cruelty of Columbus. Many boats came off to the ship, every one being anxious to pay early court to this public censor. Bobadilla remained on board all day, in the course of which he collected much of the rumors of the place, and as those who sought to secure his favor were those who had most to fear from his investigations, it is evident that the nature of the rumors must generally have been unfavorable to Columbus. In fact, before Bobadilla landed, if not before he arrived, the culpability of the admiral was decided in his mind.

The next morning he landed, with all his followers, and went to the church to attend mass, where he found Don Diego Columbus, Rodrigo Perez, the lieutenant of the admiral, and

---

[1] Las Casas, Hist. Ind., lib. i. cap. 169. Herrera, Hist. Ind., decad. i. lib. iv. cap. 5.

other persons of note. Mass being ended, and those persons, with a multitude of the populace, being assembled at the door of the church, Bobadilla ordered his letters patent to be read, authorizing him to investigate the rebellion, seize the persons and sequestrate the property of delinquents, and proceed against them with the utmost rigor of the law ; commanding also the admiral, and all others in authority, to assist him in the discharge of his duties. The letter being read, he demanded of Don Diego and the alcaldes to surrender to him the persons of Fernando Guevara, Pedro Requelme, and the other prisoners. with the depositions taken concerning them : and ordered that the parties by whom they were accused, and those by whose command they had been taken. should appear before him.

Don Diego replied, that the proceedings had emanated from the orders of the admiral, who held superior powers to any Bobadilla could possess. and without whose authority he could do nothing. He requested, at the same time, a copy of the letter patent, that he might send it to his brother, to whom alone the matter appertained. This Bobadilla refused, observing that, if Don Diego had power to do nothing, it was useless to give him a copy. He added, that since the office and authority he had proclaimed appeared to have no weight, he would try what power and consequence there was in the name of governor, and would show them that he had command, not merely over them, but over the admiral himself.

The little community remained in breathless suspense, waiting the portentous movements of Bobadilla. The next morning he appeared at mass, resolved on assuming those powers which were only to have been produced after full investigation. and ample proof of the mal-conduct of Columbus. When mass was over. and the eager populace had gathered round the door of the church, Bobadilla, in presence of Don Diego and Rodrigo Perez, ordered his other royal patent to be read. investing him with the government of the islands, and of Terra Firma.

The patent being read, Bobadilla took the customary oath, and then claimed the obedience of Don Diego, Rodrigo Perez, and all present, to this royal instrument ; on the authority of which he again demanded the prisoners confined in the fortress. In reply, they professed the utmost deference to the letter of the sovereigns, but again observed that they held the prisoners in obedience to the admiral, to whom the sovereigns had granted letters of a higher nature.

The self-importance of Bobadilla was incensed at this non-compliance, especially as he saw it had some effect upon the populace, who appeared to doubt his authority. He now produced the third mandate of the crown, ordering Columbus and his brothers to deliver up all fortresses, ships, and other royal property. To win the public completely to his side, he read also the additional mandate, issued on the 30th of May, of the same year, ordering him to pay the arrears of wages due to all persons in the royal service, and to compel the admiral to pay the arrears of those to whom he was accountable.

This last document was received with shouts by the multitude, many having long arrears due to them in consequence of the poverty of the treasury. Flushed with his growing importance, Bobadilla again demanded the prisoners; threatening, if refused, to take them by force. Meeting with the same reply, he repaired to the fortress to execute his threats. This post was commanded by Miguel Diaz, the same Arragonian cavalier who had once taken refuge among the Indians on the banks of the Ozema, won the affections of the female cacique Catalina, receiving from her information of the neighboring gold mines, and induced his countrymen to remove to those parts.

When Bobadilla came before the fortress, he found the gates closed and the alcayde, Miguel Diaz, upon the battlements. He ordered his letters patent to be read with a loud voice, the signatures and seals to be held up to view, and then demanded the surrender of the prisoners. Diaz requested a copy of the letters; but this Bobadilla refused, alleging that there was no time for delay, the prisoners being under sentence of death, and liable at any moment to be executed. He threatened at the same time, that if they were not given up, he would proceed to extremities, and Diaz should be answerable for the consequences. The wary alcayde again required time to reply, and a copy of the letters, saying that he held the fortress for the king by the command of the admiral, his lord, who had gained these territories and islands, and that when the latter arrived he should obey his orders.[1]

The whole spirit of Bobadilla was roused within him, at the refusal of the alcayde. Assembling all the people he had brought from Spain, together with the sailors of the ships and the rabble of the place, he exhorted them to aid him in getting possession of the prisoners, but to harm no one unless in case of resistance. The mob shouted assent, for Bobadilla was already the idol of the multitude. About the hour of vespers

---

[1] Las Casas, Hist. Ind., lib. 1 cap. 179.

he set out at the head of this motley army, to storm a fortress destitute of a garrison, and formidable only in name, being calculated to withstand only a naked and slightly-armed people. The accounts of this transaction have something in them bordering on the ludicrous, and give it the air of absurd rhodomontade. Bobadilla assailed the portal with great impetuosity, the frail bolts and locks of which gave way at the first shock, and allowed him easy admission. In the mean time, however, his zealous myrmidons applied ladders to the walls, as if about to carry the place by assault, and to experience a desperate defence. The alcayde, Miguel Diaz, and Don Diego de Alvarado, alone appeared on the battlements ; they had drawn swords, but offered no resistance. Bobadilla entered the fortress in triumph, and without molestation. The prisoners were found in a chamber in irons. He ordered that they should be brought up to him to the top of the fortress, where, having put a few questions to them, as a matter of form, he gave them in charge to an alguazil named Juan de Espinosa.[1]

Such was the arrogant and precipitate entrance into office of Francisco de Bobadilla. He had reversed the order of his written instructions, having seized upon the government before he had investigated the conduct of Columbus. He continued his career in the same spirit, acting as if the case had been prejudged in Spain, and he had been sent out merely to degrade the admiral from his employments, not to ascertain the manner in which he had fulfilled them. He took up his residence in the house of Columbus, seized upon his arms, gold, plate, jewels, horses, together with his letters, and various manuscripts, both public and private, even to his most secret papers. He gave no account of the property thus seized, and which he no doubt considered already confiscated to the crown, excepting that he paid out of it the wages of those to whom the admiral was in arrears.[2] To increase his favor with the people, he proclaimed, on the second day of his assumption of power, a general license for the term of twenty years, to seek for gold, paying merely one-eleventh to government, instead of a third as heretofore. At the same time he spoke in the most disrespectful and unqualified terms of Columbus, saying that he was empowered to send him home in chains, and that neither he nor any of his lineage would ever again be permitted to govern in the island.[3]

---

[1] Las Casas, ubi sup. Herrera, ubi sup.
[2] Hist. del Almirante, cap. 85. Las Casas. Herrera, ubi sup.
[3] Letters of Columbus to the Nurse of Prince Juan.

CHAPTER III.

COLUMBUS SUMMONED TO APPEAR BEFORE BOBADILLA.

[1500.]

WHEN the tidings reached Columbus at Fort Conception of the high-handed proceedings of Bobadilla, he considered them the unauthorized acts of some rash adventurer like Ojeda. Since government had apparently thrown open the door to private enterprise, he might expect to have his path continually crossed, and his jurisdiction infringed by bold intermeddlers, feigning or fancying themselves authorized to interfere in the affairs of the colony. Since the departure of Ojeda another squadron had touched upon the coast, and produced a transient alarm, being an expedition under one of the Pinzons, licensed by the sovereigns to make discoveries. There had also been a rumor of another squadron hovering about the island, which proved, however, to be unfounded [1]

The conduct of Bobadilla bore all the appearance of a lawless usurpation of some intruder of the kind. He had possessed himself forcibly of the fortress, and consequently of the town. He had issued extravagant licenses injurious to the government, and apparently intended only to make partisans among the people, and had threatened to throw Columbus himself in irons. That this man could really be sanctioned by government in such intemperate measures was repugnant to belief. The admiral's consciousness of his own services, the repeated assurances he had received of high consideration on the part of the sovereigns, and the perpetual prerogatives granted to him under their hand and seal, with all the solemnity that a compact could possess, all forbade him to consider the transactions at San Domingo otherwise than as outrages on his authority by some daring or misguided individual.

To be nearer to San Domingo, and obtain more correct information, he proceeded to Bonao, which was now beginning to assume the appearance of a settlement, several Spaniards having erected houses there, and cultivated the adjacent country. He had scarcely reached the place when an alcalde, bearing a staff of office, arrived there from San Domingo, proclaiming the ap-

---

[1] Letters of Columbus to the Nurse of Prince Juan.

pointment of Bobadilla to the government, and bearing copies of his letters-patent. There was no especial letter or message sent to the admiral, nor were any of the common forms of courtesy and ceremony observed in superseding him in the command, all the proceedings of Bobadilla toward him were abrupt and insulting.

Columbus was exceedingly embarrassed how to act. It was evident that Bobadilla was intrusted with extensive powers by the sovereigns, but that they could have exercised such a sudden, unmerited, and apparently capricious act of severity, as that of divesting him of all his commands, he could not believe. He endeavored to persuade himself that Bobadilla was some person sent out to exercise the functions of chief judge, according to the request he had written some to the sovereigns, and that they had intrusted him likewise with provisional powers to make an inquest into the late troubles of the island All beyond these powers he tried to believe were mere assumptions and exaggerations of authority, as in the case of Aguado. At all events, he was determined to act upon such presumption, and to endeavor to gain time. If the monarchs had really taken any harsh measures with respect to him, it must have been in consequence of misrepresentations The least delay might give them an opportunity of ascertaining their error, and making the necessary amends.

He wrote to Bobadilla. therefore, in guarded terms. welcoming him to the island; cautioning him against precipitate measures, especially in granting licenses to collect gold: informing him that he was on the point of going to Spain, and in a little time would leave him in command, with every thing fully and clearly explained. He wrote at the same time to the like purport to certain monks who had come out with Bobadilla, though he observes that these letters were only written to gain time.[1] He received no replies; but while an insulting silence was observed toward him, Bobadilla filled up several of the blank letters, of which he had a number signed by the sovereigns, and sent them to Roldan, and other of the admiral's enemies, the very men whom he had been sent out to judge. These letters were full of civilities and promises of favor.[2]

To prevent any mischief which might arise from the licenses and indulgences so prodigally granted by Bobadilla, Columbus published by word and letter that the powers assumed by him could not be valid, nor his licenses availing, as he himself held

---

[1] Letter of Columbus to the Nurse of Prince Juan. [2] Ibid Herrera, decad. i lib iv

superior powers granted to him in perpetuity by the crown, which could no more be superseded in this instance than they had been in that of Aguado.

For some time Columbus remained in this anxious and perplexed state of mind, uncertain what line of conduct to pursue in so singular and unlooked-for a conjuncture. He was soon brought to a decision. Francisco Velasquez, deputy treasurer, and Juan de Trasierra, a Franciscan friar, arrived at Bonao, and delivered to him the royal letter of credence, signed by the sovereigns on the 26th of May, 1499, commanding him to give implicit faith and obedience to Bobadilla; and they delivered, at the same time, a summons from the latter to appear immediately before him.

This laconic letter from the sovereigns struck at once at the root of all his dignity and power. He no longer made hesitation or demur, but complying with the peremptory summons of Bobadilla, departed, almost alone and unattended, for San Domingo.[1]

CHAPTER IV.

COLUMBUS AND HIS BROTHERS ARRESTED AND SENT TO SPAIN IN CHAINS.

[1500.]

THE tidings that a new governor had arrived, and that Columbus was in disgrace, and to be sent home in chains, circulated rapidly through the Vega, and the colonists hastened from all parts to San Domingo to make interest with Bobadilla. It was soon perceived that there was no surer way than that of vilifying his predecessor. Bobadilla felt that he had taken a rash step in seizing upon the government, and that his own safety required the conviction of Columbus. He listened eagerly, therefore, to all accusations, public or private; and welcome was he who could bring any charge, however extravagant, against the admiral and his brothers.

Hearing that the admiral was on his way to the city, he made a bustle of preparation, and armed the troops, affecting to believe a rumor that Columbus had called upon the caciques of the Vega to aid him with their subjects in a resistance to the

---

[1] Herrera, decad. i. lib. iv. cap. 9   Letter to the Nurse of Prince Juan.

commands of government. No grounds appear for this absurd report, which was probably invented to give a coloring of precaution to subsequent measures of violence and insult. The admiral's brother, Don Diego, was seized, thrown in irons, and confined on board of a caravel. without any reason being assigned for his imprisonment.

In the mean time Columbus pursued his journey to San Domingo, travelling in a lonely manner, without guards or retinue. Most of his people were with the Adelantado, and he had declined being attended by the remainder. He had heard of the rumors of the hostile intentions of Bobadilla ; and although he knew that violence was threatened to his person, he came in this unpretending manner to manifest his pacific feelings, and to remove all suspicion.[1]

No sooner did Bobadilla hear of his arrival than he gave orders to put him in irons, and confine him in the fortress. This outrage to a person of such dignified and venerable appearance and such eminent merit. seemed for the time to shock even his enemies. When the irons were brought, every one present shrank from the task of putting them on him. either from a sentiment of compassion at so great a reverse of fortune, or out of habitual reverence for his person. To fill the measure of ingratitude meted out to him, it was one of his own domestics. " a graceless and shameless cook,'' says Las Casas, " who, with unwashed front, riveted the fetters with as much readiness and alacrity as though he were serving him with choice and savory viands. I knew the fellow,'' adds the venerable historian, " and I think his name was Espinosa ''[2]

Columbus conducted himself with characteristic magnanimity under the injuries heaped upon him. There is a noble scorn which swells and supports the heart, and silences the tongue of the truly great, when enduring the insults of the unworthy. Columbus could not stoop to deprecate the arrogance of a weak and violent man like Bobadilla. He looked beyond this shallow agent and all his petty tyranny to the sovereigns who had employed him. Their injustice or ingratitude alone could wound his spirit; and he felt assured that when the truth came to be known, they would blush to find how greatly they had wronged him. With this proud assurance he bore all present indignities in silence.

Bobadilla, although he had the admiral and Don Diego in his power, and had secured the venal populace, felt anxious and ill

---

[1] Las Casas, Hist. Ind., lib. 1. cap. 186.   [2] Ibid.

at ease. The Adelantado, with an armed force under his command, was still in the distant province of Xaragua, in pursuit of the rebels. Knowing his soldier-like and determined spirit, he feared he might take some violent measure when he should hear of the ignominious treatment and imprisonment of his brothers. He doubted whether any order from himself would have any effect, except to exasperate the stern Don Bartholomew. He sent a demand, therefore, to Columbus, to write to his brother, requesting him to repair peaceably to San Domingo, and forbidding him to execute the persons he held in confinement; Columbus readily complied. He exhorted his brother to submit quietly to the authority of his sovereigns, and to endure all present wrongs and indignities, under the confidence that when they arrived at Castile, every thing would be explained and redressed.[1]

On receiving this letter, Don Bartholomew immediately complied. Relinquishing his command, he hastened peacefully to San Domingo, and on arriving experienced the same treatment with his brothers, being put in irons and confined on board of a caravel. They were kept separate from each other, and no communication permitted between them. Bobadilla did not see them himself, nor did he allow others to visit them, but kept them in ignorance of the cause of their imprisonment, the crimes with which they were charged, and the process that was going on against them.[2]

It has been questioned whether Bobadilla really had authority for the arrest and imprisonment of the admiral and his brothers,[3] and whether such violence and indignity was in any case contemplated by the sovereigns. He may have fancied himself empowered by the clause in the letter of instructions, dated

---

[1] Peter Martyr mentions a vulgar rumor of the day, that the admiral, not knowing what might happen, wrote a letter in cipher to the Adelantado, urging him to come with arms in his hands to prevent any violence that might be contrived against him, that the Adelantado advanced, in effect, with his armed force but having the imprudence to proceed some distance ahead of it, was surprised by the governor, before his men could come to his succor, and that the letter in cipher had been sent to Spain This must have been one of the groundless rumors of the day, circulated to prejudice the public mind. Nothing of the kind appears among the charges in the inquest made by Bobadilla, and which was seen, and extracts made from it, by Las Casas for his history It is, in fact, in total contradiction to the statements of Las Casas, Herrera, and Fernando Columbus.

[2] Charlevoix, in his History of San Domingo (lib iii p 199), states, that the suit against Columbus was conducted in writing, that written charges were sent to him, to which he replied in the same way. This is contrary to the statements of Las Casas, Herrera, and Fernando Columbus. The admiral himself, in his letter to the Nurse of Prince Juan, after relating the manner in which he and his brothers had been thrown into irons, and confined separately, without being visited by Bobadilla, or permitted to see any other persons, expressly adds, "I make oath that I do not know for what I am imprisoned." Again, in a letter written some time afterward from Jamaica, he says, "I was taken and thrown with two of my brothers in a ship, loaded with irons, with little clothing and much ill-treatment without being summoned or convicted by justice."

[3] Herrera, decad. i lib. iv. cap 10. Oviedo, Cronica, lib. iii. cap. 6.

March 21st, 1499. in which. speaking of the rebellion of Roldan, " he is authorized to *seize the persons and sequestrate the property* of those who appeared to be culpable, and then to proceed against them and against the absent, with the highest civil and criminal penalties." This evidently had reference to the persons of Roldan and his followers, who were then in arms, and against whom Columbus had sent home complaints: and this, by a violent construction, Bobadilla seems to have wrested into an authority for seizing the person of the admiral himself. In fact, in the whole course of his proceedings, he reversed and confounded the order of his instructions. His first step should have been to proceed against the rebels; this he made the last. His last step should have been, in case of ample evidence against the admiral. to have superseded him in office: and this he made the first, without waiting for evidence. Having predetermined. from the very outset. that Columbus was in the wrong, by the same rule he had to presume that all the opposite parties were in the right. It became indispensable to his own justification to inculpate the admiral and his brothers; and the rebels he had been sent to judge became, by this singular perversion of rule, necessary and cherished evidences, to criminate those against whom they had rebelled.

The intentions of the crown, however, are not to be vindicated at the expense of its miserable agent. If proper respect had been felt for the rights and dignities of Columbus, Bobadilla would never have been intrusted with powers so extensive, undefined, and discretionary; nor would he have dared to proceed to such lengths, with such rudeness and precipitation, had he not felt assured that it would not be displeasing to the jealous-minded Ferdinand.

The old scenes of the time of Aguado were now renewed with tenfold virulence, and the old charges revived, with others still more extravagant. From the early and never-to-be-forgotten outrage upon Castilian pride, of compelling hidalgos, in time of emergency. to labor in the construction of works necessary to the public safety, down to the recent charge of levying war against the government. there was not a hardship. abuse, nor sedition in the island, that was not imputed to the misdeeds of Columbus and his brothers. Besides the usual accusations of inflicting oppressive labor, unnecessary tasks, painful restrictions. short allowances of food. and cruel punishments upon the Spaniards, and waging unjust wars against the natives, they were now charged with preventing the conversion of the latter, that they might send them slaves to Spain, and profit by their sale. This last charge, so contrary to the pious feelings of the admiral, was founded on his having objected to the baptism of certain Indians of mature age, until they could be instructed in the doctrines of Christianity: justly considering it an abuse of that holy sacrament to administer it thus blindly.[1]

Columbus was charged, also, with having secreted pearls, and other precious articles, collected in his voyage along the coast of Paria, and with keeping the sovereigns in ignorance of the nature of his discoveries there, in order to exact new privileges from them: yet it was notorious that he had sent home specimens of the pearls and journals and charts of his voyage, by which others had been enabled to pursue his track.

Even the late tumults, now that the rebels were admitted as evidence, were all turned into matters of accusation. They were represented as spirited and loyal resistances to tyranny exercised upon the colonists and the natives. The well-merited punishments inflicted upon certain of the ringleaders were cited as proofs of a cruel and revengeful disposition, and a secret hatred of Spaniards. Bobadilla believed, or affected to believe, all these charges. He had, in a manner, made the rebels his confederates in the ruin of Columbus. It was become a common cause with them. He could no longer, therefore, conduct himself toward them as a judge. Guevara, Requelme, and their fellow-convicts, were discharged almost without the form of a trial, and it is even said were received into favor and countenance. Roldan, from the very first, had been treated with confidence by Bobadilla, and honored with his correspondence. All the others, whose conduct had rendered them liable to justice, received either a special acquittal or a general pardon. It was enough to have been opposed in any way to Columbus, to obtain full justification in the eyes of Bobadilla.

The latter had now collected a weight of testimony, and produced a crowd of witnesses, sufficient, as he conceived, to insure the condemnation of the prisoners, and his own continuance in command. He determined, therefore, to send the admiral and his brothers home in chains, in the vessels ready for sea, transmitting at the same time the inquest taken in their case, and writing private letters, enforcing the charges made against them, and advising that Columbus should on no account be restored to the command, which he had so shamefully abused.

San Domingo now swarmed with miscreants just delivered from the dungeon and the gibbet. It was a perfect jubilee of

---

1 Muñoz Hist. N Mundo. part unpublished.

triumphant villany and dastard malice. Every base spirit. which had been awed into obsequiousness by Columbus and his brothers when in power. now started up to revenge itself upon them when in chains. The most injurious slanders were loudly proclaimed in the streets; insulting pasquinades and inflammatory libels were posted up at every corner; and horns were blown in the neighborhood of their prisons, to taunt them with the exultings of the rabble.[1] When these rejoicings of his enemies reached him in his dungeon, and Columbus reflected on the inconsiderate violence already exhibited by Bobadilla, he knew not how far his rashness and confidence might carry him, and began to entertain apprehensions for his life.

The vessels being ready to make sail, Alonzo de Villejo was appointed to take charge of the prisoners, and carry them to Spain. This officer had been brought up by an uncle of Fonseca. was in the employ of that bishop. and had come out with Bobadilla. The latter instructed him, on arriving at Cadiz, to deliver his prisoners into the hands of Fonseca. or of his uncle, thinking thereby to give the malignant prelate a triumphant gratification. This circumstance gave weight with many to a report that Bobadilla was secretly instigated and encouraged in his violent measures by Fonseca, and was promised his protection and influence at court, in case of any complaints of his conduct.[2]

Villejo undertook the office assigned him, but he discharged it in a more generous manner than was intended "This Alonzo de Villejo," says the worthy Las Casas, "was a hidalgo of honorable character, and my particular friend." He certainly showed himself superior to the low malignity of his patrons. When he arrived with a guard to conduct the admiral from the prison to the ship, he found him in chains in a state of silent despondency. So violently had he been treated, and so savage were the passions let loose against him, that he feared he should be sacrificed without an opportunity of being heard. and his name go down sullied and dishonored to posterity. When he beheld the officer enter with the guard, he thought it was to conduct him to the scaffold. "Villejo," said he, mournfully, "whither are you taking me?" "To the ship. your Excellency. to embark." replied the other. "To embark!" repeated the admiral, earnestly; "Villejo, do you speak the truth?" "By the life of your Excellency." replied the honest officer, "it is true!" With these words the admiral

---

[1] Hist. del Almirante, cap. 36.   [2] Las Casas, Hist. Ind., lib 1. cap. 180, MS.

was comforted. and felt as one restored from death to life. Nothing can be more touching and expressive than this little colloquy. recorded by the venerable Las Casas. who doubtless had it from the lips of his friend Villejo.

The caravels set sail early in October, bearing off Columbus shackled like the vilest of culprits, amid the scoffs and shouts of a miscreant rabble. who took a brutal joy in heaping insults on his venerable head, and sent curses after him from the shores of the island he had so recently added to the civilized world. Fortunately the voyage was favorable, and of but moderate duration, and was rendered less disagreeable by the conduct of those to whom he was given in custody. The worthy Villejo, though in the service of Fonseca, felt deeply moved at the treatment of Columbus. The master of the caravel, Andreas Martin, was equally grieved : they both treated the admiral with profound respect and assiduous attention. They would have taken off his irons, but to this he would not consent. "No," said he proudly, "their majesties commanded me by letter to submit to whatever Bobadilla should order in their name ; by their authority he has put upon me these chains ; I will wear them until they shall order them to be taken off, and I will preserve them afterward as relics and memorials of the reward of my services."[1]

"He did so." adds his son Fernando : "I saw them always hanging in his cabinet, and he requested that when he died they might be buried with him!"[2]

---

[1] Las Casas, Hist. Ind., lib. i. cap. 180, MS   [2] Hist. del Almirante, cap. 86.

BOOK XIV.

CHAPTER I.

SENSATION IN SPAIN ON THE ARRIVAL OF COLUMBUS IN IRONS —
HIS APPEARANCE AT COURT.

[1500.]

THE arrival of Columbus at Cadiz, a prisoner and in chains, produced almost as great a sensation as his triumphant return from his first voyage. It was one of those striking and obvious facts which speak to the feelings of the multitude, and preclude the necessity of reflection. No one stopped to inquire into the case. It was sufficient to be told that Columbus was brought home in irons from the world he had discovered. There was a general burst of indignation in Cadiz, and in the powerful and opulent Seville, which was echoed throughout all Spain. If the ruin of Columbus had been the intention of his enemies, they had defeated their object by their own violence. One of those re-actions took place, so frequent in the public mind, when persecution is pushed to an unguarded length. Those of the populace who had recently been loud in their clamor against Columbus were now as loud in their reprobation of his treatment, and a strong sympathy was expressed, against which it would have been odious for the government to contend

The tidings of his arrival, and of the ignominious manner in which he had been brought, reached the court at Granada, and filled the halls of the Alhambra with murmurs of astonishment. Columbus, full of his wrongs, but ignorant how far they had been authorized by the sovereigns, had forborne to write to them In the course of his voyage, however, he had penned a long letter to Doña Juana de la Torre, the aya of Prince Juan, a lady high in favor with Queen Isabella. This letter, on his arrival at Cadiz, Andreas Martin, the captain of the caravel, permitted him to send off privately by express. It arrived, there-

461

fore, before the protocol of the proceedings instituted by Bobadilla. and from this document the sovereigns derived their first
intimation of his treatment.[1]   It contained a statement of the
late transactions of the island. and of the wrongs he had
suffered, written with his usual artlessness and energy.   To
specify the contents would be but to recapitulate circumstances already recorded.   Some expressions, however, which
burst from him in the warmth of his feelings. are worthy of
being noted.   " The slanders of worthless men," says he,
" have done me more injury than all my services have profited
me."   Speaking of the misrepresentations to which he was
subjected, he observes : " Such is the evil name which I have
acquired, that if I were to build hospitals and churches,
they would be called dens of robbers."   After relating in
indignant terms the conduct of Bobadilla, in seeking testimony
respecting his administration from the very men who had
rebelled against him, and throwing himself and his brothers
in irons, without letting them know the offences with which
they were charged, " I have been much aggrieved," he adds,
" in that a person should be sent out to investigate my conduct. who knew that if the evidence which he could send
home should appear to be of a serious nature, he would
remain in the government."   He complains that, in forming
an opinion of his administration, allowances had not been
made for the extraordinary difficulties with which he had
to contend, and the wild state of the country over which he
had to rule.   " I was judged." he observes. " as a governor who
had been sent to take charge of a well-regulated city, under the
dominion of well-established laws. where there was no danger
of every thing running to disorder and ruin ; but I ought to be
judged as a captain, sent to subdue a numerous and hostile
people, of manners and religion opposite to ours, living not in
regular towns, but in forests and mountains.   It ought to be
considered that I have brought all these under subjection to
their majesties, giving them dominion over another world. by
which Spain, heretofore poor, has suddenly become rich.
Whatever errors I may have fallen into, they were not with an
evil intention , and I believe their majesties will credit what I
say   I have known them to be merciful to those who have wil-
fully done them disservice   I am convinced that they will
have still more indulgence for me who have erred innocently,
or by compulsion, as they will hereafter be more fully in-

---

[1] Las Casas, Hist. Ind., lib. i cap. 182

formed; and I trust they will consider my great services, the advantages of which are every day more and more apparent."

When this letter was read to the noble-minded Isabella, and she found how grossly Columbus had been wronged and the royal authority abused, her heart was filled with mingled sympathy and indignation. The tidings were confirmed by a letter from the alcalde or corregidor of Cadiz, into whose hands Columbus and his brothers had been delivered, until the pleasure of the sovereigns should be known;[1] and by another letter from Alonzo de Villejo, expressed in terms accordant with his humane and honorable conduct toward his illustrious prisoner.

However Ferdinand might have secretly felt disposed against Columbus, the momentary tide of public feeling was not to be resisted. He joined with his generous queen in her reprobation of the treatment of the admiral, and both sovereigns hastened to give evidence to the world that his imprisonment had been without their authority, and contrary to their wishes. Without waiting to receive any documents that might arrive from Bobadilla, they sent orders to Cadiz that the prisoners should be instantly set at liberty, and treated with all distinction. They wrote a letter to Columbus, couched in terms of gratitude and affection, expressing their grief at all that he had suffered, and inviting him to court. They ordered, at the same time, that two thousand ducats should be advanced to defray his expenses.[2]

The loyal heart of Columbus was again cheered by this declaration of his sovereigns. He felt conscious of his integrity, and anticipated an immediate restitution of all his rights and dignities. He appeared at court in Granada on the 17th of December, not as a man ruined and disgraced, but richly dressed, and attended by an honorable retinue. He was received by the sovereigns with unqualified favor and distinction. When the queen beheld this venerable man approach, and thought on all he had deserved and all he had suffered, she was moved to tears. Columbus had borne up firmly against the rude conflicts of the world — he had endured with lofty scorn the injuries and insults of ignoble men; but he possessed strong and quick sensibility. When he found himself thus kindly received by his sovereigns, and beheld tears in the benign eyes of Isabella, his long-suppressed feelings burst forth; he threw

---

[1] Oviedo, Cronica, lib iii. cap. 6

[2] Las Casas, lib. i cap. 182. Two thousand ducats, or two thousand eight hundred and forty-six dollars, equivalent to eight thousand five hundred and thirty-eight dollars of the present day.

himself on his knees, and for some time could not utter a word for the violence of his tears and sobbings.[1]

Ferdinand and Isabella raised him from the ground, and endeavored to encourage him by the most gracious expressions. As soon as he regained self-possession he entered into an eloquent and high-minded vindication of his loyalty, and the zeal he had ever felt for the glory and advantage of the Spanish crown, declaring that if at any time he had erred, it had been through inexperience in government, and the extraordinary difficulties by which he had been surrounded

There needed no vindication on his part. The intemperance of his enemies had been his best advocate. He stood in presence of his sovereigns a deeply-injured man, and it remained for them to vindicate themselves to the world from the charge of ingratitude toward their most deserving subject. They expressed their indignation at the proceedings of Bobadilla, which they disavowed, as contrary to their instructions, and declared that he should be immediately dismissed from his command.

In fact, no public notice was taken of the charges sent home by Bobadilla, nor of the letters written in support of them. The sovereigns took every occasion to treat Columbus with favor and distinction, assuring him that his grievances should be redressed, his property restored, and he reinstated in all his privileges and dignities.

It was on the latter point that Columbus was chiefly solicitous. Mercenary considerations had scarcely any weight in his mind. Glory had been the great object of his ambition, and he felt that, as long as he remained suspended from his employments, a tacit censure rested on his name. He expected, therefore, that the moment the sovereigns should be satisfied of the rectitude of his conduct, they would be eager to make him amends; that a restitution of his viceroyalty would immediately take place, and he should return in triumph to San Domingo. Here, however, he was doomed to experience a disappointment which threw a gloom over the remainder of his days. To account for this flagrant want of justice and gratitude in the crown, it is expedient to notice a variety of events which had materially affected the interests of Columbus in the eyes of the politic Ferdinand.

---

[1] Herrera, decad. 1. lib. iv. cap. 10.

CHAPTER II.

CONTEMPORARY VOYAGES OF DISCOVERY.

The general license granted by the Spanish sovereigns in 1495, to undertake voyages of discovery, had given rise to various expeditions by enterprising individuals, chiefly persons who had sailed with Columbus in his first voyages. The government, unable to fit out many armaments itself, was pleased to have its territories thus extended, free of cost, and its treasury at the same time benefited by the share of the proceeds of these voyages, reserved as a kind of duty to the crown. These expeditions had chiefly taken place while Columbus was in partial disgrace with the sovereigns. His own charts and journal served as guides to the adventurers ; and his magnificent accounts of Paria and the adjacent coasts had chiefly excited their cupidity.

Besides the expedition of Ojeda, already noticed, in the course of which he touched at Xaragua, one had been undertaken at the same time by Pedro Alonzo Niño, native of Moguer, an able pilot, who had been with Columbus in the voyages to Cuba and Paria. Having obtained a license, he interested a rich merchant of Seville in the undertaking, who fitted out a caravel of fifty tons burden, under condition that his brother Christoval Guevra should have the command. They sailed from the bar of Saltes, a few days after Ojeda had sailed from Cadiz, in the spring of 1499, and arriving on the coast of Terra Firma, to the south of Paria, ran along it for some distance, passed through the Gulf, and thence went one hundred and thirty leagues along the shore of the present republic of Colombia, visiting what was afterward called the Pearl Coast. They landed in various places , disposed of their European trifles to immense profit, and returned with a large store of gold and pearls ; having made, in their diminutive bark, one of the most extensive and lucrative voyages yet accomplished.

About the same time the Pinzons, that family of bold and opulent navigators, fitted out an armament of four caravels at Palos, manned in a great measure by their own relations and friends. Several experienced pilots embarked in it who had been with Columbus to Paria, and it was commanded by Vicente Yañez Pinzon, who had been captain of a caravel in the squadron of the admiral on his first voyage.

Pinzon was a hardy and experienced seaman, and did not, like the others, follow closely in the track of Columbus. Sailing in December, 1499, he passed the Canary and Cape de Verde Islands, standing south-west until he lost sight of the polar star. Here he encountered a terrible storm, and was exceedingly perplexed and confounded by the new aspect of the heavens. Nothing was yet known of the southern hemisphere, nor of the beautiful constellation of the cross, which in those regions has since supplied to mariners the place of the north star. The voyagers had expected to find at the south pole a star corresponding to that of the north. They were dismayed at beholding no guide of the kind, and thought there must be some prominent swelling of the earth, which hid the pole from their view.[1]

Pinzon continued on, however, with great intrepidity. On the 26th of January, 1500, he saw, at a distance, a great headland, which he called Cape Santa Maria de la Consolacion, but which has since been named Cape St. Augustine. He landed and took possession of the country in the name of their Catholic majesties; being a part of the territories since called the Brazils. Standing thence westward, he discovered the Maragnon, since called the River of the Amazons; traversed the Gulf of Paria, and continued across the Caribbean Sea and the Gulf of Mexico, until he found himself among the Bahamas, where he lost two of his vessels on the rocks, near the island of Jumeto. He returned to Palos in September, having added to his former glory that of being the first European who had crossed the equinoctial line in the western ocean, and of having discovered the famous kingdom of Brazil, from its commencement at the River Maragnon to its most eastern point. As a reward for his achievements, power was granted to him to colonize and govern the lands which he had discovered, and which extended southward from a little beyond the River of Maragnon to Cape St. Augustine.[2]

The little port of Palos, which had been so slow in furnishing the first squadron for Columbus, was now continually agitated by the passion for discovery. Shortly after the sailing of Pinzon, another expedition was fitted out there, by Diego Lepe, a native of the place, and manned by his adventurous townsmen. He sailed in the same direction with Pinzon, but discovered more of the southern continent than any other voyager of the day, or for twelve years afterward. He doubled Cape St. Au-

---

[1] Peter Martyr, decad. i. lib. ix.
[2] Herrera, decad. i. lib. iv. cap. 12. Muñoz, Hist. N Mundo, part unpublished.

gustine, and ascertained that the coast beyond ran to the south-west. He landed and performed the usual ceremonies of taking possession in the name of the Spanish sovereigns, and in one place carved their names on a magnificent tree, of such enormous magnitude that seventeen men with their hands joined could not embrace the trunk. What enhanced the merit of his discoveries was, that he had never sailed with Columbus. He had with him, however, several skilful pilots who had accompanied the admiral in his voyage.[1]

Another expedition of two vessels sailed from Cadiz, in October, 1500, under the command of Rodrigo Bastides of Seville. He explored the coast of Terra Firma, passing Cape de la Vela, the western limits of the previous discoveries on the main-land, continuing on to a port since called The Retreat, where afterward was founded the seaport of Nombre de Dios. His vessels being nearly destroyed by the teredo, or worm which abounds in those seas, he had great difficulty in reaching Xaragua in Hispaniola, where he lost his two caravels, and proceeded with his crew by land to San Domingo. Here he was seized and imprisoned by Bobadilla, under pretext that he had treated for gold with the natives of Xaragua.[2]

Such was the swarm of Spanish expeditions immediately resulting from the enterprises of Columbus; but others were also undertaken by foreign nations. In the year 1497, Sebastian Cabot, son of a Venetian merchant resident in Bristol, sailing in the service of Henry VII. of England, navigated to the northern seas of the New World. Adopting the idea of Columbus, he sailed in quest of the shores of Cathay, and hoped to find a north-west passage to India. In this voyage he discovered Newfoundland, coasted Labrador to the fifty-sixth degree of north latitude, and then returning, ran down south-west to the Floridas, when, his provisions beginning to fail, he returned to England.[3] But vague and scanty accounts of this voyage exist, which was important, as including the first discovery of the northern continent of the New World.

The discoveries of rival nations, however, which most excited the attention and jealousy of the Spanish crown, were those of the Portuguese. Vasco de Gama, a man of rank and consummate talent and intrepidity, had, at length, accomplished the great design of the late Prince Henry of Portugal, and by doubling the Cape of Good Hope in the year 1497, had opened the long-sought-for route to India.

---

[1] Las Casas, Hist. Ind., lib. ii. cap. 2. Muñoz, part unpublished.   [2] Ibid.
[3] Hakluyt's Collection of Voyages, vol. iii. p. 7.

Immediately after Gama's return a fleet of thirteen sail was fitted out to visit the magnificent countries of which he brought accounts. This expedition sailed on the 9th of March, 1500, for Calicut, under the command of Pedro Alvarez de Cabral. Having passed the Cape de Verde Islands, he sought to avoid the calms prevalent on the coast of Guinea. by stretching far to the west. Suddenly, on the 25th of April, he came in sight of land unknown to any one in his squadron: for, as yet, they had not heard of the discoveries of Pinzon and Lepe. He at first supposed it to be some great island; but after coasting it for some time he became persuaded that it must be part of a continent. Having ranged along it somewhat beyond the fifteenth degree of southern latitude, he landed at a harbor which he called Porto Securo, and taking possession of the country for the crown of Portugal, despatched a ship to Lisbon with the important tidings.[1] In this way did the Brazils come into the possession of Portugal, being to the eastward of the conventional line settled with Spain as the boundaries of their respective territories. Dr. Robertson, in recording this voyage of Cabral, concludes with one of his just and elegant remarks:

"Columbus's discovery of the New World was," he observes, "the effort of an active genius, guided by experience, and acting upon a regular plan, executed with no less courage than perseverance. But from this adventure of the Portuguese, it appears that chance might have accomplished that great design, which it is now the pride of human reason to have formed and perfected. If the sagacity of Columbus had not conducted mankind to America, Cabral, by a fortunate accident, might have led them, a few years later, to the knowledge of that extensive continent."[2]

CHAPTER III.

NICHOLAS DE OVANDO APPOINTED TO SUPERSEDE BOBADILLA.

[1501.]

THE numerous discoveries briefly noticed in the preceding chapter had produced a powerful effect upon the mind of Ferdinand. His ambition, his avarice, and his jealousy were equally

---

[1] Lafiteau, Conquêtes des Portugais, lib. ii.
[2] Robertson, Hist America, book ii.

inflamed. He beheld boundless regions, teeming with all kinds of riches, daily opening before the enterprises of his subjects: but he beheld at the same time other nations launching forth into competition, emulous for a share of the golden world which he was eager to monopolize. The expeditions of the English and the accidental discovery of the Brazils by the Portuguese caused him much uneasiness. To secure his possession of the continent, he determined to establish local governments or commands in the most important places, all to be subject to a general government, established at San Domingo, which was to be the metropolis.

With these considerations, the government, heretofore granted to Columbus, had risen vastly in importance ; and while the restitution of it was the more desirable in his eyes, it became more and more a matter of repugnance to the selfish and jealous monarch. He had long repented having vested such great powers and prerogatives in any subject, particularly in a foreigner. At the time of granting them he had no anticipation of such boundless countries to be placed under his command. He appeared almost to consider himself outwitted by Columbus in the arrangement ; and every succeeding discovery, instead of increasing his grateful sense of the obligation, only made him repine the more at the growing magnitude of the reward. At length, however, the affair of Bobadilla had effected a temporary exclusion of Columbus from his high office, and that without any odium to the crown, and the wary monarch secretly determined that the door thus closed between him and his dignities should never again be opened.

Perhaps Ferdinand may really have entertained doubts as to the innocence of Columbus with respect to the various charges made against him He may have doubted also the sincerity of his loyalty, being a stranger, when he should find himself strong in his command, at a great distance from the parent country, with immense and opulent regions under his control. Columbus himself, in his letters, alludes to reports circulated by his enemies, that he intended either to set up an independent sovereignty, or to deliver his discoveries into the hands of other potentates ; and he appears to fear that these slanders might have made some impression on the mind of Ferdinand. But there was one other consideration which had no less force with the monarch in withholding this great act of justice — Columbus was no longer indispensable to him. He had made his great discovery ; he had struck out the route to the New World, and now any one could follow it. A number of able navigators had sprung up under his auspices, and acquired experience in his voyages. They were daily besieging the throne with offers to fit out expeditions at their own cost, and to yield a share of the profits to the crown. Why should he, therefore, confer princely dignities and prerogatives for that which men were daily offering to perform gratuitously?

Such, from his after conduct, appears to have been the jealous and selfish policy which actuated Ferdinand in forbearing to reinstate Columbus in those dignities and privileges so solemnly granted to him by treaty, and which it was acknowledged he had never forfeited by misconduct.

This deprivation, however, was declared to be but temporary, and plausible reasons were given for the delay in his re-appointment. It was observed that the elements of those violent factions, recently in arms against him, yet existed in the island; his immediate return might produce fresh exasperation, his personal safety might be endangered, and the island again thrown into confusion. Though Bobadilla, therefore, was to be immediately dismissed from command, it was deemed advisable to send out some officer of talent and discretion to supersede him, who might dispassionately investigate the recent disorders, remedy the abuses which had arisen, and expel all dissolute and factious persons from the colony. He should hold the government for two years, by which time it was trusted that all angry passions would be allayed, and turbulent individuals removed: Columbus might then resume the command with comfort to himself and advantage to the crown. With these reasons, and the promise which accompanied them, Columbus was obliged to content himself. There can be no doubt that they were sincere on the part of Isabella, and that it was her intention to reinstate him in the full enjoyment of his rights and dignities, after his apparently necessary suspension. Ferdinand, however, by his subsequent conduct, has forfeited all claim to any favorable opinion of the kind

The person chosen to supersede Bobadilla was Don Nicholas de Ovando, commander of Lares, of the order of Alcantara. He is described as of the middle size, fair complexion, with a red beard, and a modest look, yet a tone of authority. He was fluent in speech, and gracious and courteous in his manners. A man of great prudence, says Las Casas, and capable of governing many people, but not of governing the Indians, on whom he inflicted incalculable injuries. He possessed great veneration for justice, was an enemy to avarice, sober in his mode of living, and of such humility that when he rose afterward to be grand commander of the order of Alcantara, he would never allow himself to be addressed by the title of respect attached to it.[1] Such is the picture drawn of him by historians ; but his conduct in several important instances is in direct contradiction to it. He appears to have been plausible and subtle, as well as fluent and courteous ; his humility concealed a great love of command, and in his transactions with Columbus he was certainly both ungenerous and unjust.

The various arrangements to be made, according to the new plan of colonial government, delayed for some time the departure of Ovando. In the mean time every arrival brought intelligence of the disastrous state of the island under the maladministration of Bobadilla. He had commenced his career by an opposite policy to that of Columbus. Imagining that rigorous rule had been the rock on which his predecessors had split, he sought to conciliate the public by all kinds of indulgence. Having at the very outset relaxed the reins of justice and morality, he lost all command over the community ; and such disorder and licentiousness ensued that many, even of the opponents of Columbus, looked back with regret upon the strict but wholesome rule of himself and the Adelantado.

Bobadilla was not so much a bad as an imprudent and a weak man. He had not considered the dangerous excesses to which his policy would lead. Rash in grasping authority, he was feeble and temporizing in the exercise of it ; he could not look beyond the present exigency. One dangerous indulgence granted to the colonists called for another ; each was ceded in its turn, and thus he went on from error to error — showing that in government there is as much danger to be apprehended from a weak as from a bad man.

He had sold the farms and estates of the crown at low prices, observing that it was not the wish of the monarchs to enrich themselves by them, but that they should redound to the profit of their subjects. He granted universal permission to work the mines, exacting only an eleventh of the produce for the crown. To prevent any diminution in the revenue, it became necessary, of course, to increase the quantity of gold collected. He obliged the caciques, therefore, to furnish each Spaniard with Indians, to assist him both in the labors of the field and of the mine. To carry this into more complete effect, he made an enumeration of the natives of the island, reduced them into classes, and distributed them, according to his favor or caprice, among the

---

[1] Las Casas, Hist. Ind., lib. ii. cap. 3.

colonists. The latter, at his suggestion, associated themselves in partnerships of two persons each, who were to assist one another with their respective capitals and Indians, one superintending the labors of the field, and the other the search for gold. The only injunction of Bovadilla was to produce large quantities of ore. He had one saying continually in his mouth, which shows the pernicious and temporizing principle upon which he acted: "Make the most of your time," he would say; "there is no knowing how long it will last," alluding to the possibility of his being speedily recalled. The colonists acted up to his advice, and so hard did they drive the poor natives that the eleventh yielded more revenue to the crown than had ever been produced by the third under the government of Columbus. In the mean time the unhappy natives suffered under all kinds of cruelties from their inhuman taskmasters. Little used to labor, feeble of constitution, and accustomed in their beautiful and luxurious island to a life of ease and freedom, they sank under the toils imposed upon them, and the severities by which they were enforced. Las Casas gives an indignant picture of the capricious tyranny exercised over the Indians by worthless Spaniards, many of whom had been transported convicts from the dungeons of Castile. These wretches, who in their own countries had been the vilest among the vile, here assumed the tone of grand cavaliers. They insisted upon being attended by trains of servants. They took the daughters and female relations of caciques for their domestics, or rather for their concubines, nor did they limit themselves in number. When they travelled, instead of using the horses and mules with which they were provided, they obliged the natives to transport them upon their shoulders in litters, or hammocks, with others attending to hold umbrellas of palm-leaves over their heads to keep off the sun, and fans of feathers to cool them; and Las Casas affirms that he has seen the backs and shoulders of the unfortunate Indians who bore these litters, raw and bleeding from the task. When these arrogant upstarts arrived at an Indian village they consumed and lavished away the provisions of the inhabitants, seizing upon whatever pleased their caprice, and obliging the cacique and his subjects to dance before them for their amusement. Their very pleasures were attended with cruelty. They never addressed the natives but in the most degrading terms, and on the least offence, or the least freak of ill-humor, inflicted blows and lashes, and even death itself.[1]

---

[1] Las Casas, Hist. Ind., lib. ii. cap. 1, MS.

Such is but a faint picture of the evils which sprang up under the feeble rule of Bobadilla, and are sorrowfully described by Las Casas, from actual observation, as he visited the island just at the close of his administration. Bobadilla had trusted to the immense amount of gold, wrung from the miseries of the natives, to atone for all errors, and secure favor with the sovereigns; but he had totally mistaken his course. The abuses of his government soon reached the royal ear, and above all, the wrongs of the natives reached the benevolent heart of Isabella. Nothing was more calculated to arouse her indignation, and she urged the speedy departure of Ovando, to put a stop to these enormities.

In conformity to the plan already mentioned, the government of Ovando extended over the islands and Terra Firma, of which Hispaniola was to be the metropolis. He was to enter upon the exercise of his powers immediately upon his arrival, by procuration, sending home Bobadilla by the return of the fleet. He was instructed to inquire diligently into the late abuses, punishing the delinquents without favor or partiality, and removing all worthless persons from the island. He was to revoke immediately the license granted by Bobadilla for the general search after gold, it having been given without royal authority. He was to require, for the crown, a third of what was already collected, and one-half of all that should be collected in future. He was empowered to build towns, granting them the privileges enjoyed by municipal corporations of Spain, and obliging the Spaniards, and particularly the soldiers, to reside in them, instead of scattering themselves over the island. Among many sage provisions there were others injurious and illiberal, characteristic of an age when the principles of commerce were but little understood, but which were continued by Spain long after the rest of the world had discarded them as the errors of dark and unenlightened times. The crown monopolized the trade of the colonies. No one could carry merchandise there on his own account. A royal factor was appointed, through whom alone were to be obtained supplies of European articles. The crown reserved to itself not only exclusive property in the mines, but in precious stones, and like objects of extraordinary value, and also in dyewoods. No strangers, and above all no Moors nor Jews, were permitted to establish themselves in the island, nor to go upon voyages of discovery. Such were some of the restrictions upon trade which Spain imposed upon her colonies, and which were followed up by others equally illiberal. Her commercial policy has been the scoff of modern times : but may not the present restrictions on trade, imposed by the most intelligent nations, be equally the wonder and the jest of future ages?

Isabella was particularly careful in providing for the kind treatment of the Indians. Ovando was ordered to assemble the caciques, and declare to them that the sovereigns took them and their people under their special protection. They were merely to pay tribute like other subjects of the crown, and it was to be collected with the utmost mildness and gentleness. Great pains were to be taken in their religious instruction , for which purpose twelve Franciscan friars were sent out, with a prelate named Antonio de Espinal, a venerable and pious man. This was the first formal introduction of the Franciscan order into the New World.[1]

All these precautions with respect to the natives were defeated by one unwary provision. It was permitted that the Indians might be compelled to work in the mines, and in other employments : but this was limited to the royal service. They were to be engaged as hired laborers, and punctually paid. This provision led to great abuses and oppressions, and was ultimately as fatal to the natives as could have been the most absolute slavery.

But, with that inconsistency frequent in human conduct, while the sovereigns were making regulations for the relief of the Indians, they encouraged a gross invasion of the rights and welfare of another race of human beings. Among their various decrees on this occasion, we find the first trace of negro slavery in the New World. It was permitted to carry to the colony negro slaves born among Christians ;[2] that is to say, slaves born in Seville and other parts of Spain, the children and descendants of natives brought from the Atlantic coast of Africa, where such traffic had for some time been carried on by the Spaniards and Portuguese. There are signal events in the course of history, which sometimes bear the appearance of temporal judgments. It is a fact worthy of observation that Hispaniola, the place where this flagrant sin against nature and humanity was first introduced into the New World, has been the first to exhibit an awful retribution.

Amid the various concerns which claimed the attention of the sovereigns, the interests of Columbus were not forgotten. Ovando was ordered to examine into all his accounts, without undertaking to pay them off. He was to ascertain the damages

---

[1] Las Casas, Hist. Ind., lib. ii. cap. 3, MS
[2] Herrera, Hist. Ind., decad. i. lib. iv. cap. 12.

he had sustained by his imprisonment, the interruption of his privileges, and the confiscation of his effects. All the property confiscated by Bobadilla was to be restored; or if it had been sold, to be made good. If it had been employed in the royal service, Columbus was to be indemnified out of the treasury, if Bobadilla had appropriated it to his own use, he was to account for it out of his private purse. Equal care was to be taken to indemnify the brothers of the admiral for the losses they had wrongfully suffered by their arrest.

Columbus was likewise to receive the arrears of his revenues, and the same were to be punctually paid to him in future. He was permitted to have a factor resident in the island, to be present at the melting and marking of the gold, to collect his dues, and in short to attend to all his affairs. To this office he appointed Alonzo Sanchez de Carvajal; and the sovereigns commanded that his agent should be treated with great respect.

The fleet appointed to convey Ovando to his government was the largest that had yet sailed to the New World. It consisted of thirty sail, five of them from ninety to one hundred and fifty tons burden, twenty-four caravels from thirty to ninety, and one bark of twenty-five tons.[1] The number of souls embarked in this fleet was about twenty-five hundred; many of them persons of rank and distinction, with their families.

That Ovando might appear with dignity in his new office, he was allowed to use silks, brocades, precious stones, and other articles of sumptuous attire, prohibited at that time in Spain, in consequence of the ruinous ostentation of the nobility. He was permitted to have seventy-two esquires as his body-guard, ten of whom were horsemen. With this expedition sailed Don Alonzo Maldonado, appointed as alguazil mayor, or chief justice, in place of Roldan, who was to be sent to Spain. There were artisans of various kinds: to these were added a physician, surgeon, and apothecary; and seventy-three married men[2] with their families, all of respectable character, destined to be distributed in four towns, and to enjoy peculiar privileges, that they might form the basis of a sound and useful population. They were to displace an equal number of the idle and dissolute who were to be sent from the island: this excellent measure had been especially urged and entreated by Columbus. There was also live stock, artillery, arms, munitions of all kinds; every thing, in short, that was required for the supply of the island.

---

[1] Muñoz, part inedit. Las Casas says the fleet consisted of thirty-two sail. He states from memory, however; Muñoz from documents.

[2] Muñoz, H. N. Mundo, part inedit.

Such was the style in which Ovando, a favorite of Ferdinand, and a native subject of rank, was fitted out to enter upon the government withheld from Columbus. The fleet put to sea on the thirteenth of February, 1502. In the early part of the voyage it was encountered by a terrible storm; one of the ships foundered, with one hundred and twenty passengers; the others were obliged to throw overboard every thing on deck, and were completely scattered. The shores of Spain were strewn with articles from the fleet, and a rumor spread that all the ships had perished. When this reached the sovereigns, they were so overcome with grief that they shut themselves up for eight days, and admitted no one to their presence. The rumor proved to be incorrect; but one ship was lost. The others assembled again at the island of Gomera in the Canaries, and pursuing their voyage, arrived at San Domingo on the 15th of April.[1]

CHAPTER IV.

PROPOSITION OF COLUMBUS RELATIVE TO THE RECOVERY OF THE HOLY SEPULCHRE.

[1500–1501.]

COLUMBUS remained in the city of Granada upward of nine months, endeavoring to extricate his affairs from the confusion into which they had been thrown by the rash conduct of Bobadilla, and soliciting the restoration of his offices and dignities. During this time he constantly experienced the smiles and attentions of the sovereigns, and promises were repeatedly made him that he should ultimately be reinstated in all his honors. He had long since, however, ascertained the great interval that may exist between promise and performance in a court. Had he been of a morbid and repining spirit, he had ample food for misanthropy. He beheld the career of glory which he had opened, thronged by favored adventurers; he witnessed preparations making to convey with unusual pomp a successor to that government from which he had been so wrongfully and rudely ejected; in the mean while his own career was interrupted, and as far as public employ is a gauge of royal favor, he remained apparently in disgrace.

His sanguine temperament was not long to be depressed; if checked in one direction it broke forth in another. His vision-

---

[1] Las Casas, Hist. Ind., lib. ii. cap. 3, MS.

ary imagination was an internal light, which, in the darkest times, repelled all outward gloom, and filled his mind with splendid images and glorious speculations. In this time of evil, his vow to furnish, within seven years from the time of his discovery, fifty thousand foot soldiers, and five thousand horse, for the recovery of the holy sepulchre, recurred to his memory with peculiar force. The time had elapsed, but the vow remained unfulfilled, and the means to perform it had failed him. The New World, with all its treasures, had as yet produced expense instead of profit; and so far from being in a situation to set armies on foot by his own contributions, he found himself without property, without power, and without employ.

Destitute of the means of accomplishing his pious intentions, he considered it his duty to incite the sovereigns to the enterprise : and he felt emboldened to do so, from having originally proposed it as the great object to which the profits of his discoveries should be dedicated. He set to work, therefore, with his accustomed zeal, to prepare arguments for the purpose. During the intervals of business, he sought into the prophecies of the holy Scriptures, the writings of the fathers, and all kinds of sacred and speculative sources, for mystic portents and revelations which might be construed to bear upon the discovery of the New World, the conversion of the Gentiles, and the recovery of the holy sepulchre — three great events which he supposed to be predestined to succeed each other. These passages, with the assistance of a Carthusian friar, he arranged in order, illustrated by poetry, and collected into a manuscript volume, to be delivered to the sovereigns. He prepared, at the same time, a long letter, written with his usual fervor of spirit and simplicity of heart. It is one of those singular compositions which lay open the visionary part of his character, and show the mystic and speculative reading with which he was accustomed to nurture his solemn and soaring imagination.

In this letter he urged the sovereigns to set on foot a crusade for the deliverance of Jerusalem from the power of the unbelievers. He entreated them not to reject his present advice as extravagant and impracticable, nor to heed the discredit that might be cast upon it by others : reminding them that his great scheme of discovery had originally been treated with similar contempt. He avowed in the fullest manner his persuasion, that, from his earliest infancy, he had been chosen by Heaven for the accomplishment of those two great designs, the discovery of the New World, and the rescue of the holy sepulchre. For this purpose, in his tender years, he had been guided by a divine impulse to embrace the profession of the sea, a mode of life, he observes, which produces an inclination to inquire into the mysteries of nature ; and he had been gifted with a curious spirit, to read all kinds of chronicles, geographical treatises, and works of philosophy. In meditating upon these, his understanding had been opened by the Deity, " as with a palpable hand," so as to discover the navigation to the Indies, and he had been inflamed with ardor to undertake the enterprise. "Animated as by a heavenly fire," he adds, " I came to your highnesses : all who heard of my enterprise mocked at it : all the sciences I had acquired profited me nothing ; seven years did I pass in your royal court, disputing the case with persons of great authority and learned in all the arts, and in the end they decided that all was vain In your highnesses alone remained faith and constancy. Who will doubt that this light was from the holy Scriptures, illumining you as well as myself with rays of marvellous brightness?"

These ideas, so repeatedly, and solemnly, and artlessly expressed, by a man of the fervent piety of Columbus, show how truly his discovery arose from the working of his own mind, and not from information furnished by others. He considered it a divine intimation, a light from Heaven, and the fulfilment of what had been foretold by our Saviour and the prophets. Still he regarded it but as a minor event, preparatory to the great enterprise, the recovery of the holy sepulchre. He pronounced it a miracle effected by Heaven to animate himself and others to that holy undertaking ; and he assured the sovereigns that, if they had faith in his present as in his former proposition, they would assuredly be rewarded with equally triumphant success. He conjured them not to heed the sneers of such as might scoff at him as one unlearned, as an ignorant mariner, a worldly man , reminding them that the Holy Spirit works not merely in the learned, but also in the ignorant ; nay, that it reveals things to come, not merely by rational beings, but by prodigies in animals, and by mystic signs in the air and in the heavens.

The enterprise here suggested by Columbus, however idle and extravagant it may appear in the present day, was in unison with the temper of the times, and of the court to which it was proposed. The vein of mystic erudition by which it was enforced, likewise, was suited to an age when the reveries of the cloister still controlled the operations of the cabinet and the camp. The spirit of the crusades had not yet passed away. In the cause of the church, and at the instigation of its dignitaries. every cavalier was ready to draw his sword ; and religion mingled a glowing and devoted enthusiasm with the ordinary excitement of warfare. Ferdinand was a religious bigot ; and the devotion of Isabella went as near to bigotry as her liberal mind and magnanimous spirit would permit. Both the sovereigns were under the influence of ecclesiastical politicians constantly guiding their enterprises in a direction to redound to the temporal power and glory of the church. The recent conquest of Granada had been considered a European crusade, and had gained to the sovereigns the epithet of Catholic. It was natural to think of extending their sacred victories still farther, and retaliating upon the infidels their domination of Spain, and their long triumphs over the cross. In fact, the Duke of Medina Sidonia had made a recent inroad into Barbary, in the course of which he had taken the city of Melilla, and his expedition had been pronounced a renewal of the holy wars against the infidels in Africa.[1]

There was nothing, therefore, in the proposition of Columbus that could be regarded as preposterous, considering the period and circumstances in which it was made. though it strongly illustrates his own enthusiastic and visionary character. It must be recollected that it was meditated in the courts of the Alhambra, among the splendid remains of Moorish grandeur, where, but a few years before. he had beheld the standard of the faith elevated in triumph above the symbols of infidelity. It appears to have been the offspring of one of those moods of high excitement, when, as has been observed, his soul was elevated by the contemplation of his great and glorious office ; when he considered himself under divine inspiration, imparting the will of Heaven, and fulfilling the high and holy purposes for which he had been predestined.[2]

---

[1] Garibay, Hist. España, lib. xix. cap. 6. Among the collections existing in the library of the late Prince Sebastian, there is a folio which, among other things, contains a paper or letter, in which is a calculation of the probable expenses of an army of twenty thousand men, for the conquest of the Holy Land. It is dated 1509 or 1510, and the handwriting appears to be of the same time.

[2] Columbus was not singular in this belief, it was entertained by many of his zealous and learned admirers The erudite lapidary, Jayme Ferrer, in the letter written to Columbus in 1495, at the command of the sovereigns, observes. "I see in this a great mystery the divine and infallible Providence sent the great St Thomas from the west into the east, to manifest in India our holy and Catholic faith, and you, Señor, he sent in an opposite direction, from the east into the west, until you have arrived in the Orient, into the extreme part of Upper India, that the people may hear that which their ancestors neglected of the preaching of St. Thomas. Thus shall be accomplished what was written, *in omnen terram exibit sonus eorum.*" .   And again, "The office which you hold, Señor, places you in the light of an apostle and ambassador of God, sent by his divine judgment, to make known his holy name in unknown lands " — Letra de Mossen Jayme Ferrer, Navarrete Coleccion. tom. ii decad. 68. See also the opinion expressed by Agostino Giustiniani, his contemporary, in his Polyglot Psalter.

CHAPTER V.

PREPARATIONS OF COLUMBUS FOR A FOURTH VOYAGE OF DISCOVERY.

[1501–1502.]

THE speculation relative to the recovery of the holy sepulchre held but a temporary sway over the mind of Columbus. His thoughts soon returned, with renewed ardor, to their wonted channel. He became impatient of inaction, and soon conceived a leading object for another enterprise of discovery. The achievement of Vasco de Gama, of the long-attempted navigation to India by the Cape of Good Hope, was one of the signal events of the day. Pedro Alvarez Cabral, following in his track, had made a most successful voyage, and returned with his vessels laden with the precious commodities of the East. The riches of Calicut were now the theme of every tongue, and the splendid trade now opened in diamonds and precious stones from the mines of Hindostan; in pearls, gold, silver, amber, ivory, and porcelain; in silken stuffs, costly woods, gums, aromatics, and spices of all kinds. The discoveries of the savage regions of the New World, as yet, brought little revenue to Spain: but this route, suddenly opened to the luxurious countries of the East, was pouring immediate wealth into Portugal.

Columbus was roused to emulation by these accounts. He now conceived the idea of a voyage, in which, with his usual enthusiasm, he hoped to surpass not merely the discovery of Vasco de Gama, but even those of his own previous expeditions. According to his own observations in his voyage to Paria, and the reports of other navigators, who had pursued the same route to a greater distance, it appeared that the coast of Terra Firma stretched far to the west. The southern coast of Cuba, which he considered a part of the Asiatic continent, stretched onward toward the same point. The currents of the Caribbean Sea must pass between those lands. He was persuaded, therefore, that there must be a strait existing somewhere thereabout, opening into the Indian sea. The situation in which he placed his conjectural strait was somewhere about what at present is called the Isthmus of Darien.[1] Could he

---

[1] Las Casas, lib. ii. cap. 4. Las Casas specifies the vicinity of Nombre de Dios as the place.

but discover such a passage, and thus link the New World he had discovered, with the opulent Oriental regions of the Old, he felt that he should make a magnificent close to his labors, and consummate this great object of his existence.

When he unfolded his plan to the sovereigns, it was listened to with great attention. Certain of the royal council, it is said, endeavored to throw difficulties in the way, observing that the various exigencies of the times, and the low state of the royal treasury, rendered any new expedition highly inexpedient. They intimated also that Columbus ought not to be employed until his good conduct in Hispaniola was satisfactorily established by letters from Ovando. These narrow-minded suggestions failed in their aim; Isabella had implicit confidence in the integrity of Columbus. As to the expense, she felt that while furnishing so powerful a fleet and splendid retinue to Ovando, to take possession of his government, it would be ungenerous and ungrateful to refuse a few ships to the discoverer of the New World, to enable him to prosecute his illustrious enterprises. As to Ferdinand, his cupidity was roused at the idea of being soon put in possession of a more direct and safe route to those countries with which the crown of Portugal was opening so lucrative a trade. The project also would occupy the admiral for a considerable time, and, while it diverted him from claims of an inconvenient nature, would employ his talents in a way most beneficial to the crown. However the king might doubt his abilities as a legislator, he had the highest opinion of his skill and judgment as a navigator. If such a strait as the one supposed were really in existence, Columbus was, of all men in the world, the one to discover it. His proposition, therefore, was promptly acceded to; he was authorized to fit out an armament immediately; and repaired to Seville in the autumn of 1501, to make the necessary preparations.

Though this substantial enterprise diverted his attention from his romantic expedition for the recovery of the holy sepulchre, it still continued to haunt his mind. He left his manuscript collection of researches among the prophecies, in the hands of a devout friar of the name of Gaspar Gorricio, who assisted to complete it. In February, also, he wrote a letter to Pope Alexander VII., in which he apologizes on account of indispensable occupations, for not having repaired to Rome, according to his original intention, to give an account of his grand discoveries. After briefly relating them, he adds that his enterprises had been undertaken with intent of dedicating the gains to the recovery of the holy sepulchre. He mentions his vow to fur-nish, within seven years, fifty thousand foot and five thousand horse for the purpose, and another of like force within five suc-ceeding years. This pious intention, he laments, had been im-peded by the arts of the devil, and he feared, without divine aid, would be entirely frustrated, as the government which had been granted to him in perpetuity had been taken from him. He informs his Holiness of his being about to embark on an-other voyage, and promises solemnly, on his return, to repair to Rome without delay, to relate every thing by word of mouth, as well as to present him with an account of his voyages, which he had kept from the commencement to the present time, in the style of the Commentaries of Cæsar.[1]

It was about this time, also, that he sent his letter on the subject of the sepulchre to the sovereigns, together with the collection of prophecies.[2] We have no account of the manner in which the proposition was received   Ferdinand, with all his bigotry, was a shrewd and worldly prince.   Instead of a chival-rous crusade against Jerusalem, he preferred making a pacific arrangement with the Grand Soldan of Egypt, who had men-aced the destruction of the sacred edifice. He despatched, therefore, the learned Peter Martyr, so distinguished for his historical writings, as ambassador to the Soldan, by whom all ancient grievances between the two powers were satisfactorily adjusted, and arrangements made for the conservation of the holy sepulchre, and the protection of all Christian pilgrims re-sorting to it.

In the mean time Columbus went on with the preparations for his contemplated voyage, though but slowly, owing, as Charle-voix intimates, to the artifices and delays of Fonseca and his

---

[1] Navarrete, Colec. Viag., tom ii. p. 145.

[2] A manuscript volume containing a copy of this letter and of the collection of prophecies, is in the Columbian Library, in the Cathedral of Seville, where the author of this work has seen and examined it, since publishing the first edition. The title and some of the early pages of the work are in the handwriting of Fernando Columbus, the main body of the work is by a strange hand, probably by the Friar Gaspar Gorricio, or some brother of his Convent. There are trifling marginal notes or corrections, and one or two trivial additions in the handwriting of Columbus, especially a passage added after his return from his fourth voyage and shortly before his death, alluding to an eclipse of the moon which took place during his sojourn in the island of Jamaica. The handwriting of this last passage, like most of the manu script of Columbus which the author has seen, is small and delicate, but wants the firm-ness and distinctness of his earlier writing, his hand having doubtless become unsteady by age and infirmity.

This document is extremely curious as containing all the passages of Scripture and of the works of the fathers which had so powerful an influence on the enthusiastic mind of Columbus, and were construed by him into mysterious prophecies and reve-lations. The volume is in good preservation, excepting that a few pages have been cut out. The writing, though of the beginning of the fifteenth century, is very distinct and legible. The library mark of the book is Estante Z, Tab 138, No. 25.

agents. He craved permission to touch at the island of Hispaniola for supplies on his outward voyage. This, however,
the sovereigns forbade, knowing that he had many enemies
in the island, and that the place would be in great agitation from
the arrival of Ovando and the removal of Bobadilla. They
consented, however, that he should touch there briefly on his
return, by which time they hoped the island would be restored
to tranquillity. He was permitted to take with him in this expedition his brother the Adelantado, and his son Fernando, then
in his fourteenth year; also two or three persons learned in
Arabic, to serve as interpreters, in case he should arrive at the
dominions of the Grand Khan, or of any other eastern prince
where that language might be spoken, or partially known. In
reply to letters relative to the ultimate restoration of his rights,
and to matters concerning his family, the sovereigns wrote him
a letter, dated March 14th, 1502, from Valencia de Torre, in
which they again solemnly assured him that their capitulations
with him should be fulfilled to the letter, and the dignities
therein ceded enjoyed by him, and his children after him; and
if it should be necessary to confirm them anew, they would do
so, and secure them to his son. Besides which, they expressed
their disposition to bestow further honors and rewards upon
himself, his brothers, and his children. They entreated him,
therefore, to depart in peace and confidence, and to leave all
his concerns in Spain to the management of his son Diego.[1]

This was the last letter that Columbus received from the
sovereigns, and the assurances it contained were as ample and
absolute as he could desire. Recent circumstances, however,
had apparently rendered him dubious of the future. During
the time that he passed in Seville, previous to his departure,
he took measures to secure his fame, and preserve the claims
of his family, by placing them under the guardianship of his
native country. He had copies of all the letters, grants, and
privileges from the sovereigns, appointing him admiral, viceroy, and governor of the Indies, copied and authenticated before the alcaldes of Seville. Two sets of these were transcribed,
together with his letter to the nurse of Prince Juan, containing a circumstantial and eloquent vindication of his rights; and
two letters to the Bank of St. George, at Genoa, assigning to it
the tenth of his revenues, to be employed in diminishing the
duties on corn and other provisions — a truly benevolent and
patriotic donation, intended for the relief of the poor of his

---

[1] Las Casas, Hist. Ind., lib. ii. cap. 4.

native city   These two sets of documents he sent by different individuals to his friend, Doctor Nicola Oderigo, formerly ambassador from Genoa to the court of Spain, requesting him to preserve them in some safe deposit, and to apprise his son Diego of the same.   His dissatisfaction at the conduct of the Spanish court may have been the cause of this precautionary measure, that an appeal to the world, or to posterity, might be in the power of his descendants, in case he should perish in the course of his voyage.[1]

---

[1] These documents lay unknown in the Oderigo family until 1670, when Lorenzo Oderigo presented them to the government of Genoa, and they were deposited in the archives   In the disturbances and revolutions of after times, one of these copies was taken to Paris, and the other disappeared.   In 1816 the latter was discovered in the library of the deceased Count Michel Angelo Cambiaso, a senator of Genoa.   It was procured by the King of Sardinia, then sovereign of Genoa, and given up by him to the city of Genoa in 1821.   A custodia, or monument, was erected in that city for its preservation, consisting of a marble column supporting an urn, surmounted by a bust of Columbus.   The documents were deposited in the urn.   These papers have been published, together with an historical memoir of Columbus by D. Gio. Battista Spotorno, Professor of Eloquence, etc., in the University of Genoa.

BOOK XV.

CHAPTER I.

[1502.]

AGE was rapidly making its advances upon Columbus when he undertook his fourth and last voyage of discovery. He had already numbered sixty-six years, and they were years filled with care and trouble, in which age outstrips the march of time. His constitution, originally vigorous in the extreme, had been impaired by hardships and exposures in every clime, and silently preyed upon by the sufferings of the mind. His frame, once powerful and commanding, and retaining a semblance of strength and majesty even in its decay, was yet crazed by infirmities and subject to paroxysms of excruciating pain. His intellectual forces alone retained their wonted health and energy, prompting him, at a period of life when most men seek repose, to sally forth with youthful ardor, on the most toilsome and adventurous of expeditions.

His squadron for the present voyage consisted of four caravels, the smallest of fifty tons burden, the largest not exceeding seventy, and the crews amounting in all to one hundred and fifty men. With this little armament and these slender barks did the venerable discoverer undertake the search after a strait, which, if found, must conduct him into the most remote seas, and lead to a complete circumnavigation of the globe.

In this arduous voyage, however, he had a faithful counsellor, and an intrepid and vigorous coadjutor, in his brother Don Bartholomew, while his younger son Fernando cheered him with his affectionate sympathy. He had learned to appreciate such comforts, from being too often an isolated stranger, surrounded by false friends and perfidious enemies.

The squadron sailed from Cadiz on the 9th of May, and passed over to Ercilla, on the coast of Morocco. where it anchored on the 13th. Understanding that the Portuguese garrison was closely besieged in the fortress by the Moors. and exposed to great peril, Columbus was ordered to touch there, and render all the assistance in his power. Before his arrival the siege had been raised, but the governor lay ill, having been wounded in an assault. Columbus sent his brother, the Adelantado, his son Fernando, and the captains of the caravels on shore, to wait upon the governor, with expressions of friendship and civility, and offers of the services of his squadron. Their visit and message gave high satisfaction, and several cavaliers were sent to wait upon the admiral in return, some of whom were relatives of his deceased wife, Doña Felippa Muñoz After this exchange of civilities, the admiral made sail on the same day, and continued his voyage.[1] On the 25th of May, he arrived at the Grand Canary and remained at that and the adjacent islands for a few days, taking in wood and water. On the evening of the 25th he took his departure for the New World. The trade-winds were so favorable that the little squadron swept gently on its course. without shifting a sail, and arrived on the 15th of June at one of the Caribbee Islands, called by the natives Mantinino.[2] After stopping here for three days, to take in wood and water, and allow the seamen time to wash their clothes. the squadron passed to the west of the island, and sailed to Dominica, about ten leagues distant.[3] Columbus continued hence along the inside of the Antilles, to Santa Cruz, then along the south side of Porto Rico, and steered for San Domingo. This was contrary to the original plan of the admiral, who had intended to steer to Jamaica,[4] and thence to take a departure for the continent, and explore its coasts in search of the supposed strait. It was contrary to the orders of the sovereigns also, prohibiting him on his outward voyage to touch at Hispaniola. His excuse was that his principal vessel sailed extremely ill, could not carry any canvas, and continually embarrassed and delayed the rest of the squadron.[5] He wished, therefore, to exchange it for one of the fleet which had recently conveyed Ovando to his government.

---

[1] Hist. del Almirante, cap. 88
[2] Señor Navarrete supposes this island to be the same at present called Santa Lucia From the distance between it and Dominica, as stated by Fernando Columbus, it was more probably the present Martinica.
[3] Hist. del Almirante, cap. 88.
[4] Letter of Columbus from Jamaica. Journal of Porras, Navarrete, tom. i.
[5] Hist. del Almirante, cap. 88. Las Casas. lib. ii cap. 5.

or to purchase some other vessel at San Domingo; and he was persuaded that he would not be blamed for departing from his orders, in a case of such importance to the safety and success of his expedition.

It is necessary to state the situation of the island at this moment. Ovando had reached San Domingo on the 15th of April. He had been received with the accustomed ceremony on the shore, by Bobadilla, accompanied by the principal inhabitants of the town. He was escorted to the fortress, where his commission was read in form, in presence of all the authorities. The usual oaths were taken, and ceremonials observed; and the new governor was hailed with great demonstrations of obedience and satisfaction. Ovando entered upon the duties of his office with coolness and prudence, and treated Bobadilla with a courtesy totally opposite to the rudeness with which the latter had superseded Columbus. The emptiness of mere official rank, when unsustained by merit, was shown in the case of Bobadilla. The moment his authority was at an end all his importance vanished. He found himself a solitary and neglected man, deserted by those whom he had most favored, and he experienced the worthlessness of the popularity gained by courting the prejudices and passions of the multitude. Still there is no record of any suit having been instituted against him; and Las Casas, who was on the spot, declares that he never heard any harsh thing spoken of him by the colonists.[1]

The conduct of Roldan and his accomplices, however, underwent a strict investigation, and many were arrested to be sent to Spain for trial. They appeared undismayed, trusting to the influence of their friends in Spain to protect them, and many relying on the well-known disposition of the Bishop of Fonseca to favor all who had been opposed to Columbus.

The fleet which had brought out Ovando was now ready for sea; and was to take out a number of the principal delinquents, and many of the idlers and profligates of the island. Bobadilla was to embark in the principal ship, on board of which he put an immense amount of gold, the revenue collected for the crown during his government, and which he confidently expected would atone for all his faults. There was one solid mass of virgin gold on board of this ship, which is famous in the old Spanish chronicles. It had been found by a female Indian in a brook, on the estate of Francisco de Garay and Miguel Diaz, and had been taken by Bobadilla to send to the king, making

---

[1] Las Casas, Hist. Ind., lib. ii. cap. 3.

the owners a suitable compensation. It was said to weigh three thousand six hundred castellanos.[1]

Large quantities of gold were likewise shipped in the fleet, by the followers of Roldan, and other adventurers, the wealth gained by the sufferings of the unhappy natives. Among the various persons who were to sail in the principal ship was the unfortunate Guarionex, the once powerful cacique of the Vega. He had been confined in Fort Conception ever since his capture after the war of Higuey, and was now to be sent a captive in chains to Spain. In one of the ships, Alonzo Sanchez de Carvajal, the agent of Columbus, had put four thousand pieces of gold, to be remitted to him, being part of his property, either recently collected or recovered from the hands of Bobadilla.[2]

The preparations were all made, and the fleet was ready to put to sea, when, on the 29th of June, the squadron of Columbus arrived at the mouth of the river. He immediately sent Pedro de Terreros, captain of one of the caravels, on shore to wait on Ovando, and explain to him that the purpose of his coming was to procure a vessel in exchange for one of his caravels, which was extremely defective. He requested permission also to shelter his squadron in the harbor; as he apprehended, from various indications, an approaching storm. This request was refused by Ovando. Las Casas thinks it probable that he had instructions from the sovereigns not to admit Columbus, and that he was further swayed by prudent considerations, as San Domingo was at that moment crowded with the most virulent enemies of the admiral, many of them in a high state of exasperation, from recent proceedings which had taken place against them.[3]

When the ungracious refusal of Ovando was brought to Columbus, and he found all shelter denied him, he sought at least to avert the danger of the fleet, which was about to sail. He sent back the officer, therefore, to the governor, entreating him not to permit the fleet to put to sea for several days, assuring him that there were indubitable signs of an impending tempest. This second request was equally fruitless with the first. The weather, to an inexperienced eye, was fair and tranquil; the pilots and seamen were impatient to depart. They scoffed at the prediction of the admiral, ridiculing him as a false prophet, and they persuaded Ovando not to detain the fleet on so unsubstantial a pretext.

It was hard treatment of Columbus, thus to be denied the

[1] Las Casas Hist. Ind., lib. ii. cap. 5.   [2] Ibid.
[3] Las Casas, ubi sup.

relief which the state of his ships required, and to be excluded
in time of distress from the very harbor he had discovered.
He retired from the river full of grief and indignation. His
crew murmured loudly at being shut out from a port of their
own nation, where even strangers, under similar circumstances,
would be admitted. They repined at having embarked with a
commander liable to such treatment, and anticipated nothing
but evil from a voyage, in which they were exposed to the
dangers of the sea, and repulsed from the protection of the
land.

Being confident, from his observations of those natural phenomena in which he was deeply skilled, that the anticipated
storm could not be distant, and expecting it from the land side,
Columbus kept his feeble squadron close to the shore, and
sought for secure anchorage in some wild bay or river of the
island.

In the mean time the fleet of Bobadilla set sail from San Domingo, and stood out confidently to sea. Within two days the
predictions of Columbus were verified One of those tremendous hurricanes, which sometimes sweep those latitudes, had
gradually gathered up. The baleful appearance of the heavens,
the wild look of the ocean, the rising murmur of the winds, all
gave notice of its approach. The fleet had scarcely reached the
eastern point of Hispaniola when the tempest burst over it
with awful fury, involving every thing in wreck and ruin. The
ship on board of which were Bobadilla, Roldan, and a number
of the most inveterate enemies of Columbus, was swallowed up
with all its crew, and with the celebrated mass of gold, and the
principal part of the ill-gotten treasure, gained by the miseries
of the Indians. Many of the ships were entirely lost, some returned to San Domingo, in shattered condition, and only one
was enabled to continue her voyage to Spain. That one, according to Fernando Columbus, was the weakest of the fleet,
and had on board the four thousand pieces of gold, the property
of the admiral.

During the early part of this storm the little squadron of
Columbus remained tolerably well sheltered by the land. On
the second day the tempest increased in violence, and the night
coming on with unusual darkness, the ships lost sight of each
other and were separated. The admiral still kept close to the
shore, and sustained no damage. The others, fearful of the
land in such a dark and boisterous night, ran out for sea-room,
and encountered the whole fury of the elements. For several
days they were driven about at the mercy of wind and

wave, fearful each moment of shipwreck, and giving up each other as lost. The Adelantado, who commanded the ship already mentioned as being scarcely seaworthy, ran the most imminent hazard, and nothing but his consummate seamanship enabled him to keep her afloat. At length, after various vicissitudes, they all arrived safe at Port Hermoso, to the west of San Domingo. The Adelantado had lost his long-boat; and all the vessels, with the exception of that of the admiral, had sustained more or less injury.

When Columbus learnt the signal destruction that had overwhelmed his enemies, almost before his eyes, he was deeply impressed with awe, and considered his own preservation as little less than miraculous. Both his son Fernando and the venerable historian Las Casas looked upon the event as one of those awful judgments which seem at times to deal forth temporal retribution. They notice the circumstance, that while the enemies of the admiral were swallowed up by the raging sea, the only ship of the fleet which was enabled to pursue her voyage, and reach her port of destination, was the frail bark freighted with the property of Columbus. The evil, however, in this, as in most circumstances, overwhelmed the innocent as well as the guilty. In the ship with Bobadilla and Roldan, perished the captive Guarionex, the unfortunate cacique of the Vega.[1]

CHAPTER II.

VOYAGE ALONG THE COAST OF HONDURAS.

[1502.]

FOR several days Columbus remained in Port Hermoso, to repair his vessels and permit his crews to repose and refresh themselves after the late tempest. He had scarcely left this harbor when he was obliged to take shelter from another storm in Jacquemel, or as it was called by the Spaniards, Port Brazil. Hence he sailed on the 14th of July, steering for Terra Firma. The weather falling perfectly calm, he was borne away by the currents until he found himself in the vicinity of some little islands near Jamaica,[2] destitute of springs, but where the sea-

---

[1] Las Casas, Hist. Ind., lib. ii. cap 5. Hist. del Almirante, cap. 88.
[2] Supposed to be the Morant Keys.

men obtained a supply of water by digging holes in the sand on the beach.

The calm continuing, he was swept away to the group of small islands, or keys, on the southern coast of Cuba, to which, in 1494, he had given the name of The Gardens. He had scarcely touched there, however, when the wind sprang up from a favorable quarter, and he was enabled to make sail on his destined course. He now stood to the south-west, and after a few days discovered, on the 30th of July, a small but elevated island, agreeable to the eye from the variety of trees with which it was covered. Among these was a great number of lofty pines, from which circumstance Columbus named it Isla de Pinos. It has always, however, retained its Indian name of Guanaja,[1] which has been extended to a number of smaller islands surrounding it. This group is within a few leagues of the coast of Honduras, to the east of the great bay or gulf of that name.

The Adelantado, with two launches full of people, landed on the principal island, which was extremely verdant and fertile. The inhabitants resembled those of other islands, excepting that their foreheads were narrower. While the Adelantado was on shore, he beheld a great canoe arriving, as from a distant and important voyage. He was struck with its magnitude and contents. It was eight feet wide, and as long as a galley, though formed of the trunk of a single tree. In the centre was a kind of awning or cabin of palm-leaves, after the manner of those in the gondolas of Venice, and sufficiently close to exclude both sun and rain. Under this sat a cacique with his wives and children. Twenty-five Indians rowed the canoe, and it was filled with all kinds of articles of the manufacture and natural production of the adjacent countries. It is supposed that this bark had come from the province of Yucatan, which is about forty leagues distant from this island.

The Indians in the canoe appeared to have no fear of the Spaniards, and readily went alongside of the admiral's caravel. Columbus was overjoyed at thus having brought to him at once, without trouble or danger, a collection of specimens of all the important articles of this part of the New World. He examined with great curiosity and interest the contents of the canoe. Among various utensils and weapons similar to those already found among the natives, he perceived others of a much superior kind. There were hatchets for cutting wood,

---

[1] Called in some of the English maps Bonacca.

formed not of stone but copper : wooden swords, with channels on each side of the blade, in which sharp flints were firmly fixed by cords made of the intestines of fishes ; being the same kind of weapon afterward found among the Mexicans. There were copper bells, and other articles of the same metal, together with a rude kind of crucible in which to melt it, various vessels and utensils neatly formed of clay, of marble, and of hard wood ; sheets and mantles of cotton, worked and dyed with various colors : great quantities of cacao, a fruit as yet unknown to the Spaniards, but which, as they soon found, the natives held in great estimation, using it both as food and money. There was a beverage also extracted from maize or Indian corn, resembling beer. Their provisions consisted of bread made of maize, and roots of various kinds, similar to those of Hispaniola. From among these articles Columbus collected such as were important to send as specimens to Spain, giving the natives European trinkets in exchange, with which they were highly satisfied. They appeared to manifest neither astonishment nor alarm when on board of the vessels, and surrounded by people who must have been so strange and wonderful to them. The women wore mantles, with which they wrapped themselves, like the female Moors of Granada, and the men had cloths of cotton round their loins. Both sexes appeared more particular about these coverings, and to have a quicker sense of personal modesty than any Indians Columbus had yet discovered.

These circumstances, together with the superiority of their implements and manufactures, were held by the admiral as indications that he was approaching more civilized nations. He endeavored to gain particular information from these Indians about the surrounding countries : but as they spoke a different language from that of his interpreters, he could understand them but imperfectly. They informed him that they had just arrived from a country, rich, cultivated, and industrious, situated to the west. They endeavored to impress him with an idea of the wealth and magnificence of the regions, and the people in that quarter, and urged him to steer in that direction Well would it have been for Columbus had he followed their advice. Within a day or two he would have arrived at Yucatan ; the discovery of Mexico and the other opulent countries of New Spain would have necessarily followed : the Southern Ocean would have been disclosed to him, and a succession of splendid discoveries would have shed fresh glory on his declining age, instead of its sinking amidst gloom, neglect, and disappointment.

The admiral's whole mind. however. was at present intent upon discovering the strait. As the countries described by the Indians lay to the west. he supposed that he could easily visit them at some future time, by running with the trade-winds along the coast of Cuba. which he imagined must continue on, so as to join them. At present he was determined to seek the mainland, the mountains of which were visible to the south, and apparently not many leagues distant; [1] by keeping along it steadfastly to the east, he must at length arrive to where he supposed it to be severed from the coast of Paria by an intervening strait; and passing through this, he should soon make his way to the Spice Islands and the richest parts of India. [2]

He was encouraged the more to persist in his eastern course by information from the Indians, that there were many places in that direction which abounded with gold. Much of the information which he gathered among these people was derived from an old man more intelligent than the rest. who appeared to be an ancient navigator of these seas. Columbus retained him to serve as a guide along the coast, and dismissed his companions with many presents.

Leaving the island of Guanaja. he stood southwardly for the mainland, and after sailing a few leagues discovered a cape, to which he gave the name of Caxinas. from its being covered with fruit trees, so called by the natives. It is at present known as Cape Honduras. Here. on Sunday the 14th of August, the Adelantado landed with the captains of the caravels and many of the seamen, to attend mass, which was performed under the trees on the sea-shore, according to the pious custom of the admiral, whenever circumstances would permit. On the 17th the Adelantado again landed at a river about fifteen miles from the point, on the bank of which he displayed the banners of Castile, taking possession of the country in the name of their Catholic Majesties; from which circumstance he named this the River of Possession. [3]

At this place they found upward of a hundred Indians assembled, laden with bread and maize, fish and fowl, vegetables. and fruits of various kinds. These they laid down as presents before the Adelantado and his party, and drew back to a distance without speaking a word. The Adelantado distributed among them various trinkets, with which they were well pleased

---

[1] Journal of Porras, Navarrete, tom i.
[2] Las Casas, lib ii cap. 20. Letter of Columbus from Jamaica.
[3] Journal of Porras, Navarrete, Colec., tom. i.

and appeared the next day in the same place, in greater num bers, with still more abundant supplies of provisions.

The natives of this neighborhood, and for a considerable distance eastward, had higher foreheads than those of the islands. They were of different languages, and varied from each other in their decorations. Some were entirely naked; and their bodies were marked by means of fire with the figures of various animals. Some wore coverings about the loins; others short cotton jerkins without sleeves; some wore tresses of hair in front. The chieftains had caps of white or colored cotton When arrayed for any festival, they painted their faces black, or with stripes of various colors, or with circles round the eyes. The old Indian guide assured the admiral that many of them were cannibals. In one part of the coast the natives had their ears bored, and hideously distended; which caused the Spaniards to call that region *la Costa de la Oreja*, or "The Coast of the Ear." [1]

From the River of Possession, Columbus proceeded along what is at present called the coast of Honduras, beating against contrary winds, and struggling with currents, which swept from the east like the constant stream of a river. He often lost in one tack what he had laboriously gained in two, frequently making but two leagues in a day, and never more than five. At night he anchored under the land, through fear of proceeding along an unknown coast in the dark, but was often forced out to sea by the violence of the currents. [2] In all this time he experienced the same kind of weather that had prevailed on the coast of Hispaniola, and had attended him more or less for upward of sixty days. There was, he says, almost an incessant tempest of the heavens, with heavy rains, and such thunder and lightning that it seemed as if the end of the world was at hand Those who know any thing of the drenching rains and rending thunder of the tropics will not think his description of the storms exaggerated. His vessels were strained so that their seams opened; the sails and rigging were rent, and the provisions were damaged by the rain and by the leakage. The sailors were exhausted with labor and harassed with terror. They many times confessed their sins to each other, and prepared for death. "I have seen many tempests," says Columbus, "but none so violent or of such long duration." He alludes to the whole series of storms for upward of two months, since he had been refused shelter at San

---

[1] Las Casas, lib. ii. cap. 21. Hist del Almirante, cap. 90.
[2] Hist. del Almirante, cap 80.

Domingo. During a great part of this time ne had suffered extremely from the gout. aggravated by his watchfulness and anxiety. His illness did not prevent his attending to his duties : he had a small cabin or chamber constructed on the stern, whence, even when confined to his bed, he could keep a look-out and regulate the sailing of the ships. Many times he was so ill that he thought his end approaching. His anxious mind was distressed about his brother the Adelantado. whom he had persuaded against his will to come on this expedition, and who was in the worst vessel of the squadron. He lamented also having brought with him his son Fernando, exposing him at so tender an age to such perils and hardships, although the youth bore them with the courage and fortitude of a veteran. Often, too, his thoughts reverted to his son Diego, and the cares and perplexities into which his death might plunge him.[1] At length, after struggling for upward of forty days since leaving the Cape of Honduras, to make a distance of about seventy leagues, they arrived on the 14th of September at a cape where the coast, making an angle, turned directly south, so as to give them an easy wind and free navigation. Doubling the point, they swept off with flowing sails and hearts filled with joy; and the admiral, to commemorate this sudden relief from toil and peril. gave to the Cape the name of *Gracias a Dios*, or Thanks to God.[2]

CHAPTER III.

VOYAGE ALONG THE MOSQUITO COAST, AND TRANSACTIONS AT CARIARI.

[1503.]

AFTER doubling Cape Gracias a Dios, Columbus sailed directly south, along what is at present called the Mosquito shore The land was of varied character, sometimes rugged, with craggy promontories and points stretching into the sea, at other places verdant and fertile, and watered by abundant streams. In the rivers grew immense reeds, sometimes of the thickness of a man's thigh : they abounded with fish and tortoises, and alligators basked on the banks. At one place Columbus passed a cluster of twelve small islands, on which grew

---

[1] Letter from Jamaica. Navarrete Colec., tom. i.
[2] Las Casas, lib. ii. cap. 21. Hist. del Almirante, cap. 91.

a fruit resembling the lemon, on which account he called them the Limonares.[1]

After sailing about sixty-two leagues along this coast, being greatly in want of wood and water the squadron anchored on the 16th of September, near a copious river, up which the boats were sent to procure the requisite supplies. As they were returning to their ships, a sudden swelling of the sea, rushing in and encountering the rapid current of the river, caused a violent commotion, in which one of the boats was swallowed up, and all on board perished. This melancholy event had a gloomy effect upon the crews, already dispirited and careworn from the hardships they had endured, and Columbus, sharing their dejection, gave the stream the sinister name of *El Rio del Desastre*, or the River of Disaster.[2]

Leaving this unlucky neighborhood, they continued for several days along the coast, until finding both his ships and his people nearly disabled by the buffetings of the tempests, Columbus, on the 25th of September, cast anchor between a small island and the main-land, in what appeared a commodious and delightful situation. The island was covered with groves of palm-trees, cocoanut-trees, bananas, and a delicate and fragrant fruit, which the admiral continually mistook for the mirabolane of the East Indies. The fruits and flowers and odoriferous shrubs of the island sent forth grateful perfumes, so that Columbus gave it the name of La Huerta, or The Garden. It was called by the natives, Quiribiri. Immediately opposite, at a short league's distance, was an Indian village, named Cariari, situated on the bank of a beautiful river. The country around was fresh and verdant, finely diversified by noble hills and forests, with trees of such height that Las Casas says they appeared to reach the skies.

When the inhabitants beheld the ships, they gathered together on the coast, armed with bows and arrows, war-clubs, and lances, and prepared to defend their shores. The Spaniards, however, made no attempt to land during that or the succeeding day, but remained quietly on board repairing the ships, airing and drying the damaged provisions, or reposing from the fatigues of the voyage. When the savages perceived that these wonderful beings, who had arrived in this strange manner on their coast, were perfectly pacific, and made no movement to molest them, their hostility ceased, and curiosity pre-

---

[1] P. Martyr, decad. iii. lib. iv. These may have been the lime, a small and extremely acid species of the lemon.

[2] Las Casas, lib. ii. cap. 21. Hist. del Almirante, cap. 91. Journal of Porras.

dominated. They made various pacific signals, waving their mantles like banners, and inviting the Spaniards to land. Growing still more bold, they swam to the ships, bringing off mantles and tunics of cotton, and ornaments of the inferior sort of gold called guanin, which they wore about their necks. These they offered to the Spaniards. The admiral, however, forbade all traffic, making them presents, but taking nothing in exchange, wishing to impress them with a favorable idea of the liberality and disinterestedness of the white men. The pride of the savages was touched at the refusal of their proffered gifts, and this supposed contempt for their manufactures and productions. They endeavored to retaliate, by pretending like indifference. On returning to shore, they tied together all the European articles which had been given them, without retaining the least trifle, and left them lying on the strand, where the Spaniards found them on a subsequent day.

Finding the strangers still declined to come on shore, the natives tried in every way to gain their confidence, and dispel the distrust which their hostile demonstrations might have caused. A boat approaching the shore cautiously one day, in quest of some safe place to procure water, an ancient Indian, of venerable demeanor, issued from among the trees, bearing a white banner on the end of a staff, and leading two girls, one about fourteen years of age, the other about eight, having jewels of guanin about their necks. These he brought to the boat and delivered to the Spaniards, making signs that they were to be detained as hostages while the strangers should be on shore. Upon this the Spaniards sallied forth with confidence and filled their water-casks, the Indians remaining at a distance, and observing the strictest care, neither by word nor movement to cause any new distrust. When the boats were about to return to the ships, the old Indian made signs that the young girls should be taken on board, nor would he admit of any denial. On entering the ships the girls showed no signs of grief nor alarm, though surrounded by what to them must have been uncouth and formidable beings. Columbus was careful that the confidence thus placed in him should not be abused. After feasting the young females, and ordering them to be clothed and adorned with various ornaments, he sent them on shore. The night, however, had fallen, and the coast was deserted. They had to return to the ship, where they remained all night under the careful protection of the admiral. The next morning he restored them to their friends. The old Indian received them with joy, and manifested a grateful sense of the kind treatment they had experienced. In the evening, however, when the boats went on shore. the young girls appeared, accompanied by a multitude of their friends, and returned all the presents they had received. nor could they be prevailed upon to retain any of them, although they must have been precious in their eyes ; so greatly was the pride of these savages piqued at having their gifts refused.

On the following day. as the Adelantado approached the shore, two of the principal inhabitants, entering the water, took him out of the boat in their arms, and carrying him to land, seated him with great ceremony on a grassy bank.   Don Bartholomew endeavored to collect information from them respecting the country, and ordered the notary of the squadron to write down their replies   The latter immediately prepared pen, ink, and paper, and proceeded to write ; but no sooner did the Indians behold this strange and mysterious process, than mistaking it for some necromantic spell, intended to be wrought upon them, they fled with terror.   After some time they returned, cautiously scattering a fragrant powder in the air, and burning some of it in such a direction that the smoke should be borne toward the Spaniards by the wind.   This was apparently intended to counteract any baleful spell, for they regarded the strangers as beings of a mysterious and supernatural order.

The sailors looked upon these counter-charms of the Indians with equal distrust, and apprehended something of magic ; nay, Fernando Columbus, who was present. and records the scene. appears to doubt whether these Indians were not versed in sorcery, and thus led to suspect it in others.[1]

Indeed, not to conceal a foible, which was more characteristic of the superstition of the age than of the man. Columbus himself entertained an idea of the kind, and assures the sovereigns, in his letter from Jamaica, that the people of Cariari and its vicinity are great enchanters, and he intimates that the two Indian girls who had visited his ship had magic powder concealed about their persons.   He adds, that the sailors attributed all the delays and hardships experienced on that coast to their being under the influence of some evil spell, worked by the witchcraft of the natives, and that they still remained in that belief.[2]

---

[1] Hist. del Almirante, cap. 91.
[2] Letter from Jamaica

Note. — We find instances of the same kind of superstition in the work of Marco Polo, and as Columbus considered himself in the vicinity of the countries described by that traveller, he may have been influenced in this respect by his narrations. Speaking of the island of Soccotera, (Socotra), Marco Polo observes: " The inhabit

For several days the squadron remained at this place, during which time the ships were examined and repaired, and the crews enjoyed repose and the recreation of the land. The Adelantado, with a band of armed men, made excursions on shore to collect information. There was no pure gold to be met with here, all their ornaments were of guanin; but the natives assured the Adelantado, that, in proceeding along the coast, the ships would soon arrive at a country where gold was in great abundance.

In examining one of the villages, the Adelantado found, in a large house, several sepulchres. One contained a human body embalmed in another, there were two bodies wrapped in cotton, and so preserved as to be free from any disagreeable odor. They were adorned with the ornaments most precious to them when living; and the sepulchres were decorated with rude carvings and paintings representing various animals, and sometimes what appeared to be intended for portraits of the deceased.[1] Throughout most of the savage tribes there appears to have been great veneration for the dead, and an anxiety to preserve their remains undisturbed.

When about to sail, Columbus seized seven of the people, two of whom, apparently the most intelligent, he selected to serve as guides; the rest he suffered to depart. His late guide he had dismissed with presents at Cape Gracias a Dios. The inhabitants of Cariari manifested unusual sensibility at this seizure of their countrymen. They thronged the shore, and sent off four of their principal men with presents to the ships, imploring the release of the prisoners.

The admiral assured them that he only took their companions as guides, for a short distance along the coast, and would restore them soon in safety to their homes. He ordered various presents to be given to the ambassadors; but neither his promises nor gifts could soothe the grief and apprehension of the natives at beholding their friends carried away by beings of whom they had such mysterious apprehensions.[2]

---

ants deal more in sorcery and witchcraft than any other people, although forbidden by their archbishop, who excommunicates and anathematizes them for the sin. Of this, however, they make little account, and if any vessel belonging to a pirate should injure one of theirs, they do not fail to lay him under a spell, so that he cannot proceed on his cruise until he has made satisfaction for the damage; and even although he should have a fair and leading wind, they have the power of causing it to change, and thereby obliging him, in spite of himself, to return to the island. They can in like manner, cause the sea to become calm, and at their will can raise tempests, occasion shipwrecks, and produce many other extraordinary effects that need not be particularized. — Marco Polo, book iii. cap 35, Eng. translation by W. Marsden.

[1] Las Casas, lib. ii. cap. 21. Hist. del Almirante, cap 91.

[2] Ibid. Hist. del Almirante, cap. 91. Letter of Columbus from Jamaica.

CHAPTER IV.

VOYAGE ALONG COSTA RICA — SPECULATIONS CONCERNING THE
ISTHMUS AT VERAGUA.

[1502.]

ON the 5th of October the squadron departed from Cariari, and sailed along what is at present called Costa Rica (or the Rich Coast), from the gold and silver mines found in after years among its mountains. After sailing about twenty-two leagues the ships anchored in a great bay, about six leagues in length and three in breadth, full of islands, with channels opening between them, so as to present three or four entrances. It was called by the natives Caribaro,[1] and had been pointed out by the natives of Cariari as plentiful in gold.

The islands were beautifully verdant, covered with groves, and sent forth the fragrance of fruits and flowers. The channels between them were so deep and free from rocks that the ships sailed along them, as if in canals in the streets of a city, the spars and rigging brushing the overhanging branches of the trees. After anchoring, the boats landed on one of the islands, where they found twenty canoes. The people were on shore among the trees. Being encouraged by the Indians of Cariari, who accompanied the Spaniards, they soon advanced with confidence. Here, for the first time on this coast, the Spaniards met with specimens of pure gold, the natives wearing large plates of it suspended round their necks by cotton cords; they had ornaments likewise of guanin, rudely shaped like eagles. One of them exchanged a plate of gold, equal in value to ten ducats, for three hawk's bells.[2]

On the following day the boats proceeded to the main-land at the bottom of the bay. The country around was high and rough, and the villages were generally perched on the heights. They met with ten canoes of Indians, their heads decorated with garlands of flowers, and coronets formed of the claws of beasts and the quills of birds;[3] most of them had plates of gold about their necks, but refused to part with them. The Spaniards

---

[1] In some English maps this bay is called Almirante, or Carnavaco Bay. The channel by which Columbus entered is still called Boca del Almirante, or the Mouth of the Admiral.
[2] Journal of Porras, Navarrete, tom. i.   [3] P. Martyr, decad. iii. lib. v.

brought two of them to the admiral to serve as guides One had a plate of pure gold worth fourteen ducats, another an eagle worth twenty-two ducats Seeing the great value which the strangers set upon this metal, they assured them it was to be had in abundance within the distance of two days' journey; and mentioned various places along the coast whence it was procured, particularly Veragua, which was about twenty-five leagues distant.[1]

The cupidity of the Spaniards was greatly excited, and they would gladly have remained to barter. but the admiral discouraged all disposition of the kind. He barely sought to collect specimens and information of the riches of the country. and then pressed forward in quest of the great object of his enterprise. the imaginary strait.

Sailing on the 17th of October, from this bay, or rather gulf, he began to coast this region of reputed wealth, since called the coast of Veragua; and after sailing about twelve leagues arrived at a large river, which his son Fernando calls the Guaig Here, on the boats being sent to land, about two hundred Indians appeared on the shore, armed with clubs, lances, and swords of palm-wood. The forests echoed with the sound of wooden drums, and the blasts of conch-shells, their usual war signals. They rushed into the sea up to their waists, brandishing their weapons, and splashing the water at the Spaniards in token of defiance; but were soon pacified by gentle signs and the intervention of the interpreters, and willingly bartered away their ornaments. giving seventeen plates of gold, worth one hundred and fifty ducats, for a few toys and trifles.

When the Spaniards returned the next day to renew their traffic, they found the Indians relapsed into hostility, sounding their drums and shells. and rushing forward to attack the boats. An arrow from a cross-bow, which wounded one of them in the arm. checked their fury. and on the discharge of a cannon they fled with terror. Four of the Spaniards sprang on shore, pursuing and calling after them. They threw down their weapons and came, awe-struck, and gentle as lambs, bringing three plates of gold, and meekly and thankfully receiving whatever was given in exchange.

Continuing along the coast, the admiral anchored in the mouth of another river, called the Catiba. Here likewise the sound of drums and conchs from among the forests gave notice that the warriors were assembling. A canoe soon came off with

---

[1] Columbus's Letter from Jamaica.

two Indians, who, after exchanging a few words with the interpreters. entered the admiral's ship with fearless confidence: and being satisfied of the friendly intentions of the strangers, returned to their cacique with a favorable report The boats landed, and the Spaniards were kindly received by the cacique. He was naked like his subjects, nor distinguished in any way from them, except by the great deference with which he was treated; and by a trifling attention paid to his personal comfort, being protected from a shower of rain by an immense leaf of a tree. He had a large plate of gold, which he readily gave in exchange, and permitted his people to do the same. Nineteen plates of pure gold were procured at this place Here, for the first time in the New World, the Spaniards met with signs of solid architecture ; finding a great mass of stucco, formed of stone and lime, a piece of which was retained by the admiral as a specimen,[1] considering it an indication of his approach to countries where the arts were in a higher state of cultivation.

He had intended to visit other rivers along this coast, but the wind coming on to blow freshly, he ran before it, passing in sight of five towns, where his interpreters assured him he might procure great quantities of gold. One they pointed out as Veragua, which has since given its name to the whole province. Here, they said, were the richest mines, and here most of the plates of gold were fabricated. On the following day they arrived opposite a village called Cubiga, and here Columbus was informed that the country of gold terminated.[2] He resolved not to return to explore it, considering it as discovered, and its mines secured to the crown, and being anxious to arrive at the supposed strait, which he flattered himself could be at no great distance.

In fact, during his whole voyage along the coast, he had been under the influence of one of his frequent delusions. From the Indians met with at the Island of Guanaja, just arrived from Yucatan, he had received accounts of some great, and, as far as he could understand, civilized nation in the interior. This intimation had been corroborated, as he imagined, by the various tribes with which he had since communicated. In a subsequent letter to the sovereigns he informs them that all the Indians of this coast concurred in extolling the magnificence of the country of Ciguare, situated at ten days' journey, by land, to the west. The people of that region wore crowns, and bracelets, and anklets of gold, and garments embroidered with it.

---

[1] Hist. del Almirante, cap. 92.   [2] Ibid.

They used it for all their domestic purposes, even to the orna-
menting and embossing of their seats and tables On being
shown coral, the Indians declared that the women of Ciguare
wore bands of it about their heads and necks. Pepper and
other spices being shown them, were equally said to abound
there. They described it as a country of commerce, with great
fairs and seaports, in which ships arrived armed with cannon.
The people were warlike, also, armed like the Spaniards
with swords, bucklers. cuirasses. and cross-bows. and they
were mounted on horses. Above all, Columbus understood
from them that the sea continued round to Ciguare. and that
ten days beyond it was the Ganges.

These may have been vague and wandering rumors concerning the distant kingdoms of Mexico and Peru, and many of the
details may have been filled up by the imagination of Columbus.
They made, however, a strong impression on his mind. He
supposed that Ciguare must be some province belonging to the
Grand Khan, or some other eastern potentate, and as the sea
reached it, he concluded it was on the opposite side of a peninsula, bearing the same position with respect to Veragua that
Fontarabia does with Tortosa in Spain, or Pisa with Venice in
Italy. By proceeding farther eastward. therefore, he must soon
arrive at a strait, like that of Gibraltar, through which he
could pass into another sea, and visit this country of Ciguare,
and, of course, arrive at the banks of the Ganges. He accounted
for the circumstance of his having arrived so near to that river.
by the idea which he had long entertained, that geographers
were mistaken as to the circumference of the globe ; that it
was smaller than was generally imagined, and that a degree of
the equinoctial line was but fifty-six miles and two-thirds.[1]

With these ideas Columbus determined to press forward,
leaving the rich country of Veragua unexplored. Nothing
could evince more clearly his generous ambition, than hurrying in this brief manner along a coast where wealth was to be
gathered at every step, for the purpose of seeking a strait
which, however it might produce vast benefit to mankind,
could yield little else to himself than the glory of the discovery.

---

[1] Letter of Columbus from Jamaica. Navarrete Colec., tom. l.

CHAPTER V.

DISCOVERY OF PUERTO BELLO AND EL RETRETE — COLUMBUS ABANDONS THE SEARCH AFTER THE STRAIT.

[1502.]

ON the 2d of November the squadron anchored in a spacious and commodious harbor, where the vessels could approach close to the shore without danger. It was surrounded by an elevated country; open and cultivated, with houses within bow-shot of each other, surrounded by fruit-trees, groves of palms, and fields producing maize, vegetables, and the delicious pine-apple, so that the whole neighborhood had the mingled appearance of orchard and garden. Columbus was so pleased with the excellence of the harbor and the sweetness of the surrounding country that he gave it the name of Puerto Bello [1]. It is one of the few places along this coast which retain the appellation given by the illustrious discoverer. It is to be regretted that they have so generally been discontinued, as they were so often records of his feelings, and of circumstances attending the discovery.

For seven days they were detained in this port by heavy rain and stormy weather. The natives repaired from all quarters in canoes, bringing fruits and vegetables and balls of cotton. but there was no longer gold offered in traffic. The cacique and seven of his principal chieftains had small plates of gold hanging in their noses, but the rest of the natives appear to have been destitute of all ornaments of the kind They were generally naked and painted red : the cacique alone was painted black.[2]

Sailing hence, on the 9th of November, they proceeded eight leagues to the eastward, to the point since known as Nombre de Dios ; but being driven back for some distance, they anchored in a harbor in the vicinity of three small islands These, with the adjacent country of the main-land, were cultivated with fields of Indian corn, and various fruits and vegetables, whence Columbus called the harbor Puerto de Bastimentos, or Port of Provisions. Here they remained until the 23d, endeavoring to repair their vessels which leaked excessively. They were

---

[1] Las Casas, lib. ii. cap. 33. Hist. del Almirante.
[2] Peter Martyr, decad. iii. lib. iv.

pierced in all parts by the teredo or worm which abounds in the tropical seas. It is of the size of a man's finger, and bores through the stoutest planks and timbers, so as soon to destroy any vessel that is not well coppered. After leaving this port they touched at another called Guiga, where above three hundred of the natives appeared on the shore, some with provisions, and some with golden ornaments, which they offered in barter. Without making any stay, however, the admiral urged his way forward; but rough and adverse winds again obliged him to take shelter in a small port, with a narrow entrance, not above twenty paces wide, beset on each side with reefs of rocks, the sharp points of which rose above the surface. Within, there was not room for more than five or six ships; yet the port was so deep that they had no good anchorage, unless they approached near enough to the land for a man to leap on shore.

From the smallness of the harbor, Columbus gave it the name of *El Retrete*, or The Cabinet He had been betrayed into this inconvenient and dangerous port by the misrepresentations of the seamen sent to examine it, who were always eager to come to anchor and have communication with the shore.[1]

The adjacent country was level and verdant, covered with herbage, but with few trees. The port was infested with alligators, which basked in the sunshine on the beach, filling the air with a powerful and musky odor. They were timorous, and fled on being attacked, but the Indians affirmed that if they found a man sleeping on the shore they would seize and drag him into the water. These alligators Columbus pronounced to be the same as the crocodiles of the Nile. For nine days the squadron was detained in this port by tempestuous weather. The natives of this place were tall, well proportioned, and graceful: of gentle and friendly manners, and brought whatever they possessed to exchange for European trinkets.

As long as the admiral had control over the actions of his people, the Indians were treated with justice and kindness, and every thing went on amicably. The vicinity of the ships to land, however, enabled the seamen to get on shore in the night without license. The natives received them in their dwellings with their accustomed hospitality: but the rough adventurers, instigated by avarice and lust, soon committed excesses that

---

[1] Las Casas, lib. ii. cap. 23. Hist. del Almirante, cap. 92.

roused their generous hosts to revenge. Every night there were brawls and fights on shore. and blood was shed on both sides. The number of the Indians daily augmented by arrivals from the interior. They became more powerful and daring as they became more exasperated ; and seeing that the vessels lay close to the shore, approached in a great multitude to attack them.

The admiral thought at first to disperse them by discharging cannon without ball, but they were not intimidated by the sound, regarding it as a kind of harmless thunder They replied to it by yells and howlings, beating their lances and clubs against the trees and bushes in furious menace. The situation of the ships so close to the shore exposed them to assaults, and made the hostility of the natives unusually formidable. Columbus ordered a shot or two, therefore, to be discharged among them. When they saw the havoc made, they fled in terror, and offered no further hostility.[1]

The continuance of stormy winds from the east and the north-east in addition to the constant opposition of the currents. disheartened the companions of Columbus, and they began to murmur against any further prosecution of the voyage. The seamen thought that some hostile spell was operating, and the commanders remonstrated against attempting to force their way in spite of the elements, with ships crazed and worm-eaten, and continually in need of repair. Few of his companions could sympathize with Columbus in his zeal for mere discovery. They were actuated by more gainful motives, and looked back with regret on the rich coast they had left behind, to go in search of an imaginary strait It is probable that Columbus himself began to doubt the object of his enterprise. If he knew the details of the recent voyage of Bastides he must have been aware that he had arrived from an opposite quarter to about the place where that navigator's exploring voyage from the east had terminated , consequently that there was but little probability of the existence of the strait he had imagined.[2]

---

[1] Las Casas, lib. ii. cap. 23. Hist. del Almirante, cap. 92.

[2] It appears doubtful whether Columbus was acquainted with the exact particulars of that voyage, as they could scarcely have reached Spain previously to his sailing. Bastides had been seized in Hispaniola by Bobadilla, and was on board of that very fleet which was wrecked at the time that Columbus arrived off San Domingo. He escaped the fate that attended most of his companions and returned to Spain where he was rewarded by the sovereigns for his enterprise. Though some of his seamen had reached Spain previous to the sailing of Columbus, and had given a general idea of the voyage, it is doubtful whether he had transmitted his papers and charts. Porras, in his journal of the voyage of Columbus, states that they arrived at the place where the discoveries of Bastides terminated ; but this information he may have obtained subsequently at San Domingo.

At all events, he determined to relinquish the further prosecution of his voyage eastward for the present, and to return to the coast of Veragua, to search for those mines of which he had heard so much and seen so many indications. Should they prove equal to his hopes, he would have wherewithal to return to Spain in triumph, and silence the reproaches of his enemies, even though he should fail in the leading object of his expedition.

Here, then, ended the lofty anticipations which had elevated Columbus above all mercenary interests ; which had made him regardless of hardships and perils, and given an heroic character to the early part of this voyage. It is true, he had been in pursuit of a mere chimera, but it was the chimera of a splendid imagination and a penetrating judgment. If he was disappointed in his expectation of finding a strait through the Isthmus of Darien, it was because nature herself had been disappointed, for she appears to have attempted to make one, but to have attempted it in vain.

CHAPTER VI.

RETURN TO VERAGUA — THE ADELANTADO EXPLORES THE COUNTRY.

[1502.]

On the 5th of December, Columbus sailed from El Retrete, and relinquishing his course to the east, returned westward, in search of the gold mines of Veragua. On the same evening he anchored in Puerto Bello, about ten leagues distant ; whence departing on the succeeding day, the wind suddenly veered to the west, and began to blow directly adverse to the new course he had adopted. For three months he had been longing in vain for such a wind, and now it came merely to contradict him. Here was a temptation to resume his route to the east, but he did not dare trust to the continuance of the wind, which, in these parts, appeared but seldom to blow from that quarter. He resolved, therefore, to keep on in the present direction, trusting that the breeze would soon change again to the eastward.

In a little while the wind began to blow with dreadful violence, and to shift about in such manner as to baffle all seamanship. Unable to reach Veragua, the ships were obliged to

put back to Puerto Bello, and when they would have entered
that harbor, a sudden veering of the gale drove them from the
land. For nine days they were blown and tossed about, at
the mercy of a furious tempest, in an unknown sea, and often
exposed to the awful perils of a lee-shore. It is wonderful that
such open vessels, so crazed and decayed, could outlive such a
commotion of the elements. Nowhere is a storm so awful as
between the tropics. The sea, according to the description of
Columbus, boiled at times like a caldron : at other times it ran
in mountain waves, covered with foam. At night the raging
billows resembled great surges of flame, owing to those lumi-
nous particles which cover the surface of the waters in these
seas, and throughout the whole course of the Gulf Stream
For a day and night the heavens glowed as a furnace with the
incessant flashes of lightning ; while the loud claps of thunder
were often mistaken by the affrighted mariners for signal-guns
of distress from their foundering companions. During the
whole time, says Columbus, it poured down from the skies,
not rain, but as it were a second deluge. The seamen were
almost drowned in their open vessels. Haggard with toil and
affright, some gave themselves over for lost, they confessed
their sins to each other, according to the rites of the Catholic
religion, and prepared themselves for death ; many in their
desperation, called upon death as a welcome relief from such
overwhelming horrors. In the midst of this wild tumult of the
elements, they beheld a new object of alarm. The ocean in one
place became strangely agitated. The water was whirled up
into a kind of pyramid or cone, while a livid cloud, tapering to
a point, bent down to meet it. Joining together, they formed
a vast column, which rapidly approached the ships, spinning
along the surface of the deep, and drawing up the waters with
a rushing sound. The affrighted mariners when they beheld
this water-spout advancing toward them, despaired of all
human means to avert it, and began to repeat passages from
St. John the Evangelist. The water-spout passed close by the
ships without injuring them, and the trembling mariners
attributed their escape to the miraculous efficacy of their quo-
tations from the Scriptures [1]

In this same night they lost sight of one of the caravels, and
for three dark and stormy days gave it up for lost. At length,
to their great relief, it rejoined the squadron, having lost its
boat, and been obliged to cut its cable, in an attempt to anchor

---

[1] Las Casas, lib. ii. cap. 24. Hist. del Almirante, cap. 90.

on a boisterous coast, and having since been driven to and fro by the storm. For one or two days there was an interval of calm, and the tempest-tossed mariners had time to breathe. They looked upon this tranquillity, however, as deceitful, and in their gloomy mood beheld every thing with a doubtful and foreboding eye. Great numbers of sharks, so abundant and ravenous in these latitudes, were seen about the ships. This was construed into an evil omen; for among the superstitions of the seas it is believed that these voracious fish can smell dead bodies at a distance; that they have a kind of presentiment of their prey, and keep about vessels which have sick persons on board, or which are in danger of being wrecked. Several of these fish they caught, using large hooks fastened to chains, and sometimes baited merely with a piece of colored cloth. From the maw of one they took out a living tortoise, from that of another the head of a shark, recently thrown from one of the ships; such is the indiscriminate voracity of these terrors of the ocean. Notwithstanding their superstitious fancies, the seamen were glad to use a part of these sharks for food, being very short of provisions. The length of the voyage had consumed the greater part of their sea-stores; the heat and humidity of the climate and the leakage of the ships had damaged the remainder, and their biscuit was so filled with worms that, notwithstanding their hunger, they were obliged to eat it in the dark, lest their stomachs should revolt at its appearance.[1]

At length, on the 17th, they were enabled to enter a port resembling a great canal, where they enjoyed three days of repose. The natives of this vicinity built their cabins in trees, on stakes or poles laid from one branch to another. The Spaniards supposed this to be through the fear of wild beasts, or of surprisals from neighboring tribes; the different nations of these coasts being extremely hostile to one another. It may have been a precaution against inundations caused by floods from the mountains. After leaving this port they were driven backward and forward by the changeable and tempestuous winds until the day after Christmas, when they sheltered themselves in another port, where they remained until the 3d of January, 1503, repairing one of the caravels, and procuring wood, water, and a supply of maize or Indian corn. These measures being completed, they again put to sea, and on the day of Epiphany, to their great joy, anchored at the mouth of

---

[1] Hist. del Almirante, cap. 94.

a river called by the natives Yebra, within a league or two of the river Veragua, and in the country said to be so rich in mines. To this river, from arriving at it on the day of Epiphany, Columbus gave the name of Belen, or Bethlehem.

For nearly a month he had endeavored to accomplish the voyage from Puerto Bello to Veragua, a distance of about thirty leagues, and had encountered so many troubles and adversities, from changeable winds and currents, and boisterous tempests, that he gave this intermediate line of seaboard the name of *La Costa de los Contrastes*, or the Coast of Contradictions.[1]

Columbus immediately ordered the mouths of the Belen, and of its neighboring river of Veragua, to be sounded. The latter proved too shallow to admit his vessels, but the Belen was somewhat deeper, and it was thought they might enter it with safety. Seeing a village on the banks of the Belen, the admiral sent the boats on shore to procure information. On their approach the inhabitants issued forth with weapons in hand to oppose their landing, but were readily pacified. They seemed unwilling to give any intelligence about the gold-mines, but, on being importuned, declared that they lay in the vicinity of the river of Veragua. To that river the boats were despatched on the following day. They met with the reception so frequent along this coast, where many of the tribes were fierce and warlike, and are supposed to have been of Carib origin. As the boats entered the river, the natives sallied forth in their canoes, and others assembled in menacing style on the shores. The Spaniards, however, had brought with them an Indian of that coast, who put an end to this show of hostility by assuring his countrymen that the strangers came only to traffic with them.

The various accounts of the riches of these parts appeared to be confirmed by what the Spaniards saw and heard among these people. They procured in exchange for the veriest trifles twenty plates of gold, with several pipes of the same metal, and crude masses of ore. The Indians informed them that the mines lay among distant mountains; and that when they went in quest of it they were obliged to practise rigorous fasting and continence.[2]

---

[1] Hist. del Almirante, cap. 94.

[2] A superstitious notion with respect to gold appears to have been very prevalent among the natives. The Indians of Hispaniola observed the same privations when they sought for it, abstaining from food and from sexual intercourse. Columbus, who seemed to look upon gold as one of the sacred and mystic treasures of the earth, wished to encourage similar observances among the Spaniards; exhorting them to purify themselves for the research of the mines by fasting, prayer, and chastity. It is scarcely necessary to add, that his advice was but little attended to by his rapacious and sensual followers.

The favorable report brought by the boats determined the admiral to remain in the neighborhood. The river Belen having the greatest depth, two of the caravels entered it on the 9th of January, and the two others on the following day at high tide. which on that coast does not rise above half a fathom.[1] The natives came to them in the most friendly manner, bringing great quantities of fish, with which that river abounded. They brought also golden ornaments to traffic, but continued to affirm that Veragua was the place whence the ore was procured.

The Adelantado, with his usual activity and enterprise, set off on the third day, with the boats well armed, to ascend the Veragua about a league and a half, to the residence of Quibian, the principal cacique. The chieftain, hearing of his intention, met him near the entrance of the river, attended by his subjects in several canoes. He was tall, of powerful frame, and warlike demeanor; the interview was extremely amicable. The cacique presented the Adelantado with the golden ornaments which he wore, and received as magnificent presents a few European trinkets. They parted mutually well pleased. On the following day Quibian visited the ships, where he was hospitably entertained by the admiral. They could only communicate by signs, and as the chieftain was of a taciturn and cautious character, the interview was not of long duration. Columbus made him several presents; the followers of the cacique exchanged many jewels of gold for the usual trifles, and Quibian returned, without much ceremony, to his home.

On the 24th of January there was a sudden swelling of the river. The waters came rushing from the interior like a vast torrent; the ships were forced from their anchors, tossed from side to side, and driven against each other; the foremast of the admiral's vessel was carried away, and the whole squadron was in imminent danger of shipwreck. While exposed to this peril in the river, they were prevented from running out to sea by a violent storm, and by the breakers which beat upon the bar. This sudden rising of the river, Columbus attributed to some heavy fall of rain among a range of distant mountains, to which he had given the name of the mountains of San Christoval. The highest of these rose to a peak far above the clouds.[2]

The weather continued extremely boisterous for several days. At length, on the 6th of February, the sea being tolerably

---

[1] Hist. del Almirante, cap 95.
[2] Las Casas, lib. ii. cap. 25. Hist. del Almirante, cap. 95.

calm the Adelantado, attended by sixty-eight men. well armed, proceeded in the boats to explore the Veragua, and seek its reputed mines.   When he ascended the river and drew near to the village of Quibian, situated on the side of a hill, the cacique came down to the bank to meet him. with a great train of his subjects, unarmed, and making signs of peace.   Quibian was naked. and painted after the fashion of the country.   One of his attendants drew a great stone out of the river, and washed and rubbed it carefully. upon which the chieftain seated himself as upon a throne.[1]   He received the Adelantado with great courtesy : for the lofty. vigorous. and iron form of the latter, and his look of resolution and command, were calculated to inspire awe and respect in an Indian warrior   The cacique, however, was wary and politic.   His jealousy was awakened by the intrusion of these strangers into his territories ; but he saw the futility of any open attempt to resist them.   He acceded to the wishes of the Adelantado, therefore, to visit the interior of his dominions, and furnished him with three guides to conduct him to the mines.

Leaving a number of his men to guard the boats. the Adelantado departed on foot with the remainder.   After penetrating into the interior about four leagues and a half. they slept for the first night on the banks of a river, which seemed to water the whole country with its windings. as they had crossed it upward of forty times.   On the second day they proceeded a league and a half farther, and arrived among thick forests. where their guides informed them the mines were situated.   In fact, the whole soil appeared to be impregnated with gold. They gathered it from among the roots of the trees, which were of an immense height. and magnificent foliage   In the space of two hours each man had collected a little quantity of gold, gathered from the surface of the earth   Hence the guides took the Adelantado to the summit of a high hill, and showing him an extent of country as far as the eye could reach, assured him that the whole of it, to the distance of twenty days' journey westward, abounded in gold, naming to him several of the principal places.[2]   The Adelantado gazed with enraptured eye over a vast wilderness of continued forest, where only here and there a bright column of smoke from amid the trees gave sign of some savage hamlet, or solitary wigwam, and the wild, unappropriated aspect of this golden country delighted him more than if he had beheld it covered with towns and cities, and

[1] Peter Martyr, decad. iii. lib. iv.   [2] Letter of the Admiral from Jamaica.

adorned with all the graces of cultivation. He returned with his party, in high spirits, to the ships, and rejoiced the admiral with the favorable report of his expedition. It was soon discovered, however, that the politic Quibian had deceived them. His guides. by his instructions. had taken the Spaniards to the mines of a neighboring cacique, with whom he was at war. hoping to divert them into the territories of his enemy. The real mines of Veragua, it was said, were nearer and much more wealthy.

The indefatigable Adelantado set forth again on the 16th of February, with an armed band of fifty-nine men, marching along the coast westward, a boat with fourteen men keeping pace with him. In this excursion he explored an extensive tract of country, and visited the dominions of various caciques, by whom he was hospitably entertained. He met continually with proofs of abundance of gold; the natives generally wearing great plates of it suspended round their necks by cotton cords. There were tracts of land, also, cultivated with Indian corn — one of which continued for the extent of six leagues, and the country abounded with excellent fruits. He again heard of a nation in the interior, advanced in arts and arms, wearing clothing, and being armed like the Spaniards. Either these were vague and exaggerated rumors concerning the great empire of Peru, or the Adelantado had misunderstood the signs of his informants. He returned, after an absence of several days. with a great quantity of gold, and with animating accounts of the country. He had found no port, however, equal to the river of Belen, and was convinced that gold was nowhere to be met with in such abundance as in the district of Veragua.[1]

CHAPTER VII.

COMMENCEMENT OF A SETTLEMENT ON THE RIVER BELEN — CON-SPIRACY OF THE NATIVES — EXPEDITION OF THE ADELANTADO TO SURPRISE QUIBIAN.

[1503.]

THE reports brought to Columbus, from every side, of the wealth of the neighborhood ; the golden tract of twenty days' journey in extent, shown to his brother from the mountain ; the

---

[1] Las Casas, lib. ii. cap. 25. Hist. del Almirante, cap. 95.

rumors of a rich and civilized country at no great distance, all convinced him that he had reached one of the most favored parts of the Asiatic continent.   Again his ardent mind kindled up with glowing anticipations.   He fancied himself arrived at a fountain-head of riches, at one of the sources of the unbounded wealth of King Solomon.   Josephus in his work on the antiquities of the Jews, had expressed an opinion that the gold for the building of the temple of Jerusalem had been procured from the mines of the Aurea Chersonesus.   Columbus supposed the mines of Veragua to be the same.   They lay, as he observed, " within the same distance from the pole, and from the line:" and if the information which he fancied he had received from the Indians was to be depended on, they were situated about the same distance from the Ganges.[1]

Here, then, it appeared to him, was a place at which to found a colony, and establish a mart that should become the emporium of a vast tract of mines.   Within the two first days after his arrival in the country, as he wrote to the sovereigns, he had seen more signs of gold than in Hispaniola during four years. That island, so long the object of his pride and hopes, had been taken from him, and was a scene of confusion ; the pearl coast of Paria was ravaged by mere adventurers ; all his plans concerning both had been defeated ; but here was a far more wealthy region than either, and one calculated to console him for all his wrongs and deprivations.

On consulting with his brother, therefore, he resolved immediately to commence an establishment here, for the purpose of securing the possession of the country, and exploring and working the mines.   The Adelantado agreed to remain with the greater part of the people while the admiral should return to Spain for re-enforcements and supplies.   The greatest despatch was employed in carrying this plan into immediate operation. Eighty men were selected to remain.   They were separated into parties of about ten each, and commenced building houses on a small eminence, situated on the bank of a creek, about a bowshot within the mouth of the river Belen.   The houses were of wood, thatched with the leaves of palm-trees.   One larger than the rest was to serve as a magazine, to receive their ammunition, artillery, and a part of their provisions.   The principal part was stored, for greater security, on board of one of the caravels, which was to be left for the use of the colony.   It was true they had but a scanty supply of European stores remain-

----

[1] Letter of Columbus from Jamaica.

ing, consisting chiefly of biscuit, cheese, pulse, wine, oil and vinegar; but the country produced bananas, plantains, pine-apples, cocoanuts, and other fruit. There was also maize in abundance, together with various roots, such as were found in Hispaniola. The rivers and seacoast abounded with fish. The natives, too, made beverages of various kinds. One from the juice of the pineapple, having a vinous flavor; another from maize, resembling beer; and another from the fruit of a species of palm-tree.[1] There appeared to be no danger, therefore, of suffering from famine. Columbus took pains to conciliate the good-will of the Indians, that they might supply the wants of the colony during his absence, and he made many presents to Quibian, by way of reconciling him to this intrusion into his territories.[2]

The necessary arrangements being made for the colony, and a number of the houses being roofed, and sufficiently finished for occupation, the admiral prepared for his departure, when an unlooked-for obstacle presented itself. The heavy rains which had so long distressed him during this expedition had recently ceased. The torrents from the mountains were over, and the river, which had once put him to such peril by its sudden swelling, had now become so shallow that there was not above half a fathom water on the bar. Though his vessels were small, it was impossible to draw them over the sands, which choked the mouth of the river, for there was a swell rolling and tumbling upon them, enough to dash his worm-eaten barks to pieces. He was obliged, therefore, to wait with patience, and pray for the return of those rains which he had lately deplored.

In the mean time Quibian beheld with secret jealousy and indignation, these strangers erecting habitations and manifest-ing an intention of establishing themselves in his territories. He was of a bold and warlike spirit, and had a great force of warriors at his command; and being ignorant of the vast superiority of the Europeans in the art of war, thought it easy, by a well-concerted artifice, to overwhelm and destroy them. He sent messengers round, and ordered all his fighting men to assemble at his residence on the river Veragua, under pretext of making war upon a neighboring province. Numbers of the warriors, in repairing to his headquarters, passed by the har-bor. No suspicions of their real design were entertained by Columbus or his officers: but their movements attracted the attention of the chief notary, Diego Mendez, a man of a shrewd

---

[1] Hist. del Almirante. cap. 96.   [2] Letter from Jamaica.

and prying character, and zealously devoted to the admiral. Doubting some treachery, he communicated his surmises to Columbus, and offered to coast along in an armed boat to the river Veragua, and reconnoitre the Indian camp. His offer was accepted, and he sallied from the river accordingly, but had scarcely advanced a league when he descried a large force of Indians on the shore. Landing alone, and ordering that the boat should be kept afloat, he entered among them. There were about a thousand, armed and supplied with provisions, as if for an expedition. He offered to accompany them with his armed boat; his offer was declined, with evident signs of impatience. Returning to his boat, he kept watch upon them all night, until seeing they were vigilantly observed, they returned to Veragua.

Mendez hastened back to the admiral, and gave it as his opinion that the Indians had been on their way to surprise the Spaniards. The admiral was loath to believe in such treachery, and was desirous of obtaining clearer information, before he took any step that might interrupt the apparently good understanding that existed with the natives. Mendez now undertook, with a single companion, to penetrate by land to the head-quarters of Quibian, and endeavor to ascertain his intentions. Accompanied by one Rodrigo de Escobar, he proceeded on foot along the seaboard, to avoid the tangled forests, and arriving at the mouth of the Veragua, found two canoes with Indians, whom he prevailed on, by presents, to convey him and his companion to the village of the cacique. It was on the bank of the river; the houses were detached and interspersed among trees. There was a bustle of warlike preparation in the place, and the arrival of the two Spaniards evidently excited surprise and uneasiness. The residence of the cacique was larger than the others, and situated on a hill which rose from the water's edge. Quibian was confined to the house by indisposition, having been wounded in the leg by an arrow. Mendez gave himself out as a surgeon come to cure the wound; with great difficulty and by force of presents he obtained permission to proceed. On the crest of the hill and in front of the cacique's dwelling was a broad, level, open place, round which, on posts, were the heads of three hundred enemies slain in battle. Undismayed by this dismal array, Mendez and his companion crossed the place toward the den of this grim warrior. A number of women and children about the door fled into the house with piercing cries. A young and powerful Indian, son of the cacique, sallied forth in a violent rage, and struck Mendez a blow which made him recoil several paces. The latter pacified him by presents and assurances that he came to cure his father's wound. in proof of which he produced a box of ointment. It was impossible, however, to gain access to the cacique, and Mendez returned with all haste to the harbor to report to the admiral what he had seen and learned. It was evident there was a dangerous plot impending over the Spaniards, and as far as Mendez could learn from the Indians who had taken him up the river in their canoe, the body of a thousand warriors which he had seen on his previous reconnoitring expedition had actually been on a hostile enterprise against the harbor, but had given it up on finding themselves observed.

This information was confirmed by an Indian of the neighborhood. who had become attached to the Spaniards and acted as interpreter. He revealed to the admiral the designs of his countrymen, which he had overheard. Quibian intended to surprise the harbor at night with a great force, burn the ships and houses, and make a general massacre. Thus forewarned, Columbus immediately set a double watch upon the harbor. The military spirit of the Adelantado suggested a bolder expedient. The hostile plan of Quibian was doubtless delayed by his wound. and in the mean time he would maintain the semblance of friendship. The Adelantado determined to march at once to his residence, capture him, his family, and principal warriors, send them prisoners to Spain, and take possession of his village.

With the Adelantado, to conceive a plan was to carry it into immediate execution, and, in fact, the impending danger admitted of no delay. Taking with him seventy-four men, well armed, among whom was Diego Mendez, and being accompanied by the Indian interpreter who had revealed the plot, he set off on the 30th of March, in boats, to the mouth of the Veragua. ascended it rapidly, and before the Indians could have notice of his movements, landed at the foot of the hill on which the house of Quibian was situated.

Lest the cacique should take alarm and fly at the sight of a large force. he ascended the hill. accompanied by only five men. among whom was Diego Mendez ; ordering the rest to come on, with great caution and secrecy, two at a time. and at a distance from each other. On the discharge of an arquebuse, they were to surround the dwelling and suffer no one to escape.

As the Adelantado drew near to the house, Quibian came forth. and seating himself in the portal. desired the Adelantado to approach singly. Don Bartholomew now ordered Diego

Mendez and his four companions to remain at a little distance, and when they should see him take the cacique by the arm, to rush immediately to his assistance. He then advanced with his Indian interpreter, through whom a short conversation took place, relative to the surrounding country. The Adelantado then adverted to the wound of the cacique, and pretending to examine it, took him by the arm. At the concerted signal four of the Spaniards rushed forward, the fifth discharged the arquebuse. The cacique attempted to get loose, but was firmly held in the iron grasp of the Adelantado. Being both men of great muscular power, a violent struggle ensued. Don Bartholomew, however, maintained the mastery, and Diego Mendez and his companions coming to his assistance, Quibian was bound hand and foot. At the report of the arquebuse, the main body of the Spaniards surrounded the house, and seized most of those who were within, consisting of fifty persons, old and young. Among these were the wives and children of Quibian, and several of his principal subjects. No one was wounded, for there was no resistance, and the Adelantado never permitted wanton bloodshed. When the poor savages saw their prince a captive, they filled the air with lamentations, imploring his release, and offering for his ransom a great treasure, which they said lay concealed in a neighboring forest.

The Adelantado was deaf to their supplications and their offers. Quibian was too dangerous a foe to be set at liberty; as a prisoner he would be a hostage for the security of the settlement. Anxious to secure his prize, he determined to send the cacique and other prisoners on board of the boats, while he remained on shore with a part of his men to pursue the Indians who had escaped. Juan Sanchez, the principal pilot of the squadron, a powerful and spirited man, volunteered to take charge of the captives. On committing the chieftain to his care, the Adelantado warned him to be on his guard against any attempt at rescue or escape. The sturdy pilot replied that if the cacique got out of his hands, he would give them leave to pluck out his beard, hair by hair; with this vaunt he departed, bearing off Quibian bound hand and foot. On arriving at the boat, he secured him by a strong cord to one of the benches. It was a dark night. As the boat proceeded down the river, the cacique complained piteously of the painfulness of his bonds. The rough heart of the pilot was touched with compassion, and he loosened the cord by which Quibian was tied to the bench, keeping the end of it in his hand. The wily Indian watched his opportunity, and when Sanchez was looking another way plunged into the water and disappeared. So sudden and violent was his plunge that the pilot had to let go the cord lest he should be drawn in after him. The darkness of the night and the bustle which took place in preventing the escape of the other prisoners rendered it impossible to pursue the cacique. or even to ascertain his fate. Juan Sanchez hastened to the ships with the residue of the captives, deeply mortified at being thus outwitted by a savage.

The Adelantado remained all night on shore. The following morning, when he beheld the wild, broken. and mountainous nature of the country, and the scattered situation of the habitations perched on different heights, he gave up the search after the Indians, and returned to the ships with the spoils of the cacique's mansion. These consisted of bracelets, anklets, and massive plates of gold, such as were worn round the neck, together with two golden coronets. The whole amounted to the value of three hundred ducats.[1] One fifth of the booty was set apart for the crown. The residue was shared among those concerned in the enterprise. To the Adelantado one of the coronets was assigned, as a trophy of his exploit.[2]

CHAPTER VIII.

DISASTERS OF THE SETTLEMENT.

[1503.]

IT was hoped by Columbus that the vigorous measure of the Adelantado would strike terror into the Indians of the neighborhood, and prevent any further designs upon the settlement. Quibian had probably perished. If he survived, he must be disheartened by the captivity of his family, and several of his principal subjects, and fearful of their being made responsible for any act of violence on his part. The heavy rains, therefore, which fall so frequently among the mountains of this isthmus, having again swelled the river, Columbus made his final arrange-

---

[1] Equivalent to one thousand two hundred and eighty-one dollars at the present day.
[2] Hist. del Almirante. cap. 98. Las Casas, lib ii cap. 27 Many of the particulars of this chapter are from a short narrative given by Diego Mendez, and inserted in his last will and testament. It is written in a strain of simple egotism, as he represents himself as the principal and almost the sole actor in every affair. The facts, however, have all the air of veracity, and being given on such a solemn occasion, the document is entitled to high credit. He will be found to distinguish himself on another hazardous and important occasion in the course of this history. — Vide Navarrete, Colec., tom. i.

ments for the management of the colony, and having given much wholesome counsel to the Spaniards who were to remain, and taken an affectionate leave of his brother, got under weigh with three of the caravels, leaving the fourth for the use of the settlement. As the water was still shallow at the bar, the ships were lightened of a great part of their cargoes, and towed out by the boats in calm weather, grounding repeatedly. When fairly released from the river, and their cargoes reshipped, they anchored within a league of the shore, to await a favorable wind. It was the intention of the admiral to touch at Hispaniola, on his way to Spain, and send thence supplies and re-enforcements. The wind continuing adverse, he sent a boat on shore on the 6th of April, under the command of Diego Tristan, captain of one of the caravels, to procure wood and water, and make some communications to the Adelantado. The expedition of this boat proved fatal to its crew, but was providential to the settlement.

The cacique Quibian had not perished as some had supposed. Though both hands and feet were bound, yet in the water he was as in his natural element. Plunging to the bottom, he swam below the surface until sufficiently distant to be out of view in the darkness of the night, and then emerging made his way to shore. The desolation of his home, and the capture of his wives and children, filled him with anguish; but when he saw the vessels in which they were confined leaving the river, and bearing them off, he was transported with fury and despair. Determined on a signal vengeance, he assembled a great number of his warriors, and came secretly upon the settlement. The thick woods by which it was surrounded enabled the Indians to approach unseen within ten paces. The Spaniards, thinking the enemy completely discomfited and dispersed, were perfectly off their guard. Some had strayed to the sea-shore to take a farewell look at the ships, some were on board of the caravel in the river; others were scattered about the houses: on a sudden the Indians rushed from their concealment with yells and howlings, launched their javelins through the roofs of palm-leaves, hurled them in at the windows, or thrust them through the crevices of the logs which composed the walls. As the houses were small several of the inhabitants were wounded. On the first alarm the Adelantado seized a lance and sallied forth with seven or eight of his men. He was joined by Diego Mendez and several of his companions, and they drove the enemy into the forest, killing and wounding several of them. The Indians kept up a brisk fire of darts and arrows from among the trees, and made furious sallies with their war-clubs; but there was no withstanding the keen edge of the Spanish weapons, and a fierce blood-hound being let loose upon them completed their terror. They fled howling through the forest, leaving a number dead on the field, having killed one Spaniard and wounded eight Among the latter was the Adelantado, who received a slight thrust of a javelin in the breast.

Diego Tristan arrived in his boat during the contest, but feared to approach the land, lest the Spaniards should rush on board in such numbers as to sink him. When the Indians had been put to flight he proceeded up the river in quest of fresh water, disregarding the warnings of those on shore, that he might be cut off by the enemy in their canoes.

The river was deep and narrow, shut in by high banks and overhanging trees. The forests on each side were thick and impenetrable, so that there was no landing-place excepting here and there where a footpath wound down to some fishing-ground, or some place where the natives kept their canoes.

The boat had ascended about a league above the village, to a part of the river where it was completely overshadowed by lofty banks and spreading trees. Suddenly yells and war-whoops and blasts of conch-shells rose on every side. Light canoes darted forth in every direction from dark hollows and overhanging thickets each dexterously managed by a single savage, while others stood up brandishing and hurling their lances. Missiles were launched also from the banks of the river and the branches of the trees. There were eight sailors in the boat, and three soldiers. Galled and wounded by darts and arrows, confounded by the yells and blasts of conchs and the assaults which thickened from every side, they lost all presence of mind, neglected to use either oars or fire-arms, and only sought to shelter themselves with their bucklers. Diego Tristan had received several wounds, but still displayed great intrepidity, and was endeavoring to animate his men when a javelin pierced his right eye and struck him dead. The canoes now closed upon the boat, and a general massacre ensued. But one Spaniard escaped, Juan de Noya, a cooper of Seville. Having fallen overboard in the midst of the action, he dived to the bottom, swam under water, gained the bank of the river unperceived, and made his way down to the settlement, bringing tidings of the massacre of his captain and comrades.

The Spaniards were completely dismayed, were few in number, several of them were wounded, and they were in the midst of tribes of exasperated savages, far more fierce and warlike than those to whom they had been accustomed. The admiral, being ignorant of their misfortunes, would sail away without yielding them assistance, and they would be left to sink beneath the overwhelming force of barbarous foes, or to perish with hunger on this inhospitable coast. In their despair they determined to take the caravel which had been left with them, and abandon the place altogether. The Adelantado remonstrated with them in vain; nothing would content them but to put to sea immediately. Here a new alarm awaited them. The torrents having subsided, the river was again shallow, and it was impossible for the caravel to pass over the bar. They now took the boat of the caravel to bear tidings of their danger to the admiral, and implore him not to abandon them; but the wind was boisterous, a high sea was rolling, and a heavy surf, tumbling and breaking at the mouth of the river, prevented the boat from getting out. Horrors increased upon them. The mangled bodies of Diego Tristan and his men came floating down the stream, and drifting about the harbor, with flights of crows, and other carrion birds feeding on them, and hovering, and screaming, and fighting about their prey. The forlorn Spaniards contemplated this scene with shuddering: it appeared ominous of their own fate.

In the mean time the Indians, elated by their triumph over the crew of the boat, renewed their hostilities. Whoops and yells answered each other from various parts of the neighborhood. The dismal sound of conchs and war-drums in the deep bosom of the woods showed that the number of the enemy was continually augmenting. They would rush forth occasionally upon straggling parties of Spaniards, and make partial attacks upon the houses. It was considered no longer safe to remain in the settlement, the close forest which surrounded it being a covert for the approaches of the enemy. The Adelantado chose, therefore, an open place on the shore, at some distance from the wood. Here he caused a kind of bulwark to be made of the boat of the caravel, and of chests, casks, and similar articles. Two places were left open as embrasures, in which were placed a couple of falconets, or small pieces of artillery, in such a manner as to command the neighborhood. In this little fortress the Spaniards shut themselves up; its walls were sufficient to screen them from the darts and arrows of the Indians, but mostly they depended upon their fire-arms, the sound of which struck dismay into the savages, especially when they saw the effect of the balls, splintering and rending the trees around them, and carrying havoc to such a distance. The

Indians were thus kept in check for the present, and deterred from venturing from the forest , but the Spaniards, exhausted by constant watching and incessant alarms, anticipated all kinds of evil when their ammunition should be exhausted, or they should be driven forth by hunger to seek for food.[1]

CHAPTER IX.

DISTRESS OF THE ADMIRAL ON BOARD OF HIS SHIP — ULTIMATE RELIEF OF THE SETTLEMENT.

[1503.]

WHILE the Adelantado and his men were exposed to such imminent peril on shore, great anxiety prevailed on board of the ships. Day after day elapsed without the return of Diego Tristan and his party, and it was feared some disaster had befallen them. Columbus would have sent on shore to make inquiries, but there was only one boat remaining for the service of the squadron, and he dared not risk it in the rough sea and heavy surf. A dismal circumstance occurred to increase the gloom and uneasiness of the crews. On board of one of the caravels were confined the family and household of the cacique Quibian. It was the intention of Columbus to carry them to Spain, trusting that as long as they remained in the power of the Spaniards their tribe would be deterred from further hostilities. They were shut up at night in the forecastle of the caravel, the hatchway of which was secured by a strong chain and padlock. As several of the crew slept upon the hatch, and it was so high as to be considered out of reach of the prisoners, they neglected to fasten the chain The Indians discovered their negligence. Collecting a quantity of stones from the ballast of the vessel, they made a great heap directly under the hatchway. Several of the most powerful warriors mounted upon the top, and bending their backs, by a sudden and simultaneous effort, forced up the hatch, flinging the seamen who slept upon it to the opposite side of the ship. In an instant the greater part of the Indians sprang forth, plunged into the sea, and swam for shore. Several, however, were prevented from sallying forth ; others were seized on the deck and forced back

---

[1] Hist. del Almirante, cap 98. Las Casas, lib. ii. Letter of Columbus from Jamaica. Relation of Diego Mendez, Navarrete, tom. i. Journal of Porras, Navarrete, tom. i.

into the forecastle; the hatchway was carefully chained down, and a guard was set for the rest of the night. In the morning, when the Spaniards went to examine the captives, they were all found dead. Some had hanged themselves with the ends of ropes, their knees touching the floor, others had strangled themselves by straining the cords tight with their feet. Such was the fierce unconquerable spirit of these people, and their horror of the white men.[1]

The escape of the prisoners occasioned great anxiety to the admiral. fearing they would stimulate their countrymen to some violent act of vengeance, and he trembled for the safety of his brother. Still this painful mystery reigned over the land. The boat of Diego Tristan did not return, and the raging surf prevented all communication. At length, one Pedro Ledesma, a pilot of Seville, a man of about forty-five years of age, and of great strength of body and mind, offered, if the boat would take him to the edge of the surf, to swim to shore. and bring off news. He had been piqued by the achievement of the Indian captives, in swimming to land at a league's distance, in defiance of sea and surf. "Surely," he said, "if they dare venture so much to procure their individual liberties. I ought to brave at least a part of the danger, to save the lives of so many companions." His offer was gladly accepted by the admiral. and was boldly accomplished. The boat approached with him as near to the surf as safety would permit. where it was to await his return. Here, stripping himself, he plunged into the sea. and after buffeting for some time with the breakers. sometimes rising upon their surges. sometimes buried beneath them and dashed upon the sand. he succeeded in reaching the shore.

He found his countrymen shut up in their forlorn fortress, beleaguered by savage foes, and learnt the tragical fate of Diego Tristan and his companions. Many of the Spaniards, in their horror and despair, had thrown off all subordination, refused to assist in any measure that had in view a continuance in this place, and thought of nothing but escape. When they beheld Ledesma, a messenger from the ships, they surrounded him with frantic eagerness, urging him to implore the admiral to take them on board, and not abandon them on a coast where their destruction was inevitable. They were preparing canoes to take them to the ships, when the weather should moderate, the boat of the caravel being too small, and swore that, if the admiral refused to take them on board, they would embark in

---

[1] Hist. del Almirante, cap. 99.

the caravel, as soon as it could be extricated from the river, and abandon themselves to the mercy of the seas, rather than remain upon that fatal coast.

Having heard all that his forlorn countrymen had to say, and communicated with the Adelantado and his officers, Ledesma set out on his perilous return. He again braved the surf and the breakers, reached the boat which was waiting for him, and was conveyed back to the ships. The disastrous tidings from the land filled the heart of the admiral with grief and alarm. To leave his brother on shore would be to expose him to the mutiny of his own men and the ferocity of the savages. He could spare no re-enforcement from his ships, the crews being so much weakened by the loss of Tristan and his companions. Rather than the settlement should be broken up, he would gladly have joined the Adelantado with all his people, but in such case how could intelligence be conveyed to the sovereigns of this important discovery, and how could supplies be obtained from Spain? There appeared no alternative, therefore, but to embark all the people, abandon the settlement for the present, and return at some future day, with a force competent to take secure possession of the country.[1] The state of the weather rendered the practicability even of this plan doubtful. The wind continued high, the sea rough, and no boat could pass between the squadron and the land. The situation of the ships was itself a matter of extreme solicitude. Feebly manned, crazed by storms, and ready to fall to pieces from the ravages of the teredo, they were anchored on a lee-shore, with a boisterous wind and sea, in a climate subject to tempests, and where the least augmentation of the weather might drive them among the breakers. Every hour increased the anxiety of Columbus for his brother, his people, and his ships, and each hour appeared to render the impending dangers more imminent. Days of constant perturbation and nights of sleepless anxiety preyed upon a constitution broken by age, by maladies, and hardships, and produced a fever of the mind, in which he was visited by one of those mental hallucinations deemed by him mysterious and supernatural. In a letter to the sovereigns he gives a solemn account of a kind of vision by which he was comforted in a dismal night, when full of despondency and tossing on a couch of pain:

"Wearied and sighing," says he, "I fell into a slumber, when I heard a piteous voice saying to me, 'O fool, and slow

---

[1] Letter of Columbus from Jamaica.

to believe and serve thy God, who is the God of all! What did he more for Moses, or for his servant David, than he has done for thee? From the time of thy birth he has ever had thee under his peculiar care. When he saw thee of a fitting age he made thy name to resound marvellously throughout the earth, and thou wert obeyed in many lands, and didst acquire honorable fame among Christians. Of the gates of the Ocean Sea, shut up with such mighty chains, he delivered thee the keys; the Indies, those wealthy regions of the world, he gave thee for thine own, and empowered thee to dispose of them to others, according to thy pleasure. What did he more for the great people of Israel when he led them forth from Egypt? Or for David, whom, from being a shepherd, he made a king in Judea? Turn to him, then, and acknowledge thine error; his mercy is infinite. He has many and vast inheritances yet in reserve. Fear not to seek them. Thine age shall be no impediment to any great undertaking. Abraham was above an hundred years when he begat Isaac: and was Sarah youthful? Thou urgest despondingly for succor. Answer! who hath afflicted thee so much, and so many times?— God, or the world? The privileges and promises which God hath made thee he hath never broken: neither hath he said, after having received thy services, that his meaning was different, and to be understood in a different sense. He performs to the very letter. He fulfils all that he promises, and with increase. Such is his custom. I have shown thee what thy Creator hath done for thee, and what he doeth for all. The present is the reward of the toils and perils thou hast endured in serving others.' I heard all this," adds Columbus, "as one almost dead, and had no power to reply to words so true, excepting to weep for my errors. Whoever it was that spake to me, finished by saying, 'Fear not! Confide! All these tribulations are written in marble, and not without cause.'"

Such is the singular statement which Columbus gave to the sovereigns of his supposed vision. It has been suggested that this was a mere ingenious fiction, adroitly devised by him to convey a lesson to his prince; but such an idea is inconsistent with his character. He was too deeply imbued with awe of the Deity, and with reverence for his sovereign, to make use of such an artifice. The words here spoken to him by the supposed voice are truths which dwelt upon his mind and grieved his spirit during his waking hours. It is natural that they should recur vividly and coherently in his feverish dreams: and in recalling and relating a dream one is unconsciously apt to give it a little coherency. Besides, Columbus had a solemn belief that he was a peculiar instrument in the hands of Providence, which, together with a deep tinge of superstition common to the age, made him prone to mistake every striking dream for a revelation. He is not to be measured by the same standard with ordinary men in ordinary circumstances. It is difficult for the mind to realize his situation, and to conceive the exaltations of spirit to which he must have been subjected. The artless manner in which, in his letter to the sovereigns, he mingles up the rhapsodies and dreams of his imagination, with simple facts, and sound practical observations, pouring them forth with a kind of scriptural solemnity and poetry of language, is one of the most striking illustrations of a character richly compounded of extraordinary and apparently contradictory elements.

Immediately after this supposed vision, and after a duration of nine days, the boisterous weather subsided, the sea became calm, and the communication with the land was restored. It was found impossible to extricate the remaining caravel from the river; but every exertion was made to bring off the people and the property before there should be a return of bad weather. In this, the exertions of the zealous Diego Mendez were eminently efficient. He had been for some days preparing for such an emergency. Cutting up the sails of the caravel, he made great sacks to receive the biscuit. He lashed two Indian canoes together with spars, so that they could not be overturned by the waves, and made a platform on them capable of sustaining a great burden. This kind of raft was laden repeatedly with the stores, arms, and ammunition, which had been left on shore, and with the furniture of the caravel, which was entirely dismantled. When well freighted, it was towed by the boat to the ships. In this way, by constant and sleepless exertions, in the space of two days, almost every thing of value was transported on board the squadron, and little else left than the hull of the caravel, stranded, decayed, and rotting in the river. Diego Mendez superintended the whole embarkation with unwearied watchfulness and activity. He and five companions, were the last to leave the shore, remaining all night at their perilous post, and embarking in the morning with the last cargo of effects.

Nothing could equal the transports of the Spaniards, when they found themselves once more on board of the ships, and saw a space of ocean between them and those forests which had lately seemed destined to be their graves. The joy of their comrades seemed little inferior to their own, and the perils and hardships which yet surrounded them were forgotten for a time in mutual congratulations. The admiral was so much impressed with a sense of the high services rendered by Diego Mendez, throughout the late time of danger and disaster, that he gave him the command of the caravel, vacant by the death of the unfortunate Diego Tristan.[1]

CHAPTER X.

DEPARTURE FROM THE COAST OF VERAGUA — ARRIVAL AT JAMAICA — STRANDING OF THE SHIPS.

[1503.]

THE wind at length becoming favorable, Columbus set sail, toward the end of April, from the disastrous coast of Veragua. The wretched condition of the ships, the enfeebled state of the crews, and the scarcity of provisions determined him to make the best of his way to Hispaniola, where he might refit his vessels and procure the necessary supplies for the voyage to Europe. To the surprise of his pilot and crews, however, on making sail, he stood again along the coast to the eastward, instead of steering north, which they considered the direct route to Hispaniola. They fancied that he intended to proceed immediately for Spain, and murmured loudly at the madness of attempting so long a voyage, with ships destitute of stores and consumed by the worms. Columbus and his brother, however, had studied the navigation of those seas with a more observant and experienced eye. They considered it advisable to gain a considerable distance to the east, before standing across for Hispaniola, to avoid being swept away, far below their destined port, by the strong currents setting constantly to the west.[2] The admiral, however, did not impart his reasons to the pilots, being anxious to keep the knowledge of his routes as much to himself as possible, seeing that there were so many adventurers crowding into the field, and ready to follow on his track. He even took from the mariners their charts,[3]

---

[1] Hist. del Almirante, cap. 99, 100. Las Casas, lib. ii. cap. 29. Relacion por Diego Mendez. Letter of Columbus from Jamaica. Journal of Porras, Navarrete Colec., tom. i.

[2] Hist. del Almirante. Letter from Jamaica.

[3] Journal of Porras, Navarrete, Colec., tom. i.

and boasts, in a letter to the sovereigns, that none of his pilots would be able to retrace the route to and from Veragua, nor to describe where it was situated.

Disregarding the murmurs of his men, therefore, he continued along the coast eastward as far as Puerto Bello. Here he was obliged to leave one of the caravels, being so pierced by worms that it was impossible to keep her afloat. All the crews were now crowded into two caravels, and these were little better than mere wrecks. The utmost exertions were necessary to keep them free from water; while the incessant labor of the pumps bore hard on men enfeebled by scanty diet and dejected by various hardships. Continuing onward, they passed Port Retrete, and a number of islands to which the admiral gave the name of Las Barbas, now termed the Mulatas, a little beyond Point Blas. Here he supposed that he had arrived at the province of Mangi in the territories of the Grand Khan, described by Marco Polo as adjoining to Cathay.[1] He continued on about ten leagues farther, until he approached the entrance of what is at present called the Gulf of Darien. Here he had a consultation with his captains and pilots, who remonstrated at his persisting in this struggle against contrary winds and currents, representing the lamentable plight of the ships and the infirm state of the crews.[2] Bidding farewell, therefore, to the main-land, he stood northward on the 1st of May, in quest of Hispaniola. As the wind was easterly, with a strong current setting to the west, he kept as near the wind as possible. So little did his pilots know of their situation, that they supposed themselves to the east of the Caribbee Islands, whereas the admiral feared that, with all his exertions, he should fall to the westward of Hispaniola.[3] His apprehensions proved to be well founded; for, on the 10th of the month, he came in sight of two small low islands to the north-west of Hispaniola, to which, from the great quantities of tortoises seen about them, he gave the name of the Tortugas; they are now known as the Caymans. Passing wide of these, and continuing directly north, he found himself, on the 30th of May, among the cluster of islands on the south side of Cuba, to which he had formerly given the name of the Queen's Gardens; having been carried between eight and nine degrees west of his destined port. Here he cast anchor near one of the keys, about ten leagues from the main island. His crews were suffering excessively

---

[1] Letter from Jamaica.
[2] Testimony of Pedro de Ledesma. Pleito de los Colones.
[3] Letter from Jamaica.

through scanty provisions and great fatigue : nothing was left
of the sea-stores but a little biscuit, oil, and vinegar ; and they
were obliged to labor incessantly at the pumps to keep the vessels afloat.   They had scarcely anchored at these islands when
there came on, at midnight, a sudden tempest, of such violence
that, according to the strong expression of Columbus, it seemed
as if the world would dissolve.[1]   They lost three of their anchors almost immediately, and the caravel Bermuda was driven
with such violence upon the ship of the admiral that the bow
of the one and the stern of the other were greatly shattered.
The sea running high, and the wind being boisterous, the vessels chafed and injured each other dreadfully, and it was with
great difficulty that they were separated.   One anchor only
remained to the admiral's ship, and this saved him from being
driven upon the rocks ; but at daylight the cable was found
nearly worn asunder.   Had the darkness continued an hour
longer, he could scarcely have escaped shipwreck.[2]

At the end of six days, the weather having moderated, he
resumed his course, standing eastward for Hispaniola ; " his
people," as he says, " dismayed and down-hearted ; almost all
his anchors lost, and his vessels bored as full of holes as a
honey-comb."   After struggling against contrary winds and the
usual currents from the east, he reached Cape Cruz, and anchored at a village in the province of Macaca,[3] where he had
touched in 1494, in his voyage along the southern coast of Cuba.
Here he was detained by head winds for several days, during
which he was supplied with cassava bread by the natives.
Making sail again, he endeavored to beat up to Hispaniola ; but
every effort was in vain.   The winds and currents continued
adverse ; the leaks continually gained upon his vessels, though
the pumps were kept incessantly going, and the seamen even
bailed the water out with buckets and kettles.   The admiral
now stood, in despair, for the island of Jamaica, to seek some
secure port ; for there was imminent danger of foundering at
sea.   On the eve of St. John, the 23d of June, they put into
Puerto Bueno, now called Dry Harbor, but met with none of
the natives from whom they could obtain provisions, nor was
there any fresh water to be had in the neighborhood.   Suffering from hunger and thirst, they sailed eastward, on the following day, to another harbor, to which the admiral on his first
visit to the island had given the name of Port Santa Gloria.

[1] Letter from Jamaica.
[2] Hist. del Almirante, cap 100.   Letter of Columbus from Jamaica.
[3] Hist. del Almirante.   Journal of Porras.

Here, at last, Columbus had to give up his long and arduous struggle against the unremitting persecution of the elements. His ships, reduced to mere wrecks, could no longer keep the sea, and were ready to sink even in port. He ordered them, therefore, to be run aground, within a bow-shot of the shore, and fastened together, side by side. They soon filled with water to the decks. Thatched cabins were then erected at the prow and stern for the accommodation of the crews, and the wreck was placed in the best possible state of defence. Thus castled in the sea, he trusted to be able to repel any sudden attack of the natives, and at the same time to keep his men from roving about the neighborhood and indulging in their usual excesses. No one was allowed to go on shore without especial license, and the utmost precaution was taken to prevent any offence being given to the Indians. Any exasperation of them might be fatal to the Spaniards in their present forlorn situation. A firebrand thrown into their wooden fortress might wrap it in flames, and leave them defenceless amid hostile thousands.

BOOK XVI.

CHAPTER I.

[1503.]

THE island of Jamaica was extremely populous and fertile, and the harbor soon swarmed with Indians. who brought provisions to barter with the Spaniards. To prevent any disputes in purchasing or sharing these supplies, two persons were appointed to superintend all bargains, and the provisions thus obtained were divided. every evening among the people. This arrangement had a happy effect in promoting a peaceful intercourse. The stores thus furnished. however. coming from a limited neighborhood of improvident beings, were not sufficient for the necessities of the Spaniards. and were so irregular as often to leave them in pinching want. They feared, too, that the neighborhood might soon be exhausted. in which case they should be reduced to famine. In this emergency Diego Mendez stepped forward with his accustomed zeal. and volunteered to set off, with three men, on a foraging expedition about the island. His offer being gladly accepted by the admiral, he departed with his comrades well armed. He was everywhere treated with the utmost kindness by the natives They took him to their houses, set meat and drink before him and his companions, and performed all the rites of savage hospitality. Mendez made an arrangement with the cacique of a numerous tribe, that his subjects should hunt and fish, and make cassava bread, and bring a quantity of provisions every day to the harbor. They were to receive in exchange knives, combs, beads, fish-hooks, hawk's bells, and other articles, from a Spaniard, who was to reside among them for that purpose. The agreement being made, Mendez despatched one of his com-

532

rades to apprise the admiral. He then pursued his journey three leagues farther, when he made a similar arrangement, and despatched another of his companions to the admiral. Proceeding onward, about thirteen leagues from the ships, he arrived at the residence of another cacique, called Huarco, where he was generously entertained. The cacique ordered his subjects to bring a large quantity of provisions, for which Mendez paid him on the spot, and made arrangements for a like supply at stated intervals. He despatched his third companion with this supply to the admiral, requesting, as usual, that an agent might be sent to receive and pay for the regular deliveries of provisions.

Mendez was now left alone, but he was fond of any enterprise that gave individual distinction. He requested of the cacique two Indians to accompany him to the end of the island; one to carry his provisions and the other to bear the hammock, or cotton net in which he slept. These being granted, he pushed resolutely forward along the coast until he reached the eastern extremity of Jamaica. Here he found a powerful cacique of the name of Ameyro. Mendez had buoyant spirits. great address, and an ingratiating manner with the savages. He and the cacique became great friends, exchanged names, which is a kind of token of brotherhood, and Mendez engaged him to furnish provisions to the ships. He then bought an excellent canoe of the cacique, for which he gave a splendid brass basin, a short frock or cassock. and one of the two shirts which formed his stock of linen. The cacique furnished him with six Indians to navigate his bark, and they parted mutually well pleased. Diego Mendez coasted his way back, touching at the various places where he had made his arrangements. He found the Spanish agents already arrived at them, loaded his canoe with provisions, and returned in triumph to the harbor, where he was received with acclamations by his comrades, and with open arms by the admiral. The provisions he brought were a most seasonable supply, for the Spaniards were absolutely fasting ; and thenceforward Indians arrived daily, well laden, from the marts which he had established.[1] The immediate wants of his people being thus provided for, Columbus revolved, in his anxious mind, the means of getting from this island. His ships were beyond the possibility of repair, and there was no hope of any chance sail arriving to his relief, on the shores of a savage island, in an unfrequented sea. The most likely measure ap-

---

[1] Relacion por Diego Mendez. Navarrete, tom. 1.

peared to be to send notice of his situation to Ovando, the governor at San Domingo, entreating him to despatch a vessel to his relief. But how was this message to be conveyed? The distance between Jamaica and Hispaniola was forty leagues, across a gulf swept by contrary currents; there were no means of transporting a messenger, except in the light canoes of the savages; and who would undertake so hazardous a voyage in a frail bark of the kind? Suddenly the idea of Diego Mendez, and the canoe he had recently purchased, presented itself to the mind of Columbus. He knew the ardor and intrepidity of Mendez, and his love of distinction by any hazardous exploit. Taking him aside, therefore, he addressed him in a manner calculated both to stimulate his zeal and flatter his self-love. Mendez himself gives an artless account of this interesting conversation, which is full of character.

"Diego Mendez, my son," said the venerable admiral, "none of those whom I have here understand the great peril in which we are placed, excepting you and myself. We are few in number, and these savage Indians are many, and of fickle and irritable natures. On the least provocation they may throw firebrands from the shore, and consume us in our straw-thatched cabins. The arrangement which you have made with them for provisions, and which at present they fulfil so cheerfully, to-morrow they may break in their caprice, and may refuse to bring us any thing; nor have we the means to compel them by force, but are entirely at their pleasure. I have thought of a remedy, if it meets with your views. In this canoe, which you have purchased, some one may pass over to Hispaniola, and procure a ship, by which we may all be delivered from this great peril into which we have fallen. Tell me your opinion on the matter."

"To this," says Diego Mendez, "I replied: 'Señor, the danger in which we are placed, I well know, is far greater than is easily conceived. As to passing from this island to Hispaniola, in so small a vessel as a canoe, I hold it not merely difficult, but impossible; since it is necessary to traverse a gulf of forty leagues, and between islands where the sea is extremely impetuous and seldom in repose. I know not who there is would adventure upon so extreme a peril.'"

Columbus made no reply, but from his looks and the nature of his silence, Mendez plainly perceived himself to be the person whom the admiral had in view; "Whereupon," continues he, "I added: 'Señor, I have many times put my life in peril of death to save you and all those who are here, and God has hitherto preserved me in a miraculous manner. There are, nevertheless, murmurers, who say that your Excellency intrusts to me all affairs wherein honor is to be gained, while there are others in your company who would execute them as well as I do. Therefore I beg that you would summon all the people, and propose this enterprise to them, to see if among them there is any one who will undertake it, which I doubt. If all decline it, I will then come forward and risk my life in your service, as I many times have done.' " [1]

The admiral gladly humored the wishes of the worthy Mendez, for never was simple egotism accompanied by more generous and devoted loyalty. On the following morning the crew was assembled, and the proposition publicly made. Every one drew back at the thoughts of it, pronouncing it the height of rashness. Upon this, Diego Mendez stepped forward. "Señor," said he. "I have but one life to lose, yet I am willing to venture it for your service and for the good of all here present, and I trust in the protection of God, which I have experienced on so many other occasions."

Columbus embraced his zealous follower, who immediately set about preparing for his expedition. Drawing his canoe on shore, he put on a false keel, nailed weather-boards along the bow and stern, to prevent the sea from breaking over it; payed it with a coat of tar; furnished it with a mast and sail; and put in provisions for himself, a Spanish comrade, and six Indians.

In the mean time Columbus wrote letters to Ovando, requesting that a ship might be immediately sent to bring him and his men to Hispaniola. He wrote a letter likewise to the sovereigns; for, after fulfilling his mission at San Domingo, Diego Mendez was to proceed to Spain on the admiral's affairs. In the letter to the sovereigns Columbus depicted his deplorable situation, and entreated that a vessel might be despatched to Hispaniola, to convey himself and his crew to Spain. He gave a comprehensive account of his voyage, most particulars of which have already been incorporated in this history, and he insisted greatly on the importance of the discovery of Veragua. He gave it as his opinion, that here were the mines of the Aurea Chersonesus, whence Solomon had derived such wealth for the building of the Temple. He entreated that this golden coast might not, like other places which he had discovered, be abandoned to adventurers, or placed under the government of men

---

[1] Relacion por Diego Mendez. Navarrete, Colec., tom. 1.

who felt no interest in the cause. "This is not a child," he adds, "to be abandoned to a step-mother. I never think of Hispaniola and Paria without weeping. Their case is desperate and past cure; I hope their example may cause this region to be treated in a different manner." His imagination becomes heated. He magnifies the supposed importance of Veragua, as transcending all his former discoveries; and he alludes to his favorite project for the deliverance of the Holy Sepulchre: "Jerusalem," he says, "and Mount Sion are to be rebuilt by the hand of a Christian. Who is he to be? God, by the mouth of the Prophet, in the fourteenth Psalm, declares it. The abbot Joachim [1] says that he is to come out of Spain." His thoughts then revert to the ancient story of the Grand Khan, who had requested that sages might be sent to instruct him in the Christian faith. Columbus, thinking that he had been in the very vicinity of Cathay, exclaims, with sudden zeal, "Who will offer himself for this task? If our Lord permit me to return to Spain, I engage to take him there, God helping, in safety."

Nothing is more characteristic of Columbus than his earnest, artless, at times eloquent, and at times almost incoherent letters. What an instance of soaring enthusiasm and irrepressible enterprise is here exhibited! At the time that he was indulging in these visions, and proposing new and romantic enterprises, he was broken down by age and infirmities, racked by pain, confined to his bed, and shut up in a wreck on the coast of a remote and savage island. No stronger picture can be given of his situation, than that which shortly follows this transient glow of excitement, when with one of his sudden transitions of thought, he awakens, as it were, to his actual condition.

"Hitherto," says he, "I have wept for others: but now, have pity upon me, heaven, and weep for me, O earth! In my temporal concerns, without a farthing to offer for a mass; cast away here in the Indies; surrounded by cruel and hostile savages: isolated, infirm, expecting each day will be my last; in spiritual concerns, separated from the holy sacraments of the

---

[1] Joachim, native of the burgh of Celico, near Cozenza, travelled in the Holy Land. Returning to Calabria, he took the habit of the Cistercians in the monastery of Corazzo, of which he became prior and abbot, and afterward rose to higher monastic importance. He died in 1202, having attained seventy-two years of age, leaving a great number of works; among the most known are commentaries on Isaiah, Jeremiah, and the Apocalypse. There are also prophecies by him, "which" (says the Dictionnaire Historique), "during his lifetime, made him to be admired by fools and despised by men of sense, at present the latter sentiment prevails. He was either very weak or very presumptuous, to flatter himself that he had the keys of things of which God reserves the knowledge to himself." — Dict. Hist. tom. 5, Caen, 1785.

church, so that my soul, if parted here from my body, must be forever lost! Weep for me, whoever has charity, truth, and justice! I came not on this voyage to gain honor or estate, that is most certain, for all hope of the kind was already dead within me. I came to serve your majesties with a sound intention and an honest zeal, and I speak no falsehood. If it should please God to deliver me hence, I humbly supplicate your majesties to permit me to repair to Rome, and perform other pilgrimages."

The despatches being ready, and the preparations of the canoe completed, Diego Mendez embarked, with his Spanish comrade and his six Indians, and departed along the coast to the eastward. The voyage was toilsome and perilous. They had to make their way against strong currents. Once they were taken by roving canoes of Indians, but made their escape, and at length arrived at the end of the island, a distance of thirty-four leagues from the harbor. Here they remained waiting for calm weather to venture upon the broad gulf, when they were suddenly surrounded and taken prisoners by a number of hostile Indians, who carried them off a distance of three leagues, where they determined to kill them. Some dispute arose about the division of the spoils taken from the Spaniards, whereupon the savages agreed to settle it by a game of chance. While they were thus engaged Diego Mendez escaped, found his way to his canoe, embarked in it, and returned alone to the harbor after fifteen days' absence. What became of his companions he does not mention, being seldom apt to speak of any person but himself. This account is taken from the narrative inserted in his last will and testament.

Columbus, though grieved at the failure of his message, was rejoiced at the escape of the faithful Mendez. The latter, nothing daunted by the perils and hardships he had undergone, offered to depart immediately on a second attempt, provided he could have persons to accompany him to the end of the island, and protect him from the natives. This the Adelantado offered to undertake, with a large party well armed. Bartholomew Fiesco, a Genoese, who had been captain of one of the caravels, was associated with Mendez in this second expedition. He was a man of great worth, strongly attached to the admiral, and much esteemed by him. Each had a large canoe under his command, in which were six Spaniards and ten Indians — the latter were to serve as oarsmen. The canoes were to keep in company. On reaching Hispaniola, Fiesco was to return immediately to Jamaica, to relieve the anxiety of the admiral and his crew, by tidings of the safe arrival of their messenger. In the mean time Diego Mendez was to proceed to San Domingo, deliver his letter to Ovando, procure and despatch a ship, and then depart for Spain with a letter to the sovereigns.

All arrangements being made, the Indians placed in the canoes their frugal provision of cassava bread, and each his calabash of water. The Spaniards, besides their bread, had a supply of the flesh of utias, and each his sword and target. In this way they launched forth upon their long and perilous voyage, followed by the prayers of their countrymen.

The Adelantado, with his armed band, kept pace with them along the coast. There was no attempt of the natives to molest them, and they arrived in safety at the end of the island. Here they remained three days before the sea was sufficiently calm for them to venture forth in their feeble barks. At length, the weather being quite serene, they bade farewell to their comrades, and committed themselves to the broad sea. The Adelantado remained watching them, until they became mere specks on the ocean, and the evening hid them from his view. The next day he set out on his return to the harbor. stopping at various villages on the way, and endeavoring to confirm the good-will of the natives.[1]

CHAPTER II.

MUTINY OF PORRAS.

[1503.]

It might have been thought that the adverse fortune which had so long persecuted Columbus was now exhausted. The envy which had once sickened at his glory and prosperity could scarcely have devised for him a more forlorn heritage in the world he had discovered. The tenant of a wreck on a savage coast, in an untraversed ocean, at the mercy of barbarous hordes. who, in a moment, from precarious friends, might be transformed into ferocious enemies ; afflicted, too, by excruciating maladies which confined him to his bed, and by the pains and infirmities which hardship and anxiety had heaped upon his

---

· Hist. del Almirante, cap. 101.

advancing age. But he had not yet exhausted his cup of bitterness. He had yet to experience an evil worse than storm, or shipwreck, or bodily anguish, or the violence of savage hordes — the perfidy of those in whom he confided.

Mendez and Fiesco had not long departed when the Spaniards in the wreck began to grow sickly, partly from the toils and exposures of the recent voyage, partly from being crowded in narrow quarters in a moist and sultry climate, and partly from want of their accustomed food, for they could not habituate themselves to the vegetable diet of the Indians. Their maladies were rendered more insupportable by mental suffering, by that suspense which frets the spirit, and that hope deferred which corrodes the heart. Accustomed to a life of bustle and variety, they had now nothing to do but loiter about the dreary hulk, look out upon the sea, watch for the canoe of Fiesco, wonder at his protracted absence, and doubt its return. A long time elapsed, much more than sufficient for the voyage, but nothing was seen or heard of the canoe. Fears were entertained that their messenger had perished. If so, how long were they to remain here, vainly looking for relief which was never to arrive? Some sank into deep despondency, others became peevish and impatient. Murmurs broke forth, and, as usual with men in distress, murmurs of the most unreasonable kind. Instead of sympathizing with their aged and infirm commander, who was involved in the same calamity, who in suffering transcended them all, and yet who was incessantly studious of their welfare, they began to rail against him as the cause of all their misfortunes.

The factious feeling of an unreasonable multitude would be of little importance if left to itself, and might end in idle clamor; it is the industry of one or two evil spirits which generally directs it to an object, and makes it mischievous. Among the officers of Columbus were two brothers, Francisco and Diego de Porras. They were related to the royal treasurer Morales, who had married their sister, and had made interest with the admiral to give them some employment in the expedition.[1] To gratify the treasurer, he had appointed Francisco de Porras captain of one of the caravels, and had obtained for his brother Diego the situation of notary and accountant-general of the squadron. He had treated them, as he declares, with the kindness of relatives, though both proved incompetent to their situations. They were vain and insolent men, and, like many

---

[1] Hist. del Almirante, cap. 102.

others whom Columbus had benefited, requited his kindness with black ingratitude.[1]

These men, finding the common people in a highly impatient and discontented state, wrought upon them with seditious insinuations, assuring them that all hope of relief through the agency of Mendez was idle it being a mere delusion of the admiral to keep them quiet, and render them subservient to his purposes. He had no desire nor intention to return to Spain, and in fact was banished thence. Hispaniola was equally closed to him, as had been proved by the exclusion of his ships from its harbor in a time of peril. To him, at present, all places were alike, and he was content to remain in Jamaica until his friends could make interest at court, and procure his recall from banishment. As to Mendez and Fiesco, they had been sent to Spain by Columbus on his own private affairs, not to procure a ship for the relief of his followers. If this were not the case, why did not the ships arrive, or why did not Fiesco return, as had been promised? Or if the canoes had really been sent for succor, the long time that had elapsed without tidings of them gave reason to believe they had perished by the way. In such case, their only alternative would be to take the canoes of the Indians and endeavor to reach Hispaniola. There was no hope, however, of persuading the admiral to such an undertaking; he was too old, and too helpless from the gout, to expose himself to the hardships of such a voyage. What then? were they to be sacrificed to his interests or his infirmities? — to give up their only chance for escape, and linger and perish with him in this desolate wreck? If they succeeded in reaching Hispaniola, they would be the better received for having left the admiral behind. Ovando was secretly hostile to him, fearing that he would regain the government of the island, on their arrival in Spain, the Bishop Fonseca, from his enmity to Columbus, would be sure to take their part; the brothers Porras had powerful friends and relatives at court, to counteract any representations that might be made by the admiral, and they cited the case of Roldan's rebellion, to show that the prejudices of the public and of men in power would always be against him. Nay, they insinuated that the sovereigns, who, on that occasion, had deprived him of part of his dignities and privileges, would rejoice at a pretext for stripping him of the remainder.[2]

Columbus was aware that the minds of his people were imbittered against him. He had repeatedly been treated with

---

[1] Letter of Columbus to his son Diego. Navarrete Colec.
[2] Hist. del Almirante, cap. 102.

insolent impatience, and reproached with being the cause of their disasters. Accustomed, however, to the unreasonableness of men in adversity, and exercised, by many trials, in the mastery of his passions, he bore with their petulance, soothed their irritation, and endeavored to cheer their spirits by the hopes of speedy succor. A little while longer, and he trusted that Fiesco would arrive with good tidings, when the certainty of relief would put an end to all these clamors. The mischief, however, was deeper than he apprehended; a complete mutiny had been organized.

On the 2d of January, 1504, he was in his small cabin, on the stern of his vessel, being confined to his bed by the gout, which had now rendered him a complete cripple. While ruminating on his disastrous situation, Francisco de Porras suddenly entered. His abrupt and agitated manner betrayed the evil nature of his visit. He had the flurried impudence of a man about to perpetrate an open crime. Breaking forth into bitter complaints, at their being kept, week after week, and month after month, to perish piecemeal in that desolate place, he accused the admiral of having no intention to return to Spain. Columbus suspected something sinister from his unusual arrogance; he maintained, however, his calmness, and, raising himself in his bed, endeavored to reason with Porras. He pointed out the impossibility of departing until those who had gone to Hispaniola should send them vessels. He represented how much more urgent must be his desire to depart, since he had not merely his own safety to provide for, but was accountable to God and his sovereigns for the welfare of all who had been committed to his charge. He reminded Porras that he had always consulted with them all, as to the measures to be taken for the common safety, and that what he had done had been with the general approbation: still, if any other measure appeared advisable, he recommended that they should assemble together, and consult upon it, and adopt whatever course appeared most judicious.

The measures of Porras and his comrades, however, were already concerted, and when men are determined on mutiny they are deaf to reason. He bluntly replied that there was no time for further consultations. "Embark immediately or remain in God's name, were the only alternatives." "For my part," said he, turning his back upon the admiral, and elevating his voice so that it resounded all over the vessel. "I am for Castile! those who choose may follow me! Shouts arose immediately from all sides. "I will follow you! and I! and I!'

Numbers of the crew sprang upon the most conspicuous parts of the ship, brandishing weapons, and uttering mingled threats and cries of rebellion. Some called upon Porras for orders what to do; others shouted "To Castile! to Castile!" while, amid the general uproar, the voices of some desperadoes were heard menacing the life of the admiral.

Columbus, hearing the tumult, leaped from his bed, ill and infirm as he was, and tottered out of the cabin, stumbling and falling in the exertion, hoping by his presence to pacify the mutineers. Three or four of his faithful adherents, however, fearing some violence might be offered him, threw themselves between him and the throng, and taking him in their arms compelled him to return to his cabin.

The Adelantado likewise sallied forth, but in a different mood. He planted himself, with lance in hand, in a situation to take the whole brunt of the assault. It was with the greatest difficulty that several of the loyal part of the crew could appease his fury, and prevail upon him to relinquish his weapon, and retire to the cabin of his brother. They now entreated Porras and his companions to depart peaceably, since no one sought to oppose them. No advantage could be gained by violence; but should they cause the death of the admiral, they would draw upon themselves the severest punishment from the sovereigns. [1]

These representations moderated the turbulence of the mutineers, and they now proceeded to carry their plans into execution. Taking ten canoes, which the admiral had purchased of the Indians, they embarked in them with as much exultation as if certain of immediately landing on the shores of Spain. Others, who had not been concerned in the mutiny, seeing so large a force departing, and fearing to remain behind, when so reduced in number, hastily collected their effects and entered likewise into the canoes. In this way forty-eight abandoned the admiral. Many of those who remained were only detained by sickness, for had they been well, most of them would have accompanied the deserters. [2] The few who remained faithful to the admiral, and the sick, who crawled forth from their cabins, saw the departure of the mutineers with tears and lamentations, giving themselves up for lost. Notwithstanding his malady, Columbus left his bed, mingling among those who were loyal, and visiting those who were ill, endeavoring in every way to cheer and comfort them. He

[1] Las Casas, Hist. Ind., lib. ii. cap. 32. Hist. del Almirante, cap. 102.
[2] Hist. del Almirante, cap. 102.

entreated them to put their trust in God, who would yet relieve them; and he promised, on his return to Spain, to throw himself at the feet of the queen, represent their loyalty and constancy, and obtain for them rewards that should compensate for all their sufferings.[1]

In the mean time Francisco de Porras and his followers, in their squadron of canoes. coasted the island to the eastward, following the route taken by Mendez and Fiesco. Wherever they landed they committed outrages upon the Indians, robbing them of their provisions, and of whatever they coveted of their effects. They endeavored to make their own crimes redound to the prejudice of Columbus, pretending to act under his authority. and affirming that he would pay for every thing they took. If he refused, they told the natives to kill him. They represented him as an implacable foe to the Indians; as one who had tyrannized over other islands, causing the misery and death of the natives, and who only sought to gain a sway here for the purpose of inflicting like calamities.

Having reached the eastern extremity of the island, they waited until the weather should be perfectly calm before they ventured to cross the gulf. Being unskilled in the management of canoes. they procured several Indians to accompany them. The sea being at length quite smooth, they set forth upon their voyage. Scarcely had they proceeded four leagues from land when a contrary wind arose, and the waves began to swell. They turned immediately for shore. The canoes. from their light structure, and being nearly round and without keels, were easily overturned, and required to be carefully balanced. They were now deeply freighted by men unaccustomed to them, and as the sea rose they frequently let in the water. The Spaniards were alarmed, and endeavored to lighten them by throwing overboard every thing that could be spared; retaining only their arms and a part of their provisions. The danger augmented with the wind. They now compelled the Indians to leap into the sea, excepting such as were absolutely necessary to navigate the canoes. If they hesitated, they drove them overboard with the edge of the sword. The Indians were skilful swimmers, but the distance to land was too great for their strength. They kept about the canoes, therefore, taking hold of them occasionally to rest themselves and recover breath. As their weight disturbed the balance of the canoes, and endangered their overturning, the Spaniards cut off their hands

---

[1] Las Casas, lib. ii. cap. 32.

and stabbed them with their swords. Some died by the weapons of these cruel men, others were exhausted and sank beneath the waves , thus eighteen perished miserably, and none survived but such as had been retained to manage the canoes.

When the Spaniards got back to land, different opinions arose as to what course they should next pursue. Some were for crossing to Cuba, for which island the wind was favorable. It was thought they might easily cross thence to the end of Hispaniola. Others advised that they should return and make their peace with the admiral. or take from him what remained of arms and stores, having thrown almost every thing overboard during their late danger. Others counselled another attempt to cross over to Hispaniola, as soon as the sea should become tranquil.

This last advice was adopted. They remained for a month at an Indian village near the eastern point of the island, living on the substance of the natives, and treating them in the most arbitrary and capricious manner When at length the weather became serene, they made a second attempt, but were again driven back by adverse winds. Losing all patience, therefore, and despairing of the enterprise, they abandoned their canoes, and returned westward, wandering from village to village, a dissolute and lawless gang, supporting themselves by fair means or foul, according as they met with kindness or hostility, and passing like a pestilence through the island.[1]

CHAPTER III.

SCARCITY OF PROVISIONS — STRATAGEM OF COLUMBUS TO OBTAIN SUPPLIES FROM THE NATIVES.

[1504.]

WHILE Porras and his crew were raging about with that desperate and joyless licentiousness which attends the abandonment of principle, Columbus presented the opposite picture of a man true to others and to himself and supported, amid hardships and difficulties, by conscious rectitude. Deserted by the healthful and vigorous portion of his garrison, he exerted himself to soothe and encourage the infirm and desponding remnant

---

[1] Hist. del Almirante, cap. 102. Las Casas, lib. ii. cap. 32.

which remained. Regardless of his own painful maladies, he was only attentive to relieve their sufferings. The few who were fit for service were required to mount guard on the wreck or attend upon the sick : there were none to forage for provisions. The scrupulous good faith and amicable conduct maintained by Columbus toward the natives had now their effect. Considerable supplies of provisions were brought by them from time to time, which he purchased at a reasonable rate. The most palatable and nourishing of these, together with the small stock of European biscuit that remained, he ordered to be appropriated to the sustenance of the infirm. Knowing how much the body is affected by the operations of the mind, he endeavored to rouse the spirits and animate the hopes of the drooping sufferers. Concealing his own anxiety, he maintained a serene and even cheerful countenance, encouraging his men by kind words, and holding forth confident anticipations of speedy relief. By his friendly and careful treatment, he soon recruited both the health and spirits of his people, and brought them into a condition to contribute to the common safety. Judicious regulations, calmly but firmly enforced, maintained every thing in order. The men became sensible of the advantages of wholesome discipline, and perceived that the restraints imposed upon them by their commander were for their own good, and ultimately productive of their own comfort.

Columbus had thus succeeded in guarding against internal ills, when alarming evils began to menace from without. The Indians, unused to lay up any stock of provisions, and unwilling to subject themselves to extra labor, found it difficult to furnish the quantity of food daily required for so many hungry men. The European trinkets, once so precious, lost their value in proportion as they became common. The importance of the admiral had been greatly diminished by the desertion of so many of his followers, and the malignant instigations of the rebels had awakened jealousy and enmity in several of the villages, which had been accustomed to furnish provisions.

By degrees, therefore, the supplies fell off. The arrangements for the daily delivery of certain quantities, made by Diego Mendez, were irregularly attended to, and at length ceased entirely. The Indians no longer thronged to the harbor with provisions, and often refused them when applied for. The Spaniards were obliged to forage about the neighborhood for their daily food, but found more and more difficulty in procuring it ; thus, in addition to their other causes for despondency, they began to entertain horrible apprehensions of famine

The admiral heard their melancholy forebodings, and beheld the growing evil, but was at a loss for a remedy. To resort to force was an alternative full of danger, and of but temporary efficacy. It would require all those who were well enough to bear arms to sally forth, while he and the rest of the infirm would be left defenceless on board of the wreck, exposed to the vengeance of the natives.

In the mean time the scarcity daily increased. The Indians perceived the wants of the white men, and had learnt from them the art of making bargains. They asked ten times the former quantity of European articles for any amount of provisions, and brought their supplies in scanty quantities, to enhance the eagerness of the hungry Spaniards. At length even this relief ceased, and there was an absolute distress for food. The jealousy of the natives had been universally roused by Porras and his followers, and they withheld all provisions, in hopes either of starving the admiral and his people, or of driving them from the island.

In this extremity a fortunate idea presented itself to Columbus. From his knowledge of astronomy, he ascertained that, within three days, there would be a total eclipse of the moon in the early part of the night. He sent, therefore, an Indian of Hispaniola, who served as his interpreter, to summon the principal caciques to a grand conference, appointing for it the day of the eclipse. When all were assembled he told them by his interpreter, that he and his followers were worshippers of a Deity who dwelt in the skies; who favored such as did well, but punished all transgressors. That, as they must all have noticed, he had protected Diego Mendez and his companions in their voyage, because they went in obedience to the orders of their commander, but had visited Porras and his companions with all kinds of afflictions, in consequence of their rebellion. This great Deity, he added, was incensed against the Indians who refused to furnish his faithful worshippers with provisions, and intended to chastise them with famine and pestilence. Lest they should disbelieve this warning, a signal would be given that night. They would behold the moon change its color and gradually lose its light; a token of the fearful punishment which awaited them.

Many of the Indians were alarmed at the prediction, others treated it with derision — all, however, awaited with solicitude the coming of the night. When they beheld a dark shadow stealing over the moon they began to tremble; with the progress of the eclipse their fears increased, and when they saw a mysterious darkness covering the whole face of nature, there were no bounds to their terror. Seizing upon whatever provisions were at hand, they hurried to the ships, threw themselves at the feet of Columbus, and implored him to intercede with his God to withhold the threatened calamities, assuring him they would henceforth bring him whatever he required. Columbus shut himself up in his cabin, as if to commune with the Deity, and remained there during the increase of the eclipse, the forests and shores all the while resounding with the howlings and supplications of the savages. When the eclipse was about to diminish he came forth and informed the natives that his God had deigned to pardon them, on condition of their fulfilling their promises; in sign of which he would withdraw the darkness from the moon.

When the Indians saw that planet restored to its brightness, and rolling in all its beauty through the firmament, they overwhelmed the admiral with thanks for his intercession, and repaired to their homes, joyful at having escaped such great disasters. Regarding Columbus with awe and reverence, as a man in the peculiar favor and confidence of the Deity, since he knew upon earth what was passing in the heavens, they hastened to propitiate him with gifts, supplies again arrived daily at the harbor, and from that time forward there was no want of provisions.[1]

CHAPTER IV.

MISSION OF DIEGO DE ESCOBAR TO THE ADMIRAL.

[1504.]

EIGHT months had now elapsed since the departure of Mendez and Fiesco, without any tidings of their fate. For a long time the Spaniards had kept a wistful look-out upon the ocean, flattering themselves that every Indian canoe, gliding at a distance, might be the harbinger of deliverance. The hopes of the most sanguine were now fast sinking into despondency. What thousand perils awaited such frail barks, and so weak a party, on an expedition of the kind! Either the canoes had been swallowed up by boisterous waves and adverse currents, or their crews had perished among the rugged mountains and

---

[1] Hist. del Almirante, cap. 103. Las Casas, Hist. Ind., lib. ii. cap. 33.

savage tribes of Hispaniola. To increase their despondency, they were informed that a vessel had been seen, bottom upward, drifting with the currents along the coasts of Jamaica. This might be the vessel sent to their relief; and if so, all their hopes were shipwrecked with it. This rumor, it is affirmed, was invented and circulated in the island by the rebels, that it might reach the ears of those who remained faithful to the admiral, and reduce them to despair.[1] It no doubt had its effect. Losing all hope of aid from a distance, and considering themselves abandoned and forgotten by the world, many grew wild and desperate in their plans. Another conspiracy was formed by one Bernardo, an apothecary of Valencia, with two confederates, Alonzo de Zamora and Pedro de Villatoro. They designed to seize upon the remaining canoes, and seek their way to Hispaniola.[2]

The mutiny was on the very point of breaking out, when one evening, toward dusk, a sail was seen standing toward the harbor. The transports of the poor Spaniards may be more easily conceived than described. The vessel was of small size: it kept out to sea, but sent its boat to visit the ships. Every eye was eagerly bent to hail the countenances of Christians and deliverers. As the boat approached, they descried in it Diego de Escobar, a man who had been one of the most active confederates of Roldan in his rebellion, who had been condemned to death under the administration of Columbus, and pardoned by his successor Bobadilla. There was bad omen in such a messenger.

Coming alongside of the ships. Escobar put a letter on board from Ovando, governor of Hispaniola, together with a barrel of wine and a side of bacon, sent as presents to the admiral. He then drew off, and talked with Columbus from a distance. He told him that he was sent by the governor to express his great concern at his misfortunes, and his regret at not having in port a vessel of sufficient size to bring off himself and his people, but that he would send one as soon as possible. Escobar gave the admiral assurances likewise that his concerns in Hispaniola had been faithfully attended to. He requested him, if he had any letter to write to the governor in reply, to give it to him as soon as possible, as he wished to return immediately.

There was something extremely singular in this mission, but there was no time for comments, Escobar was urgent to depart. Columbus hastened, therefore, to write a reply to Ovando, de-

---

[1] Hist. del Almirante, cap. 104.   [2] Las Casas, Hist. Ind., lib ii cap. 33.

picting the dangers and distresses of his situation, increased as they were by the rebellion of Porras, but expressing his reliance on his promise to send him relief, confiding in which he should remain patiently on board of his wreck. He recommended Diego Mendez and Bartholomew Fiesco to his favor, assuring him that they were not sent to San Domingo with any artful design, but simply to represent his perilous situation, and to apply for succor.[1] When Escobar received this letter, he returned immediately on board of his vessel, which made all sail, and soon disappeared in the gathering gloom of the night.

If the Spaniards had hailed the arrival of this vessel with transport, its sudden departure and the mysterious conduct of Escobar inspired no less wonder and consternation. He had kept aloof from all communication with them, as if he felt no interest in their welfare, or sympathy in their misfortunes. Columbus saw the gloom that had gathered in their countenances, and feared the consequences. He eagerly sought, therefore, to dispel their suspicions, professing himself satisfied with the communications received from Ovando, and assuring them that vessels would soon arrive to take them all away. In confidence of this, he said, he had declined to depart with Escobar. because his vessel was too small to take the whole, preferring to remain with them and share their lot, and had despatched the caravel in such haste that no time might be lost in expediting the necessary ships. These assurances, and the certainty that their situation was known in San Domingo, cheered the hearts of the people. Their hopes again revived, and the conspiracy, which had been on the point of breaking forth, was completely disconcerted.

In secret, however, Columbus was exceedingly indignant at the conduct of Ovando. He had left him for many months in a state of the utmost danger, and most distressing uncertainty, exposed to the hostilities of the natives, the seditions of his men, and the suggestions of his own despair. He had, at length, sent a mere tantalizing message, by a man known to be one of his bitterest enemies, with a present of food, which, from its scantiness, seemed intended to mock their necessities.

Columbus believed that Ovando had purposely neglected him, hoping that he might perish on the island, being apprehensive that, should he return in safety, he would be reinstated in the government of Hispaniola: and he considered

---

[1] Las Casas, Hist Ind., lib. ii. cap 34.

Escobar merely as a spy sent to ascertain the state of himself and his crew, and whether they were yet in existence. Las Casas, who was then at San Domingo, expresses similar suspicions. He says that Escobar was chosen because Ovando was certain that, from ancient enmity, he would have no sympathy for the admiral. That he was ordered not to go on board of the vessels, nor to land, neither was he to hold conversation with any of the crew, nor to receive any letters, except those of the admiral. In a word, that he was a mere scout to collect information.[1]

Others have ascribed the long neglect of Ovando to extreme caution. There was a rumor prevalent that Columbus, irritated at the suspension of his dignities by the court of Spain, intended to transfer his newly-discovered countries into the hands of his native republic Genoa, or of some other power. Such rumors had long been current, and to their recent circulation Columbus himself alludes in his letter sent to the sovereigns by Diego Mendez. The most plausible apology given is, that Ovando was absent for several months in the interior, occupied in wars with the natives, and that there were no ships at San Domingo of sufficient burden to take Columbus and his crew to Spain. He may have feared that, should they come to reside for any length of time on the island, either the admiral would interfere in public affairs, or endeavor to make a party in his favor; or that, in consequence of the number of his old enemies still resident there, former scenes of faction and turbulence might be revived.[2] In the mean time the situation of Columbus in Jamaica, while it disposed of him quietly until vessels should arrive from Spain, could not, he may have thought, be hazardous. He had sufficient force and arms for defence, and he had made amicable arrangements with the natives for the supply of provisions, as Diego Mendez, who had made those arrangements, had no doubt informed him. Such may have been the reasoning by which Ovando, under the real influence of his interest, may have reconciled his conscience to a measure which excited the strong reprobation of his contemporaries, and has continued to draw upon him the suspicions of mankind.

---

[1] Las Casas, Hist. Ind., lib. ii. cap. 33   Hist. del Almirante, cap. 108
[2] Las Casas, ubi sup.   Hist. del Almirante, ubi sup.

CHAPTER V.

VOYAGE OF DIEGO MENDEZ AND BARTHOLOMEW FIESCO IN A
CANOE TO HISPANIOLA.

[1504.]

It is proper to give here some account of the mission of Diego Mendez and Bartholomew Fiesco, and of the circumstances which prevented the latter from returning to Jamaica. Having taken leave of the Adelantado at the east end of the island, they continued all day in a direct course, animating the Indians who navigated their canoes, and who frequently paused at their labor. There was no wind, the sky was without a cloud, and the sea perfectly calm; the heat was intolerable, and the rays of the sun reflected from the surface of the ocean seemed to scorch their very eyes. The Indians, exhausted by heat and toil, would often leap into the water to cool and refresh themselves, and, after remaining there a short time, would return with new vigor to their labors. At the going down of the sun they lost sight of land. During the night the Indians took turns, one-half to row while the others slept. The Spaniards, in like manner, divided their forces: while one-half took repose the others kept guard with their weapons in hand, ready to defend themselves in case of any perfidy on the part of their savage companions.

Watching and toiling in this way through the night, they were exceedingly fatigued at the return of day. Nothing was to be seen but sea and sky. Their frail canoes, heaving up and down with the swelling and sinking of the ocean, seemed scarcely capable of sustaining the broad undulations of a calm; how would they be able to live amid waves and surges, should the wind arise? The commanders did all they could to keep up the flagging spirits of the men. Sometimes they permitted them a respite; at other times they took the paddles and shared their toils. But labor and fatigue were soon forgotten in a new source of suffering. During the preceding sultry day and night, the Indians, parched and fatigued, had drunk up all the water. They now began to experience the torments of thirst. In proportion as the day advanced, their thirst increased: the calm, which favored the navigation of the canoes, rendered this misery the more intense. There was not a breeze to fan the air, nor counteract the ardent rays of a tropical sun. Their sufferings were irritated by the prospect around them — nothing but water, while they were perishing with thirst. At mid-day their strength failed them, and they could work no longer. Fortunately, at this time the commanders of the canoes found, or pretended to find, two small kegs of water, which they had perhaps secretly reserved for such an extremity. Administering the precious contents from time to time, in sparing mouthfuls to their companions, and particularly to the laboring Indians, they enabled them to resume their toils. They cheered them with the hopes of soon arriving at a small island called Navasa, which lay directly in their way, and was only eight leagues from Hispaniola. Here they would be able to procure water, and might take repose.

For the rest of the day they continued faintly and wearily laboring forward, and keeping an anxious look-out for the island. The day passed away, the sun went down, yet there was no sign of land, not even a cloud on the horizon that might deceive them into a hope. According to their calculations, they had certainly come the distance from Jamaica at which Navasa lay. They began to fear that they had deviated from their course. If so, they should miss the island entirely, and perish with thirst before they could reach Hispaniola.

The night closed upon them without any sight of the island. They now despaired of touching at it, for it was so small and low that, even if they were to pass near, they would scarcely be able to perceive it in the dark. One of the Indians sank and died, under the accumulated sufferings of labor, heat, and raging thirst. His body was thrown into the sea. Others lay panting and gasping at the bottom of the canoes. Their companions, troubled in spirit, and exhausted in strength, feebly continued their toils. Sometimes they endeavored to cool their parched palates by taking sea-water in their mouths, but its briny acrimony rather increased their thirst. Now and then, but very sparingly, they were allowed a drop of water from the kegs; but this was only in cases of the utmost extremity, and principally to those who were employed in rowing. The night had far advanced, but those whose turn it was to take repose were unable to sleep, from the intensity of their thirst, or if they slept, it was but to be tantalized with dreams of cool fountains and running brooks, and to awaken in redoubled torment. The last drop of water had been dealt out to the Indian rowers, but it only served to irritate their sufferings. They scarce could move their paddles; one after another gave up, and it seemed impossible they should live to reach Hispaniola.

The commanders, by admirable management, had hitherto kept up this weary struggle with suffering and despair ; they now, too, began to despond. Diego Mendez sat watching the horizon. which was gradually lighting up with those faint rays which precede the rising of the moon. As that planet rose, he perceived it to emerge from behind some dark mass elevated above the level of the ocean. He immediately gave the animating cry of 'land!' His almost expiring companions were roused by it to new life. It proved to be the island of Navasa, but so small. and low. and distant. that had it not been thus revealed by the rising of the moon, they would never have discovered it. The error in their reckoning with respect to the island had arisen from miscalculating the rate of sailing of the canoes and from not making sufficient allowance for the fatigue of the rowers and the opposition of the current.

New vigor was now diffused throughout the crews. They exerted themselves with feverish impatience ; by the dawn of day they reached the land, and, springing on shore, returned thanks to God for such signal deliverance. The island was a mere mass of rocks half a league in circuit There was neither tree, nor shrub, nor herbage, nor stream, nor fountain. Hurrying about, however, with anxious search, they found to their joy abundance of rain-water in the hollows of the rocks. Eagerly scooping it up, with their calabashes, they quenched their burning thirst by immoderate draughts. In vain the more prudent warned the others of their danger. The Spaniards were in some degree restrained ; but the poor Indians. whose toils had increased the fever of their thirst, gave way to a kind of frantic indulgence. Several died upon the spot. and others fell dangerously ill.[1]

Having allayed their thirst, they now looked about in search of food. A few shell fish were found along the shore, and Diego Mendez. striking a light. and gathering drift-wood. they were enabled to boil them, and to make a delicious banquet. All day they remained reposing in the shade of the rocks. refreshing themselves after their intolerable sufferings, and gazing upon Hispaniola, whose mountains rose above the horizon, at eight leagues' distance.

In the cool of the evening they once more embarked, invigorated by repose, and arrived safely at Cape Tiburon on the following day, the fourth since their departure from Jamaica.

---

[1] Not far from the island of Navasa there gushes up in the sea a pure fountain of fresh water that sweetens the surface for some distance ; this circumstance was of course unknown to the Spaniards at the time. (Oviedo, Cronica, lib. vi cap. 12.)

Here they landed on the banks of a beautiful river, where they were kindly received and treated by the natives. Such are the particulars, collected from different sources, of this adventurous and interesting voyage, on the precarious success of which depended the deliverance of Columbus and his crews.[1] The voyagers remained for two days among the hospitable natives on the banks of the river to refresh themselves. Fiesco would have returned to Jamaica, according to promise, to give assurance to the admiral and his companions of the safe arrival of their messenger ; but both Spaniards and Indians had suffered so much during the voyage, that nothing could induce them to encounter the perils of a return in the canoes.

Parting with his companions. Diego Mendez took six Indians of the island, and set off resolutely to coast in his canoe one hundred and thirty leagues to San Domingo. After proceeding for eighty leagues, with infinite toil, always against the currents, and subject to perils from the native tribes. he was informed that the governor had departed for Xaragua, fifty leagues distant. Still undaunted by fatigues and difficulties. he abandoned his canoe, and proceeded alone and on foot through forests and over mountains, until he arrived at Xaragua. achieving one of the most perilous expeditions ever undertaken by a devoted follower for the safety of his commander.

Ovando received him with great kindness, expressing the utmost concern at the unfortunate situation of Columbus. He made many promises of sending immediate relief, but suffered day after day, week after week, and even month after month to elapse, without carrying his promises into effect. He was at that time completely engrossed by wars with the natives, and had a ready plea that there were no ships of sufficient burden at San Domingo. Had he felt a proper zeal, however, for the safety of a man like Columbus, it would have been easy, within eight months, to have devised some means, if not of delivering him from his situation, at least of conveying to him ample re-enforcements and supplies.

The faithful Mendez remained for seven months in Xaragua. detained there under various pretexts by Ovando, who was unwilling that he should proceed to San Domingo ; partly. as is intimated, from his having some jealousy of his being employed in secret agency for the admiral, and partly from a desire to throw impediments in the way of his obtaining the required relief. At length. by daily importunity. he obtained permission

Hist. del Almirante, cap. 105. Las Casas, lib. ii cap. 31 Testament of Diego Mendez Navarrete, tom. i.

to go to San Domingo and await the arrival of certain ships which were expected, of which he proposed to purchase one on the account of the admiral. He immediately set out on foot a distance of seventy leagues, part of his toilsome journey lying through forests and among mountains infested by hostile and exasperated Indians. It was after his departure that Ovando despatched the caravel commanded by the pardoned rebel Escobar, on that singular and equivocal visit, which, in the eyes of Columbus, had the air of a mere scouting expedition to spy into the camp of an enemy.

CHAPTER VI.

OVERTURES OF COLUMBUS TO THE MUTINEERS — BATTLE OF THE ADELANTADO WITH PORRAS AND HIS FOLLOWERS.

[1503.]

WHEN Columbus had soothed the disappointment of his men at the brief and unsatisfactory visit and sudden departure of Escobar, he endeavored to turn the event to some advantage with the rebels. He knew them to be disheartened by the inevitable miseries attending a lawless and dissolute life; that many longed to return to the safe and quiet path of duty; and that the most malignant, seeing how he had foiled all their intrigues among the natives to produce a famine, began to fear his ultimate triumph and consequent vengeance. A favorable opportunity, he thought, now presented to take advantage of these feelings, and by gentle means to bring them back to their allegiance. He sent two of his people, therefore, who were most intimate with the rebels, to inform them of the recent arrival of Escobar with letters from the Governor of Hispaniola, promising him a speedy deliverance from the island. He now offered a free pardon, kind treatment, and a passage with him in the expected ships, on condition of their immediate return to obedience. To convince them of the arrival of the vessel, he sent them a part of the bacon which had been brought by Escobar.

On the approach of these ambassadors, Francisco de Porras came forth to meet them, accompanied solely by a few of the ringleaders of his party. He imagined that there might be some propositions from the admiral, and he was fearful of their

being heard by the mass of his people, who, in their dissatisfied
and repentant mood, would be likely to desert him on the least
prospect of pardon   Having listened to the tidings and overtures brought by the messengers, he and his confidential confederates consulted for some time together   Perfidious in their
own nature, they suspected the sincerity of the admiral; and
conscious of the extent of their offences, doubted his having
the magnanimity to pardon them.   Determined, therefore, not
to confide in his proffered amnesty, they replied to the messengers that they had no wish to return to the ships, but preferred
living at large about the island.   They offered to engage, however, to conduct themselves peaceably and amicably, on receiving a solemn promise from the admiral, that should two
vessels arrive, they should have one to depart in; should but
one arrive, that half of it should be granted to them, and that,
moreover, the admiral should share with them the stores and
articles of Indian traffic remaining in the ships; having lost all
that they had, in the sea.   These demands were pronounced
extravagant and inadmissible, upon which they replied inso
lently that, if they were not peaceably conceded, they would
take them by force; and with this menace they dismissed the
ambassadors.[1]

This conference was not conducted so privately but that the
rest of the rebels learnt the purport of the mission; and the
offer of pardon and deliverance occasioned great tumult and
agitation.   Porras, fearful of their desertion assured them that
these offers of the admiral were all deceitful, that he was naturally cruel and vindictive, and only sought to get them into
his power to wreak on them his vengeance.   He exhorted them
to persist in their opposition to his tyranny; reminding them
that those who had formerly done so in Hispaniola had eventually triumphed, and sent him home in irons; he assured them
that they might do the same, and again made vaunting promises
of protection in Spain, through the influence of his relatives.
But the boldest of his assertions was with respect to the caravel
of Escobar.   It shows the ignorance of the age, and the superstitious awe which the common people entertained with respect
to Columbus and his astronomical knowledge.   Porras assured
them that no real caravel had arrived, but a mere phantasm
conjured up by the admiral, who was deeply versed in necro-
mancy.   In proof of this he adverted to its arriving in the dusk
of the evening; its holding communication with no one but the

---

[1] Las Casas, lib. ii. cap 35   Hist del Almirante, cap. 106.

admiral, and its sudden disappearance in the night. Had it been a real caravel, the crew would have sought to talk with their countrymen; the admiral, his son, and brother, would have eagerly embarked on board, and it would at any rate have remained a little while in port, and not have vanished so suddenly and mysteriously.[1]

By these and similar delusions Porras succeeded in working upon the feelings and credulity of his followers. Fearful, however, that they might yield to after reflection, and to further offers from the admiral, he determined to involve them in some act of violence which would commit them beyond all hopes of forgiveness. He marched them, therefore, to an Indian village called Maima,[2] about a quarter of a league from the ships, intending to plunder the stores remaining on board the wreck, and to take the admiral prisoner.[3]

Columbus had notice of the designs of the rebels, and of their approach. Being confined by his infirmities, he sent his brother to endeavor with mild words to persuade them from their purpose, and win them to obedience; but with sufficient force to resist any violence. The Adelantado, who was a man rather of deeds than of words, took with him fifty followers, men of tried resolution, and ready to fight in any cause. They were well armed and full of courage, though many were pale and debilitated from recent sickness, and from long confinement to the ships. Arriving on the side of a hill, within a bow-shot of the village, the Adelantado discovered the rebels, and despatched the same two messengers to treat with them, who had already carried them the offer of pardon. Porras and his fellow-leaders, however, would not permit them to approach. They confided in the superiority of their numbers, and in their men being, for the most part, hardy sailors, rendered robust and vigorous by the roving life they had been leading in the forests and the open air. They knew that many of those who were with the Adelantado were men brought up in a softer mode of life. They pointed to their pale countenances, and persuaded their followers that they were mere household men, fair-weather troops, who could never stand before them. They did not reflect that, with such men, pride and lofty spirit often more than supply the place of bodily force, and they forgot that their adversaries had the incalculable advantage of justice and law upon their side. Deluded by their words, their followers were excited to a tran-

---

[1] Hist del Almirante, cap. 106. Las Casas, lib. 11. cap. 35.
[2] At present Mammee Bay.   [3] Hist. del Almirante, ubi sup.

sient glow of courage, and brandishing their weapons, refused
to listen to the messengers.

Six of the stoutest rebels made a league to stand by one another and attack the Adelantado ; for, he being killed, the rest
would be easily defeated. The main body formed themselves
into a squadron, drawing their swords and shaking their lances.
They did not wait to be assailed, but, uttering shouts and menaces, rushed upon the enemy. They were so well received,
however, that at the first shock four or five were killed, most
of them the confederates who had leagued to attack the Adelantado. The latter, with his own hand killed Juan Sanchez,
the same powerful mariner who had carried off the cacique
Quibian ; and Juan Barber also, who had first drawn a sword
against the admiral in this rebellion. The Adelantado with his
usual vigor and courage was dealing his blows about him in the
thickest of the affray, where several lay killed and wounded,
when he was assailed by Francisco de Porras. The rebel with
a blow of his sword cleft the buckler of Don Bartholomew, and
wounded the hand which grasped it. The sword remained
wedged in the shield, and before Porras could withdraw it, the
Adelantado closed upon him, grappled him, and, being assisted
by others, after a severe struggle took him prisoner.[1]

When the rebels beheld their leader a captive, their transient
courage was at an end, and they fled in confusion. The Adelantado would have pursued them, but was persuaded to let
them escape with the punishment they had received ; especially
as it was necessary to guard against the possibility of an attack
from the Indians.

The latter had taken arms and drawn up in battle array,
gazing with astonishment at this fight between white men, but
without taking part on either side. When the battle was over,
they approached the field, gazing upon the dead bodies of the
beings they had once fancied immortal. They were curious in
examining the wounds made by the Christian weapons. Among
the wounded insurgents was Pedro Ledesma, the same pilot
who so bravely swam ashore at Veragua, to procure tidings of
the colony. He was a man of prodigious muscular force and a
hoarse, deep voice. As the Indians, who thought him dead,
were inspecting the wounds with which he was literally covered, he suddenly uttered an ejaculation in his tremendous
voice, at the sound of which the savages fled in dismay. This
man, having fallen into a cleft or ravine, was not discovered by

---

[1] Hist. del Almirante, cap. 107. Las Casas, Hist. Ind., lib. ii. cap. 35.

the white men until the dawning of the following day, having remained all that time without a drop of water. The number and severity of the wounds he is said to have received would seem incredible, but they are mentioned by Fernando Columbus, who was an eye-witness, and by Las Casas, who had the account from Ledesma himself. For want of proper remedies his wounds were treated in the roughest manner, yet, through the aid of a vigorous constitution, he completely recovered. Las Casas conversed with him several years afterward at Seville, when he obtained from him various particulars concerning this voyage of Columbus. Some few days after this conversation, however, he heard that Ledesma had fallen under the knife of an assassin.[1]

The Adelantado returned in triumph to the ships, where he was received by the admiral in the most affectionate manner; thanking him as his deliverer. He brought Porras and several of his followers prisoners. Of his own party only two had been wounded; himself in the hand, and the admiral's steward, who had received an apparently slight wound with a lance, equal to one of the most insignificant of those with which Ledesma was covered; yet, in spite of careful treatment, he died.

On the next day, the 20th of May, the fugitives sent a petition to the admiral, signed with all their names, in which, says Las Casas, they confessed all their misdeeds and cruelties, and evil intentions, supplicating the admiral to have pity on them and pardon them for their rebellion, for which God had already punished them. They offered to return to their obedience, and to serve him faithfully in future, making an oath to that effect upon a cross and a missal, accompanied by an imprecation worthy of being recorded "They hoped, should they break their oath, that no priest nor other Christian might ever confess them; that repentance might be of no avail; that they might be deprived of the holy sacraments of the church; that at their death they might receive no benefit from bulls nor indulgences; that their bodies might be cast out into the fields, like those of heretics and renegadoes, instead of being buried in holy ground; and that they might not receive absolution from the pope, nor from cardinals, nor archbishops, nor bishops, nor any other Christian priests."[2] Such were the awful imprecations by which these men endeavored to add validity to an oath. The worthlessness of a man's word may always be known by the extravagant means he uses to enforce it.

---

[1] Las Casas, Hist. Ind., lib. ii. cap. 35.   [2] Ibid., cap. 32

The admiral saw, by the abject nature of this petition, how completely the spirit of these misguided men was broken; with his wonted magnanimity, he readily granted their prayer, and pardoned their offences; but on one condition, that their ringleader, Francisco Porras, should remain a prisoner.

As it was difficult to maintain so many persons on board of the ships, and as quarrels might take place between persons who had so recently been at blows, Columbus put the late followers of Porras under the command of a discreet and faithful man; and giving in his charge a quantity of European articles for the purpose of purchasing food of the natives, directed him to forage about the island until the expected vessels should arrive.

At length, after a long year of alternate hope and despondency, the doubts of the Spaniards were joyfully dispelled by the sight of two vessels standing into the harbor. One proved to be a ship hired and well victualled, at the expense of the admiral, by the faithful and indefatigable Diego Mendez: the other had been subsequently fitted out by Ovando, and put under the command of Diego de Salcedo, the admiral's agent employed to collect his rents in San Domingo.

The long neglect of Ovando to attend to the relief of Columbus had, it seems, roused the public indignation, insomuch that animadversions had been made upon his conduct even in the pulpits. This is affirmed by Las Casas, who was at San Domingo at the time. If the governor had really entertained hopes that, during the delay of relief, Columbus might perish in the island, the report brought back by Escobar must have completely disappointed him. No time was to be lost if he wished to claim any merit in his deliverance, or to avoid the disgrace of having totally neglected him. He exerted himself, therefore, at the eleventh hour, and despatched a caravel at the same time with the ship sent by Diego Mendez. The latter having faithfully discharged this part of his mission, and seen the ships depart, proceeded to Spain on the further concerns of the admiral.[1]

---

[1] Some brief notice of the further fortunes of Diego Mendez may be interesting to the reader When King Ferdinand heard of his faithful services, says Oviedo, he bestowed rewards upon Mendez, and permitted him to bear a canoe in his coat of arms, as a memento of his loyalty. He continued devotedly attached to the admiral, serving him zealously after his return to Spain, and during his last illness Columbus retained the most grateful and affectionate sense of his fidelity. On his death-bed he promised Mendez that, in reward for his services, he should be appointed principal alguazil of the island of Hispaniola, an engagement which the admiral's son, Don Diego, who was present, cheerfully undertook to perform A few years afterward, when the latter succeeded to the office of his father, Mendez reminded him of the promise but Don Diego informed him that he had given the office to his uncle, Don Bartholomew; he assured him how

BOOK XVII.

CHAPTER I.

ADMINISTRATION OF OVANDO IN HISPANIOLA — OPPRESSION OF THE
NATIVES.

[1503.]

BEFORE relating the return of Columbus to Hispaniola, it is
proper to notice some of the principal occurrences which took
place in that island under the government of Ovando. A great
crowd of adventurers of various ranks had thronged his fleet —
eager speculators, credulous dreamers, and broken-down gentlemen of desperate fortunes; all expecting to enrich themselves
suddenly in an island where gold was to be picked up from the

---

ever, that he should receive something equivalent. Mendez shrewdly replied, that the
equivalent had better be given to Don Bartholomew, and the office to himself, according
to agreement   The promise, however, remained unperformed, and Diego Mendez unre-
warded. He was afterward engaged on voyages of discovery in vessels of his own but
met with many vicissitudes, and appears to have died in impoverished circumstances.
His last will, from which these particulars are principally gathered, was dated in Valladolid, the 19th of June, 1536, by which it is evident he must have been in the prime of
life at the time of his voyage with the admiral In this will he requested that the reward
which had been promised to him should be paid to his children, by making his eldest
son principal alguazil for life of the city of San Domingo, and his other son lieutenant
to the admiral for the same city. It does not appear whether this request was complied
with under the successors of Don Diego.
    In another clause of his will he desired that a large stone should be placed upon his
sepulchre, on which should be engraved, "Here lies the honorable Cavalier Diego Mendez,
who served greatly the royal crown of Spain, in the conquest of the Indies, with the
admiral Don Christopher Columbus of glorious memory, who made the discovery, and
afterward by himself, with ships at his own cost He died, etc., etc. Bestow in charity
a Paternoster, and an Ave Maria."
    He ordered that in the midst of this stone there should be carved an Indian canoe, as
given him by the king for armorial bearings in memorial of his voyage from Jamaica to
Hispaniola, and above it should be engraved, in large letters, the word "CANOA." He
enjoined upon his heirs to be loyal to the admiral (Don Diego Columbus), and his lady,
and gave them much ghostly counsel, mingled with pious benedictions. As an heirloom
in his family, he bequeathed his library, consisting of a few volumes, which accompanied him in his wanderings — viz · "The Art of Holy Dying, by Erasmus; A Sermon
of the same author, in Spanish, The Lingua and the Colloquies of the same, The History of Josephus; The Moral Philosophy of Aristotle; The Book of the Holy Land; A
Book called the Contemplation of the Passion of our Saviour; A Tract on the Vengeance
of the Death of Agamemnon, and several other short treatises." This curious and characteristic testament is in the archives of the Duke of Veragua in Madrid.

surface of the soil or gathered from the mountain brooks. They had scarcely landed, says Las Casas, who accompanied the expedition, when they all hurried off to the mines, about eight leagues' distance. The roads swarmed like ant-hills, with adventurers of all classes. Every one had his knapsack stored with biscuit or flour, and his mining implements on his shoulders. Those hidalgos, or gentlemen, who had no servants to carry their burdens, bore them on their own backs, and lucky was he who had a horse for the journey: he would be able to bring back the greater load of treasure. They all set out in high spirits, eager who should first reach the golden land: thinking they had but to arrive at the mines and collect riches; "for they fancied," says Las Casas, "that gold was to be gathered as easily and readily as fruit from the trees." When they arrived, however, they discovered, to their dismay, that it was necessary to dig painfully into the bowels of the earth — a labor to which most of them had never been accustomed; that it required experience and sagacity to detect the veins of ore, that, in fact, the whole process of mining was exceedingly toilsome, demanded vast patience and much experience, and, after all, was full of uncertainty. They digged eagerly for a time, but found no ore. They grew hungry, threw by their implements, sat down to eat, and then returned to work. It was all in vain. "Their labor," says Las Casas, "gave them a keen appetite and quick digestion, but no gold." They soon consumed their provisions, exhausted their patience, cursed their infatuation, and in eight days set off drearily on their return along the roads they had lately trod so exultingly. They arrived at San Domingo without an ounce of gold, half-famished, downcast, and despairing.[1] Such is too often the case of those who ignorantly engage in mining — of all speculations the most brilliant, promising, and fallacious.

Poverty soon fell upon these misguided men. They exhausted the little property brought from Spain. Many suffered extremely from hunger, and were obliged to exchange even their apparel for bread. Some formed connections with the old settlers of the island; but the greater part were like men lost and bewildered, and just awakened from a dream. The miseries of the mind, as usual, heightened the sufferings of the body. Some wasted away and died broken-hearted; others were hurried off by raging fevers, so that there soon perished upward of a thousand men.

---

[1] Las Casas, Hist. Ind., lib. ii. cap. 6.

Ovando was reputed a man of great prudence and sagacity, and he certainly took several judicious measures for the regulation of the island and the relief of the colonists. He made arrangements for distributing the married persons and the families which had come out in his fleet, in four towns in the interior, granting them important privileges. He revived the drooping zeal for mining, by reducing the royal share of the product from one-half to a third, and shortly after to a fifth; but he empowered the Spaniards to avail themselves, in the most oppressive manner, of the labor of the unhappy natives in working the mines. The charge of treating the natives with severity had been one of those chiefly urged against Columbus. It is proper, therefore, to notice in this respect the conduct of his successor, a man chosen for his prudence and his supposed capacity to govern.

It will be recollected that when Columbus was in a manner compelled to assign lands to the rebellious followers of Francisco Roldan, in 1499, he had made an arrangement that the caciques in their vicinity should, in lieu of tribute, furnish a number of their subjects to assist them in cultivating their estates. This, as has been observed, was the commencement of the disastrous system of repartimientos, or distributions of Indians. When Bobadilla administered the government, he constrained the caciques to furnish a certain number of Indians to each Spaniard, for the purpose of working the mines, where they were employed like beasts of burden. He made an enumeration of the natives, to prevent evasion; reduced them into classes, and distributed them among the Spanish inhabitants. The enormous oppressions which ensued have been noticed. They roused the indignation of Isabella; and when Ovando was sent out to supersede Bobadilla, in 1502, the natives were pronounced free: they immediately refused to labor in the mines.

Ovando represented to the Spanish sovereigns, in 1503, that ruinous consequences resulted to the colony from this entire liberty granted to the Indians. He stated that the tribute could not be collected, for the Indians were lazy and improvident; that they could only be kept from vices and irregularities by occupation; that they now kept aloof from the Spaniards, and from all instruction in the Christian faith.

The last representation had an influence with Isabella, and drew a letter from the sovereigns to Ovando, in 1503, in which he was ordered to spare no pains to attach the natives to the Spanish nation and the Catholic religion. To make them labor moderately, if absolutely essential to their own good, but to temper authority with persuasion and kindness. To pay them regularly and fairly for their labor, and to have them instructed in religion on certain days.

Ovando availed himself of the powers given him by this letter to their fullest extent. He assigned to each Castilian a certain number of Indians, according to the quality of the applicant, the nature of the application, or his own pleasure. It was arranged in the form of an order on a cacique for a certain number of Indians, who were to be paid by their employer, and instructed in the Catholic faith. The pay was so small as to be little better than nominal; the instruction was little more than the mere ceremony of baptism; and the term of labor was at first six months, and then eight months in the year. Under cover of this hired labor, intended for the good both of their bodies and their souls, more intolerable toil was exacted from them, and more horrible cruelties were inflicted, than in the worst days of Bobadilla. They were separated often the distance of several days' journey from their wives and children, and doomed to intolerable labor of all kinds, extorted by the cruel infliction of the lash. For food they had the cassava bread, an unsubstantial support for men obliged to labor; sometimes a scanty portion of pork was distributed among a great number of them, scarce a mouthful to each. When the Spaniards who superintended the mines were at their repast, says Las Casas, the famished Indians scrambled under the table, like dogs, for any bone thrown to them. After they had gnawed and sucked it, they pounded it between stones and mixed it with their cassava bread, that nothing of so precious a morsel might be lost. As to those who labored in the fields, they never tasted either flesh or fish; a little cassava bread and a few roots were their support. While the Spaniards thus withheld the nourishment necessary to sustain their health and strength, they exacted a degree of labor sufficient to break down the most vigorous man. If the Indians fled from this incessant toil and barbarous coercion, and took refuge in the mountains, they were hunted out like wild beasts, scourged in the most inhuman manner, and laden with chains to prevent a second escape. Many perished long before their term of labor had expired. Those who survived their term of six or eight months were permitted to return to their homes until the next term commenced. But their homes were often forty, sixty, and eighty leagues distant. They had nothing to sustain them through the journey but a few roots or agi peppers, or a little cassava bread. Worn down by long toil and cruel hardships, which their feeble constitutions were incapable of sustaining, many had not strength to perform the journey, but sank down and died by the way; some by the side of a brook, others under the shade of a tree, where they had crawled for shelter from the sun. "I have found many dead in the road," says Las Casas, "others gasping under the trees, and others in the pangs of death, faintly crying Hunger! hunger!"[1] Those who reached their homes most commonly found them desolate. During the eight months they had been absent, their wives and children had either perished or wandered away; the fields on which they depended for food were overrun with weeds, and nothing was left them but to lie down, exhausted and despairing, and die at the threshold of their habitations.[2]

It is impossible to pursue any farther the picture drawn by the venerable Las Casas, not of what he had heard, but of what he had seen; nature and humanity revolt at the details. Suffice it to say, that so intolerable were the toils and sufferings inflicted upon this weak and unoffending race, that they sank under them, dissolving, as it were, from the face of the earth. Many killed themselves in despair, and even mothers overcame the powerful instinct of nature, and destroyed the infants at their breasts, to spare them a life of wretchedness. Twelve years had not elapsed since the discovery of the island, and several hundred thousand of its native inhabitants had perished, miserable victims to the grasping avarice of the white men.

CHAPTER II.

MASSACRE AT XARAGUA — FATE OF ANACAONA.

[1503.]

THE sufferings of the natives under the civil policy of Ovando have been briefly shown; it remains to give a concise view of the military operations of this commander, so lauded by certain of the early historians for his prudence. By this notice a portion of the eventful history of this island will be recounted which is connected with the fortunes of Columbus, and which comprises the thorough subjugation, and, it may almost be said, extermination of the native inhabitants. And first, we

---

[1] Las Casas, Hist. Ind., lib. ii. cap. 14, MS. [2] Ibid., ubi sup.

must treat of the disasters of the beautiful province of **Xaragua**, the seat of hospitality. the refuge of the suffering Spaniards; and of the fate of the female cacique, Anacaona, once the pride of the island, and the generous friend of white men

Behechio, the ancient cacique of this province, being dead, Anacaona, his sister, had succeeded to the government. The marked partiality which she once manifested for the Spaniards had been greatly weakened by the general misery they had produced in her country, and by the brutal profligacy exhibited in her immediate dominions by the followers of Roldan. The unhappy story of the loves of her beautiful daughter Higuenamota, with the young Spaniard Hernando de Guevara, had also caused her great affliction: and, finally, the various and enduring hardships inflicted on her once happy subjects by the grinding systems of labor enforced by Bobadilla and Ovando. had at length, it is said, converted her friendship into absolute detestation.

This disgust was kept alive and aggravated by the Spaniards who lived in her immediate neighborhood, and had obtained grants of land there; a remnant of the rebel faction of Roldan, who retained the gross licentiousness and open profligacy in which they had been indulged under the loose misrule of that commander, and who made themselves odious to the inferior caciques, by exacting services tyrannically and capriciously under the baneful system of repartimientos.

The Indians of this province were uniformly represented as a more intelligent, polite, and generous-spirited race than any others of the islands. They were the more prone to feel and resent the overbearing treatment to which they were subjected. Quarrels sometimes took place between the caciques and their oppressors. These were immediately reported to the governor as dangerous mutinies. and a resistance to any capricious and extortionate exaction was magnified into a rebellious resistance to the authority of government. Complaints of this kind were continually pouring in upon Ovando, until he was persuaded by some alarmists. or some designing mischief-maker, that there was a deep-laid conspiracy among the Indians of this province to rise upon the Spaniards.

Ovando immediately set out for Xaragua at the head of three hundred foot-soldiers, armed with swords, arquebuses, and cross-bows, and seventy horsemen, with cuirasses, bucklers, and lances. He pretended that he was going on a mere visit of friendship to Anacaona, and to make arrangements about the payment of tribute.

When Anacaona heard of the intended visit, she summoned all her tributary caciques and principal subjects, to assemble at her chief town, that they might receive the commander of the Spaniards with becoming homage and distinction. As Ovando, at the head of his little army, approached, she went forth to meet him. according to the custom of her nation. attended by a great train of her most distinguished subjects, male and female : who. as has been before observed, were noted for superior grace and beauty. They received the Spaniards with their popular areytos, their national songs ; the young women waving palm branches and dancing before them, in the way that had so much charmed the followers of the Adelantado, on his first visit to the province.

Anacaona treated the governor with that natural graciousness and dignity for which she was celebrated. She gave him the largest house in the place for his residence, and his people were quartered in the houses adjoining. For several days the Spaniards were entertained with all the natural luxuries that the province afforded. National songs and dances and games were performed for their amusement, and there was every outward demonstration of the same hospitality, the same amity. that Anacaona had uniformly shown to white men.

Notwithstanding all this kindness. and notwithstanding her uniform integrity of conduct and open generosity of character, Ovando was persuaded that Anacaona was secretly meditating a massacre of himself and his followers. Historians tell us nothing of the grounds for such a belief. It was too probably produced by the misrepresentations of the unprincipled adventurers who infested the province. Ovando should have paused and reflected before he acted upon it. He should have considered the improbability of such an attempt by naked Indians against so large a force of steel-clad troops, armed with European weapons; and he should have reflected upon the general character and conduct of Anacaona. At any rate, the example set repeatedly by Columbus and his brother the Adelantado should have convinced him that it was a sufficient safeguard against the machinations of the natives, to seize upon their caciques and detain them as hostages. The policy of Ovando, however, was of a more rash and sanguinary nature , he acted upon suspicion as upon conviction. He determined to anticipate the alleged plot by a counter artifice, and to overwhelm this defenceless people in an indiscriminate and bloody vengeance.

As the Indians had entertained their guests with various

national games, Ovando invited them in return to witness
certain games of his country. Among these was a tilting
match or joust with reeds; a chivalrous game which the Spaniards had learnt from the Moors of Granada. The Spanish
cavalry, in those days, were as remarkable for the skilful
management as for the ostentatious caparison of their horses.
Among the troops brought out from Spain by Ovando, one
horseman had disciplined his horse to prance and curvet in
time to the music of a viol.[1] The joust was appointed to take
place of a Sunday after dinner, in the public square, before the
house where Ovando was quartered The cavalry and foot-
soldiers had their secret instructions. The former were to
parade, not merely with reeds or blunted tilting-lances, but with
weapons of a more deadly character. The foot-soldiers were
to come apparently as mere spectators, but likewise armed and
ready for action at a concerted signal.

At the appointed time the square was crowded with the
Indians. waiting to see this military spectacle. The caciques
were assembled in the house of Ovando, which looked upon
the square. None were armed; an unreserved confidence
prevailed among them, totally incompatible with the dark
treachery of which they were accused. To prevent all suspicion, and take off all appearance of sinister design, Ovando,
after dinner. was playing at quoits with some of his principal
officers, when the cavalry having arrived in the square, the
caciques begged the governor to order the joust to commence.[2]
Anacaona, and her beautiful daughter Higuenamota, with several of her female attendants. were present and joined in the
request.

Ovando left his game and came forward to a conspicuous
place. When he saw that every thing was disposed according
to his orders, he gave the fatal signal. Some say it was by
taking hold of a piece of gold which was suspended about his
neck;[3] others by laying his hand on the cross of Alcantara,
which was embroidered on his habit.[4] A trumpet was immediately sounded. The house in which Anacaona, and all the
principal caciques were assembled was surrounded by soldiery,
commanded by Diego Valasquez and Rodrigo Mexiatrillo, and
no one was permitted to escape. They entered, and seizing
upon the caciques, bound them to the posts which supported

---

[1] Las Casas, Hist. Ind., lib. ii. cap. 9.
[2] Oviedo, Cronica de las Indias, lib iii. cap. 12.
[3] Las Casas, Hist. Ind., lib. ii. cap. 9.
[4] Charlevoix, Hist. San Domingo, lib. xxiv. p. 235.

the roof. Anacaona was led forth a prisoner. The unhappy caciques were then put to horrible tortures, until some of them, in the extremity of anguish, were made to accuse their queen and themselves of the plot with which they were charged. When this cruel mockery of judicial form had been executed, instead of preserving them for after-examination, fire was set to the house, and all the caciques perished miserably in the flames.

While these barbarities were practised upon the chieftains, a horrible massacre took place among the populace. At the signal of Ovando, the horsemen rushed into the midst of the naked and defenceless throng, trampling them under the hoofs of their steeds, cutting them down with their swords, and transfixing them with their spears. No mercy was shown to age or sex; it was a savage and indiscriminate butchery. Now and then a Spanish horseman, either through an emotion of pity or an impulse of avarice, caught up a child, to bear it off in safety, but it was barbarously pierced by the lances of his companions. Humanity turns with horror from such atrocities, and would fain discredit them; but they are circumstantially and still more minutely recorded by the venerable bishop Las Casas, who was resident in the island at the time, and conversant with the principal actors in this tragedy. He may have colored the picture strongly, in his usual indignation when the wrongs of the Indians are in question; yet, from all concurring accounts, and from many precise facts which speak for themselves, the scene must have been most sanguinary and atrocious. Oviedo, who is loud in extolling the justice, and devotion, and charity, and meekness of Ovando, and his kind treatment of the Indians, and who visited the province of Xaragua a few years afterward, records several of the preceding circumstances; especially the cold-blooded game of quoits played by the governor on the verge of such a horrible scene, and the burning of the caciques, to the number, he says, of more than forty. Diego Mendez, who was at Xaragua at the time, and doubtless present on such an important occasion, says incidentally, in his last will and testament, that there were eighty-four caciques either burnt or hanged.[1] Las Casas says that there were eighty who entered the house with Anacaona. The slaughter of the multitude must have been great; and this was inflicted on an unarmed and unresisting throng. Several who escaped from the massacre fled in their canoes to an island

---

[1] Relacion hecha por Don Diego Mendez. Navarrete Col., tom. i. p. 314.

about eight leagues distant, called Guanabo. They were pursued and taken, and condemned to slavery.

As to the princess Anacaona, she was carried in chains to San Domingo. The mockery of a trial was given her, in which she was found guilty on the confessions wrung by tortures from her subjects, and on the testimony of their butchers; and she was ignominiously hanged in the presence of the people whom she had so long and so signally befriended.[1] Oviedo has sought to throw a stigma on the character of this unfortunate princess accusing her of great licentiousness; but he was prone to criminate the character of the native princes, who fell victims to the ingratitude and injustice of his countrymen. Contemporary writers of great authority have concurred in representing Anacaona as remarkable for her native propriety and dignity. She was adored by her subjects, so as to hold a kind of dominion over them even during the lifetime of her brother; she is said to have been skilled in composing the areytos, or legendary ballads of her nation, and may have conduced much toward producing that superior degree of refinement remarked among her people. Her grace and beauty had made her renowned throughout the island, and had excited the admiration both of the savage and the Spaniard. Her magnanimous spirit was evinced in her amicable treatment of the white men, although her husband, the brave Caonabo, had perished a prisoner in their hands; and defenceless parties of them had been repeatedly in her power, and lived at large in her dominions. After having for several years neglected all safe opportunities of vengeance, she fell a victim to the absurd charge of having conspired against an armed body of nearly four hundred men, seventy of them horsemen; a force sufficient to have subjugated large armies of naked Indians.

After the massacre of Xaragua the destruction of its inhabitants still continued. The favorite nephew of Anacaona, the cacique Guaora, who had fled to the mountains, was hunted like a wild beast, until he was taken, and likewise hanged. For six months the Spaniards continued ravaging the country with horse and foot, under pretext of quelling insurrections; for, wherever the affrighted natives took refuge in their despair, herding in dismal caverns and in the fastnesses of the mountains, they were represented as assembling in arms to make a head of rebellion. Having at length hunted them out of their retreats, destroyed many, and reduced the survivors to the most

---

[1] Oviedo, Cronica de las Indias, lib. iii. cap 12.   Las Casas, Hist. Ind., lib. ii. cap. 9.

deplorable misery and abject submission, the whole of that part of the island was considered as restored to good order; and in commemoration of this great triumph Ovando founded a town near to the lake, which he called Santa Maria de la Verdadera Paz (St. Mary of the True Peace).[1]

Such is the tragical history of the delightful region of Xaragua, and of its amiable and hospitable people. A place which the Europeans, by their own account, found a perfect paradise, but which, by their vile passions, they filled with horror and desolation.

CHAPTER III.

WAR WITH THE NATIVES OF HIGUEY.

[1504.]

THE subjugation of four of the Indian sovereignties of Hispaniola, and the disastrous fate of their caciques, have been already related. Under the administration of Ovando was also accomplished the downfall of Higuey, the last of those independent districts; a fertile province which comprised the eastern extremity of the island.

The people of Higuey were of a more warlike spirit than those of the other provinces, having learned the effectual use of their weapons, from frequent contests with their Carib invaders. They were governed by a cacique named Cotabanama. Las Casas describes this chieftain from actual observation, and draws the picture of a native hero. He was, he says, the strongest of his tribe, and more perfectly formed than one man in a thousand, of any nation whatever. He was taller in stature than the tallest of his countrymen, a yard in breadth from shoulder to shoulder, and the rest of his body in admirable proportion. His aspect was not handsome, but grave and courageous. His bow was not easily bent by a common man: his arrows were three pronged, tipped with the bones of fishes, and his weapons appeared to be intended for a giant. In a word, he was so nobly proportioned as to be the admiration even of the Spaniards.

While Columbus was engaged in his fourth voyage, and shortly after the accession of Ovando to office, there was an

---

[1] Oviedo, Cronica de las Indias, lib. iii. cap. 12.

insurrection of this cacique and his people   A shallop, with eight Spaniards, was surprised at the small island of Saona, adjacent to Higuey, and all the crew slaughtered. This was in revenge for the death of a cacique, torn to pieces by a dog wantonly set upon him by a Spaniard, and for which the natives had in vain sued for redress.

Ovando immediately despatched Juan de Esquibel, a courageous officer, at the head of four hundred men, to quell the insurrection and punish the massacre. Cotabanama assembled his warriors, and prepared for vigorous resistance. Distrustful of the mercy of the Spaniards, the chieftain rejected all overtures of peace, and the war was prosecuted with some advantage to the natives. The Indians had now overcome their superstitious awe of the white men as supernatural beings, and though they could ill withstand the superiority of European arms, they manifested a courage and dexterity that rendered them enemies not to be despised. Las Casas and other historians relate a bold and romantic encounter between a single Indian and two mounted cavaliers named Valtenebro and Portevedra, in which the Indian, though pierced through the body by the lances and swords of both his assailants, retained his fierceness, and continued the combat until he fell dead in the possession of all their weapons.[1] This gallant action, says Las Casas, was public and notorious

The Indians were soon defeated and driven to their mountain retreats. The Spaniards pursued them into their recesses, discovered their wives and children, wreaked on them the most indiscriminate slaughter, and committed their chieftains to the flames. An aged female cacique of great distinction, named Higuanama, being taken prisoner, was hanged.

A detachment was sent in a caravel to the island of Saona, to take particular vengeance for the destruction of the shallop and its crew. The natives made a desperate defence and fled. The island was mountainous and full of caverns, in which the Indians vainly sought for refuge. Six or seven hundred were imprisoned in a dwelling, and all put to the sword or poniarded. Those of the inhabitants who were spared were carried off as slaves, and the island was left desolate and deserted.

The natives of Higuey were driven to despair, seeing that there was no escape for them even in the bowels of the earth ;[2] they sued for peace, which was granted them, and protection promised on condition of their cultivating a large tract of land,

---

[1] Las Casas, Hist. Ind., lib. ii. cap. 8.   [2] Ibid., ubi sup.

and paying a great quantity of bread in tribute. The peace being concluded, Cotabanama visited the Spanish camp, where his gigantic proportions and martial demeanor made him an object of curiosity and admiration. He was received with great distinction by Esquibel, and they exchanged names, an Indian league of fraternity and perpetual friendship. The natives thenceforward called the cacique Juan de Esquibel, and the Spanish commander Cotabanama. Esquibel then built a wooden fortress in an Indian village near the sea, and left in it nine men, with a captain, named Martin de Villaman. After this the troops dispersed, every man returning home, with his proportion of slaves gained in this expedition.

The pacification was not of long continuance. About the time that succors were sent to Columbus, to rescue him from the wrecks of his vessels at Jamaica, a new revolt broke out in Higuey, in consequence of the oppressions of the Spaniards, and a violation of the treaty made by Esquibel. Martin de Villaman demanded that the natives should not only raise the grain stipulated for by the treaty, but convey it to San Domingo. and he treated them with the greatest severity on their refusal. He connived also at the licentious conduct of his men toward the Indian women : the Spaniards often taking from the natives their daughters and sisters, and even their wives.[1] The Indians, roused at last to fury, rose on their tyrants, slaughtered them, and burnt their wooden fortress to the ground. Only one of the Spaniards escaped, and bore the tidings of this catastrophe to the city of San Domingo.

Ovando gave immediate orders to carry fire and sword into the province of Higuey. The Spanish troops mustered from various quarters on the confines of that province, when Juan de Esquibel took the command, and had a great number of Indians with him as allies. The towns of Higuey were generally built among the mountains. Those mountains rose in terraces from ten to fifteen leagues in length and breadth ; rough and rocky, interspersed with glens of a red soil, remarkably fertile, where they raised their cassava bread. The ascent from terrace to terrace was about fifty feet ; steep and precipitous, formed of the living rock, and resembling a wall wrought with tools into rough diamond points. Each village had four wide streets, a stone's throw in length, forming a cross, the trees being cleared away from them, and from a public square in the centre.

---

[1] Las Casas, ubi sup.

When the Spanish troops arrived on the frontiers, alarm fires along the mountains and columns of smoke spread the intelligence by night and day. The old men, the women, and children, were sent off to the forests and caverns, and the warriors prepared for battle. The Castilians paused in one of the plains clear of forests, where their horses could be of use. They made prisoners of several of the natives, and tried to learn from them the plans and forces of the enemy. They applied tortures for the purpose, but in vain, so devoted was the loyalty of these people to their caciques. The Spaniards penetrated into the interior. They found the warriors of several towns assembled in one, and drawn up in the streets with their bows and arrows, but perfectly naked, and without defensive armor. They uttered tremendous yells, and discharged a shower of arrows; but from such a distance that they fell short of their foe. The Spaniards replied with their cross-bows, and with two or three arquebuses, for at this time they had but few fire-arms. When the Indians saw several of their comrades fall dead, they took to flight, rarely waiting for the attack with swords; some of the wounded, in whose bodies the arrows from the cross-bows had penetrated to the very feather, drew them out with their hands, broke them with their teeth, and hurling them at the Spaniards with impotent fury, fell dead upon the spot.

The whole force of the Indians was routed and dispersed: each family, or band of neighbors, fled in its own direction, and concealed itself in the fastness of the mountains. The Spaniards pursued them, but found the chase difficult amid the close forests, and the broken and stony heights. They took several prisoners as guides, and inflicted incredible torments on them, to compel them to betray their countrymen. They drove them before them, secured by cords fastened round their necks; and some of them, as they passed along the brinks of precipices, suddenly threw themselves headlong down, in hopes of dragging after them the Spaniards. When at length the pursuers came upon the unhappy Indians in their concealments, they spared neither age nor sex; even pregnant women, and mothers with infants in their arms, fell beneath their merciless swords. The cold-blooded acts of cruelty which followed this first slaughter would be shocking to relate.

Hence Esquibel marched to attack the town where Cotabanama resided, and where that cacique had collected a great force to resist him. He proceeded direct for the place along the seacoast, and came to where two roads led up the mountain to the town. One of the roads was open and inviting; the branches of the trees being lopped, and all the underwood cleared away. Here the Indians had stationed an ambuscade to take the Spaniards in the rear. The other road was almost closed up by trees and bushes cut down and thrown across each other. Esquibel was wary and distrustful: he suspected the stratagem, and chose the encumbered road. The town was about a league and a half from the sea. The Spaniards made their way with great difficulty for the first half league. The rest of the road was free from all embarrassment, which confirmed their suspicion of a stratagem. They now advanced with great rapidity, and, having arrived near the village, suddenly turned into the other road, took the party in ambush by surprise, and made great havoc among them with their crossbows.

The warriors now sallied from their concealment, others rushed out of the houses into the streets, and discharged flights of arrows, but from such a distance as generally to fall harmless. They then approached nearer, and hurled stones with their hands, being unacquainted with the use of slings. Instead of being dismayed at seeing their companions fall, it rather increased their fury. An irregular battle, probably little else than wild skirmishing and bush-fighting, was kept up from two o'clock in the afternoon until night. Las Casas was present on the occasion, and, from his account, the Indians must have shown instances of great personal bravery, though the inferiority of their weapons, and the want of all defensive armor, rendered their valor totally ineffectual. As the evening shut in, their hostilities gradually ceased, and they disappeared in the profound gloom and closed thickets of the surrounding forest. A deep silence succeeded to their yells and war-whoops, and throughout the night the Spaniards remained in undisturbed possession of the village.

CHAPTER IV.

CLOSE OF THE WAR WITH HIGUEY — FATE OF COTABANAMA.

[1504.]

ON the morning after the battle not an Indian was to be seen. Finding that even their great chief, Cotabanama, was incapable of vying with the prowess of the white men, they had given up the contest in despair, and fled to the mountains, The Spaniards, separating into small parties, hunted them with the utmost diligence, their object was to seize the caciques, and, above all, Cotabanama. They explored all the glens and concealed paths leading into the wild recesses where the fugitives had taken refuge. The Indians were cautious and stealthy in their mode of retreating, treading in each other's footprints, so that twenty would make no more track than one, and stepping so lightly as scarce to disturb the herbage; yet there were Spaniards so skilled in hunting Indians that they could trace them even by the turn of a withered leaf, and among the confused tracks of a thousand animals.

They could scent afar off also the smoke of the fires which the Indians made whenever they halted, and thus they would come upon them in their most secret haunts. Sometimes they would hunt down a straggling Indian, and compel him, by torments, to betray the hiding-place of his companions, binding him, and driving him before them as a guide. Wherever they discovered one of these places of refuge, filled with the aged and the infirm, with feeble women and helpless children, they massacred them without mercy. They wished to inspire terror throughout the land, and to frighten the whole tribe into submission. They cut off the hands of those whom they took roving at large, and sent them, as they said, to deliver them as letters to their friends, demanding their surrender. Numberless were those, says Las Casas, whose hands were amputated in this manner, and many of them sank down and died by the way, through anguish and loss of blood.

The conquerors delighted in exercising strange and ingenious cruelties. They mingled horrible levity with their blood-thirstiness. They erected gibbets long and low, so that the feet of the sufferers might reach the ground, and their death be lingering. They hanged thirteen together, in reverence, says the indignant Las Casas, of our blessed Saviour and the twelve apostles. While their victims were suspended, and still living, they hacked them with their swords, to prove the strength of their arms and the edge of their weapons. They wrapped them in dry straw, and setting fire to it terminated their existence by the fiercest agony.

These are horrible details, yet a veil is drawn over others still more detestable. They are related circumstantially by Las Casas, who was an eye-witness. He was young at the time, but records them in his advanced years. " All these things," said the venerable bishop, " and others revolting to human nature, did my own eyes behold; and now I almost fear to repeat them. scarce believing myself. or whether I have not dreamt them.''[1]

These details would have been withheld from the present work as disgraceful to human nature, and from an unwillingness to advance any thing which might convey a stigma upon a brave and generous nation. But it would be a departure from historical veracity. having the documents before my eyes, to pass silently over transactions so atrocious, and vouched for by witnesses beyond all suspicion of falsehood. Such occurrences show the extremity to which human cruelty may extend, when stimulated by avidity of gain, by a thirst of vengeance, or even by a perverted zeal in the holy cause of religion. Every nation has in turn furnished proofs of this disgraceful truth. As in the present instance, they are commonly the crimes of individuals rather than of the nation. Yet it behooves governments to keep a vigilant eye upon those to whom they delegate power in remote and helpless colonies. It is the imperious duty of the historian to place these matters upon record, that they may serve as warning beacons to future generations.

Juan de Esquibel found that, with all his severities. it would be impossible to subjugate the tribe of Higuey as long as the cacique Cotabanama was at large. That chieftain had retired to the little island of Saona, about two leagues from the coast of Higuey. in the centre of which, amid a labyrinth of rocks and forests, he had taken shelter, with his wife and children, in a vast cavern.

A caravel, recently arrived from the city of San Domingo with supplies for the camp, was employed by Esquibel to entrap the cacique. He knew that the latter kept a vigilant look-out, stationing scouts upon the lofty rocks of his island to watch the movements of the caravel. Esquibel departed by night, therefore, in the vessel, with fifty followers, and keeping under the deep shadows cast by the land. arrived at Saona unperceived, at the dawn of morning Here he anchored close in with the shore, hid by its cliffs and forests, and landed forty men, before the spies of Cotabanama had taken their station. Two of these were surprised and brought to Esquibel, who, having learnt from them that the cacique was at hand, poniarded one of the spies, and bound the other, making him serve as guide.

A number of Spaniards ran in advance, each anxious to sig-

---

[1] Las Casas lib. d cap. 17, MS.

nalize himself by the capture of the cacique. They came to two roads, and the whole party pursued that to the right, excepting one Juan Lopez, a powerful man, skilful in Indian warfare. He proceeded in a foot-path to the left, winding among little hills, so thickly wooded that it was impossible to see any one at a distance of half a bow-shot. Suddenly, in a narrow pass, overshadowed by rocks and trees, he encountered twelve Indian warriors, armed with bows and arrows, and following each other in single file according to their custom. The Indians were confounded at the sight of Lopez, imagining that there must be a party of soldiers behind him. They might readily have transfixed him with their arrows, but they had lost all presence of mind. He demanded their chieftain. They replied that he was behind, and opening to let him pass, Lopez beheld the cacique in the rear. At sight of the Spaniard Cotabanama bent his gigantic bow, and was on the point of launching one of his three-pronged arrows, but Lopez rushed upon him and wounded him with his sword. The other Indians, struck with panic, had already fled. Cotabanama, dismayed at the keenness of the sword, cried out that he was Juan de Esquibel, claiming respect as having exchanged names with the Spanish commander. Lopez seized him with one hand by the hair, and with the other aimed a thrust at his body; but the cacique struck down the sword with his hand, and, grappling with his antagonist, threw him with his back upon the rocks. As they were both men of great power, the struggle was long and violent. The sword was beneath them, but Cotabanama, seizing the Spaniard by the throat with his mighty hand, attempted to strangle him. The sound of the contest brought the other Spaniards to the spot. They found their companion writhing and gasping, and almost dead, in the gripe of the gigantic Indian. They seized the cacique, bound him, and carried him captive to a deserted Indian village in the vicinity. They found the way to his secret cave, but his wife and children having received notice of his capture by the fugitive Indians, had taken refuge in another part of the island. In the cavern was found the chain with which a number of Indian captives had been bound, who had risen upon and slain three Spaniards who had them in charge, and had made their escape to this island. There were also the swords of the same Spaniards, which they had brought off as trophies to their cacique. The chain was now employed to manacle Cotabanama.

The Spaniards prepared to execute the chieftain on the spot, in the centre of the deserted village. For this purpose a pyre was built of logs of wood laid crossways, in form of a gridiron, on which he was to be slowly broiled to death. On further consultation, however, they were induced to forego the pleasure of this horrible sacrifice. Perhaps they thought the cacique too important a personage to be executed thus obscurely. Granting him, therefore, a transient reprieve, they conveyed him to the caravel and sent him, bound with heavy chains, to San Domingo. Ovando saw him in his power, and incapable of doing further harm; but he had not the magnanimity to forgive a fallen enemy, whose only crime was the defence of his native soil and lawful territory. He ordered him to be publicly hanged like a common culprit.[1] In this ignominious manner was the cacique Cotabanama executed, the last of the five sovereign princes of Hayti. His death was followed by the complete subjugation of his people, and sealed the last struggle of the natives against their oppressors. The island was almost un-peopled of its original inhabitants, and meek and mournful submission and mute despair settled upon the scanty remnant that survived.

Such was the ruthless system which had been pursued, during the absence of the admiral, by the commander Ovando: this man of boasted prudence and moderation, who was sent to re-form the abuses of the island, and above all, to redress the wrongs of the natives. The system of Columbus may have borne hard upon the Indians, born and brought up in untasked freedom, but it was never cruel or sanguinary. He inflicted no wanton massacres nor vindictive punishments: his desire was to cherish and civilize the Indians, and to render them use-ful subjects; not to oppress, and persecute, and destroy them. When he beheld the desolation that had swept them from the land during his suspension from authority, he could not restrain the strong expression of his feelings. In a letter written to the king after his return to Spain, he thus expresses himself on the subject: "The Indians of Hispaniola were and are the riches of the island; for it is they who cultivate and make the bread and the provisions for the Christians; who dig the gold from the mines, and perform all the offices and labors both of men and beasts. I am informed that, since I left this island, six parts out of seven of the natives are dead; all through ill treatment and inhumanity; some by the sword, others by blows and cruel usage, others through hunger. The greater part have

---

Las Casas, Hist Ind., lib. ii. cap. 18.

perished in the mountains and glens, whither they have fled, from not being able to support the labor imposed upon them." For his own part, he added, although he had sent many Indians to Spain to be sold, it was always with a view to their being instructed in the Christian faith, and in civilized arts and usages, and afterward sent back to their island to assist in civilizing their countrymen.[1]

The brief view that has been given of the policy of Ovando on certain points on which Columbus was censured, may enable the reader to judge more correctly of the conduct of the latter It is not to be measured by the standard of right and wrong established in the present more enlightened age We must consider him in connection with the era in which he lived. By comparing his measures with those of men of his own times praised for their virtues and abilities, placed in precisely his own situation, and placed there expressly to correct his faults, we shall be the better able to judge how virtuously and wisely, under the peculiar circumstances of the case, he may be considered to have governed.

---

[1] Las Casas, Hist. Ind., lib. ii. cap 36.

BOOK XVIII.

CHAPTER I.

DEPARTURE OF COLUMBUS FOR SAN DOMINGO — HIS RETURN TO SPAIN.

THE arrival at Jamaica of the two vessels under the command of Salcedo had caused a joyful reverse in the situation of Columbus. He hastened to leave the wreck in which he had been so long immured, and hoisting his flag on board of one of the ships, felt as if the career of enterprise and glory were once more open to him. The late partisans of Porras, when they heard of the arrival of the ships, came wistful and abject to the harbor, doubting how far they might trust to the magnanimity of a man whom they had so greatly injured, and who had now an opportunity of vengeance. The generous mind, however, never harbors revenge in the hour of returning prosperity; but feels noble satisfaction in sharing its happiness even with its enemies. Columbus forgot, in his present felicity, all that he had suffered from these men; he ceased to consider them enemies, now that they had lost the power to injure; and he not only fulfilled all that he had promised them, by taking them on board the ships, but relieved their necessities from his own purse, until their return to Spain; and afterward took unwearied pains to recommend them to the bounty of the sovereigns Francisco Porras alone continued a prisoner, to be tried by the tribunals of his country.

Oviedo assures us that the Indians wept when they beheld the departure of the Spaniards; still considering them as beings from the skies. From the admiral, it is true, they had experienced nothing but just and gentle treatment, and continual benefits; and the idea of his immediate influence with the Deity, manifested on the memorable occasion of the eclipse, may have made them consider him as more than human, and his presence as propitious to their island; but it is not easy to believe that a lawless gang like that of Porras could have been ranging for months among their villages, without giving cause for the greatest joy at their departure.

On the 28th of June the vessels set sail for San Domingo. The adverse winds and currents which had opposed Columbus throughout this ill-starred expedition still continued to harass him. After a weary struggle of several weeks he reached, on the 3d of August, the little island of Beata, on the coast of Hispaniola. Between this place and San Domingo the currents are so violent that vessels are often detained months, waiting for sufficient wind to enable them to stem the stream. Hence Columbus despatched a letter by land to Ovando, to inform him of his approach, and to remove certain absurd suspicions of his views, which he had learnt from Salcedo were still entertained by the governor; who feared his arrival in the island might produce factions and disturbances. In this letter he expresses, with his usual warmth and simplicity, the joy he felt at his deliverance, which was so great, he says, that, since the arrival of Diego de Salcedo with succor, he had scarcely been able to sleep. The letter had barely time to precede the writer, for, a favorable wind springing up, the vessels again made sail, and, on the 13th of August, anchored in the harbor of San Domingo.

If it is the lot of prosperity to awaken envy and excite detraction, it is certainly the lot of misfortune to atone for a multitude of faults. San Domingo had been the very hot-bed of sedition against Columbus in the day of his power; he had been hurried from it in ignominious chains, amid the shouts and taunts of the triumphant rabble; he had been excluded from its harbor when, as commander of a squadron, he craved shelter from an impending tempest; but now that he arrived in its waters, a broken down and shipwrecked man, all past hostility was overpowered by the popular sense of his late disasters. There was a momentary burst of enthusiasm in his favor; what had been denied to his merits was granted to his misfortunes; and even the envious, appeased by his present reverses, seemed to forgive him for having once been so triumphant.

The governor and principal inhabitants came forth to meet him, and received him with signal distinction. He was lodged as a guest in the house of Ovando, who treated him with the utmost courtesy and attention. The governor was a shrewd and discreet man and much of a courtier; but there were causes of jealousy and distrust between him and Columbus too deep to permit of cordial intercourse. The admiral and his son Fernando always pronounced the civility of Ovando over-strained and hypocritical; intended to obliterate the remembrance of past neglect, and to conceal lurking enmity. While he professed the utmost friendship and sympathy for the admiral, he set at liberty the traitor Porras, who was still a prisoner, to be taken to Spain for trial. He also talked of punishing those of the admiral's people who had taken arms in his defence, and in the affray at Jamaica had killed several of the mutineers. These circumstances were loudly complained of by Columbus; but, in fact, they rose out of a question of jurisdiction between him and the governor. Their powers were so undefined as to clash with each other, and they were both disposed to be extremely punctilious. Ovando assumed a right to take cognizance of all transactions at Jamaica; as happening within the limits of his government, which included all the islands and Terra Firma. Columbus, on the other hand, asserted the absolute command, and the jurisdiction both civil and criminal given to him by the sovereigns, over all persons who sailed in his expedition, from the time of departure until they returned to Spain. To prove this he produced his letter of instructions. The governor heard him with great courtesy and a smiling countenance; but observed that the letter of instructions gave him no authority within the bounds of his government.[1] He relinquished the idea, however, of investigating the conduct of the followers of Columbus, and sent Porras to Spain, to be examined by the board which had charge of the affairs of the Indies.

The sojourn of Columbus at San Domingo was but little calculated to yield him satisfaction. He was grieved at the desolation of the island by the oppressive treatment of the natives, and the horrible massacre which had been perpetrated by Ovando and his agents. He had fondly hoped, at one time, to render the natives civilized, industrious, and tributary subjects to the crown, and to derive from their well-regulated labor a great and steady revenue. How different had been the event! The five great tribes which peopled the mountains and the valleys at the time of the discovery, and rendered, by their mingled towns and villages and tracts of cultivation, the rich levels of the Vega so many " painted gardens," had almost all passed away, and the native princes had perished chiefly by violent or ignominious deaths. Columbus regarded the affairs of the island with a different eye from Ovando. He had a paternal feeling for its prosperity, and his fortunes were implicated in its judicious management. He complained, in subse-

---

[1] Letter of Columbus to his son Diego, Seville, Nov. 21, 1504. Navarrete, Colec., tom. i

quent letters to the sovereigns, that all the public affairs were ill conducted; that the ore collected lay unguarded in large quantities in houses slightly built, and thatched, inviting depredation; that Ovando was unpopular, the people were dissolute, and the property of the crown and the security of the island in continual risk from mutiny and sedition.[1] While he saw all this, he had no power to interfere, and any observation or remonstrance on his part was ill received by the governor.

He found his own immediate concerns in great confusion. His rents and dues were either uncollected, or he could not obtain a clear account and a full liquidation of them. Whatever he could collect was appropriated to the fitting out of the vessels which were to convey himself and his crews to Spain. He accuses Ovando, in his subsequent letters, of having neglected, if not sacrificed, his interests during his long absence, and of having impeded those who were appointed to attend to his concerns. That he had some grounds for these complaints would appear from two letters still extant,[2] written by Queen Isabella to Ovando, on the 27th of November, 1503, in which she informs him of the complaint of Alonzo Sanchez de Carvajal, that he was impeded in collecting the rents of the admiral; and expressly commands Ovando to observe the capitulations granted to Columbus; to respect his agents, and to facilitate, instead of obstructing his concerns. These letters, while they imply ungenerous conduct on the part of the governor toward his illustrious predecessor, evince likewise the personal interest taken by Isabella in the affairs of Columbus, during his absence. She had, in fact, signified her displeasure at his being excluded from the port of San Domingo, when he applied there for succor for his squadron, and for shelter from a storm, and had censured Ovando for not taking his advice and detaining the fleet of Bobadilla, by which it would have escaped its disastrous fate.[3] And here it may be observed that the sanguinary acts of Ovando toward the natives, in particular the massacre at Xaragua and the execution of the unfortunate Anacaona, awakened equal horror and indignation in Isabella; she was languishing on her death-bed when she received the intelligence, and with her dying breath she exacted a promise from King Ferdinand that Ovando should immediately be recalled from his government. The promise was tardily and

[1] Letter of Columbus to his son Diego, dated Seville, 3d Dec., 1504. Navarrete, tom. i. p. 341

[2] Navarrete, Colec., tom. ii. decad. 151, 152.

[3] Herrera, Hist. Ind., decad i. lib. v. cap 12.

reluctantly fulfilled, after an interval of about four years, and not until induced by other circumstances ; for Ovando contrived to propitiate the monarch, by forcing a revenue from the island.

The continual misunderstandings between the admiral and the governor, though always qualified on the part of the latter with great complaisance, induced Columbus to hasten as much as possible his departure from the island. The ship in which he had returned from Jamaica was repaired and fitted out, and put under the command of the Adelantado ; another vessel was freighted, in which Columbus embarked with his son and his domestics. The greater part of his late crews remained at San Domingo ; as they were in great poverty, he relieved their necessities from his own purse, and advanced the funds necessary for the voyage home of those who chose to return. Many thus relieved by his generosity had been among the most violent of the rebels.

On the 12th of September he set sail : but had scarcely left the harbor when, in a sudden squall, the mast of his ship was carried away. He immediately went with his family on board of the vessel commanded by the Adelantado, and, sending back the damaged ship to port, continued on his course. Throughout the voyage he experienced the most tempestuous weather. In one storm the main-mast was sprung in four places. He was confined to his bed at the time by the gout ; by his advice, however, and the activity of the Adelantado, the damage was skilfully repaired ; the mast was shortened ; the weak parts were fortified by wood taken from the castles or cabins, which the vessels in those days carried on the prow and stern ; and the whole was well secured by cords. They were still more damaged in a succeeding tempest, in which the ship sprung her fore-mast. In this crippled state they had to traverse seven hundred leagues of a stormy ocean. Fortune continued to persecute Columbus to the end of this, his last and most disastrous expedition. For several weeks he was tempest-tossed — suffering at the same time the most excruciating pains from his malady — until, on the seventh day of November, his crazy and shattered bark anchored in the harbor of San Lucar. Hence he had himself conveyed to Seville, where he hoped to enjoy repose of mind and body, and to recruit his health after such a long series of fatigues, anxieties, and hardships.[1]

---

[1] Hist. del Almirante, cap. 108. Las Casas, Hist. Ind., lib. ii cap. 36.

CHAPTER II.

ILLNESS OF COLUMBUS AT SEVILLE — APPLICATION TO THE CROWN
FOR A RESTITUTION OF HIS HONORS — DEATH OF ISABELLA.

[1504.]

BROKEN by age and infirmities, and worn down by the toils
and hardships of his recent expedition, Columbus had looked
forward to Seville as to a haven of rest, where he might repose
a while from his troubles. Care and sorrow, however, followed
him by sea and land. In varying the scene he but varied the
nature of his distress. "Wearisome days and nights" were
appointed to him for the remainder of his life; and the very
margin of his grave was destined to be strewed with thorns.

On arriving at Seville, he found all his affairs in confusion.
Ever since he had been sent home in chains from San Domingo,
when his house and effects had been taken possession of by
Bobadilla, his rents and dues had never been properly collected;
and such as had been gathered had been retained in the hands
of the governor Ovando. "I have much vexation from the
governor," says he in a letter to his son Diego.[2] "All tell me
that I have there eleven or twelve thousand castellanos; and I
have not received a quarto. * * * I know well that, since
my departure he must have received upward of five thousand
castellanos." He entreated that a letter might be written by
the king, commanding the payment of these arrears without
delay; for his agents would not venture even to speak to
Ovando on the subject, unless empowered by a letter from the
sovereign.

Columbus was not of a mercenary spirit; but his rank and
situation required large expenditure. The world thought him
in the possession of sources of inexhaustible wealth; but as
yet those sources had furnished him but precarious and scanty
streams. His last voyage had exhausted his finances, and involved him in perplexities. All that he had been able to collect
of the money due to him in Hispaniola, to the amount of twelve
hundred castellanos, had been expended in bringing home
many of his late crew, who were in distress; and for the
greater part of the sum the crown remained his debtor.

---

[2] Let. Seville, 15 Dec., 1504. Navarrete, v. 1. p. 343.

While struggling to obtain his mere pecuniary dues, he was absolutely suffering a degree of penury. He repeatedly urges the necessity of economy to his son Diego, until he can obtain a restitution of his property, and the payment of his arrears. " I receive nothing of the revenue due to me," says he, in one letter ; " I live by borrowing." " Little have I profited," he adds, in another, " by twenty years of service, with such toils and perils : since, at present, I do not own a roof in Spain. If I desire to eat or sleep, I have no resort but an inn ; and, for the most times, have not wherewithal to pay my bill."

Yet in the midst of these personal distresses he was more solicitous for the payment of his seamen than of himself. He wrote strongly and repeatedly to the sovereigns, entreating the discharge of their arrears, and urged his son Diego, who was at court, to exert himself in their behalf. " They are poor," said he, " and it is now nearly three years since they left their homes. They have endured infinite toils and perils, and they bring invaluable tidings, for which their majesties ought to give thanks to God and rejoice." Notwithstanding his generous solicitude for these men, he knew several of them to have been his enemies ; nay, that some of them were at this very time disposed to do him harm rather than good ; such was the magnanimity of his spirit and his forgiving disposition.

The same zeal, also, for the interests of his sovereigns, which had ever actuated his loyal mind, mingled with his other causes of solicitude. He represented, in his letter to the king, the mismanagement of the royal rents in Hispaniola, under the administration of Ovando. Immense quantities of ore lay unprotected in slightly built houses, and liable to depredations. It required a person of vigor, and one who had an individual interest in the property of the island, to restore its affairs to order, and draw from it the immense revenues which it was capable of yielding ; and Columbus plainly intimated that he was the proper person.

In fact, as to himself, it was not so much pecuniary indemnification that he sought, as the restoration of his offices and dignities He regarded them as the trophies of his illustrious achievements ; he had received the royal promise that he should be reinstated in them ; and he felt that as long as they were withheld, a tacit censure rested upon his name. Had he not been proudly impatient on this subject he would have belied the loftiest part of his character ; for he who can be indifferent to the wreath of triumph is deficient in the noble ambition which incites to glorious deeds.

The unsatisfactory replies received to his letters disquieted his mind. He knew that he had active enemies at court ready to turn all things to his disadvantage, and felt the importance of being there in person to defeat their machinations; but his infirmities detained him at Seville. He made an attempt to set forth on the journey, but the severity of the winter and the virulence of his malady obliged him to relinquish it in despair. All that he could do was to reiterate his letters to the sovereigns, and to entreat the intervention of his few but faithful friends. He feared the disastrous occurrences of the last voyage might be represented to his prejudice. The great object of the expedition, the discovery of a strait opening from the Caribbean to a southern sea, had failed. The secondary object, the acquisition of gold, had not been completed. He had discovered the gold mines of Veragua, it is true; but he had brought home no treasure; because, as he said, in one of his letters, " I would not rob nor outrage the country; since reason requires that it should be settled, and then the gold may be procured without violence "

He was especially apprehensive that the violent scenes in the island of Jamaica might, by the perversity of his enemies and the effrontery of the delinquents, be wrested into matters of accusation against him, as had been the case with the rebellion of Roldan. Porras, the ringleader of the late faction, had been sent home by Ovando, to appear before the board of the Indies, but without any written process, setting forth the offences charged against him. While at Jamaica Columbus had ordered an inquest of the affair to be taken; but the notary of the squadron who took it, and the papers which he drew up, were on board of the ship in which the admiral had sailed from Hispaniola, but which had put back dismasted. No cognizance of the case, therefore, was taken by the Council of the Indies: and Porras went at large, armed with the power and the disposition to do mischief. Being related to Morales, the royal treasurer, he had access to people in place, and an opportunity of enlisting their opinions and prejudices on his side. Columbus wrote to Morales, enclosing a copy of the petition which the rebels had sent to him when in Jamaica, in which they acknowledged their culpability, and implored his forgiveness, and he entreated the treasurer not to be swayed by the representations of his relative, nor to pronounce an opinion unfavorable to him, until he had an opportunity of being heard

The faithful and indefatigable Diego Mendez was at this time at the court, as well as Alonzo Sanchez de Carvajal, and an active friend of Columbus named Geronimo. They could bear the most important testimony as to his conduct, and he wrote to his son Diego to call upon them for their good offices. "I trust," said he, "that the truth and diligence of Diego Mendez will be of as much avail as the lies of Porras." Nothing can surpass the affecting earnestness and simplicity of the general declaration of loyalty, contained in one of his letters. "I have served their majesties," says he, "with as much zeal and diligence as if it had been to gain Paradise; and if I have failed in any thing, it has been because my knowledge and powers went no further."

While reading these touching appeals we can scarcely realize the fact that the dejected individual thus wearily and vainly applying for unquestionable rights, and pleading almost like a culprit, in cases wherein he had been flagrantly injured, was the same who but a few years previously had been received at this very court with almost regal honors, and idolized as a national benefactor; that this, in a word, was Columbus, the discoverer of the New World; broken in health, and impoverished in his old days by his very discoveries.

At length the caravel bringing the official proceedings relative to the brothers Porras arrived at the Algarves, in Portugal, and Columbus looked forward with hope that all matters would soon be placed in a proper light. His anxiety to get to court became every day more intense. A litter was provided to convey him thither, and was actually at the door, but the inclemency of the weather and his increasing infirmities obliged him again to abandon the journey. His resource of letter-writing began to fail him: he could only write at night, for in the daytime the severity of his malady deprived him of the use of his hands. The tidings from the court were every day more and more adverse to his hopes; the intrigues of his enemies were prevailing, the cold-hearted Ferdinand treated all his applications with indifference; the generous Isabella lay dangerously ill. On her justice and magnanimity he still relied for the full restoration of his rights, and the redress of all his grievances. "May it please the Holy Trinity," says he, "to restore our sovereign queen to health; for by her will every thing be adjusted which is now in confusion." Alas! while writing that letter, his noble benefactress was a corpse!

The health of Isabella had long been undermined by the shocks of repeated domestic calamities. The death of her only son, the Prince Juan; of her beloved daughter and bosom friend, the Princess Isabella; and of her grandson and prospective heir, the Prince Miguel, had been three cruel wounds to a heart full of the tenderest sensibility. To these was added the constant grief caused by the evident infirmity of intellect of her daughter Juana, and the domestic unhappiness of that princess with her husband, the archduke Philip. The desolation which walks through palaces admits not the familiar sympathies and sweet consolations which alleviate the sorrows of common life. Isabella pined in state, amidst the obsequious homages of a court, surrounded by the trophies of a glorious and successful reign, and placed at the summit of earthly grandeur. A deep and incurable melancholy settled upon her, which undermined her constitution, and gave a fatal acuteness to her bodily maladies. After four months of illness she died, on the 26th of November, 1504, at Medina del Campo, in the fifty-fourth year of her age; but long before her eyes closed upon the world, her heart had closed on all its pomps and vanities. " Let my body," said she in her will, " be interred in the monastery of San Francisco, which is in the Alhambra of the city of Granada, in a low sepulchre, without any monument except a plain stone, with the inscription cut on it. But I desire and command, that if the king, my lord, should choose a sepulchre in any church or monastery in any other part or place of these my kingdoms, my body be transported thither, and buried beside the body of his highness; so that the union we have enjoyed while living, and which, through the mercy of God, we hope our souls will experience in heaven, may be represented by our bodies in the earth." [1]

Such was one of several passages in the will of this admirable woman, which bespoke the chastened humility of her heart; and in which, as has been well observed, the affections of conjugal love were delicately intwined with piety, and with the most tender melancholy.[2] She was one of the purest spirits that ever ruled over the destinies of a nation. Had she been spared, her benignant vigilance would have prevented many a scene of horror in the colonization of the New World, and might have softened the lot of its native inhabitants. As it is, her fair name will ever shine with celestial radiance in the dawning of its history

The news of the death of Isabella reached Columbus when he

---

[1] The dying command of Isabella has been obeyed. The author of this work has seen her tomb in the royal chapel of the Cathedral of Granada, in which her remains are interred with those of Ferdinand. Their effigies, sculptured in white marble, lie side by side on a magnificent sepulchre. The altar of the chapel is adorned with bas-reliefs representing the conquest and surrender of Granada.

[2] Elogio de la Reina Catolica por D. Diego Clemencid. Illustration 19.

was writing a letter to his son Diego. He notices it in a postscript or memorandum, written in the haste and brevity of the moment, but in beautifully touching and mournful terms. " A memorial," he writes, " for thee, my dear son Diego, of what is at present to be done. The principal thing is to commend affectionately, and with great devotion, the soul of the queen our sovereign to God. Her life was always catholic and holy, and prompt to all things in his holy service ; for this reason we may rest assured that she is received into his glory, and beyond the cares of this rough and weary world. The next thing is to watch and labor in all matters for the service of our sovereign the king, and to endeavor to alleviate his grief. His majesty is the head of Christendom. Remember the proverb which says, when the head suffers all the members suffer. Therefore. all good Christians should pray for his health and long life ; and we who are in his employ ought more than others to do this with all study and diligence." [1]

It is impossible to read this mournful letter without being moved by the simply eloquent yet artless language in which Columbus expresses his tenderness for the memory of his benefactress, his weariness under the gathering cares and ills of life, and his persevering and enduring loyalty toward the sovereign who was so ungratefully neglecting him. It is in these unstudied and confidential letters that we read the heart of Columbus

---

CHAPTER III.

COLUMBUS ARRIVES AT COURT — FRUITLESS APPLICATION TO THE KING FOR REDRESS.

[1505.]

THE death of Isabella was a fatal blow to the fortunes of Columbus. While she lived he had every thing to anticipate from her high sense of justice. her regard for her royal word, her gratitude for his services, and her admiration of his character. With her illness. however. his interests had languished, and when she died he was left to the justice and generosity of Ferdinand !

During the remainder of the winter and a part of the spring he

---

[1] Letter to his son Diego. Dec. 3. 1504.

continued at Seville, detained by painful illness, and endeavoring to obtain redress from the government by ineffectual letters. His brother the Adelantado, who supported him with his accustomed fondness and devotion through all his trials, proceeded to court to attend to his interests, taking with him the admiral's younger son Fernando, then aged about seventeen. The latter, the affectionate father repeatedly represents to his son Diego as a man in understanding and conduct, though but a stripling in years, and inculcates the strongest fraternal attachment, alluding to his own brethren with one of those simply eloquent and affecting expressions which stamp his heart upon his letters. "To thy brother conduct thyself as the elder brother should unto the younger. Thou hast no other, and I praise God that this is such a one as thou dost need. Ten brothers would not be too many for thee. Never have I found a better friend to right or left, than my brothers."

Among the persons whom Columbus employed at this time in his missions to the court was Amerigo Vespucci. He describes him as a worthy but unfortunate man, who had not profited as much as he deserved by his undertakings, and who had always been disposed to render him service. His object in employing him appears to have been to prove the value of his last voyage, and that he had been in the most opulent parts of the New World; Vespucci having since touched upon the same coast, in a voyage with Alonzo de Ojeda.

One circumstance occurred at this time which shed a gleam of hope and consolation over his gloomy prospects. Diego de Deza, who had been for some time Bishop of Palencia, was expected at court. This was the same worthy friar who had aided him to advocate his theory before the board of learned men at Salamanca, and had assisted him with his purse when making his proposals to the Spanish court. He had just been promoted and made Archbishop of Seville, but had not yet been installed in office. Columbus directs his son Diego to intrust his interests to this worthy prelate. "Two things," says he, "require particular attention. Ascertain whether the queen, who is now with God, has said any thing concerning me in her testament, and stimulate the Bishop of Palencia, he who was the cause that their highnesses obtained possession of the Indies, who induced me to remain in Castile when I was on the road to leave it."[1] In another letter he says: "If the Bishop of Palencia has arrived, or should arrive, tell him how much I

---

[1] Letter of December 21 1504. Navarrete tom i. p. 346

have been gratified by his prosperity, and that if I come, I shall lodge with his grace, even though he should not invite me, for we must return to our ancient fraternal affection."

The incessant applications of Columbus, both by letter and by the intervention of friends, appear to have been listened to with cool indifference. No compliance was yielded to his requests, and no deference was paid to his opinions, on various points, concerning which he interested himself. New instructions were sent out to Ovando, but not a word of their purport was mentioned to the admiral. It was proposed to send out three bishops, and he entreated in vain to be heard previous to their election. In short, he was not in any way consulted in the affairs of the New World. He felt deeply this neglect, and became every day more impatient of his absence from court. To enable himself to perform the journey with more ease, he applied for permission to use a mule, a royal ordinance having prohibited the employment of those animals under the saddle, in consequence of their universal use having occasioned a decline in the breed of horses. A royal permission was accordingly granted to Columbus, in consideration that his age and infirmities incapacitated him from riding on horseback; but it was a considerable time before the state of his health would permit him to avail himself of that privilege.

The foregoing particulars, gleaned from letters of Columbus recently discovered, show the real state of his affairs, and the mental and bodily affliction sustained by him during his winter's residence at Seville, on his return from his last disastrous voyage. He has generally been represented as reposing there from his toils and troubles. Never was honorable repose more merited, more desired, and less enjoyed.

It was not until the month of May that he was able, in company with his brother the Adelantado, to accomplish his journey to court, at that time held at Segovia. He who but a few years before had entered the city of Barcelona in triumph, attended by the nobility and chivalry of Spain, and hailed with rapture by the multitude, now arrived within the gates of Segovia, a way-worn, melancholy, and neglected man; oppressed more by sorrow than even by his years and infirmities. When he presented himself at court he met with none of that distinguished attention, that cordial kindness, that cherishing sympathy, which his unparalleled services and his recent sufferings had merited.[1]

---

[1] Las Casas, Hist. Ind., lib. ii. cap. 37. Herrera, Hist. Ind., decad. i. lib. vi. cap. 13.

The selfish Ferdinand had lost sight of his past services, in what appeared to him the inconvenience of his present demands. He received him with many professions of kindness, but with those cold, ineffectual smiles which pass like wintry sunshine over the countenance, and convey no warmth to the heart.

The admiral now gave a particular account of his late voyage, describing the great tract of Terra Firma, which he had explored, and the riches of the province of Veragua. He related also the disaster sustained in the island of Jamaica; the insurrection of the Porras and their band; and all the other griefs and troubles of this unfortunate expedition. He had but a cold-hearted auditor in the king; and the benignant Isabella was no more at hand to soothe him with a smile of kindness or a tear of sympathy. "I know not," says the venerable Las Casas, "what could cause this dislike and this want of princely countenance in the king toward one who had rendered him such pre-eminent benefits; unless it was that his mind was swayed by the false testimonies which had been brought against the admiral; of which I have been enabled to learn something from persons much in favor with the sovereigns."[1]

After a few days had elapsed Columbus urged his suit in form, reminding the king of all that he had done, and all that had been promised him under the royal word and seal, and supplicating that the restitutions and indemnifications which had been so frequently solicited, might be awarded to him: offering in return to serve his majesty devotedly for the short time he had yet to live; and trusting, from what he felt within him, and from what he thought he knew with certainty, to render services which should surpass all that he had yet performed a hundred-fold. The king, in reply, acknowledged the greatness of his merits, and the importance of his services, but observed that, for the more satisfactory adjustment of his claims, it would be advisable to refer all points in dispute to the decision of some discreet and able person. The admiral immediately proposed as arbiter his friend the archbishop of Seville, Don Diego de Deza, one of the most able and upright men about the court, devotedly loyal, high in the confidence of the king, and one who had always taken great interest in the affairs of the New World. The king consented to the arbitration, but artfully extended it to questions which he knew would never be put at issue by Columbus, among these was his claim to the restoration of his office of viceroy. To this Colum-

<hr>

[1] Las Casas, Hist. Ind., lib. ii. cap. 37, MS.

bus objected with becoming spirit, as compromising a right which was too clearly defined and solemnly established, to be put for a moment in dispute. It was the question of rents and revenues alone, he observed, which he was willing to submit to the decision of a learned man, not that of the government of the Indies. As the monarch persisted, however, in embracing both questions in the arbitration, the proposed measure was never carried into effect.

It was, in fact, on the subject of his dignities alone that Columbus was tenacious; all other matters he considered of minor importance. In a conversation with the king, he absolutely disavowed all wish of entering into any suit or pleading as to his pecuniary dues; on the contrary, he offered to put all his privileges and writings into the hands of his sovereign, and to receive out of the dues arising from them, whatever his majesty might think proper to award. All that he claimed without qualification or reserve, were his official dignities, assured to him under the royal seal with all the solemnity of a treaty. He entreated, at all events, that these matters might speedily be decided, so that he might be released from a state of miserable suspense, and enabled to retire to some quiet corner, in search of that tranquillity and repose necessary to his fatigues and his infirmities.

To this frank appeal to his justice and generosity, Ferdinand replied with many courteous expressions, and with those general evasive promises, which beguile the ear of the court applicant, but convey no comfort to his heart. "As far as actions went," observes Las Casas, "the king not merely showed him no signs of favor. but, on the contrary. discountenanced him as much as possible, yet he was never wanting in complimentary expressions."

Many months were passed by Columbus in unavailing solicitation, during which he continued to receive outward demonstrations of respect from the king, and due attention from Cardinal Ximenes, Archbishop of Toledo, and other principal personages; but he had learned to appreciate and distrust the hollow civilities of a court. His claims were referred to a tribunal, called, "The council of the discharges of the conscience of the deceased queen, and of the king." This is a kind of tribunal commonly known by the name of the Junta de Descargos, composed of persons nominated by the sovereign, to superintend the accomplishment of the last will of his predecessor, and the discharge of his debts. Two consultations were held by this body, but nothing was determined. The wishes of the king were too well known to be thwarted. "It was believed," says Las Casas, "that if the king could have done so with a safe conscience, and without detriment to his fame, he would have respected few or none of the privileges which he and the queen had conceded to the admiral, and which had been so justly merited."[1]

Columbus still flattered himself that, his claims being of such importance, and touching a question of sovereignty, the adjustment of them might be only postponed by the king until he could consult with his daughter Juana, who had succeeded to her mother as Queen of Castile, and who was daily expected from Flanders with her husband, King Philip. He endeavored, therefore, to bear his delays with patience, but he had no longer the physical strength and glorious anticipations which once sustained him through his long application at this court. Life itself was drawing to a close.

He was once more confined to his bed by a tormenting attack of the gout, aggravated by the sorrows and disappointments which preyed upon his heart. From this couch of anguish he addressed one more appeal to the justice of the king. He no longer petitioned for himself; it was for his son Diego. Nor did he dwell upon his pecuniary dues; it was the honorable trophies of his services which he wished to secure and perpetuate in his family. He entreated that his son Diego might be appointed, in his place, to the government of which he had been so wrongfully deprived. "This," he said, "is a matter which concerns my honor; as to all the rest, do as your majesty may think proper; give or withhold, as may be most for your interest, and I shall be content. I believe the anxiety caused by the delay of this affair is the principal cause of my ill health." A petition to the same purpose was presented at the same time by his son Diego, offering to take with him such persons for counsellors as the king should appoint, and to be guided by their advice.

These petitions were treated by Ferdinand with his usual professions and evasions. "The more applications were made to him," observes Las Casas, "the more favorably did he reply; but still he delayed, hoping, by exhausting their patience, to induce them to waive their privileges, and accept in place thereof titles and estates in Castile." Columbus rejected all propositions of the kind with indignation, as calculated to compromise those titles which were the trophies of his achievements.

[1] Las Casas, Hist. Ind., lib. ii. cap. 37.

He saw, however, that all further hope of redress from Ferdinand was vain. From the bed to which he was confined he addressed a letter to his constant friend Diego de Deza, expressive of his despair. "It appears that his majesty does not think fit to fulfil that which he, with the queen, who is now in glory, promised me by word and seal. For me to contend for the contrary would be to contend with the wind. I have done all that I could do. I leave the rest to God, whom I have ever found propitious to me in my necessities." [1]

The cold and calculating Ferdinand beheld this illustrious man sinking under infirmity of body, heightened by that deferred hope which "maketh the heart sick." A little more delay, a little more disappointment, and a little longer infliction of ingratitude, and this loyal and generous heart would cease to beat: he should then be delivered from the just claims of a well-tried servant, who, in ceasing to be useful, was considered by him to have become importunate.

CHAPTER IV.

DEATH OF COLUMBUS.

In the midst of illness and despondency, when both life and hope were expiring in the bosom of Columbus, a new gleam was awakened and blazed up for the moment with characteristic fervor. He heard with joy of the landing of King Philip and Queen Juana, who had just arrived from Flanders to take possession of their throne of Castile. In the daughter of Isabella he trusted once more to find a patroness and a friend. King Ferdinand and all the court repaired to Laredo to receive the youthful sovereigns. Columbus would gladly have done the same, but he was confined to his bed by a severe return of his malady; neither in his painful and helpless situation could he dispense with the aid and ministry of his son Diego. His brother, the Adelantado, therefore, his main dependence in all emergencies, was sent to represent him, and to present his homage and congratulations. Columbus wrote by him to the new king and queen expressing his grief at being prevented by illness from coming in person to manifest his devotion, but begging to be considered among the most faithful of their

---

[1] Navarrete, Colec., tom. I.

subjects. He expressed a hope that he should receive at their hands the restitution of his honors and estates, and assured them that, though cruelly tortured at present by disease, he would yet be able to render them services, the like of which had never been witnessed.

Such was the last sally of his sanguine and unconquerable spirit; which, disregarding age and infirmities, and all past sorrows and disappointments, spoke from his dying bed with all the confidence of youthful hope, and talked of still greater enterprises, as if he had a long and vigorous life before him. The Adelantado took leave of his brother, whom he was never to behold again. and set out on his mission to the new sovereigns. He experienced the most gracious reception. The claims of the admiral were treated with great attention by the young king and queen, and flattering hopes were given of a speedy and prosperous termination to his suit

In the mean time the cares and troubles of Columbus were drawing to a close. The momentary fire which had reanimated him was soon quenched by accumulating infirmities Immediately after the departure of the Adelantado. his illness increased in violence His last voyage had shattered beyond repair a frame already worn and wasted by a life of hardship: and continual anxieties robbed him of that sweet repose so necessary to recruit the weariness and debility of age The cold ingratitude of his sovereign chilled his heart. The continued suspension of his honors, and the enmity and defamation experienced at every turn, seemed to throw a shadow over that glory which had been the great object of his ambition. This shadow, it is true, could be but of transient duration, but it is difficult for the most illustrious man to look beyond the present cloud which may obscure his fame, and anticipate its permanent lustre in the admiration of posterity.

Being admonished by failing strength and increasing sufferings that his end was approaching, he prepared to leave his affairs in order for the benefit of his successors.

It is said that on the 4th of May he wrote an informal testamentary codicil on the blank page of a little breviary. given him by Pope Alexander VI. In this he bequeathed that book to the Republic of Genoa. which he also appointed successor to his privileges and dignities, on the extinction of his male line. He directed likewise the erection of an hospital in that city with the produce of his possessions in Italy. The authenticity of this document is questioned. and has become a point of warm contest among commentators. It is not, however, of much importance. The paper is such as might readily have been written by a person like Columbus in the paroxysm of disease, when he imagined his end suddenly approaching, and shows the affection with which his thoughts were bent on his native city. It is termed among commentators a military codicil, because testamentary dispositions of this kind are executed by the soldier at the point of death, without the usual formalities required by the civil law. About two weeks afterward, on the eve of his death, he executed a final and regularly authenticated codicil, in which he bequeathed his dignities and estates with better judgment.

In these last and awful moments, when the soul has but a brief space in which to make up its accounts between heaven and earth, all dissimulation is at an end, and we read unequivocal evidences of character. The last codicil of Columbus, made at the very verge of the grave, is stamped with his ruling passion and his benignant virtues. He repeats and enforces several clauses of his original testament, constituting his son Diego his universal heir. The entailed inheritance, or mayorazgo, in case he died without male issue, was to go to his brother Don Fernando, and from him, in like case, to pass to his uncle Don Bartholomew, descending always to the nearest male heir; in failure of which it was to pass to the female nearest in lineage to the admiral. He enjoined upon whoever should inherit his estate never to alienate or diminish it, but to endeavor by all means to augment its prosperity and importance. He likewise enjoined upon his heirs to be prompt and devoted at all times, with person and estate, to serve their sovereign and promote the Christian faith. He ordered that Don Diego should devote one tenth of the revenues which might arise from his estate, when it came to be productive, to the relief of indigent relatives, and of other persons in necessity; that, out of the remainder he should yield certain yearly proportions to his brother Don Fernando, and his uncles Don Bartholomew and Don Diego; and that the part allotted to Don Fernando should be settled upon him and his male heirs in an entailed and unalienable inheritance. Having thus provided for the maintenance and perpetuity of his family and dignities, he ordered that Don Diego, when his estates should be sufficiently productive, should erect a chapel in the island of Hispaniola, which God had given to him so marvellously, at the town of Conception, in the Vega, where masses should be daily performed for the repose of the souls of himself, his father, his mother, his wife, and of all who died in the faith.

Another clause recommends to the care of Don Diego, Beatrix Enriquez, the mother of his natural son Fernando His connection with her had never been sanctioned by matrimony, and either this circumstance, or some neglect of her, seems to have awakened deep compunction in his dying moments. He orders Don Diego to provide for her respectable maintenance ; "and let this be done," he adds, "for the discharge of my conscience, for it weighs heavy on my soul."[1] Finally he noted with his own hand several minute sums, to be paid to persons at different and distant places, without their being told whence they received them. These appear to have been trivial debts of conscience, or rewards for petty services received in times long past. Among them is one of half a mark of silver to a poor Jew, who lived at the gate of the Jewry, in the city of Lisbon. These minute provisions evince the scrupulous attention to justice in all his dealings, and that love of punctuality in the fulfilment of duties, for which he was remarked. In the same spirit he gave much advice to his son Diego, as to the conduct of his affairs, enjoining upon him to take every month an account with his own hand of the expenses of his household, and to sign it with his name ; for a want of regularity in this he observed, lost both property and servants, and turned the last into enemies.[2] His dying bequests were made in presence of a few faithful followers and servants, and among them we find the name of Bartholomeo Fiesco, who had accompanied Diego Mendez in the perilous voyage in a canoe from Jamaica to Hispaniola.

Having thus scrupulously attended to all the claims of affection, loyalty, and justice upon earth, Columbus turned his thoughts to heaven ; and having received the holy sacrament, and performed all the pious offices of a devout Christian, he expired with great resignation on the day of Ascension, the 20th of May, 1506, being about seventy years of age.[3] His last words were, "*In manus tuas Domine, commendo spiritum meum:*" Into thy hands, O Lord, I commend my spirit.[4]

His body was deposited in the convent of St. Francisco, and his obsequies were celebrated with funeral pomp at Vallado-

---

[1] Diego, the son of the admiral, notes in his own testament this bequest of his father and says, that he was charged by him to pay Beatrix Enriquez 10,000 maravedis a year, which for some time he had faithfully performed; but as he believes that for three or four years previous to her death he had neglected to do so, he orders that the deficiency shall be ascertained and paid to her heirs. Memorial ajustado sobre la propriedad del mayorazgo que fondo D Christ. Colon. § 245

[2] Memorial ajustado, § 245.

[3] Cura de los Palacios. cap. 121

[4] Las Casas, Hist. Ind., lib. ii. cap. 38. Hist. del Almirante, cap. 105

lid, in the parochial church of Santa Maria de la Antigua. His remains were transported afterward. in 1513. to the Carthusian monastery of Las Cuevas of Seville, to the chapel of St. Ann or of Santo Christo, in which chapel were likewise deposited those of his son Don Diego, who died in the village of Montalban, on the 23d of February, 1526. In the year 1536 the bodies of Columbus and his son Diego were removed to Hispaniola, and interred in the principal chapel of the cathedral of the city of San Domingo; but even here they did not rest in quiet, having since been again disinterred and conveyed to the Havana, in the island of Cuba.

We are told that Ferdinand, after the death of Columbus, showed a sense of his merits by ordering a monument to be erected to his memory, on which was inscribed the motto already cited, which had formerly been granted to him by the sovereigns: A CASTILLA Y A LEON NUEVO MUNDO DIO COLON (*To Castile and Leon Columbus gave a new world*). However great an honor a monument may be for a subject to receive, it is certainly but a cheap reward for a sovereign to bestow. As to the motto inscribed upon it, it remains engraved in the memory of mankind. more indelibly than in brass or marble: a record of the great debt of gratitude due to the discoverer, which the monarch had so faithlessly neglected to discharge.

Attempts have been made in recent days, by loyal Spanish writers, to vindicate the conduct of Ferdinand toward Columbus. They were doubtless well intended, but they have been futile, nor is their failure to be regretted. To screen such injustice in so eminent a character from the reprobation of mankind is to deprive history of one of its most important uses. Let the ingratitude of Ferdinand stand recorded in its full extent, and endure throughout all time. The dark shadow which it casts upon his brilliant renown will be a lesson to all rulers, teaching them what is important to their own fame in their treatment of illustrious men.

CHAPTER V.

OBSERVATIONS ON THE CHARACTER OF COLUMBUS.

IN narrating the story of Columbus, it has been the endeavor of the author to place him in a clear and familiar point of view: for this purpose he has rejected no circumstance, however trivial. which appeared to evolve some point of character; and he has sought all kinds of collateral facts which might throw light upon his views and motives. With this view also he has detailed many facts hitherto passed over in silence, or vaguely noticed by historians. probably because they might be deemed instances of error or misconduct on the part of Columbus; but he who paints a great man merely in great and heroic traits, though he may produce a fine picture, will never present a faithful portrait. Great men are compounds of great and little qualities. Indeed, much of their greatness arises from their mastery over the imperfections of their nature, and their noblest actions are sometimes struck forth by the collision of their merits and their defects

In Columbus were singularly combined the practical and the poetical. His mind had grasped all kinds of knowledge, whether procured by study or observation. which bore upon his theories: impatient of the scanty aliment of the day. " his impetuous ardor," as has well been observed, " threw him into the study of the fathers of the church, the Arabian Jews, and the ancient geographers;" while his daring but irregular genius. bursting from the limits of imperfect science, bore him to conclusions far beyond the intellectual vision of his contemporaries. If some of his conclusions were erroneous, they were at least ingenious and splendid: and their error resulted from the clouds which still hung over his peculiar path of enterprise. His own discoveries enlightened the ignorance of the age: guided conjecture to certainty, and dispelled that very darkness with which he had been obliged to struggle.

In the progress of his discoveries he has been remarked for the extreme sagacity and the admirable justness with which he seized upon the phenomena of the exterior world. The variations, for instance, of terrestrial magnetism, the direction of currents, the groupings of marine plants, fixing one of the grand climacteric divisions of the ocean, the temperatures changing not solely with the distance to the equator, but also with the difference of meridians : these and similar phenomena, as they broke upon him were discerned with wonderful quickness of perception, and made to contribute important principles to the stock of general knowledge. This lucidity of spirit, this quick convertibility of facts to principles, distinguish him from the dawn to the close of his sublime enterprise, insomuch that, with all the sallying ardor of his imagination, his ultimate success has been admirably characterized as a " conquest of reflection." [1]

It has been said that mercenary views mingled with the ambition of Columbus, and that his stipulations with the Spanish court were selfish and avaricious. The charge is inconsiderate and unjust. He aimed at dignity and wealth in the same lofty spirit in which he sought renown ; they were to be part and parcel of his achievement, and palpable evidence of its success ; they were to arise from the territories he should discover, and be commensurate in importance. No condition could be more just. He asked nothing of the sovereigns but a command of the countries he hoped to give them, and a share of the profits to support the dignity of his command. If there should be no country discovered, his stipulated viceroyalty would be of no avail ; and if no revenues should be produced, his labor and peril would produce no gain. If his command and revenues ultimately proved magnificent, it was from the magnificence of the regions he had attached to the Castilian crown. What monarch would not rejoice to gain empire on such conditions? But he did not risk merely a loss of labor, and a disappointment of ambition, in the enterprise ; — on his motives being questioned, he voluntarily undertook, and, with the assistance of his coadjutors, actually defrayed one-eighth of the whole charge of the first expedition.

It was, in fact, this rare union already noticed, of the practical man of business with the poetical projector. which enabled him to carry his grand enterprises into effect through so many difficulties ; but the pecuniary calculations and cares, which gave feasibility to his schemes, were never suffered to chill the glowing aspirations of his soul. The gains that promised to arise from his discoveries he intended to appropriate in the same princely and pious spirit in which they were demanded. He contemplated works and achievements of benevolence and religion ; vast contributions for the relief of the poor of his native city ; the foundation of churches, where masses should

---

[1] D. Humboldt. Examen Critique.

be said for the souls of the departed ; and armies for the recovery of the holy sepulchre in Palestine Thus his ambition was truly noble and lofty ; instinct with high thought and prone to generous deed.

In the discharge of his office he maintained the state and ceremonial of a viceroy, and was tenacious of his rank and privileges ; not from a mere vulgar love of titles, but because he prized them as testimonals and trophies of his achievements : these he jealously cherished as his great rewards. In his repeated applications to the king, he insisted merely on the restitution of his dignities. As to his pecuniary dues and all questions relative to mere revenue, he offered to leave them to arbitration or even to the absolute disposition of the monarch : but not so his official dignities : " these things," said he nobly, " affect my honor." In his testament, he enjoined on his son Diego, and whoever after him should inherit his estates, whatever dignities and titles might afterward be granted by the king, always to sign himself simply " the admiral," by way of perpetuating in the family its real source of greatness.

His conduct was characterized by the grandeur of his views and the magnanimity of his spirit. Instead of scouring the newly-found countries, like a grasping adventurer eager only for immediate gain, as was too generally the case with contemporary discoverers, he sought to ascertain their soil and productions, their rivers and harbors ; he was desirous of colonizing and cultivating them ; of conciliating and civilizing the natives ; of building cities ; introducing the useful arts ; subjecting every thing to the control of law, order, and religion ; and thus of founding regular and prosperous empires. In this glorious plan he was constantly defeated by the dissolute rabble which it was his misfortune to command ; with whom all law was tyranny, and all order restraint. They interrupted all useful works by their seditions ; provoked the peaceful Indians to hostility ; and after they had thus drawn down misery and warfare upon their own heads, and overwhelmed Columbus with the ruins of the edifice he was building, they charged him with being the cause of the confusion.

Well would it have been for Spain had those who followed in the track of Columbus possessed his sound policy and liberal views. The New World, in such cases, would have been settled by pacific colonists, and civilized by enlightened legislators ; instead of being overrun by desperate adventurers, and desolated by avaricious conquerors.

Columbus was a man of quick sensibility, liable to great ex citement, to sudden and strong impressions, and powerful impulses. He was naturally irritable and impetuous, and keenly sensible to injury and injustice : yet the quickness of his temper was counteracted by the benevolence and generosity of his heart. The magnanimity of his nature shone forth through all the troubles of his stormy career. Though continually outraged in his dignity, and braved in the exercise of his command ; though foiled in his plans, and endangered in his person by the seditions of turbulent and worthless men, and that too at times when suffering under anxiety of mind and anguish of body sufficient to exasperate the most patient, yet he restrained his valiant and indignant spirit, by the strong powers of his mind, and brought himself to forbear, and reason, and even to supplicate ; nor should we fail to notice how free he was from all feeling of revenge, how ready to forgive and forget, on the least sign of repentance and atonement. He has been extolled for his skill in controlling others ; but far greater praise is due to him for his firmness in governing himself.

His natural benignity made him accessible to all kinds of pleasurable sensations from external objects. In his letters and journals, instead of detailing circumstances with the technical precision of a mere navigator, he notices the beauties of nature with the enthusiasm of a poet or a painter. As he coasts the shores of the New World, the reader participates in the enjoyment with which he describes in his imperfect but picturesque Spanish, the varied objects around him ; the blandness of the temperature, the purity of the atmosphere, the fragrance of the air, ·· full of dew and sweetness,'' the verdure of the forests, the magnificence of the trees, the grandeur of the mountains, and the limpidity and freshness of the running streams. New delight springs up for him in every scene. He extols each new discovery as more beautiful than the last, and each as the most beautiful in the world ; until, with his simple earnestness, he tells the sovereigns that, having spoken so highly of the preceding islands, he fears that they will not credit him, when he declares that the one he is actually describing surpasses them all in excellence.

In the same ardent and unstudied way he expresses his emotions on various occasions, readily affected by impulses of joy or grief, of pleasure or indignation. When surrounded and overwhelmed by the ingratitude and violence of worthless men, he often, in the retirement of his cabin, gave way to bursts of sorrow, and relieved his overladen heart by sighs and groans. When he returned in chains to Spain, and came into the presence of Isabella, instead of continuing the lofty pride with which he had hitherto sustained his injuries, he was touched with grief and tenderness at her sympathy, and burst forth into sobs and tears.

He was devoutly pious: religion mingled with the whole course of his thoughts and actions, and shone forth in his most private and unstudied writings. Whenever he made any great discovery, he celebrated it by solemn thanks to God. The voice of prayer and melody of praise rose from his ships when they first beheld the New World, and his first action on landing was to prostrate himself upon the earth and return thanksgivings. Every evening the *Salve Regina* and other vesper hymns were chanted by his crew, and masses were performed in the beautiful groves bordering the wild shores of this heathen land. All his great enterprises were undertaken in the name of the Holy Trinity, and he partook of the communion previous to embarkation. He was a firm believer in the efficacy of vows and penances and pilgrimages, and resorted to them in times of difficulty and danger. The religion thus deeply seated in his soul diffused a sober dignity and benign composure over his whole demeanor. His language was pure and guarded, and free from all imprecations, oaths and other irreverent expressions.

It cannot be denied, however, that his piety was mingled with superstition, and darkened by the bigotry of the age. He evidently concurred in the opinion, that all nations which did not acknowledge the Christian faith were destitute of natural rights; that the sternest measures might be used for their conversion, and the severest punishments inflicted upon their obstinacy in unbelief. In this spirit of bigotry he considered himself justified in making captives of the Indians, and transporting them to Spain to have them taught the doctrines of Christianity, and in selling them for slaves if they pretended to resist his invasions. In so doing he sinned against the natural goodness of his character, and against the feelings which he had originally entertained and expressed toward this gentle and hospitable people; but he was goaded on by the mercenary impatience of the crown, and by the sneers of his enemies at the unprofitable result of his enterprises. It is but justice to his character to observe, that the enslavement of the Indians thus taken in battle was at first openly countenanced by the crown, and that, when the question of right came to be discussed at the entreaty of the queen, several of the most distinguished jurists and theologians advocated the practice: so that the question was finally settled in favor of the Indians solely by the humanity of Isabella. As the venerable Bishop Las Casas observes, where the most learned men have doubted, it is not surprising that an unlearned mariner should err.

These remarks, in palliation of the conduct of Columbus, are required by candor. It is proper to show him in connection with the age in which he lived, lest the errors of the times should be considered as his individual faults. It is not the intention of the author, however, to justify Columbus on a point where it is inexcusable to err. Let it remain a blot on his illustrious name, and let others derive a lesson from it.

We have already hinted at a peculiar trait in his rich and varied character; that ardent and enthusiastic imagination which threw a magnificence over his whole course of thought. Herrera intimates that he had a talent for poetry, and some slight traces of it are on record in the book of prophecies which he presented to the Catholic sovereigns. But his poetical temperament is discernible throughout all his writings and in all his actions. It spread a golden and glorious world around him, and tinged every thing with its own gorgeous colors. It betrayed him into visionary speculations, which subjected him to the sneers and cavillings of men of cooler and safer, but more grovelling minds. Such were the conjectures formed on the coast of Paria about the form of the earth, and the situation of the terrestrial paradise: about the mines of Ophir in Hispaniola, and the Aurea Chersonesus in Veragua, and such was the heroic scheme of a crusade for the recovery of the holy sepulchre. It mingled with his religion, and filled his mind with solemn and visionary meditations on mystic passages of the Scriptures, and the shadowy portents of the prophecies. It exalted his office in his eyes, and made him conceive himself an agent sent forth upon a sublime and awful mission, subject to impulses and supernatural intimations from the Deity; such as the voice which he imagined spoke to him in comfort amidst the troubles of Hispaniola and in the silence of the night on the disastrous coast of Veragua.

He was decidedly a visionary, but a visionary of an uncommon and successful kind. The manner in which his ardent, imaginative, and mercurial nature was controlled by a powerful judgment, and directed by an acute sagacity, is the most extraordinary feature in his character. Thus governed, his imagination, instead of exhausting itself in idle flights, lent aid to his judgment, and enabled him to form conclusions at which common minds could never have arrived, nay, which they could not perceive when pointed out.

To his intellectual vision it was given to read the signs of the times, and to trace, in the conjectures and reveries of past ages, the indications of an unknown world; as soothsayers were said to read predictions in the stars, and to foretell events from the visions of the night.   " His soul, " observes a Spanish writer, " was superior to the age in which he lived.   For him was reserved the great enterprise of traversing that sea which had given rise to so many fables, and of deciphering the mystery of his time.[1]

With all the visionary fervor of his imagination. its fondest dreams fell short of the reality.   He died in ignorance of the real grandeur of his discovery.   Until his last breath he entertained the idea that he had merely opened a new way to the old resorts of opulent commerce, and had discovered some of the wild regions of the East.   He supposed Hispaniola to be the ancient Ophir which had been visited by the ships of Solomon, and that Cuba and Terra Firma were but remote parts of Asia. What visions of glory would have broken upon his mind could he have known that he had indeed discovered a, new continent, equal to the whole of the Old World in magnitude, and separated by two vast oceans from all the earth hitherto known by civilized man !   And how would his magnanimous spirit have been consoled, amidst the afflictions of age and the cares of penury, the neglect of a fickle public and the injustice of an ungrateful king. could he have anticipated the splendid empires which were to spread over the beautiful world he had discovered ; and the nations, and tongues, and languages which were to fill its lands with his renown, and revere and bless his name to the latest posterity !

---

[1] Cladera. Investigaciones historias, p. 11.

APPENDIX.

No. I.

AT the termination of a war between France and Spain, in 1795, all the Spanish possessions in the island of Hispaniola were ceded to France, by the 9th article of the treaty of peace. To assist in the accomplishment of this cession, a Spanish squadron was despatched to the island at the appointed time, commanded by Don Gabriel de Aristizabal, lieutenant-general of the royal armada. On the 11th of December, 1795, that commander wrote to the field-marshal and governor, Don Joaquin Garcia, resident at St. Domingo, that, being informed that the remains of the celebrated admiral Don Christopher Columbus lay in the cathedral of that city, he felt it incumbent on him as a Spaniard, and as commander-in-chief of his majesty's squadron of operations, to solicit the translation of the ashes of that hero to the island of Cuba, which had likewise been discovered by him, and where he had first planted the standard of the cross. He expressed a desire that this should be done officially, and with great care and formality, that it might not remain in the power of any one, by a careless transportation of these honored remains, to lose a relic connected with an event which formed the most glorious epoch of Spanish history, and that it might be manifested to all nations that Spaniards, notwithstanding the lapse of ages, never ceased to pay all honors to the remains of that " worthy and adventurous general of the seas; " nor abandoned them, when the various public bodies, representing the Spanish dominion, emigrated from the island. As he had not time, without great inconvenience, to consult the sovereign on this subject, he had recourse to the governor, as royal vice-patron of the island, hoping that his solicitation might be granted, and the remains of the admiral exhumed and conveyed to the island of Cuba, in the ship San Lorenzo.

The generous wishes of this high-minded Spaniard met with warm concurrence on the part of the governor. He informed him, in reply, that the Duke of Veraguas, lineal successor of Columbus, had manifested the same solicitude, and had sent directions that the necessary measures should be taken at his expense; and had at the same time expressed a wish that the bones of the Adelantado, Don Bartholomew Columbus, should likewise be exhumed; transmitting inscriptions to be put upon the sepulchres of both. He added, that although the king had given no orders on the subject, yet the proposition being so accordant with the grateful feelings of the Spanish nation, and meeting with the concurrence of all the authorities of the island, he was ready on his part to carry it into execution.

The commandant-general Aristizabal then made a similar communication to the archbishop of Cuba, Don Fernando Portillo y Torres, whose metropolis was then the city of St. Domingo, hoping to receive his countenance and aid in this pious undertaking.

The reply of the archbishop was couched in terms of high courtesy toward the gallant commander, and deep reverence for the memory of Columbus, and expressed a zeal in rendering this tribute of gratitude and respect to the remains of one who had done so much for the glory of the nation.

The persons empowered to act for the Duke of Veraguas, the venerable dean and chapter of the cathedral, and all the other persons and authorities to whom Don Gabriel de Aristizabal made similar communications, manifested the same eagerness to assist in the performance of this solemn and affecting rite.

The worthy commander Aristizabal, having taken all these preparatory steps with great form and punctilio, so as that the ceremony should be performed in a public and striking manner, suitable to the fame of Columbus, the whole was carried into effect with becoming pomp and solemnity.

On the 20th of December, 1795, the most distinguished persons of the place, the dignitaries of the church, and civil and military officers, assembled in the metropolitan cathedral. In the presence of this august assemblage, a small vault was opened above the chancel, in the principal wall on the right side of the high altar. Within were found the fragments of a leaden coffin, a number of bones, and a quantity of mould, evidently the remains of a human body. These were carefully collected and put into a case of gilded lead, about half an ell in length and breadth, and a third in height, secured by an iron lock, the key of which was delivered to the archbishop. The case was enclosed in a coffin covered with black velvet, and ornamented with lace and fringe of gold. The whole was then placed in a temporary tomb or mausoleum.

On the following day there was another grand convocation at the cathedral, when the vigils and masses for the dead were solemnly chanted by the archbishop, accompanied by the commandant-general of the armada, the Dominican and Franciscan friars, and the friars of the Order of Mercy, together with the rest of the distinguished assemblage. After this a funeral sermon was preached by the archbishop.

On the same day, at four o'clock in the afternoon, the coffin was transported to the ship with the utmost state and ceremony, with a civil, religious, and military procession, banners wrapped in mourning, chants and responses and discharges of artillery. The most distinguished persons of the several orders took turn to support the coffin. The key was taken with great formality from the hands of the archbishop by the governor, and given into the hands of the commander of the armada, to be delivered by him to the governor of the Havana, to be held in deposit until the pleasure of the king should be known. The coffin was received on board of a brigantine called the Discoverer, which, with all the other shipping, displayed mourning signals, and saluted the remains with the honors paid to an admiral.

From the port of St. Domingo the coffin was conveyed to the bay of Ocoa and there transferred to the ship San Lorenzo. It was accompanied by a portrait of Columbus, sent from Spain by the Duke of Veraguas, to be suspended close by the place where the remains of his illustrious ancestor should be deposited.

The ship immediately made sail, and arrived at Havana, in Cuba, on the 15th of January, 1796. Here the same deep feeling of reverence to the memory of the discoverer was evinced. The principal authorities repaired on board of the ship, accompanied by the superior naval and military officers. Every thing was conducted with the same circum stantial and solemn ceremonial. The remains were removed with great reverence, and placed in a felucca, in which they were conveyed to land in the midst of a procession of three columns of feluccas and boats in the royal service, all properly decorated, containing distinguished military and ministerial officers. Two feluccas followed, in one of which was a marine guard of honor, with mourning banners and muffled drums: and in the other were the commandant-general, the principal minister of marine, and the military staff. In passing the vessels of war in the harbor, they all paid the honors due to an admiral and captain-general of the navy. On arriving at the mole the remains were met by the governor of the island, accompanied by the generals and the military staff. The coffin was then conveyed, between files of soldiery which lined the streets, to the obelisk, in the place of arms, where it was received in a hearse prepared for the purpose. Here the remains were formally delivered to the governor and captain-general of the island, the key given up to him, the coffin opened and examined, and the safe transportation of its contents authenticated. This ceremony being concluded, it was conveyed in grand procession and with the utmost pomp to the cathedral. Masses and the solemn ceremonies of the dead were performed by the bishop, and the mortal remains of Columbus deposited with great reverence in the wall on the right side of the grand altar. "All these honors and ceremonies," says the document, from whence this notice is digested,[1] "were attended by the ecclesiastical and secular dignitaries, the public bodies and all the nobility and gentry of Havana, in proof of the high estimation and respectful remembrance in which they held the hero who had discovered the New World, and had been the first to plant the standard of the cross on that island."

This is the last occasion that the Spanish nation has had to testify its feelings toward the memory of Columbus, and it is with deep satisfaction that the author of this work has been able to cite at large a ceremonial so solemn, affecting, and noble in its details, and so honorable to the national character.

When we read of the remains of Columbus, thus conveyed from the port of St. Domingo, after an interval of nearly three hundred years, as sacred national relics, with civic and military pomp, and high religious ceremonial; the most dignified and illustrious men striving who most should pay them reverence, we cannot but reflect that it was from this very port he was carried off loaded with ignominious chains, blasted apparently in fame and fortune, and followed by the revilings of the rabble. Such honors, it is true, are nothing to the dead, nor can they atone to the heart, now dust and ashes for all the wrongs and sorrows it may have suffered; but they speak volumes of comfort to the illustrious, yet slandered and persecuted living, encouraging them bravely to bear with present injuries, by showing them how true merit outlives all calumny, and receives its glorious reward in the admiration of after ages.

---

[1] Navarrete, Colec., tom ii. p. 365.

No. II.

NOTICE OF THE DESCENDANTS OF COLUMBUS.

ON the death of Columbus his son Diego succeeded to his rights, as viceroy and governor of the New World, according to the express capitulations between the sovereigns and his father He appears by the general consent of historians to have been a man of great integrity, of respectable talents, and of a frank and generous nature. Herrera speaks repeatedly of the gentleness and urbanity of his manners, and pronounces him of a noble disposition, and without deceit. This absence of all guile frequently laid him open to the stratagems of crafty men, grown old in deception, who rendered his life a continued series of embarrassments; but the probity of his character, with the irresistible power of truth, bore him through difficulties in which more politic and subtle men would have been entangled and completely lost.

Immediately after the death of the admiral, Don Diego came forward as lineal successor, and urged the restitution of the family offices and privileges, which had been suspended during the latter years of his father's life If the cold and wary Ferdinand, however, could forget his obligations of gratitude and justice to Columbus, he had less difficulty in turning a deaf ear to the solicitations of his son. For two years Don Diego pressed his suit with fruitless diligence. He felt the apparent distrust of the monarch the more sensibly, from having been brought up under his eye, as a page in the royal household, where his character ought to be well known and appreciated. At length, on the return of Ferdinand from Naples in 1508, he put to him a direct question, with the frankness attributed to his character. He demanded "why his majesty would not grant to him as a favor, that which was his right, and why he hesitated to confide in the fidelity of one who had been reared in his house." Ferdinand replied that he could fully confide in him, but could not repose so great a trust at a venture in his children and successors To this Don Diego rejoined, that it was contrary to all justice and reason to make him suffer for the sins of his children, who might never be born.[1]

Still, though he had reason and justice on his side, the young admiral found it impossible to bring the wary monarch to a compliance Finding all appeal to all his ideas of equity or sentiments of generosity in vain, he solicited permission to pursue his claim in the ordinary course of law. The king could not refuse so reasonable a request, and Don Diego commenced a process against King Ferdinand before the council of the Indies, founded on the repeated capitulations between the crown and his father, and embracing all the dignities and immunities ceded by them.

One ground of opposition to these claims was, that if the capitulation, made by the sovereigns in 1492, had granted a perpetual viceroyalty to the admiral and his heirs, such grant could not stand; being contrary to the interests of the state, and to an express law promulgated in Toledo in 1480; wherein it was ordained that no office, involving the administration of justice, should be given in perpetuity; that therefore, the viceroyalty granted to the admiral could only have been for his life; and that even, during that term, it had justly been taken from him for his misconduct. That such concessions were contrary to the inherent pre-

---

[1] Herrera, Hist Ind., decad. ii. lib. vii. cap. 4

rogatives of the crown, of which the government could not divest itself. To this Don Diego replied, that as to the validity of the capitulation, it was a binding contract, and none of its privileges ought to be restricted. That as by royal schedules dated in Villa Franca, June 2d, 1506, and Almazan, August 28th, 1507, it had been ordered that he, Don Diego, should receive the tenths, so equally ought the other privileges to be accorded to him. As to the allegation that his father had been deprived of his viceroyalty for his demerits, it was contrary to all truth. It had been audacity on the part of Bobadilla to send him a prisoner to Spain in 1500, and contrary to the will and command of the sovereigns, as was proved by their letter, dated from Valencia de la Torre in 1502, in which they expressed grief at his arrest, and assured him that it should be redressed, and his privileges guarded entire to himself and his children.[1]

This memorable suit was commenced in 1508, and continued for several years. In the course of it the claims of Don Diego were disputed, likewise, on the plea that his father was not the original discoverer of Terra Firma, but only subsequently of certain portions of it. This, however, was completely controverted by overwhelming testimony. The claims of Don Diego were minutely discussed and rigidly examined, and the unanimous decision of the Council of the Indies in his favor, while it reflected honor on the justice and independence of that body, silenced many petty cavilers at the fair fame of Columbus.[2] Notwithstanding this decision, the wily monarch wanted neither means nor pretexts to delay the ceding of such vast powers, so repugnant to his cautious policy. The young admiral was finally indebted for his success in this suit to previous success attained in a suit of a different nature. He had become enamoured of Doña Maria de Toledo, daughter of Fernando de Toledo. grand commander of Leon, and niece to Don Fadrique Toledo, the celebrated Duke of Alva, chief favorite of the king. This was aspiring to a high connection. The father and uncle of the lady were the most powerful grandees of the proud kingdom of Spain. and cousins German to Ferdinand. The glory. however, which Columbus had left behind, rested upon his children. and the claims of Don Diego, recently confirmed by the council, involved dignities and wealth sufficient to raise him to a level with the loftiest alliance. He found no difficulty in obtaining the hand of the lady, and thus was the foreign family of Columbus ingrafted on one of the proudest races of Spain. The natural consequences followed. Diego had secured that magical power called "connections;" and the favor of Ferdinand. which had been so long withheld from him. as the son of Columbus, shone upon him, though coldly. as the nephew of the Duke of Alva. The father and uncle of his bride succeeded. though with great difficulty, in conquering the repugnance of the monarch, and after all he but granted in part the justice they required. He ceded to Don Diego merely the dignities and powers enjoyed by Nicholas de Ovando. who was recalled, and he cautiously withheld the title of viceroy.

The recall of Ovando was not merely a measure to make room for Don Diego; it was the tardy performance of a promise made to Isabella on her death-bed. The expiring queen had demanded it as a punishment for the massacre of her poor Indian subjects at Xaragua, and the cruel and ignominious execution of the female cacique Anacaona. Thus retribution was continually going its rounds in the checkered destinies of this

---

[1] Extracts from the minutes of the process taken by the historian Muñoz, MS.
[2] Further mention will be found of this lawsuit in the article relative to Amerigo Vespucci.

island, which has ever presented a little epitome of human history, its errors and crimes, and consequent disasters.

In complying with the request of the queen, however, Ferdinand was favorable toward Ovando. He did not feel the same generous sympathies with his late consort, and, however Ovando had sinned against humanity in his treatment of the Indians, he had been a vigilant officer, and his very oppressions had in general proved profitable to the crown Ferdinand directed that the fleet which took out the new governor should return under the command of Ovando, and that he should retain undisturbed enjoyment of any property or Indian slaves that might be found in his possession. Some have represented Ovando as a man far from mercenary; that the wealth wrung from the miseries of the natives was for his sovereign, not for himself; and it is intimated that one secret cause of his disgrace was his having made an enemy of the all-powerful and unforgiving Fonseca.[1]

The new admiral embarked at St. Lucar, June 9th 1509. with his wife, his brother Don Fernando, who was now grown to man's estate, and had been well educated. and his two uncles. Don Bartholomew and Don Diego. They were accompanied by a numerous retinue of cavaliers. with their wives, and of young ladies of rank and family more distinguished it is hinted. for high blood than large fortune. and who were sent out to find wealthy husbands in the New World.[2]

Though the king had not granted Don Diego the dignity of viceroy. the title was generally given to him by courtesy, and his wife was universally addressed by that of vice-queen.

Don Diego commenced his rule with a degree of splendor hitherto unknown in the colony The vice-queen, who was a lady of great desert, surrounded by the noble cavaliers and the young ladies of family who had come in her retinue. established a sort of court. which threw a degree of lustre over the half-savage island. The young ladies were soon married to the wealthiest colonists, and contributed greatly to soften those rude manners which had grown up in a state of society hitherto destitute of the salutary restraint and pleasing decorum produced by female influence.

Don Diego had considered his appointment in the light of a viceroyalty, but the king soon took measures which showed that he admitted of no such pretension. Without any reference to Don Diego, he divided the coast of Darien into two great provinces, separated by an imaginary line running through the Gulf of Uraba, appointing Alonzo de Ojeda governor of the eastern province, which he called New Andalusia, and Diego de Nicuessa, governor of the western province, which included the rich coast of Veragua, and which he called Castilla del Oro, or Golden Castile. Had the monarch been swayed by principles of justice and gratitude. the settlement of this coast would have been given to the Adelantado, Don Bartholomew Columbus, who had assisted in the discovery of the country, and, together with his brother the admiral, had suffered so greatly in the enterprise. Even his superior abilities for the task should have pointed him out to the policy of the monarch, but the cautious and calculating Ferdinand knew the lofty spirit of the Adelantado, and that he would be disposed to demand high and dignified terms. He passed him by, therefore, and preferred more eager and accommodating adventurers.

Don Diego was greatly aggrieved at this measure, thus adopted without his participation or knowledge. He justly considered it an infringement of the capitulations granted and repeatedly confirmed to his father and

---

[1] Charlevoix, ut supra, v. i. p. 272, id. 274
[2] Las Casas, lib. ii. cap. 49, MS.

his heirs   He had further vexations and difficulties with respect to the government of the island of St. Juan, or Porto Rico, which was conquered and settled about this time; but after a variety of cross purposes, the officers whom he appointed were ultimately recognized by the crown

Like his father, he had to contend with malignant factions in his government; for the enemies of the father transferred their enmity to the son.   There was one Miguel Pasamonte, the king's treasurer, who became his avowed enemy, under the support and chiefly at the instigation of the Bishop Fonseca, who continued to the son the implacable hostility which he had manifested to the father.   A variety of trivial circumstances contributed to embroil him with some of the petty officers of the colony, and there was a remnant of the followers of Roldan who arrayed themselves against him [1]

Two factions soon arose in the island; one of the admiral, the other of the treasurer Pasamonte   The latter affected to call themselves the party of the king.   They gave all possible molestation to Don Diego, and sent home the most virulent and absurd misrepresentations of his conduct. Among others, they represented a large house with many windows which he was building, as intended for a fortress, and asserted that he had a design to make himself sovereign of the island.   King Ferdinand, who was now advancing in years, had devolved the affairs of the Indies in a great measure on Fonseca,[2] who had superintended them from the first, and he was greatly guided by the advice of that prelate, which was not likely to be favorable to the descendants of Columbus.   The complaints from the colonies were so artfully enforced, therefore, that he established in 1510 a sovereign court at St. Domingo, called the royal audience, to which an appeal might be made from all sentences of the admiral, even in cases reserved hitherto exclusively for the crown.   Don Diego considered this a suspicious and injurious measure intended to demolish his authority.

Frank, open, and unsuspicious, the young admiral was not formed for a contest with the crafty politicians arrayed against him, who were ready and adroit in seizing upon his slightest errors, and magnifying them into crimes.   Difficulties were multiplied in his path which it was out of his power to overcome.   He had entered upon office full of magnanimous intentions. determined to put an end to oppression, and correct all abuses; all good men therefore had rejoiced at his appointment; but he soon found that he had overrated his strength. and undervalued the difficulties awaiting him.   He calculated from his own good heart. but he had no idea of the wicked hearts of others.   He was opposed to the repartimientos of Indians, that source of all kinds of inhumanity; but he found all the men of wealth in the colony. and most of the important persons of the court, interested in maintaining them.   He perceived that the attempt to abolish them would be dangerous, and the result questionable: at the same time this abuse was the source of immense profit to himself. Self-interest, therefore. combined with other considerations. and what at first appeared difficult, seemed presently impracticable.   The repartimientos continued in the state in which he found them. excepting that he removed such of the superintendents as had been cruel and oppressive, and substituted men of his own appointment. who probably proved equally worthless. His friends were disappointed, his enemies encouraged; a hue and cry was raised against him by the friends of those he had displaced; and it was even said that if Ovando had not died about this time. he would have been sent out to supplant Don Diego.

---

[1] Herrera. decad. i. lib. vii. cap. 12.   [2] Ibid.

The subjugation and settlement of the Island of Cuba, in 1510, was a fortunate event in the administration of the present admiral. He congratulated King Ferdinand on having acquired the largest and most beautiful island in the world without losing a single man. The intelligence was highly acceptable to the king; but it was accompanied by a great number of complaints against the admiral. Little affection as Ferdinand felt for Don Diego, he was still aware that most of these representations were false, and had their origin in the jealousy and envy of his enemies. He judged it expedient, however, in 1512, to send out Don Bartholomew Columbus with minute instructions to his nephew the admiral.

Don Bartholomew still retained the office of Adelantado of the Indies; although Ferdinand, through selfish motives, detained him in Spain, while he employed inferior men in voyages of discovery. He now added to his appointments the property and government of the little island of Mona during life, and assigned him a repartimiento of two hundred Indians, with the superintendence of the mines which might be discovered in Cuba; an office which proved very lucrative.[1]

Among the instructions given by the king to Don Diego, he directed that, in consequence of the representations of the Dominican friars, the labor of the natives should be reduced to one-third; that negro slaves should be procured from Guinea as a relief to the Indians,[2] and that Carib slaves should be branded on the leg, to prevent other Indians from being confounded with them and subjected to harsh treatment.[3]

The two governors, Ojeda and Nicuessa, whom the king had appointed to colonize and command at the Isthmus of Darien, in Terra Firma, having failed in their undertaking, the sovereign, in 1514, wrote to Hispaniola, permitting the Adelantado, Don Bartholomew, if so inclined, to take charge of settling the coast of Veragua, and to govern that country under the admiral Don Diego conformably to his privileges. Had the king consulted his own interest, and the deference due to the talents and services of the Adelantado, this measure would have been taken at an earlier date. It was now too late: illness prevented Don Bartholomew from executing the enterprise, and his active and toilsome life was drawing to a close.

Many calumnies having been sent home to Spain by Pasamonte and other enemies of Don Diego, and various measures being taken by government, which he conceived derogatory to his dignity, and injurious to his privileges, he requested and obtained permission to repair to court, that he might explain and vindicate his conduct. He departed, accordingly, on April 9th, 1515, leaving the Adelantado with the vice-queen Doña Maria. He was received with great honor by the king, and he merited such a reception. He had succeeded in every enterprise he had undertaken or directed. The pearl fishery had been successfully established on the coast of Cubagua; the islands of Cuba and of Jamaica had been subjected and brought under cultivation without bloodshed; his conduct as governor had been upright; and he had only excited the representations made against him, by endeavoring to lessen the oppression of the natives. The king ordered that all processes against him in the court of appeal and elsewhere, for damages done to individuals in regulating the repartimientos, should be discontinued, and the cases sent to himself for consideration. But with all these favors, as the admiral claimed a share of the profits of the provinces of Castilla del Oro, saying that it was discovered by his father, as the names of its places, such as Nombre de Dios, Porto Bello, and el Retrete, plainly proved, the king ordered that interrogato-

---

[1] Charlevoix, Hist. St. Domingo, p. 321
[2] Herrera, Hist. Ind., decad i. lib. ix cap. 5.   [3] Ibid.

ries should be made among the mariners who had sailed with Christopher Columbus, in the hope of proving that he had not discovered the coast of Darien nor the Gulf of Uraba. "Thus," adds Herrera, "Don Diego was always involved in litigations with the fiscal, so that he might truly say that he was heir to the troubles of his father."[1]

Not long after the departure of Don Diego from St. Domingo, his uncle, Don Bartholomew, ended his active and laborious life. No particulars are given of his death, nor is there mention made of his age, which must have been advanced. King Ferdinand is said to have expressed great concern at the event, for he had a high opinion of the character and talents of the Adelantado: "a man," says Herrera, "of not less worth than his brother the admiral, and who if he had been employed, would have given great proofs of it; for he was an excellent seaman, valiant and of great heart."[2] Charlevoix attributes the inaction in which Don Bartholomew had been suffered to remain for several years, to the jealousy and parsimony of the king. He found the house already too powerful; and the Adelantado, had he discovered Mexico, was a man to make as good conditions as had been made by the admiral his brother.[3] It was said, observed Herrera, that the king rather preferred to employ him in his European affairs, though it could only have been to divert him from other objects. On his death the king resumed to himself the island of Mona, which he had given to him for life, and transferred his repartimiento of two hundred Indians to the vice-queen Doña Maria.

While the admiral Don Diego was pressing for an audience in his vindication at court, King Ferdinand died, on the 23d of January, 1516. His grandson and successor, Prince Charles, afterward the Emperor Charles V., was in Flanders. The government rested for a time with Cardinal Ximenes, who would not undertake to decide on the representations and claims of the admiral. It was not until 1520 that he obtained from the Emperor Charles V. a recognition of his innocence of all the charges against him. The emperor finding that what Pasamonte and his party had written were notorious calumnies, ordered Don Diego to resume his charge, although the process with the fiscal was still pending, and that Pasamonte should be written to, requesting him to forget all past passions and differences, and to enter into amicable relations with Don Diego. Among other acts of indemnification he acknowledged his right to exercise his office of viceroy and governor in the island of Hispaniola, and in all parts discovered by his father.[4] His authority was, however, much diminished by new regulations, and a supervisor appointed over him with the right to give information to the council against him, but with no other powers. Don Diego sailed in the beginning of September, 1520, and on his arrival at St. Domingo, finding that several of the governors, presuming on his long absence, had arrogated to themselves independence, and had abused their powers, he immediately sent persons to supersede them, and demanded an account of their administration. This made him a host of active and powerful enemies both in the colonies and in Spain.

Considerable changes had taken place in the island of Hispaniola during the absence of the admiral. The mines had fallen into neglect, the cultivation of the sugar-cane having been found a more certain source of wealth. It became a by-word in Spain that the magnificent palaces

---

[1] Herrera, Hist. Ind., decad. ii. lib. ii. cap. 7.
[2] Ibid., decad. i. lib. x. cap 16.
[3] Charlevoix, Hist. St Domingo, lib. 5.
[4] Herrera, Hist Ind., decad. ii lib. ix. cap. 7.

erected by Charles V. at Madrid and Toledo were built of the sugar of Hispaniola. Slaves had been imported in great numbers from Africa, being found more serviceable in the culture of the cane than the feeble Indians. The treatment of the poor negroes was cruel in the extreme; and they seem to have had no advocates even among the humane. The slavery of the Indians had been founded on the right of the strong; but it was thought that the negroes, from their color, were born to slavery; and that from being bought and sold in their own country, it was their natural condition. Though a patient and enduring race, the barbarities inflicted on them at length roused them to revenge, and on the 27th of December, 1522, there was the first African revolt in Hispaniola. It began in a sugar plantation of the Admiral Don Diego, where about twenty slaves, joined by an equal number from a neighboring plantation, got possession of arms, rose on their superintendents, massacred them, and sallied forth upon the country. It was their intention to pillage certain plantations, to kill the whites, re enforce themselves by freeing their countrymen, and either to possess themselves of the town of Agua, or to escape to the mountains.

Don Diego set out from St. Domingo in search of the rebels, followed by several of the principal inhabitants. On the second day he stopped on the banks of the River Nizao to rest his party and suffer re-enforcements to overtake him. Here one Melcher de Castro, who accompanied the admiral, learned that the negroes had ravaged his plantation, sacked his house, killed one of his men, and carried off his Indian slaves. Without asking leave of the admiral, he departed in the night with two companions, visited his plantation, found all in confusion, and pursuing the negroes, sent to the admiral for aid. Eight horsemen were hastily despatched to his assistance, armed with bucklers and lances, and having six of the infantry mounted behind them. De Castro had three horsemen beside this re-enforcement, and at the head of this little band overtook the negroes at break of day. The insurgents put themselves in battle array, armed with stones and Indian spears, and uttering loud shouts and outcries. The Spanish horsemen braced their bucklers, couched their lances, and charged them at full speed. The negroes were soon routed, and fled to the rocks, leaving six dead and several wounded. De Castro also was wounded in the arm. The admiral coming up, assisted in the pursuit of the fugitives. As fast as they were taken they were hanged on the nearest trees, and remained suspended as spectacles of terror to their countrymen. This prompt severity checked all further attempts at revolt among the African slaves.[1]

In the mean time the various enemies whom Don Diego had created, both in the colonies and in Spain, were actively and successfully employed. His old antagonist, the treasurer Pasamonte, had charged him with usurping almost all the powers of the royal audience, and with having given to the royal declaration, re-establishing him in his office of viceroy, an extent never intended by the sovereign. These representations had weight at court, and in 1523 Don Diego received a most severe letter from the Council of the Indies, charging him with the various abuses and excesses alleged against him, and commanding him, on pain of forfeiting all his privileges and titles, to revoke the innovations he had made, and restore things to their former state. To prevent any plea of ignorance of this mandate, the royal audience was enjoined to promulgate it and to call upon all persons to conform to it, and to see that it was properly obeyed. The admiral received also a letter from the council,

---

[1] Herrera Hist Ind., decad iii. lib. iv cap. 9.

Informing him that his presence was necessary in Spain, to give information of the foregoing matters. and advice relative to the reformation of various abuses and to the treatment and preservation of the Indians; he was requested. therefore, to repair to court without waiting for further orders.[1]

Don Diego understood this to be a peremptory recall, and obeyed accordingly. On his arrival in Spain. he immediately presented himself before the court at Victoria, with the frank and fearless spirit of an upright man, and pleaded his cause so well that the sovereign and council acknowledged his innocence on all the points of accusation. He convinced them, moreover, of the exactitude with which he had discharged his duties; of his zeal for the public good, and the glory of the crown; and that all the representations against him rose from the jealousy and enmity of Pasamonte and other royal officers in the colonies, who were impatient of any superior authority in the island to restrain them.

Having completely established his innocence. and exposed the calumnies of his enemies. Don Diego trusted that he would soon obtain justice as to all his claims. As these however, involved a participation in the profits of vast and richly productive provinces, he experienced the delays and difficulties usual with such demands, for it is only when justice costs nothing that it is readily rendered. His earnest solicitations at length obtained an order from the emperor, that a commission should be formed, composed of the grand chancellor, the Friar Loyasa, confessor to the emperor. and president of the royal Council of the Indies, and a number of other distinguished personages. They were to inquire into the various points in dispute between the admiral and the fiscal, and into the proceedings which had taken place in the Council of the Indies, with the power of determining what justice required in the case.

The affair, however, was protracted to such a length, and accompanied by so many toils, vexations, and disappointments, that the unfortunate Diego, like his father. died in the pursuit. For two years he had followed the court from city to city, during its migrations from Victoria to Burgos, Valladolid, Madrid and Toledo. In the winter of 1525, the emperor set out from Toledo for Seville. The admiral undertook to follow him, though his constitution was broken by fatigue and vexation, and he was wasting under the attack of a slow fever. Oviedo, the historian, saw him at Toledo two days before his departure, and joined with his friends in endeavoring to dissuade him from a journey in such a state of health, and at such a season. Their persuasions were in vain. Don Diego was not aware of the extent of his malady: he told them that he should repair to Seville by the Church of our Lady of Guadaloupe, to offer up his devotions at that shrine; and he trusted, through the intercession of the mother of God, soon to be restored to health.[2] He accordingly left Toledo in a litter on the 21st of February, 1526, having previously confessed and taken the communion, and arrived the same day at Montalvan, distant about six leagues. There his illness increased to such a degree that he saw his end approaching. He employed the following day in arranging the affairs of his conscience, and expired on February 23d, being little more than fifty years of age, his premature death having been hastened by the griefs and troubles he had experienced. " He was worn out," says Herrera, " by following up his claims, and defending himself from the calumnies of his competitors, who, with many stratagems and devices, sought to obscure the glory of the father and the virtue of the son."[3]

---

[1] Herrera, Hist. Ind., decad lib. v cap. 4.
[2] Charlevoix, Hist. St. Domingo, lib. vi.   [3] Herrera, decad. iii. lib. viii. cap. 15.

We have seen how the discovery of the New World rendered the residue of the life of Columbus a tissue of wrongs, hardships and afflictions, and how the jealousy and enmity he had awakened were inherited by his son. It remains to show briefly in what degree the anticipations of perpetuity, wealth, and honor to his family were fulfilled.

When Don Diego Columbus died, his wife and family were at St. Domingo. He left two sons, Luis and Christopher, and three daughters — Maria, who afterwards married Don Sancho de Cardono; Juana, who married Don Luis de Cueva; and Isabella, who married Don George of Portugal, Count of Gelves. He had also a natural son named Christopher.[1]

Charlevoix mentions another son called Diego, and calls one of the daughters Phillipine. Spotorno says that the daughter Maria took the veil; confounding her with a niece. These are trivial errors, merely noticed to avoid the imputation of inaccuracy. The account of the descendants of Columbus here given, accords with a genealogical tree of the family, produced before the Council of the Indies in a great lawsuit for the estates.

After the death of Don Diego, his noble-spirited vice-queen, left with a number of young children, endeavored to assert and maintain the rights of the family. Understanding that, according to the privileges accorded to Christopher Columbus, they had a just claim to the viceroyalty of the province of Veragua, as having been discovered by him, she demanded a license from the royal audience of Hispaniola, to recruit men and fit out an armada to colonize that country. This the audience refused, and sent information of the demand to the emperor. He replied that the vice-queen should be kept in suspense until the justice of her claim could be ascertained; as, although he had at various times given commissions to different persons to examine the doubts and objections which had been opposed by the fiscal, no decision had ever been made.[2] The enterprise thus contemplated by the vice-queen was never carried into effect.

Shortly afterwards she sailed for Spain, to protect the claim of her eldest son, Don Luis, then six years of age. Charles V. was absent, but she was most graciously received by the empress. The title of admiral of the Indies was immediately conferred on her son, Don Luis, and the emperor augmented his revenues, and conferred other favors on the family. Charles V., however, could never be prevailed on to give Don Luis the title of viceroy, although that dignity had been decreed to his father, a few years previous to his death, as an hereditary right.[3]

In 1538 the young admiral, Don Luis, then about eighteen years of age, was at court, having instituted proceedings before the proper tribunals for the recovery of the viceroyalty. Two years afterward the suit was settled by arbitration, his uncle Don Fernando and Cardinal Loyasa, president of the Council of the Indies, being umpires. By a compromise Don Luis was declared captain-general of Hispaniola, but with such limitations that it was little better than a bare title. Don Luis sailed for Hispaniola, but did not remain there long. He found his dignities and privileges mere sources of vexation, and finally entered into a compromise, which relieved himself and gratified the emperor. He gave up all pretensions to the viceroyalty of the New World, receiving in its stead the titles of Duke of Veragua and Marquis of Jamaica.[4] He commuted also

---

[1] Memorial ajustado sobre el estado de Veragua.
[2] Herrera, decad. iv. lib. ii cap. 6.
[3] Charlevoix, Hist. St. Domingo, lib. vi. p. 443.
[4] Ibid., tom. i. lib. vi. p. 446.

the claim to the tenth of the produce of the Indies for a pension of one thousand doubloons of gold.[1]

Don Luis did not long enjoy the substitution of a certain, though moderate, revenue for a magnificent but unproductive claim. He died shortly afterward, leaving no other male issue than an illegitimate son, named Christopher. He left two daughters by his wife, Doña Maria de Mosquera, one named Phillippa, and the other Maria, which last became a nun in the convent of St. Quirce, at Valladolid.

Don Luis having no legitimate son, was succeeded by his nephew Diego, son to his brother Christopher. A litigation took place between this young heir and his cousin Phillippa, daughter of the late Don Luis. The convent of St. Quirce also put in a claim, on behalf of its inmate, Doña Maria, who had taken the veil. Christopher, natural son to Don Luis, likewise became a prosecutor in the suit, but was set aside on account of his illegitimacy. Don Diego and his cousin Phillippa soon thought it better to join claims and persons in wedlock, than to pursue a tedious contest. They were married, and their union was happy, though not fruitful. Diego died without issue in 1578, and with him the legitimate male line of Columbus became extinct.

One of the most important lawsuits that the world has ever witnessed now arose for the estates and dignities descended from the great discoverer. Don Diego had two sisters, Francisca and Maria, the former of whom, and the children of the latter, advanced their several claims. To these parties was added Bernard Colombo of Cogoleto, who claimed as lineal descendant from Bartholomew Columbus, the Adelantado, brother to the discoverer. He was, however, pronounced ineligible, as the Adelantado had no acknowledged, and certainly no legitimate offspring.

Baldassar, or Balthazar Colombo, of the house of Cuccaro and Conzano, in the dukedom of Montferrat, in Piedmont, was an active and persevering claimant. He came from Italy into Spain, where he devoted himself for many years to the prosecution of this suit. He produced a genealogical tree of his family, in which was contained one Domenico Colombo, Lord of Cuccaro, whom he maintained to be the identical father of Christopher Columbus, the admiral. He proved that this Domenico was living at the requisite era, and produced many witnesses who had heard that the navigator was born in the castle of Cuccaro; whence, it was added, he and his two brothers had eloped at an early age, and had never returned.[2] A monk is also mentioned among the witnesses, who made oath that Christopher and his brothers were born in that castle of Cuccaro. This testimony was afterward withdrawn by the prosecutor; as it was found that the monk's recollection must have extended back considerably upward of a century.[3] The claim of Balthazar was negatived. His proofs that Christopher Columbus was a native of Cuccaro were rejected, as only hearsay, or traditionary evidence. His ancestor Domenico, it appeared from his own showing, died in 1456; whereas it was established that Domenico, the father of the admiral, was living upward of thirty years after that date.

The cause was finally decided by the Council of the Indies, on the second of December. 1608. The male line was declared to be extinct. Don Nuño or Nugno Gelves de Portugallo was put in possession, and became Duke of Veragua. He was grandson to Isabella, third daughter of Don Diego (son of the discoverer) by his vice-queen, Doña Maria de

---

[1] Spotorno, Hist. Colom., p. 123.
[2] Bossi, Hist. Colomb. Dissert., p. 67.
[3] Ibid., Dissert on the Country of Columbus. p. 63.

Toledo. The descendants of the two elder sisters of Isabella had a prior claim, but their lines became extinct previous to this decision of the suit.

The Isabella just named had married Don George of Portugal, Count of Gelves. "Thus," says Charlevoix, "the dignities and wealth of Columbus passed into a branch of the Portuguese house of Braganza, established in Spain, of which the heirs are entitled *De Portugallo, Colon, Duke de Veragua, Marques de la Jamaica, y Almirante de las Indias.*[1]

The suit of Balthazar Colombo of Cuccaro was rejected under three different forms, by the Council of the Indies; and his application for an allowance of support, under the legacy of Columbus, in favor of poor relations, was also refused: although the other parties had assented to the demand.[2] He died in Spain, where he had resided many years in prosecution of this suit. His son returned to Italy persisting in the validity of his claim: he said that it was in vain to seek justice in Spain; they were too much interested to keep those dignities and estates among themselves; but he gave out that he had received twelve thousand doubloons of gold in compromise from the other parties. Spotorno, under sanction of Ignazio de Giovanni, a learned canon, treats this assertion as a bravado, to cover his defeat, being contradicted by his evident poverty.[3] The family of Cuccaro, however, still maintain their right, and express great veneration for the memory of their illustrious ancestor, the admiral; and travellers occasionally visit their old castle in Piedmont with great reverence, as the birthplace of the discoverer of the New World.

No. III.

FERNANDO COLUMBUS.

FERNANDO COLUMBUS (or Colon, as he is called in Spain), the natural son and historian of the admiral, was born in Cordova. There is an uncertainty about the exact time of his birth. According to his epitaph, it must have been on the 28th September, 1488; but according to his original papers preserved in the library of the cathedral of Seville, and which were examined by Don Diego Ortiz de Zuñiga, historian of that city, it would appear to have been on the 29th of August, 1487. His mother, Doña Beatrix Enriquez, was of a respectable family, but was never married to the admiral, as has been stated by some of his biographers.

Early in 1494 Fernando was carried to court, together with his elder brother Diego, by his uncle Don Bartholomew, to enter the royal household in quality of page to the Prince Don Juan, son and heir to Ferdinand and Isabella. He and his brother remained in this situation until the death of the prince, when they were taken by Queen Isabella as pages into her own service. Their education, of course, was well attended to, and Fernando in after-life gave proofs of being a learned man.

In the year 1502, at the tender age of thirteen or fourteen years, Fernando accompanied his father in his fourth voyage of discovery, and encountered all its singular and varied hardships with a fortitude that is mentioned with praise and admiration by the admiral.

After the death of his father it would appear that Fernando made two voyages to the New World. He accompanied the Emperor Charles V.

---

[1] Charlevoix, Hist. St Domingo, tom i. lib. vi. p. 447.
[2] Bossi, Dissertation on the Country of Columbus.
[3] Spotorno, p. 127.

also to Italy, Flanders, and Germany; and according to Zuñiga (Anales de Seville de 1539, No. 3) travelled over all Europe and a part of Africa and Asia. Possessing talents, judgment, and industry, these opportunities were not lost upon him, and he acquired much information in geography, navigation, and natural history. Being of a studious habit, and fond of books, he formed a select, yet copious library, of more than twenty thousand volumes, in print and in manuscript. With the sanction of the Emperor Charles V. he undertook to establish an academy and college of mathematics at Seville; and for this purpose commenced the construction of a sumptuous edifice, without the walls of the city, facing the Guadalquiver, in the place where the monastery of San Laureano is now situated. His constitution, however, had been broken by the sufferings he had experienced in his travels and voyages, and a premature death prevented the completion of his plan of the academy, and broke off other useful labors. He died in Seville on the 12th of July, 1539, at the age, according to his epitaph, of fifty years, nine months and fourteen days. He left no issue, and was never married. His body was interred according to his request, in the cathedral of Seville. He bequeathed his valuable library to the same establishment.

Don Fernando devoted himself much to letters. According to the inscription on his tomb, he composed a work in four books, or volumes, the title of which is defaced on the monument, and the work itself is lost. This is much to be regretted, as, according to Zuñiga, the fragments of the inscription specify it to have contained, among a variety of matter, historical, moral, and geographical notices of the countries he had visited, but especially of the New World, and of the voyages and discoveries of his father.

His most important and permanent work, however, was a history of the admiral, composed in Spanish. It was translated into Italian by Alonzo de Ulloa, and from this Italian translation have proceeded the editions which have since appeared in various languages. It is singular that the work only exists in Spanish, in the form of a re-translation from that of Ulloa, and full of errors in the orthography of proper names, and in dates and distances.

Don Fernando was an eye-witness of some of the facts which he relates, particularly of the fourth voyage wherein he accompanied his father. He had also the papers and charts of his father, and recent documents of all kinds to extract from, as well as familiar acquaintance with the principal personages who were concerned in the events which he records. He was a man of probity and discernment, and writes more dispassionately than could be expected, when treating of matters which affected the honor, the interests, and happiness of his father. It is to be regretted, however. that he should have suffered the whole of his father's life, previous to his discoveries (a period of about fifty-six years). to remain in obscurity He appears to have wished to cast a cloud over it, and only to have presented his father to the reader after he had rendered himself illustrious by his actions, and his history had become in a manner identified with the history of the world. His work, however, is an invaluable document. entitled to great faith, and is the corner-stone of the history of the American Continent

No. IV.

AGE OF COLUMBUS.

As the date I have assigned for the birth of Columbus makes him about ten years older than he is generally represented, at the time of his discoveries, it is proper to state precisely my authority. In the valuable manuscript chronicle of the reign of the Catholic sovereigns, written by Andres Bernaldes, the curate of Los Palacios, there is a long tract on the subject of the discoveries of Columbus; it concludes with these words: *Murió en Valladolid, el año de 1506, en el mes de Mayo, in senectute bona, de edad 70 años, poco mas ó menos.* (He died in Valladolid in the year 1506, in the month of May, in a good old age, being seventy years old, a little more or less.) The curate of Los Palacios was a contemporary, and an intimate friend of Columbus, who was occasionally a guest in his house; no one was more competent, therefore, to form a correct idea of his age. It is singular that, while the biographers of Columbus have been seeking to establish the epoch of his birth by various calculations and conjectures, this direct testimony of honest Andre Bernaldes has entirely escaped their notice, though some of them had his manuscript in their hands. It was first observed by my accurate friend Don Antonio Uguina in the course of his exact investigations, and has been pointed out and ably supported by Don Martin Fernandez de Navarrete, in the introduction to his valuable collection of voyages.

Various circumstances in the life of Columbus will be found to corroborate the statement of the curate; such, for example, as the increasing infirmities with which he struggled during his voyages, and which at last rendered him a cripple and confined him to his bed. The allusion to his advanced age in one of his letters to the sovereigns, wherein he relates the consolation he had received from a secret voice in the night season: *Tu vejez no impedira a toda cosa grande. Abraham pasaba cien años cuando engendro a Isaac, etc.* (Thy old age shall be no impediment to any great undertaking. Abraham was above a hundred years old when he begat Isaac, etc.) The permission granted him by the king the year previous to his death to travel on a mule, instead of a horse, on account of his *age* and infirmities; and the assertion of Oviedo. that at the time of his death he was quite old (*era ya viego*).

This fact of the advanced age of Columbus throws quite a new coloring over his character and history. How much more extraordinary is the ardent enthusiasm which sustained him through his long career of solicitation, and the noble pride with which he refused to descend from his dignified demands, and to bargain about his proposition. though life was rapidly wasting in delays. How much more extraordinary is the hardihood with which he undertook repeated voyages into unknown seas. amid all kinds of perils and hardships; the fortitude with which he bore up against an accumulation of mental and bodily afflictions, enough to have disheartened and destroyed the most youthful and robust, and the irrepressible buoyancy of spirit with which to the last he still rose from under the ruined concerns and disappointed hopes and blasted projects of one enterprise, to launch into another, still more difficult and perilous

We have been accustomed to admire all these things in Columbus when we considered him in the full vigor of his life; how much more are they entitled to our wonder as the achievements of a man whom the weight of years and infirmities was pressing into the grave.

No. V.

LINEAGE OF COLUMBUS.

THE ancestry of Christopher Columbus has formed a point of zealous controversy which is not yet satisfactorily settled. Several honorable families, possessing domains in Placentia, Montferrat, and the different parts of the Genoese territories, claim him as belonging to their houses; and to these has recently been added the noble family of Colombo in Modena.[1] The natural desire to prove consanguinity with a man of distinguished renown has excited this rivalry: but it has been heightened, in particular instances, by the hope of succeeding to titles and situations of wealth and honor, when his male line of descendants became extinct. The investigation is involved in particular obscurity, as even his immediate relatives appear to have been in ignorance on the subject.

Fernando Columbus in his biography of the admiral, after a pompous prelude, in which he attempts to throw a vague and cloudy magnificence about the origin of his father, notices slightly the attempts of some to obscure his fame, by making him a native of various small and insignificant villages; and dwells with more complacency upon others who make him a native of places in which there were persons of much honor of the name, and many sepulchral monuments with arms and epitaphs of the Colombos. He relates his having himself gone to the castle of Cucureo, to visit two brothers of the family of Colombo, who were rich and noble, the youngest of whom was above one hundred years of age, and who he had heard were relatives of his father; but they could give him no information upon the subject; whereupon he breaks forth into his professed contempt for these adventitious claims, declaring, that he thinks it better to content himself with dating from the glory of the admiral, than to go about inquiring whether his father "were a merchant, or one who kept his hawks;"[2] since, adds he, of persons of similar pursuits, there are thousands who die every day, whose memory, even among their own neighbors and relatives, perishes immediately, without its being possible afterward to ascertain even whether they existed.

After this, and a few more expressions of similar disdain for these empty distinctions, he indulges in vehement abuse of Agostino Guistiniani, whom he calls a false historian, an inconsiderate, partial, or malignant compatriot, for having, in his psalter, traduced his father, by saying, that in his youth he had been employed in mechanical occupations.

As, after all this discussion, Fernando leaves the question of his father's parentage in all its original obscurity, yet appears irritably sensitive to any derogatory suggestions of others, his whole evidence tends to the conviction that he really knew nothing to boast of in his ancestry.

Of the nobility and antiquity of the Colombo family, of which the admiral probably was a remote descendant, we have some account in Herrera. "We learn," he says, "that the Emperor Otto the Second, in 940, confirmed to the counts Pietro, Giovanni, and Alexandro Colombo, brothers, the feudatory possessions which they held within the jurisdiction of the cities of Ayqui, Savona, Aste, Montferrato, Turin, Viceli, Parma, Cremona, and Bergamo, and all others which they held in Italy. It

---

[1] Spotorno, Hist. Mem., p. 5

[2] Literally, in the original, *Cazador de Volateria*, a falconer. Hawking was in those days an amusement of the highest classes; and to keep hawks was almost a sign of nobility

appears that the Colombos of Cuccaro, Cucureo, and Placentia were the same, and that the Emperor in the same year, 940, made donation to the said three brothers of the castles of Cuccaro, Conzano, Rosignano, and others, and of the fourth part of Bistanio, which appertained to the empire.[1]

One of the boldest attempts of those biographers bent on ennobling Columbus, has been to make him son of the Lord of Cuccaro, a burgh of Montferrat, in Piedmont, and to prove that he was born in his father's castle at that place, whence he and his brothers eloped at an early age, and never returned. This was asserted in the course of a process brought by a certain Baldassar or Balthazar Colombo, resident in Genoa, but originally of Cuccaro, claiming the title and estates, on the death of Diego Colon, Duke of Veragua, in 1578, the great-grandson and last legitimate male descendant of the admiral. The council of the Indies decided against this claim to relationship. Some account of the lawsuit will be found in another part of the work

This romantic story, like all others of the nobility of his parentage, is at utter variance with the subsequent events of his life, his long struggles with indigence and obscurity, and the difficulties he endured from the want of family connections. How can it be believed, says Bossi, that this same man, who, in his most cruel adversities, was incessantly taunted by his enemies with the obscurity of his birth, should not reply to this reproach, by declaring his origin, if he were really descended from the Lords of Cuccaro, Conzano, and Rosignano? a circumstance which would have obtained him the highest credit with the Spanish nobility.[2]

The different families of Colombo which lay claim to the great navigator seem to be various branches of one tree, and there is little doubt of his appertaining remotely to the same respectable stock.

It appears evident, however, that Columbus sprang immediately from a line of humble but industrious citizens, which had existed in Genoa, even from the time of Giacomo Colombo, the wool-carder, in 1311, mentioned by Spotorno; nor is this in any wise incompatible with the intimation of Fernando Columbus, that the family had been reduced from high estate to great poverty, by the wars of Lombardy. The feuds of Italy, in those ages, had broken down and scattered many of the noblest families; and while some branches remained in the lordly heritage of castles and domains, others were confounded with the humblest population of the cities.

No. VI.

BIRTHPLACE OF COLUMBUS.

THERE has been much controversy about the birthplace of Columbus. The greatness of his renown has induced various places to lay claim to him as a native, and from motives of laudable pride, for nothing reflects greater lustre upon a city than to have given birth to distinguished men. The original and long-established opinion was in favor of Genoa; but such strenuous claims were asserted by the states of Placentia, and in particular of Piedmont, that the Academy of Sciences and Letters of Genoa was induced, in 1812, to nominate three of its members, Signors Serra, Carrega, and Piaggio, commissioners to examine into these pretensions.

The claims of Placentia had been first advanced in 1662, by Pietro Maria

---

[1] Herrera decad i. lib. i. cap 7.   [2] Dissertation etc.

Campi, in the ecclesiastical history of that place, who maintained that Columbus was a native of the village of Pradello, in that vicinity. It appeared probable, on investigation, that Bertolino Colombo, great-grand-father to the admiral, had owned a small property in Pradello, the rent of which had been received by Domenico Colombo of Genoa, and after his death by his sons Christopher and Bartholomew. Admitting this assertion to be correct, there was no proof that either the admiral, his father, or grandfather had ever resided on that estate. The very circum-stances of the case indicated, on the contrary, that their home was in Genoa.

The claim of Piedmont was maintained with more plausibility. It was shown that a Domenico Colombo was lord of the castle of Cuccaro in Montferrat, at the time of the birth of Christopher Columbus, who, it was asserted, was his son, and born in his castle. Balthazar Colombo, a descendant of this person, instituted a lawsuit before the Council of the Indies for the inheritance of the admiral, when his male line became ex-tinct. The Council of the Indies decided against him, as is shown in an account of that process given among the illustrations of this history. It was proved that Domenico Colombo, father of the admiral, was resident in Genoa both before and many years after the death of this lord of Cuc-caro, who bore the same name.

The three commissioners appointed by the Academy of Science and Letters of Genoa to examine into these pretensions, after a long and diligent investigation, gave a voluminous and circumstantial report in favor of Genoa. An ample digest of their inquest may be found in the History of Columbus by Signor Bossi, who, in an able dissertation on the question, confirms their opinion. It may be added, in further corrobora-tion, that Peter Martyr and Bartholomew Las Casas, who were contem-poraries and acquaintances of Columbus, and Juan de Barros, the Portuguese historian, all make Columbus a native of the Genoese terri-tories.

There has been a question fruitful of discussion among the Genoese themselves, whether Columbus was born in the city of Genoa, or in some other part of the territory. Finale, and Oneglia, and Savona, towns on the Ligurian coast to the west, Boggiasco, Cogoleto, and several other towns and villages, claim him as their own. His family possessed a small property at a village or hamlet between Quinto and Nervi, called Terra Rossa; in Latin, Terra Rubra; which has induced some writers to assign his birth to one of those places. Bossi says that there is still a tower between Quinto and Nervi which bears the title of Torre dei Colombi.[1] Barthol-omew Columbus, brother to the admiral, styled himself of Terra Rubra, in a Latin inscription on a map which he presented to Henry VII. of England, and Fernando Columbus states, in his history of the admiral, that he was accustomed to subscribe himself in the same manner before he attained to his dignities.

Cogoleto at one time bore away the palm. The families there claim the discoverer, and preserve a portrait of him. One or both of the two admirals named Colombo, with whom he sailed, are stated to have come from that place, and to have been confounded with him so as to have given support to this idea.[2]

Savona, a city in the Genoese territories, has claimed the same honor, and this claim has recently been very strongly brought forward. Signor Giovanni Battista Belloro, an advocate of Savona, has strenuously main-tained this claim in an ingenious disputation, dated May 12th, 1826, in

---

[1] Bossi. French Translation, Paris, 1824, p. 69.   [2] Ibid.

form of a letter to the Baron du Zach, editor of a valuable astronomical and geographical journal, published monthly at Genoa.[1]

Signor Belloro claims it as an admitted fact, that Domenico Colombo was for many years a resident and citizen of Savona, in which place one Christopher Columbus is shown to have signed a document in 1472.

He states that a public square in that city bore the name of Platea Columbi, toward the end of the 14th century; that the Ligurian government gave the name of Jurisdizione di Colombi to that district of the republic, under the persuasion that the great navigator was a native of Savona, and that Columbus gave the name of Saona to a little island adjacent to Hispaniola, among his earliest discoveries.

He quotes many Savonese writers, principally poets, and various historians and poets of other countries, and thus establishes the point that Columbus was held to be a native of Savona by persons of respectable authority. He lays particular stress on the testimony of the Magnifico Francisco Spinola, as related by the learned prelate Felippo Alberto Pollero, stating that he had seen the sepulchre of Christopher Columbus in the cathedral at Seville, and that the epitaph states him expressly to be a native of Savona: " Hic jacet Christophorus Columbus Savonensis." [2]

The proofs advanced by Signor Belloro show his zeal for the honor of his native city, but do not authenticate the fact he undertakes to establish. He shows clearly that many respectable writers believed Columbus to be a native of Savona; but a far greater number can be adduced, and many of them contemporary with the admiral, some of them his intimate friends, others his fellow-citizens, who state him to have been born in the city of Genoa. Among the Savonese writers, Giulio Salinorio, who investigated the subject, comes expressly to the same conclusion: " *Genova, città nobilissima, era la patria de Colombo.*"

Signor Belloro appears to be correct in stating that Domenico, the father of the admiral, was several years resident in Savona. But it appears from his own dissertation, that the Christopher who witnessed the testament in 1472, styled himself of Genoa: " *Christophorus Columbus lanerius de Janua.*" This incident is stated by other writers, who presume this Christopher to have been the navigator on a visit to his father, in the interval of his early voyages. In as far as the circumstance bears on the point, it supports the idea that he was born at Genoa.

The epitaph, on which Signor Belloro places his principal reliance, entirely fails. Christopher Columbus was not interred in the cathedral of Seville, nor was any monument erected to him in that edifice. The tomb to which the learned prelate Felippo Alberto Pollero alludes may have been that of Fernando Columbus, son to the admiral, who, as has been already observed, was buried in the cathedral of Seville, to which he bequeathed his noble library. The place of his sepulture is designated by a broad slab of white marble, inserted in the pavement, with an inscription, partly in Spanish, partly in Latin, recording the merits of Fernando and the achievements of his father. On either side of the epitaph is engraved an ancient Spanish Galley. The inscription quoted by Signor Belloro may have been erroneously written from memory by the Magnifico Francisco Spinola, under the mistaken idea that he had beheld the sepulchre of the great discoverer. As Fernando was born at Cordova, the term

---

[1] Correspondence Astronom Geograph etc., de Baron du Zach, vol. 14, cahier 6, lettera 29. 1826.

[2] Felippo Alberto Pollero, Epicherema, cioé breve discorso per difesa di sua persona e carrattere. Torino, per Gio Battista Zappata MCDXCVI. (read 1696) in l°. pag. 47

Savonensis must have been another error of memory in the Magnifico; no such word is to be found in the inscription.

This question of birthplace has also been investigated with considerable minuteness, and a decision given in favor of Genoa, by D. Gio Battista Spotorno, of the royal university in that city, in his historical memoir of Columbus He shows that the family of the Columbi had long been resident in Genoa. By an extract from the notarial register, it appeared that one Giacomo Colombo, a wool-carder, resided without the gate of St. Andria, in the year 1311. An agreement, also, published by the academy of Genoa, proved, that in 1489, Domenico Colombo possessed a house and shop, and a garden with a well, in the street of St. Andrew's gate, anciently without the walls, presumed to have been the same residence with that of Giacomo Colombo. He rented also another house from the monks of St. Stephen, in the Via Mulcento, leading from the street of St Andrew to the Strada Giulia.[1]

Signor Bossi states, that documents lately found in the archives of the monastery of St. Stephen, present the name of Domenico Colombo several times, from 1456 to 1459, and designate him as son of Giovanni Colombo, husband of Susanna Fontanarossa, and father of Christopher, Bartholomew, and Giacomo,[2] (or Diego). He states also that the receipts of the canons show that the last payment of rent was made by Domenico Colombo for his dwelling in 1489. He surmises that the admiral was born in the before-mentioned house belonging to those monks, in Via Mulcento, and that he was baptized in the church of St. Stephen. He adds that an ancient manuscript was submitted to the commissioners of the Genoese academy, in the margin of which the notary had stated that the name of Christopher was on the register of the parish as having been baptized in that church.[3]

Andres Bernaldez, the curate of los Palacios, who was an intimate friend of Columbus, says that he was of Genoa.[4] Agostino Giustiniani, a contemporary of Columbus, likewise asserts it in his Polyglot Psalter, published in Genoa, in 1516. Antonio de Herrera, an author of great accuracy, who, though not a contemporary, had access to the best documents, asserts decidedly that he was born in the city of Genoa.

To these names may be added that of Alexander Geraldini, brother to the nuncio, and instructor to the children of Ferdinand and Isabella, a most intimate friend of Columbus.[5] Also Antonio Gallo.[6] Bartolomeo Senarega,[7] and Uberto Foglieta,[8] all contemporaries with the admiral, and natives of Genoa, together with an anonymous writer, who published an account of his voyage of discovery at Venice in 1509.[9] It is unnecessary to mention historians of later date agreeing in the same fact, as they must have derived their information from some of these authorities.

The question in regard to the birthplace of Columbus has been treated thus minutely, because it has been, and still continues to be, a point of warm controversy. It may be considered, however, as conclusively decided by the highest authority, the evidence of Columbus himself. In a testament executed in 1498, which has been admitted in evidence before the Spanish tribunals in certain lawsuits among his descendants, he twice declares that he was a native of the city of Genoa : " *Siendo yo nacido en Genova.*" " I being born in Genoa." And again, he repeats the assertion, as a reason for enjoining certain conditions on his heirs, which

[1] Spotorno, Eng. trans. p. xl. xii. [2] Bossi, French trans. p. 76. [3] Ibid., p 88.
[4] Cura de los Palacios, MS. cap. 118. [5] Alex. Geraldini. Itin. ad. Reg. sub. Aquinor
[6] Antonio Gallo, Anales of Genoa, Muratori, tom. 23.
[7] Senaregi. Muratori, tom. 24 [8] Foglieta. Elog. Clar. Ligur
[9] Grineus, Nov. Orb.

manifest the interest he takes in his native place. " I command the said Diego, my son, or the person who inherits the said mayorazgo (or entailed estate), that he maintain always in the city of Genoa a person of our lineage, who shall have a house and a wife there, and to furnish him with an income on which he can live decently as a person connected with our family, and hold footing and root in that city as a native of it, so that he may have aid and favor in that city in case of need, *for from thence I came and there was born* " [1]

In another part of his testament he expresses himself with a filial fondness in respect to Genoa. " I command the said Don Diego, or whoever shall possess the said mavorazgo, that he labor and strive always for the honor, and welfare, and increase of the city of Genoa, and employ all his abilities and means in defending and augmenting the welfare and honor of her republic, in all matters which are not contrary to the service of the church of God, and the state of the king and queen our sovereigns, and their successors."

An informal codicil, executed by Columbus at Valladolid, May 4th, 1506, sixteen days before his death, was discovered about 1785, in the Corsini library at Rome. It is termed a military codicil, from being made in the manner which the civil law allows to the soldier who executes such an instrument on the eve of battle, or in expectation of death. It was written on the blank page of a little breviary presented to Columbus by Pope Alexander VII. Columbus leaves the book " to his beloved country, the Republic of Genoa."

He directs the erection of a hospital in that city for the poor, with provision for its support; and he declares that republic his successor in the admiralty of the Indies, in the event of his male line becoming extinct.

The authenticity of this paper has been questioned. It has been said, that there was no probability of Columbus having resort to a usage with which he was most likely unacquainted. The objections are not cogent. Columbus was accustomed to the peculiarities of a military life, and he repeatedly wrote letters in critical moments as a precaution against some fatal occurrence that seemed to impend. The present codicil, from its date, must have been written a few days previous to his death, perhaps at a moment when he imagined himself at extremity. This may account for any difference in the handwriting, especially as he was, at times, so affected by the gout in his hands as not to be able to write except at night. Particular stress has been laid on the signature; but it does not appear that he was uniform in regard to that, and it is a point to which any one who attempted a forgery would be attentive. It does not appear, likewise, that any advantage could have been obtained by forging the paper, or that any such was attempted.

In 1502, when Columbus was about to depart on his fourth and last voyage, he wrote to his friend, Doctor Nicolo Oderigo, formerly ambassador from Genoa to Spain, and forwarded to him copies of all his grants and commissions from the Spanish sovereigns, authenticated before the alcaldes of Seville. He, at the same time, wrote to the bank of San Giorgio, at Genoa, assigning a tenth of his revenues to be paid to that city, in diminution of the duties on corn, wine, and other provisions.

Why should Columbus feel this strong interest in Genoa, had he been

---

[1] " Item. Mando e, dicho Don Diego mi hijo, á la persona que heredare el dicho mayorazgo, que tenga y sostenga siempre en la ciudad de Genova una persona le nuestro linage que tenga alli casa é le ordene renta con que pueda vivir honestamente, como persona tar llegada á nuestro linage, y haga pie , raiz en la dicha ciudad como natural della, porque podrá haber de la dicha ciudad ayuda e favor en las cosas del menester suyo, *pues que della saii y en ella naci* "

born in any of the other Italian states which have laid claim to him? He was under no obligation to Genoa. He had resided there but a brief portion of his early life; and his proposition for discovery, according to some writers, had been scornfully rejected by that republic. There is nothing to warrant so strong an interest in Genoa but the filial tie which links the heart of man to his native place, however he may be separated from it by time or distance, and however little he may be indebted to it for favors.

Again, had Columbus been born in any of the towns and villages of the Genoese coast which have claimed him for a native, why should he have made these bequests in favor of the *city* of Genoa, and not of his native town or village?

These bequests were evidently dictated by a mingled sentiment of pride and affection, which would be without all object if not directed to his native place. He was at this time elevated above all petty pride on the subject. His renown was so brilliant, that it would have shed a lustre on any hamlet, however obscure; and the strong love of country here manifested would never have felt satisfied, until it had singled out the spot, and nestled down in the very cradle of his infancy. These appear to be powerful reasons, drawn from natural feeling, for deciding in favor of Genoa.

No. VII.

THE COLOMBOS.

DURING the early part of the life of Columbus there were two other navigators, bearing the same name, of some rank and celebrity, with whom he occasionally sailed; their names occurring vaguely from time to time, during the obscure part of his career, have caused much perplexity to some of his biographers, who have supposed that they designated the discoverer. Fernando Columbus affirms them to have been family connections,[1] and his father says, in one of his letters, " I am not the first admiral of our family "

These two were uncle and nephew: the latter being termed by historians Colombo the younger (by the Spanish historians Colombo el mozo). They were in the Genoese service, but are mentioned, occasionally, in old chronicles as French commanders, because Genoa, during a great part of their time, was under the protection, or rather the sovereignty of France, and her ships and captains, being engaged in the expeditions of that power, were indentified with the French marine.

Mention is made of the elder Colombo in Zurita's Annals of Aragon (L. xix. p. 261), in the war between Spain and Portugal, on the subject of the claim of the Princess Juana to the crown of Castile. In 1476, the King of Portugal determined to go to the Mediterranean coast of France, to incite his ally, Louis XI., to prosecute the war in the province of Guipuzcoa.

The king left Toro, says Zurita, on the 13th of June, and went by the river to the city of Porto, in order to await the armada of the king of France, the captain of which was Colon (Colombo), who was to navigate by the Straits of Gibraltar to pass to Marseilles.

After some delays Colombo arrived in the latter part of July with the French armada at Bermeo, on the coast of Biscay, where he encountered a violent storm, lost his principal ship, and ran to the coast of Galicia, with an intention of attacking Ribaldo, and lost a great many of his men.

---

[1] Hist del Almirante, cap I

Thence he went to Lisbon to receive the King of Portugal, who embarked in the fleet in August, with a number of his noblemen, and took two thousand two hundred foot soldiers, and four hundred and seventy horse, to strengthen the Portuguese garrisons along the Barbary coast. There were in the squadron twelve ships and five caravels. After touching at Ceuta the fleet proceeded to Colibre, where the king disembarked in the middle of September, the weather not permitting them to proceed to Marseilles. (Zurita, L. xix. Ch. 51.)

This Colombo is evidently the naval commander of whom the following mention is made by Jacques George de Chaufepie, in his supplement to Bayle (vol. 2, p. 126 of letter C).

"I do not know what dependence," says Chaufepie, "is to be placed on a fact reported in the *Ducatiana* (Part 1, p. 143), that Columbus was in 1474 captain of several ships for Louis XI., and that, as the Spaniards had made at that time an irruption into Roussillon, he thought that, for reprisal, and without contravening the peace between the two crowns, he could run down Spanish vessels. He attacked, therefore, and took two galleys of that nation, freighted on the account of various individuals. On complaints of this action being made to King Ferdinand, he wrote on the subject to Louis XI.; his letter is dated the 9th of December, 1474. Ferdinand terms Christopher Columbus a subject of Louis; it was because, as is known, Columbus was a Genoese, and Louis was sovereign of Genoa: although that city and Savona were held of him in fief by the Duke of Milan."

It is highly probable that it was the squadron of this same Colombo of whom the circumstance is related by Bossi, and after him by Spotorno on the authority of a letter found in the archives of Milan, and written in 1476 by two illustrious Milanese gentlemen, on their return from Jerusalem. The letter states that in the previous year, 1475, as the Venetian fleet was stationed off Cyprus to guard the island, a Genoese squadron, commanded by one Colombo, sailed by them with an air of defiance, shouting "Viva San Giorgia!" As the republics were then at peace they were permitted to pass unmolested.

Bossi supposes that the Colombo here mentioned was Christopher Columbus the discoverer: but it appears rather to have been the old Genoese admiral of that name. who according to Zurita was about that time cruising in the Mediterranean: and who, in all probability, was the hero of both the preceding occurrences.

The nephew of this Colombo, called by the Spanish Colombo el mozo, commanded a few years afterward a squadron in the French service, as will appear in a subsequent illustration, and Columbus may at various times have held an inferior command under both uncle and nephew, and been present on the above cited occasions.

No. VIII.

EXPEDITION OF JOHN OF ANJOU.

ABOUT the time that Columbus attained his twenty-fourth year, his native city was in a state of great alarm and peril from the threatened invasion of Alphonso V. of Aragon, King of Naples. Finding itself too weak to contend singly with such a foe, and having in vain looked for assistance from Italy it placed itself under the protection of Charles the VIIth of France. That monarch sent to its assistance John of Anjou son of Rene or Renato, king of Naples, who had been dispossessed of his crown by Alphonso. John of Anjou, otherwise called the Duke of Calabria,[1] immediately took upon himself the command of the place, repaired its fortifications, and defended the entrance of the harbor with strong chains. In the mean time, Alphonso had prepared a large land force, and assembled an armament of twenty ships and ten galleys at Ancona, on the frontiers of Genoa. The situation of the latter was considered eminently perilous, when Alphonso suddenly fell ill of a calenture and died, leaving the kingdoms of Anjou and Sicily to his brother John, and the kingdom of Naples to his son Ferdinand.

The death of Alphonso, and the subsequent division of his dominions, while they relieved the fears of the Genoese, gave rise to new hopes on the part of the house of Anjou; and the Duke John, encouraged by emissaries from various powerful partisans among the Neapolitan nobility, determined to make a bold attempt upon Naples for the recovery of the crown. The Genoese entered into his cause with spirit, furnishing him with ships, galleys, and money. His father René, or Renato, fitted out twelve galleys for the expedition in the harbor of Marseilles, and sent him assurance of an abundant supply of money, and of the assistance of the King of France. The brilliant nature of the enterprise attracted the attention of the daring and restless spirits of the times. The chivalrous nobleman, the soldier of fortune, the hardy corsair, the bold adventurer or the military partisan, enlisted under the banners of the Duke of Calabria. It is stated by historians that Columbus served in the armament from Genoa, in a squadron commanded by one of the Colombos, his relations.

The expedition sailed in October, 1459, and arrived at Sessa between the mouths of the Garigliano and the Volturno. The news of its arrival was the signal of universal revolt; the factious barons, and their vassals, hastened to join the standard of Anjou, and the duke soon saw the finest provinces of the Neapolitan dominions at his command, and with his army and squadron menaced the city of Naples itself.

In the history of this expedition we meet with one hazardous action of the fleet in which Columbus had embarked.

The army of John of Anjou being closely invested by a superior force, was in a perilous predicament at the mouth of the Sarno. In this conjuncture, the captain of the armada landed with his men, and scoured the neighborhood, hoping to awaken in the populace their former enthusiasm for the banner of Anjou, and perhaps to take Naples by surprise. A chosen company of Neapolitan infantry was sent against them. The troops from the fleet having little of the discipline of regular soldiery, and much of the freebooting disposition of maritime rovers, had scattered themselves about the country, intent chiefly upon spoil. They were attacked by the infantry and put to rout, with the loss of many killed and wounded. Endeavoring to make their way back to the ships, they found the passes seized and blocked up by the people of Sorento, who assailed them with dreadful havoc. Their flight now became desperate and headlong, many threw themselves from rocks and precipices into the sea, and but a small portion regained the ships.

The contest of John of Anjou for the crown of Naples lasted four years. For a time fortune favored him, and the prize seemed almost within his grasp, but reverses succeeded: he was defeated at various points ; the factious nobles, one by one, deserted him, and returned to their allegiance to Alphonso, and the duke was finally compelled to retire to the island of Ischia. Here he remained for some time,

---

[1] Duke of Calabria was a title of the heir apparent to the crown of Naples

guarded by eight galleys, which likewise harassed the bay of Naples.[1] In this squadron, which loyally adhered to him, until he ultimately abandoned this unfortunate enterprise, Columbus is stated to have served.

No. IX.

CAPTURE OF THE VENETIAN GALLEYS BY COLOMBO THE YOUNGER.

As the account of the sea-fight by which Fernando Columbus asserts that his father was first thrown upon the shores of Portugal has been adopted by various respectable historians, it is proper to give particular reasons for discrediting it.

Fernando expressly says that it was in an action mentioned by Marco Antonio Sabelico, in the eighth book of his tenth Decade; that the squadron in which Columbus served was commanded by a famous corsair, called Columbus the younger (Colombo el mozo), and that an embassy was sent from Venice to thank the King of Portugal for the succor he afforded to the Venetian captains and crews. All this is certainly recorded in Sabellicus, but the battle took place in 1485, after Columbus had *left* Portugal. Zurita in his annals of Aragon, under the date of 1685, mentions this same action. He says, "At this time four Venetian galleys sailed from the island of Cadiz, and took the route for Flanders; they were laden with merchandise from the Levant, especially from the island of Sicily, and passing by Cape St. Vincent, they were attacked by a French corsair, son of captain Colon (Colombo), who had seven vessels in his armada; and the galleys were captured the twenty-first of August." [2]

A much fuller account is given in the life of King John II of Portugal, by Garcia de Resende, who likewise records it as happening in 1485. He says the Venetian galleys were taken and robbed by the French and the captains and crews, wounded, plundered, and maltreated, were turned on shore at Cascoes. Here they were succored by Doña Maria de Meneses, Countess of Monsanto.

When King John II heard of the circumstance, being much grieved that such an event should have happened on his coast, and being disposed to show his friendship for the Republic of Venice, he ordered that the Venetian captains should be furnished with rich raiment of silks and costly cloths, and provided with horses and mules, that they might make their appearance before him in a style befitting themselves and their country. He received them with great kindness and distinction, expressing himself with princely courtesy, both as to themselves and the Republic of Venice; and having heard their account of the battle, and of their destitute situation, he assisted them with a large sum of money to ransom their galleys from the French cruisers. The latter took all the merchandises on board of their ships, but King John prohibited any of the spoil from being purchased within his dominions. Having thus generously relieved and assisted the captains, and administered to the necessities of their crews, he enabled them all to return in their own galleys to Venice.

The dignitaries of the republic were so highly sensible of this munificence on the part of King John, that they sent a stately embassy to that monarch, with rich presents and warm expressions of gratitude. Gero-

---

[1] Colenuccio, Hist. Nap., lib. vii. cap. 17.
[2] Zurita, Anales de Aragon, lib. ix. cap. 64.

nimo Donate was charged with this mission. a man eminent for learning
and eloquence: he was honorably received and entertained by King John
and dismissed with royal presents. among which were genets, and mules
with sumptuous trappings and caparisons. and many negro slaves richly
clad.[1]

The following is the account of this action as given by Sabellicus. in
his history of Venice.[2]

Erano andate quattro Galee delle quali Bartolommeo Minio era capitano. Queste navigando per l'Iberico mare. Colombo il piu giovane,
nipote di quel Colombo famoso corsale. fecesi incontro a' Veniziani di
notte. appresso il sacro Promontorio, che chiamasi ora capo di san Vin-
cenzo, con sette navi guernite da combattere. Egli quantunque nel primo
incontro avesse seco disposto d' opprimere le navi Veniziane, si ritenne
però dal combattere sin al giorno: tuttavia per esser alla battaglia piu
acconcio così le seguia, che le prode del corsale toccavano le poppe de
Veniziani. Venuto il giorno incontanente i Barbari diedero l' assalto.
Sostennero i Veniziani allora l' empito del nemico, per numero di navi e
di combattenti superiore, e durò il conflitto atroce per molte ore. Rare
fiate fu combattuto contro simili nemici con tanta uccisione. perche a
pena si costuma d' attaccarsi contro di loro, se non per occasione. Affer-
mano alcuni, che vi furono presenti. esser morte delle ciurme Veniziane
da trecento uomini. Altri dicono che fu meno: morì in quella zuffa Lorenzo Michele capitano d' una galera e Giovanni Delfino. d' altro capitano
fratello. Era durata la zuffa dal fare del giorno fin' ad ore venti. e erano le genti Veneziane mal trattate. Era gia la nave Delfina in potere
de' nemici quando le altre ad una ad una si renderono. Narrano alcuni,
che furono di quel aspro conflitto partecipi, aver numerato nelle loro navi
da prode a poppe ottanta valorosi uomini estinti, i quali dal nemico ve-
duti lo mossero a gemere e dire con sdegno. che così avevano voluto, i
Veniziani. I corpi morti furono gettati nel mare. e i feriti posti nel lido.
Quei che rimasero vivi seguirono con e navi il capitano vittorioso sin' a
Lisbona e ivi furono tutti licenziati. . . Quivi furono i Veneziani be-
nignamente ricevuti dal Re, gli infermi furono medicati, gli altri ebbero
abiti e denari secondo la loro condizione. . . . Oltre ciò vietò in tutto il
Regno, che alcuno non comprasse della preda Veniziana, portata dai corsali.
La nuova dell' avuta rovina non poco afflisse la città, erano perduti in quella
mercatanzia da ducento, mila ducati, ma il danno particolare degli
uomini uccisi diede maggior afflizione. — *Marc. Ant. Sabelico, Hist.
Venet.,* decad. iv. lib. iii.

No. X.

AMERIGO VESPUCCI.

AMONG the earliest and most intelligent of the voyagers who followed
the track of Columbus, was Amerigo Vespucci He has been considered
by many as the first discoverer of the southern continent, and by a singular caprice of fortune, his name has been given to the whole of the

---

[1] Obras de Garcia de Resende, cap. 58, Avora, 1554.
[2] Marco Antonio Coccio, better known under the name of Sabellicus, a cognomen
which he adopted on being crowned poet in the pedantic academy of Pomponius
Lætus. He was a contemporary of Columbus, and makes brief mention of his dis
coveries in the eighth book of the tenth Ennead of his universal history By some
writers he is called the Livy of his time; others accuse him of being full of misrepresentations in favor of Venice The older Scaliger charges him with venality, and
with being swayed by Venetian gold.

New World. It has been strenuously insisted, however, that he had no claim to the title of a discoverer: that he merely sailed in a subordinate capacity in a squadron commanded by others; that the account of his first voyage is a fabrication: and that he did not visit the main-land until after it had been discovered and coasted by Columbus. As this question has been made a matter of warm and voluminous controversy, it is proper to take a summary view of it in the present work.

Amerigo Vespucci was born in Florence, March 9th, 1451, of a noble, but not at that time wealthy family; his father's name was Anastatio; his mother's was Elizabetta Mini He was the third of their sons, and received an excellent education under his uncle, Georgio Antonio Vespucci, a learned friar of the fraternity of San Marco, who was instructor to several illustrious personages of that period.

Amerigo Vespucci visited Spain, and took up his residence in Seville, to attend to some commercial transactions on account of the family of the Medici of Florence, and to repair, by his ingenuity, the losses and misfortunes of an unskilful brother.[1]

The date of his arrival in Spain is uncertain, but from comparing dates and circumstances mentioned in his letters, he must have been at Seville when Columbus returned from his first voyage.

Padre Stanislaus Canovai, Professor of Mathematics at Florence, who has published the life and voyages of Amerigo Vespucci, says that he was commissioned by King Ferdinand, and sent with Columbus in his second voyage in 1493. He states this on the authority of a passage in the Cosmography of Sebastian Munster, published at Basle in 1550;[2] but Munster mentions Vespucci as having accompanied Columbus in his first voyage, the reference of Canovai is therefore incorrect; and the suggestion of Munster is disproved by the letters of Vespucci, in which he states his having been stimulated by the accounts brought of the newly discovered regions. He never mentions such a voyage in any of his letters, which he most probably would have done, or rather would have made it the subject of a copious letter, had he actually performed it.

The first notice of a positive form which we have of Vespucci, as resident in Spain, is early in 1496. He appears, from documents in the royal archives at Seville, to have acted as agent or factor for the house of Juanoto Berardi, a rich Florentine merchant, resident in Seville, who had contracted to furnish the Spanish sovereigns with three several armaments, of four vessels each, for the service of the newly discovered countries. He may have been one of the principals in this affair, which was transacted in the name of this established house Berardi died in December, 1495, and in the following January we find Amerigo Vespucci attending to the concerns of the expeditions and settling with the masters of the ships for their pay and maintenance, according to the agreements made between them and the late Juanoto Berardi. On the 12th January, 1496, he received on this account 10,000 maravedies from Bernardo Pinelo the royal treasurer He went on preparing all things for the despatch of four caravels to sail under the same contract between the sovereigns and the house of Berardi and sent them to sea on the 3d February, 1496; but on the 8th they met with a storm and were wrecked: the crews were saved with the loss of only three men.[3] While thus employed. Amerigo Vespucci, of course. had occasional opportunity of conversing with Columbus, with whom, according to the expression of the admiral

[1] Bandini vita d'Amerigo Vespucci　　　　　　[2] Cosm. Munst. p 1108.
[3] These particulars are from manuscript memoranda, extracted from the royal archives, by the late accurate historian Muñoz.

imself, in one of his letters to his son Diego, he appears to have been always on friendly terms. From these conversations, and from his agency in these expeditions, he soon became excited to visit the newly discovered countries, and to participate in enterprises which were the theme of every tongue. Having made himself well acquainted with geographical and nautical science, he prepared to launch into the career of discovery. It was not very long before he carried this design into execution.

In 1498 Columbus, in his third voyage, discovered the coast of Paria on Terra Firma; which he at that time imagined to be a great island, but that a vast continent lay immediately adjacent. He sent to Spain specimens of pearls found on this coast, and gave the most sanguine accounts of the supposed riches of the country.

In 1499 an expedition of four vessels, under command of Alonzo de Ojeda, was fitted out from Spain, and sailed for Paria, guided by charts and letters sent to the government by Columbus. These were communicated to Ojeda, by his patron, the Bishop Fonseca, who had the superintendence of India affairs, and who furnished him also with a warrant to undertake the voyage.

It is presumed that Vespucci aided in fitting out the armament, and sailed in a vessel belonging to the house of Berardi, and in this way was enabled to take a share in the gains and losses of the expedition; for Isabella, as Queen of Castile, had rigorously forbidden all strangers to trade with her transatlantic possessions, not even excepting the natives of the kingdom of Aragon.

This squadron visited Paria and several hundred miles of the coast, which they ascertained to be Terra Firma. They returned in June, 1500; and on the 18th of July, in that year, Amerigo Vespucci wrote an account of his voyage to Lorenzo de Pier Francisco de Medici of Florence, which remained concealed in manuscript until brought to light and published by Bandini in 1745.

In his account of this voyage, and in every other narrative of his different expeditions, Vespucci never mentions any other person concerned in the enterprise. He gives the time of his sailing, and states that he went with two caravels, which were probably his share of the expedition, or rather vessels sent by the house of Berardi. He gives an interesting narrative of the voyage, and of the various transactions with the natives, which corresponds, in many substantial points, with the accounts furnished by Ojeda and his mariners of their voyage, in a lawsuit hereafter mentioned.

In May, 1501, Vespucci, having suddenly left Spain, sailed in the service of Emanuel, King of Portugal, in the course of which expedition he visited the coast of Brazil. He gives an account of this voyage in a second letter to Lorenzo de Pier Francisco de Medici, which also remained in manuscript until published by Bartolozzi in 1789.[1]

No record nor notice of any such voyage undertaken by Amerigo Vespucci, at the command of Emanuel, is to be found in the archives of the Torre do Tombo, the general archives of Portugal, which have been repeatedly and diligently searched for the purpose. It is singular also that his name is not to be found in any of the Portuguese historians, who in general were very particular in naming all navigators who held any important station among them, or rendered any distinguished services. That Vespucci did sail along the coasts, however, is not questioned. His nephew, after his death, in the course of evidence on some points in dis-

---

[1] Bartolozzi, Recherche Historico. Firenze, 1789.

pute, gave the correct latitude of Cape St. Augustine, which he said he had extracted from his uncle's journal.

In 1504 Vespucci wrote a third letter to the same Lorenzo de Medici, containing a more extended account of the voyage just alluded to in the service of Portugal. This was the first of his narratives that appeared in print. It appears to have been published in Latin, at Strasburgh, as early as 1505, under the title "Americus Vesputius de Orbe Antarctica per Regem Portugalliæ pridem inventa." [1]

An edition of this letter was printed in Vicenza in 1507, in an anonymous collection of voyages edited by Francanzio di Monte Alboddo, an inhabitant of Vicenza. It was reprinted in Italian in 1508, at Milan, and also in Latin, in a book entitled "Itinerarium Portugalensium." In making the present illustration, the Milan edition in Italian [2] has been consulted, and also a Latin translation of it by Simon Grinæus, in his "Novus Orbis," published at Basle in 1532. It relates entirely the first voyage of Vespucci from Lisbon to the Brazils in 1501.

It is from this voyage to the Brazils that Amerigo Vespucci was first considered the discoverer of Terra Firma; and his name was at first applied to these southern regions, though afterward extended to the whole continent. The merits of his voyage were, however, greatly exaggerated. The Brazils had been previously discovered, and formally taken possession of for Spain in 1500, by Vicente Yañez Pinzon, and also in the same year, by Pedro Alvarez Cabral, on the part of Portugal; circumstances unknown, however, to Vespucci and his associates. The country remained in possession of Portugal, in conformity to the line of demarcation agreed on between the two nations.

Vespucci made a second voyage in the service of Portugal. He says that he commanded a caravel in a squadron of six vessels destined for the discovery of Malacca, which they had heard to be the great depot and magazine of all the trade between the Ganges and the Indian sea. Such an expedition did sail about this time, under the command of Gonzalo Coelho. The squadron sailed according to Vespucci, on the 10th of May, 1503. It stopped at the Cape de Verde islands for refreshments, and afterward sailed by the coast of Sierra Leone, but was prevented from landing by contrary winds and a turbulent sea. Standing to the south-west, they ran three hundred leagues until they were three degrees to the southward of the equinoctial line, where they discovered an uninhabited island about two leagues in length and one in breadth. Here, on the 10th of August, by mismanagement, the commander of the squadron ran his vessel on a rock and lost her. While the other vessels were assisting to save the crew and property from the wreck, Amerigo Vespucci was despatched in his caravel to search for a safe harbor in the land. He departed in his vessel without his long boat, and with less

---

[1] Panzer, tom. vi. p. 33, apud Esame Critico, p. 88, Anotazione [1]

[2] This rare book, in the possession of O. Rich Esq., is believed to be the oldest printed collection of voyages extant. It has not the pages numbered, the sheets are merely marked with a letter of the alphabet at the foot of each eighth page. It contains the earliest account of the voyages of Columbus, from his first departure until his arrival at Cadiz in chains. The letter of Vespucci to Lorenzo de Medici occupies the fifth book of this little volume. It is stated to have been originally written in Spanish, and translated into Italian by a person of the name of Jocondo. An earlier edition is stated to have been printed in Venice by Alberto Vercellese, in 1504. The author is said to have been Angelo Trivigiani, secretary to the Venetian ambassador in Spain. This Trivigiani appears to have collected many of the particulars of the voyages of Columbus from the manuscript decades of Peter Martyr, who erroneously lays the charge of the plagiarism to Aloysius Cadamosto, whose voyages are inserted in the same collection. The book was entitled '*Libretto di tutta la navigazione del Re di Espagna, delta Isole e terreni nuovamente trovati.*"

than half of his crew, the rest having gone in the boat to the assistance of the wreck. Vespucci found a harbor, but waited in vain for several days for the arrival of the ships. Standing out to sea he met with a solitary vessel, and learned that the ship of the commander had sunk, and the rest had proceeded onward. In company with this vessel he stood for the Brazils, according to a command of the king, in case that any vessel should be parted from the fleet. Arriving on the coast he discovered the famous bay of All Saints, where he remained upward of two months, in hopes of being joined by the rest of the fleet. He at length ran two hundred and sixty leagues farther south, where he remained five months building a fort and taking in a cargo of Brazil wood. Then, leaving in the fortress a garrison of twenty-four men with arms and ammunition, he set sail for Lisbon, where he arrived in June, 1504.[1] The commander of the squadron and the other four ships were never heard of afterward.

Vespucci does not appear to have received the reward from the King of Portugal that his services merited, for we find him at Seville early in 1505, on his way to the Spanish court, in quest of employment; and he was bearer of a letter from Columbus to his son Diego, dated February 5th, which, while it speaks warmly of him as a friend, intimates his having been unfortunate. The following is the letter:

"MY DEAR SON: Diego Mendez departed hence on Monday, the third of this month. After his departure I conversed with Amerigo Vespucci, the bearer of this, who goes there (to court) summoned on affairs of navigation. Fortune has been adverse to him as to many others. His labors have not profited him as much as they reasonably should have done. He goes on my account, and with much desire to do something that may result to my advantage, if within his power. I cannot ascertain here in what I can employ him, that will be serviceable to me, for I do not know what may be there required. He goes with the determination to do all that is possible for me; see in what he may be of advantage and co-operate with him, that he may say and do every thing, and put his plans in operation; and let all be done secretly, that he may not be suspected: I have said every thing to him that I can say touching the business, and have informed him of the pay I have received, and what is due, etc."[2]

About this time Amerigo Vespucci received letters of naturalization from King Ferdinand, and shortly afterward he and Vincente Yañez Pinzon were named captains of an armada about to be sent out in the spice trade and to make discoveries. There is a royal order, dated Toro, 11th of April, 1507, for 12,000 maravedies for an outfit for "Americo de Vespuche, resident of Seville." Preparations were made for this voyage, and vessels procured and fitted out, but it was eventually abandoned. There are memoranda existing concerning it, dated in 1506, 1507, and 1508, from which it appears that Amerigo Vespucci remained at Seville, attending to the fluctuating concerns of this squadron, until the destination of the vessels was changed, their equipments were sold, and the accounts settled. During this time he had a salary of 30,000 maravedies. On the 22d of March, 1508, he received the appointment of principal pilot, with a salary of 70,000 maravedies. His chief duties were to prepare charts, examine pilots, superintend the fitting out of expeditions, and prescribe the route that vessels were to pursue in their voyages to the New World. He appears to have remained at Seville, and to have

---

[1] Letter of Vespucci to Soderini or Renato — Edit. of Canoval.
[2] Navarrete, Colec. Viag., tom. i. p. 351.

retained this office until his death, on the 22d of February, 1512. His widow, Maria Corezo, enjoyed a pension of 10,000 maravedies. After his death, his nephew, Juan Vespucci, was nominated pilot with a salary of 20,000 maravedies, commencing on the 22d of May, 1512. Peter Martyr speaks with high commendation of this young man. "Young Vesputius is one to whom Americus Vesputius his uncle left the exact knowledge of the mariner's faculties, as it were by inheritance, after his death; for he was a very expert master in the knowledge of his carde, his compasse, and the elevation of the pole starre by the quadrant. . . . Vesputius is my very familiar friend, and a wittie young man, in whose company I take great pleasure, and therefore use him oftentymes for my guest. He hath also made many voyages into these coasts, and diligently noted such things as he hath seen." [1]

Vespucci, the nephew, continued in this situation during the lifetime of Fonseca, who had been the patron of his uncle and his family. He was divested of his pay and his employ by a letter of the council, dated the 18th of March, 1525, shortly after the death of the bishop. No further notice of Vespucci is to be found in the archives of the Indies.

Such is a brief view of the career of Amerigo Vespucci; it remains to notice the points of controversy. Shortly after his return from his last expedition to the Brazils, he wrote a letter dated Lisbon, 4th September, 1504, containing a summary account of all his voyages. This letter is of special importance to the matters under investigation, as it is the only one known that relates to the disputed voyage, which would establish him as the discoverer of Terra Firma. It is presumed to have been written in Latin, and was addressed to René, Duke of Lorraine, who assumed the title of King of Sicily and Jerusalem.

The earliest known edition of this letter was published in Latin, in 1507, at St. Diez in Lorraine. A copy of it has been found in the library of the Vatican (No. 9688) by the Abbe Cancelleri. In preparing the present illustration a reprint of this letter in Latin has been consulted, inserted in the Novus Orbis of Grinæus, published at Bath in 1532. The letter contains a spirited narrative of four voyages which he asserts to have made to the New World. In the prologue he excuses the liberty of addressing King Rene by calling to his recollection the ancient intimacy of their youth when studying the rudiments of science together, under the paternal uncle of the voyager: and adds that if the present narrative should not altogether please his majesty he must plead to him as Pliny said to Mæcenus, that he used formerly to be amused with his triflings.

In the prologue to this letter, he informs King Rene that affairs of commerce had brought him to Spain, where he had experienced the various changes of fortune attendant on such transactions and was induced to abandon that pursuit and direct his labors to objects of a more elevated and stable nature. He therefore purposed to contemplate various parts of the world, and to behold the marvels which it contains. To this object both time and place were favorable; for King Ferdinand was then preparing four vessels for the discovery of new lands in the west and appointed him among the number of those who went in the expedition. "We departed," he adds, "from the port of Cadiz, May 20th, 1497, taking our course on the great gulf of ocean; in which voyage we employed eighteen months, discovering many lands and innumerable islands, chiefly inhabited, of which our ancestors make no mention."

A duplicate of this letter appears to have been sent at the same time (written, it is said, in Italian) to Piere Soderini, afterward Gonfalonier

---

[1] Peter Martyr, decad. iii. lib. v. Eden's English tr.

of Florence, which was some years subsequently published in Italy not
earlier than 1510, and entitled " Lettera de Amerigo Vespucci delle Isole
nuovamente trovate in quatro suoi viaggi " We have consulted the
edition of this letter in Italian, inserted in the publication of Padre Stanislaus Canovai, already referred to.

It has been suggested by an Italian writer, that this letter was written
by Vespucci to Soderini only, and the address altered to King René
through the flattery or mistake of the Lorraine editor, without perceiving
how unsuitable the reference to former intimacy, intended for Soderini,
was, when applied to a sovereign. The person making this remark can
hardly have read the prologue to the Latin edition, in which the title of
" your majesty " is frequently repeated, and the term "illustrious king"
employed. It was first published also in Lorraine, the domains of René,
and the publisher would not probably have presumed to take such a liberty
with his sovereign's name. It becomes a question, whether Vespucci
addressed the same letter to King René and to Piere Soderini, both of
them having been educated with him, or whether he sent a copy of this
letter to Soderini, which subsequently found its way into print. The
address to Soderini may have been substituted, through mistake, by the
Italian publisher. Neither of the publications could have been made
under the supervision of Vespucci.

The voyage specified in this letter as having taken place in 1497, is the
great point in controversy. It is strenuously asserted that no such voyage
took place, and that the first expedition of Vespucci to the coast of Paria
was in the enterprise commanded by Ojeda, in 1499. The books of the
armadas existing in the archives of the Indies at Seville have been diligently examined, but no record of such voyage has been found, nor any
official documents relating to it. Those most experienced in Spanish
colonial regulations insist that no command like that pretended by Vespucci could have been given to a stranger, till he had first received letters
of naturalization from the sovereigns for the kingdom of Castile, and he
did not obtain such till 1505, when they were granted to him as preparatory to giving him the command in conjunction with Pinzon.

His account of a voyage made by him in 1497, therefore, is alleged to
be a fabrication for the purpose of claiming the discovery of Paria; or
rather it is affirmed that he has divided the voyage which he actually
made with Ojeda, in 1499, into two, taking a number of incidents from
his real voyage, altering them a little, and enlarging them with descriptions of the countries and people, so as to make a plausible narrative, which
he gives as a distinct voyage; and antedating his departure to 1497, so as
to make himself appear the first discoverer of Paria.

In support of this charge various coincidences have been pointed out
between his voyage said to have taken place in 1497, and that described
in his first letter to Lorenzo de Medici in 1499 These coincidences are
with respect to places visited, transactions and battles with the natives,
and the number of Indians carried to Spain and sold as slaves.

But the credibility of this voyage has been put to a stronger test.
About 1508 a suit was instituted against the crown of Spain by Don Diego,
son and heir of Columbus, for the government of certain parts of Terra
Firma, and for a share in the revenue arising from them, conformably to
the capitulations made between the sovereign and his father. It was the
object of the crown to disprove the discovery of the coast of Paria and
the pearl islands by Columbus, as it was maintained that unless he had
discovered them, the claim of his heir with respect to them would be of
no validity

In the course of this suit, a particular examination of witnesses took place in 1512–13 in the fiscal court. Alonzo de Ojeda, and nearly a hundred other persons, were interrogated on oath; that voyager having been the first to visit the coast of Paria after Columbus had left it, and that within a very few months. The interrogatories of these witnesses, and their replies, are still extant, in the archives of the Indies at Seville in a packet of papers entitled " Papers belonging to the Admiral Don Luis Colon, about the conservation of his privileges, from ann. 1515 to 1564." The author of the present work has two several copies of these interrogatories lying before him. One made by the late historian Muñoz, and the other made in 1826, and signed·by John Jose de la Higueray Lara keeper of the general archives of the Indies in Seville. In the course of this testimony, the fact that Amerigo Vespucci accompanied Ojeda in this voyage of 1499, appears manifest, first from the deposition of Ojeda himself. The following are the words of the record: " In this voyage which this said witness made, he took with him Juan de la Cosa and Morego Vespuche [Amerigo Vespucci] and other pilots." [1] Secondly, from the coincidence of many parts of the narrative of Vespucci with events in this voyage of Ojeda. Among these coincidences, one is particularly striking. Vespucci, in his letter to Lorenzo de Medici, and also in that to René or Soderini, says that his ships, after leaving the coast of Terra Firma, stopped at Hispaniola, where they remained about two months and a half, procuring provisions, during which time, he adds, " we had many perils and troubles with the very Christians who were in that island with Columbus, and I believe through envy." [2]

Now it is well known that Ojeda passed some time on the western end of the island victualling his ships; and that serious dissensions took place between him and the Spaniards in those parts, and the party sent by Columbus under Roldan to keep a watch upon his movements. If then Vespucci, as is stated upon oath, really accompanied Ojeda in this voyage, the inference appears almost irresistible, that he had not made the previous voyage of 1497, for the fact would have been well known to Ojeda; he would have considered Vespucci as the original discoverer and would have had no motive for depriving him of the merit of it, to give it to Columbus, with whom Ojeda was not upon friendly terms.

Ojeda, however, expressly declares that the coast had been discovered by Columbus. On being asked how he knew the fact, he replied, because he saw the chart of the country discovered, which Columbus sent at the time to the king and queen, and that he came off immediately on a voyage of discovery, and found what was therein set down as discovered by the admiral was correct. [3]

Another witness, Bernaldo de Haro, states that he had been with the admiral, and had written (or rather copied) a letter for the admiral to the king and queen designating, in an accompanying sea-chart, the courses and steerings and winds by which he had arrived at Paria and that this witness had heard that from this chart others had been made, and that

---

[1] En este viage que este dicho testigo hizo trujo consigo a Juan de la Cosa, piloto, e Morego Vespuche, e otros pilotos.

[2] Per la necessità del mantenimento fummo all' Isola d'Antiglia (Hispaniola) che è questa che descoperse Christoval Colombo più anni fa, dove facemmo molto mantenimento, e stemmo due mesi e 17 giorni; dove passammo moti pericoli e travagli con li medesimi christiani que in questa isola stavanno col Colombo (credo per invidia). Letter of Vespucci – Edit. of Canovai.

[3] Preguntado como lo sabe, dijo—que lo sabe porque vió este testigo la figura que el dicho Almirante al dicho tiempo embió á Castilla al Rey e Reyna, nuestros Señores, de lo que habia descubierto, y porque este testigo luego vino á descubrir y halló que era verdad lo que dicho tiene que el dicho Almirante descubrió. MS Process of D. Diego Colon, pregunta 2.

Pedro Alonzo Niño and Ojeda, and others, who had since visited these countries, had been guided by the same.[1]

Francisco de Molares, one of the best and most credible of all the pilots, testified that he saw a sea-chart which Columbus had made of the coast of Paria, *and he believed that all governed themselves by it.*[2]

Numerous witnesses in this process testify to the fact that Paria was first discovered by Columbus. Las Casas, who has been at the pains of counting them, says that the fact was established by twenty-five eye-witnesses and sixty ear-witnesses. Many of them testify also that the coast south of Paria, and that extending west of the island of Margarita, away to Venezuela, which Vespucci states to have been discovered by himself in 1497, was now first discovered by Ojeda, and had never before been visited either by the admiral " or any other Christian whatever."

Alonzo Sanchez de Carvajal says that all the voyages of discovery which were made to the Terra Firma, were made by persons who had sailed with the admiral, or been benefited by his instructions and directions, following the course he had laid down;[3] and the same is testified by many other pilots and mariners of reputation and experience.

It would be a singular circumstance, if none of these witnesses, many of whom must have sailed in the same squadron with Vespucci along this coast in 1499, should have known that he had discovered and explored it two years previously. If that had really been the case, what motive could he have for concealing the fact? and why, if they knew it, should they not proclaim it? Vespucci states his voyage in 1497 to have been made with four caravels; that they returned in October, 1498, and that he sailed again with two caravels in May, 1499 (the date of Ojeda's departure). Many of the mariners would therefore have been present in both voyages. Why, too, should Ojeda and the other pilots guide themselves by the charts of Columbus, when they had a man on board so learned in nautical science, and who, from his own recent observations, was practically acquainted with the coast? Not a word, however, is mentioned of the voyage and discovery of Vespucci by any of the pilots, though every other voyage and discovery is cited; nor does there even a seaman appear who had accompanied him in his asserted voyage.

Another strong circumstance against the reality of this voyage is, that it was not brought forward in this trial to defeat the claims of the heirs of Columbus. Vespucci states the voyage to have been undertaken with the knowledge and countenance of King Ferdinand; it must, therefore, have been avowed and notorious. Vespucci was living at Seville in 1508, at the time of the commencement of this suit, and for four years afterward, a salaried servant of the crown. Many of the pilots and mariners must have been at hand, who sailed with him in his pretended enterprise. If this voyage had once been proved, it would completely have settled the question, as far as concerned the coast of Paria, in favor of the crown. Yet no testimony appears ever to have been taken from Vespucci while

---

[1] Este testigo escrivio una carta que el Almirante escriviera al Rey a Reyna N.N.S.S. haciendo les saber las perlas e cosas que habia hallado, y le embió señaldo con la dicha carta, en una carta de marear, los rumbos y vientos por donde habia llegado á la Paria, e que este testigo oyó decir como pr. aquella carte se habian hecho otras e por ellas habian venido Pedro Alonzo Merino [Niño] Ojeda e otros que despues han ido á aquellas partes. Idem, pregunta 9

[2] Process of D. Diego Colon, pregunta 10.

[3] Que en todos los viages que algunos hicieron descubriendo en la dicha tierra, iban personas que ovieron navegado con el dicho Almirante, y ellos mostró muchas cosas de marear, y ellos por imitacion é industria del dicho Almirante las aprendian y aprendieron, e seguendo ag° que el dicho Almirante les habia mostrado, hicieron los viages que descubrieron en la Tierra Firma. Process pregunta 10

living; and when the interrogatories were made in the fiscal court in 1512–13, not one of his seamen is brought up to give evidence. A voyage so important in its nature, and so essential to the question in dispute, is not even alluded to, while useless pains are taken to wrest evidence from the voyage of Ojeda, undertaken at a subsequent period.

It is a circumstance worthy of notice, that Vespucci commences his first letters to Lorenzo de Medici in 1500, within a month after his return from the voyage he had actually made to Paria, and apologizes for his long silence, by saying that nothing had occurred worthy of mention ("e gran tempo che non ho scritto á vostro magnifizensa, e non lo ha causato altra cosa ne nessuna salvo non mi essere occorso cosa degna di memoria"), and proceeds eagerly to tell him the wonders he had witnessed in the expedition from which he had but just returned. It would be a singular forgetfulness to say that nothing had occurred of importance, if he had made a previous voyage of eighteen months in 1497–8 to this newly discovered world; and it would be almost equally strange that he should not make the slightest allusion to it in this letter.

It has been the endeavor of the author to examine this question dispassionately; and after considering the statements and arguments advanced on either side, he cannot resist a conviction, that the voyage stated to have been made in 1497 did not take place, and that Vespucci has no title to the first discovery of the coast of Paria.

The question is extremely perplexing from the difficulty of assigning sufficient motives for so gross a deception. When Vespucci wrote his letters there was no doubt entertained but that Columbus had discovered the main-land in his first voyage; Cuba being always considered the extremity of Asia, until circumnavigated in 1508. Vespucci may have supposed Brazil, Paria, and the rest of that coast, part of a distinct continent, and have been anxious to arrogate to himself the fame of its discovery. It has been asserted that, on his return from his voyage to the Brazils, he prepared a maritime chart, in which he gave his name to that part of the main-land; but this assertion does not appear to be well substantiated. It would rather seem that his name was given to that part of the continent by others, as a tribute paid to his supposed merit, in consequence of having read his own account of his voyages.[1]

It is singular that Fernando, the son of Columbus, in his biography of his father, should bring no charge against Vespucci of endeavoring to supplant the admiral in this discovery. Herrera has been cited as the first to bring the accusation, in his history of the Indies, first published in 1601, and has been much criticised in consequence, by the advocates of Vespucci, as making the charge on his mere assertion. But, in fact, Herrera did but copy what he found written by Las Casas, who had the proceedings of the fiscal court lying before him, and was moved to indignation against Vespucci, by what he considered proofs of great imposture.

It has been suggested that Vespucci was instigated to this deception at the time when he was seeking employment in the colonial service of Spain; and that he did it to conciliate the Bishop Fonseca, who was desirous of any thing that might injure the interests of Columbus. In corroboration of this opinion, the patronage is cited, which was ever shown by Fonseca to Vespucci and his family. This is not, however, a satisfactory reason, since it does not appear that the bishop ever made any use

---

[1] The first suggestion of the name appears to have been in the Latin work already cited published in St. Diez, in Lorraine, in 1507, in which was inserted the letter of Vespucci to king René. The author after speaking of the other three parts of the world Asia, Africa, and Europe, recommends that the fourth shall be called Amerigo, or America, after Vespucci whom he imagined its discoverer

of the fabrication. Perhaps some other means might be found of accounting for this spurious narration, without implicating the veracity of Vespucci. It may have been the blunder of some editor, or the interpolation of some book-maker, eager, as in the case of Trivigiani with the manuscripts of Peter Martyr, to gather together disjointed materials, and fabricate a work to gratify the prevalent passion of the day.

In the various editions of the letters of Vespucci, the grossest variations and inconsistencies in dates will be found, evidently the errors of hasty and careless publishers. Several of these have been corrected by the modern authors who have inserted these letters in their works.[1] The same disregard to exactness which led to these blunders may have produced the interpolation of this voyage, garbled out of the letters of Vespucci and the accounts of other voyagers. This is merely suggested as a possible mode of accounting for what appears so decidedly to be a fabrication, yet which we are loath to attribute to a man of the good sense, the character, and the reputed merit of Vespucci.

After all, this is a question more of curiosity than of real moment, although it is one of those perplexing points about which grave men will continue to write weary volumes, until the subject acquires a fictitious importance from the mountain of controversy heaped upon it. It has become a question of local pride with the literati of Florence and they emulate each other with patriotic zeal, to vindicate the fame of their distinguished countryman. This zeal is laudable when kept within proper limits, but it is to be regretted that some of them have so far been heated by controversy as to become irascible against the very memory of Columbus, and to seek to disparage his general fame, as if the ruin of it would add any thing to the reputation of Vespucci. This is discreditable to their discernment and their liberality; it injures their cause, and shocks the feelings of mankind, who will not willingly see a name like that of Columbus, lightly or petulantly assailed in the course of these literary contests. It is a name consecrated in history, and is no longer the property of a city, or a state, or a nation, but of the whole world.

Neither should those who have a proper sense of the merit of Columbus put any part of his great renown at issue upon this minor dispute. Whether or not he was the discoverer of Paria, was a question of interest to his heirs, as a share of the government and revenues of that country depended upon it; but it is of no importance to his fame. In fact, the European who first reached the main land of the New World was most probably Sebastian Cabot, a native of Venice, sailing in the employ of England. In 1497 he coasted its shores from Labrador to Florida, yet the English have never set up any pretensions on his account.

The glory of Columbus does not depend upon the parts of the country he visited or the extent of coast along which he sailed; it embraces the discovery of the whole western world. With respect to him, Vespucci is as Yañez Pinzon, Bastides, Ojeda, Cabot, and the crowd of secondary discoverers who followed in his track, and explored the realms to which he had led the way. When Columbus first touched a shore of the New

[1] An instance of these errors may be cited in the edition of the letter of Amerigo Vespucci to king René, inserted by Grinæus in his Novus Orbis, in 1532. In this Vespucci is made to state that he sailed from Cadiz, May 20, MCCCCXCVII. (1497) that he was eighteen months absent, and returned to Cadiz October 15, MCCCCXCIX. (1499), which would constitute an absence of twenty nine months. He states his departure from Cadiz, on his second voyage, Sunday, May 11, MCCCCLXXXIX. (1489), which would have made his second voyage precede his first by eight years. If we substitute 1499 for 1489, the departure on his second voyage would still precede his return from his first by five months. Canovai, in his edition, has altered the date of the first return to 1498, to limit the voyage to eighteen months.

World, even though a frontier island, he had achieved his enterprises; he had accomplished all that was necessary to his fame the great problem of the ocean was solved, the world which lay beyond its Western waters was discovered.

Note to the Revised Edition, 1848 — Humboldt, in his EXAMEN CRITIQUE, published in Paris, in 1837, says "I have been so happy as to discover, very recently, the name and the literary relations of the mysterious personage who (in 1507) was the first to propose the name of America to designate the new continent, and who concealed himself under the Grecianized name of Hylacomylas" He then by a long and ingenious investigation, shows that the real name of this personage was Martin Waldseemüller, of Fribourg, an eminent cosmographer, patronized by René, Duke of Lorraine; who, no doubt, put in his hands the letter received by him from Amerigo Vespucci The geographical works of Waldseemüller, under the assumed name of Hylacomylas, had a wide circulation, went through repeated editions, and propagated the use of the name America throughout the world.   There is no reason to suppose that this application of the name was in anywise suggested by Amerigo Vespucci. It appears to have been entirely gratuitous on the part of Waldseemüller

No. XI.

MARTIN ALÒNZO PINZON.

IN the course of the trial in the fiscal court, between Don Diego and the crown, an attempt was made to depreciate the merit of Columbus, and to ascribe the success of the great enterprise of discovery to the intelligence and spirit of Martin Alonzo Pinzon It was the interest of the crown to do so to justify itself in withholding from the heirs of Columbus the extent of his stipulated reward.   The examinations of witnesses in this trial were made at various times and places, and upon a set of interrogatories formally drawn up by order of the fiscal.   They took place upwards of twenty years after the first voyage of Columbus and the witnesses testified from recollection.

In reply to one of the interrogatories, Arias Perez Pinzon son of Martin Alonzo, declared. that. being once in Rome with his father on commercial affairs. before the time of the discovery. they had frequent conversations with a person learned in cosmography who was in the service of Pope Innocent VIII.. and that being in the library of the pope. this person showed them many manuscripts, from one of which his father gathered intimation of these new lands: for there was a passage by an historian as old as the time of Solomon, which said, "Navigate the Mediterranean Sea to the end of Spain and thence towards the setting sun, in a direction between north and south. until ninety-five degrees of longitude. and you will find the land of Cipango. fertile and abundant, and equal in greatness to Africa and Europe."   A copy of this writing, he added, his father brought from Rome with an intention of going in search of that land. and frequently expressed such determination; and that, when Columbus came to Palos with his project of discovery. Martin Alonzo Pinzon showed him the manuscript, and ultimately gave it to him just before they sailed.

It is extremely probable that this manuscript, of which Arias Perez gives so vague an account from recollection. but which he appears to think the main thing that prompted Columbus to his undertaking, was no other than the work of Marco Polo, which, at that time, existed in manuscript in most of the Italian libraries.   Martin Alonzo was evidently acquainted with the work of the Venetian, and it would appear, from various circumstances, that Columbus had a copy of it with him in his voyages. which may have been the manuscript above mentioned.   Columbus had long before, however, had a knowledge of the work, if not by actual inspection, at least through his correspondence with Toscanelli in 1474, and had derived from it all the light it was capable of furnishing, before he ever came to Palos. It is questionable, also, whether the visit of Martin Alonzo to Rome was not after his mind had been heated by conversations with Columbus in the convent of La Rabida. The testimony of Arias Perez is so worded as to leave it in doubt whether the visit was not in the very year prior to the discovery· "fue el dicho su padre à Roma aquel dicho año antes que fuese a descubrir." Arias Perez always mentions the manuscript as having been imparted to Columbus, after he had come to Palos with an intention of proceeding on the discovery.

Certain witnesses who were examined on behalf of the crown, and to whom specific interrogatories were put, asserted, as has already been mentioned in a note to this work, that had it not been for Martin Alonzo Pinzon and his brothers, Columbus would have turned back for Spain, after having run seven or eight hundred leagues; being disheartened at not finding land, and dismayed by the mutiny and menaces of his crew. This is stated by two or three as from personal knowledge, and by others from hearsay. It is said especially to have occurred on the 6th of October. On this day, according to the journal of Columbus, he had some conversation with Martin Alonzo, who was anxious that they should stand more to the south-west. The admiral refused to do so, and it is very probable that some angry words may have passed between them. Various disputes appear to have taken place between Columbus and his colleagues respecting their route, previous to the discovery of land; in one or two instances he acceded to their wishes and altered his course, but in general he was inflexible in standing to the west. The Pinzons also, in all probability, exerted their influence in quelling the murmurs of their townsmen and encouraging them to proceed, when ready to rebel against Columbus These circumstances may have become mixed up in the vague recollections of the seamen who gave the foregoing extravagant testimony, and who were evidently disposed to exalt the merits of the Pinzons at the expense of Columbus. They were in some measure prompted also in their replies by the written interrogatories put by order of the fiscal, which specified the conversation said to have passed between Columbus and the Pinzons, and notwithstanding these guides they differed widely in their statements, and ran into many absurdities. In a manuscript record in possession of the Pinzon family, I have even read the assertion of an old seaman, that Columbus, in his eagerness to compel the Pinzons to turn back to Spain, *fired upon their ships*, but, they continuing on, he was obliged to follow, and within two days afterward discovered the island of Hispaniola.

It is evident the old sailor, if he really spoke conscientiously, mingled in his cloudy remembrance the disputes in the early part of the voyage, about altering their course to the south-west, and the desertion of Martin Alonzo, subsequent to the discovery of the Lucayos and Cuba, when, after parting company with the admiral, he made the island of Hispaniola.

The witness most to be depended upon as to these points of inquiry, is the physician of Palos, Garcia Fernandez a man of education, who sailed with Martin Alonzo Pinzon as steward of his ship, and of course was present at all the conversations which passed between the commanders. He testifies that Martin Alonzo urged Columbus to stand more to the south-west, and that the admiral at length complied, but, finding no land in that direction, they turned again to the west: a statement which completely coincides with the journal of Columbus. He adds that the admiral continually comforted and animated Martin Alonzo, and all others in his company. (Siempre los consolaba el dicho Almirante esforzandolos al dicho Martin Alonzo e à todos los que en su compania iban) When the physician was specifically questioned as to the conversations pretended to have passed between the commanders, in which Columbus expressed a desire to turn back to Spain, he referred to the preceding statement as the only answer he had to make to these interrogatories.

The extravagant testimony before mentioned appears never to have had any weight with the fiscal: and the accurate historian Muñoz, who extracted all these points of evidence from the papers of the lawsuit, has not deemed them worthy of mention in his work. As these matters, however, remain on record in the archives of the Indies, and in the archives of the Pinzon family, in both of which I have had a full opportunity of inspecting them, I have thought it advisable to make these few observations on the subject, lest, in the rage for research, they might hereafter be drawn forth as a new discovery, on the strength of which to impugn the merits of Columbus.

No. XII.

RUMOR OF THE PILOT SAID TO HAVE DIED IN THE HOUSE OF COLUMBUS.

AMONG the various attempts to injure Columbus by those who were envious of his fame, was one intended to destroy all his merit as an original discoverer. It was said that he had received information of the existence of land in the western parts of the ocean from a tempest-tossed pilot, who had been driven there by violent easterly winds, and who, on his return to Europe, had died in the house of Columbus, leaving in his possession the chart and journal of his voyage, by which he was guided to his discovery.

This story was first noticed by Oviedo, a contemporary of Columbus, in his history of the Indies, published in 1535. He mentions it as a rumor circulating among the vulgar, without foundation in truth.

Fernando Lopez de Gomara first brought it forward against Columbus. In his history of the Indies, published in 1552, he repeats the rumor in the vaguest terms, manifestly from Oviedo, but without the contradiction given to it by that author. He says that the name and country of the pilot were unknown, some terming him an Andalusian, sailing between the Canaries and Madeira, others a Biscayan, trading to England and France; and others a Portuguese, voyaging between Lisbon and Nina, on the coast of Guinea. He expresses equal uncertainty whether the pilot brought the caravel to Portugal, to Madeira, or to one of the Azores. The only point on which the circulators of the rumor agreed was, that he died in the house of Columbus. Gomara adds that by this event Columbus was led to undertake his voyage to the new countries.[1]

The other early historians who mention Columbus and his voyages, and were his contemporaries, viz., Sabellicus, Peter Martyr, Gustiniani, Bernaldez, commonly called the curate of los Palacios, Las Casas, Fernando, the son of the admiral, and the anonymous author of a voyage of Columbus, translated from the Italian into Latin by Madrignano,[2] are all silent in regard to this report.

Benzoni, whose history of the New World was published in 1565, repeats the story from Gomara, with whom he was contemporary but decidedly expresses his opinion that Gomara had mingled up much false-

[1] Gomara. Hist. Ind. cap. 14
[2] Navigatio Christophori Columbi, Madrignano Interprete. It is contained in a collection of voyages called Novus Orbis Regionum, edition of 1555, but was originally published in Italian a written by Montalbodo Francanzano or Francapano de Montaldo, in a collection of voyages entitled Nuovo Mundo. in Vicenza. 1507.

hood with some truth, for the purpose of detracting from the fame of Columbus, through jealousy that any one but a Spaniard should enjoy the honor of the discovery.[1]

Acosta notices the circumstance slightly in his Natural and Moral History of the Indies, published in 1591, and takes it evidently from Gomara.[2]

Mariana, in his history of Spain, published in 1592, also mentions it, but expresses a doubt of its truth, and derives his information manifestly from Gomara.[3]

Herrera, who published his history of the Indies in 1601, takes no notice of the story. In not noticing it, he may be considered as rejecting it; for he is distinguished for his minuteness, and was well acquainted with Gomara's history, which he expressly contradicts on a point of considerable interest.[4]

Garcilaso de la Vega, a native of Cusco in Peru, revived the tale with very minute particulars, in his Commentaries of the Incas, published in 1609. He tells it smoothly and circumstantially; fixes the date of the occurrence 1484, "one year more or less;" states the name of the unfortunate pilot, Alonzo Sanchez de Huelva; the destination of his vessel, from the Canaries to Madeira; and the unknown land to which they were driven, the island of Hispaniola. The pilot, he says, landed, took an altitude, and wrote an account of all he saw, and all that had occurred in the voyage. He then took in wood and water, and set out to seek his way home. He succeeded in returning, but the voyage was long and tempestuous, and twelve died of hunger and fatigue, out of seventeen, the original number of the crew. The five survivors arrived at Tercera, where they were hospitably entertained by Columbus, but all died in his house in consequence of the hardships they had sustained; the pilot was the last that died, leaving his host heir to his papers. Columbus kept them profoundly secret, and by pursuing the route therein prescribed, obtained the credit of discovering the New World.[5]

Such are the material points of the circumstantial relation furnished by Garcilaso de la Vega, one hundred and twenty years after the event. In regard to authority, he recollects to have heard the story when he was a child, as a subject of conversation between his father and the neighbors, and he refers to the histories of the Indies, by Acosta and Gomara, for confirmation. As the conversations to which he listened must have taken place sixty or seventy years after the date of the report, there had been sufficient time for the vague rumors to become arranged into a regular narrative and thus we have not only the name, country, and destination of the pilot, but also the name of the unknown land to which his vessel was driven.

This account given by Garcilaso de la Vega, has been adopted by many old historians, who have felt a confidence in the peremptory manner in which he relates it and in the authorities to whom he refers.[6] These

---

[1] Girolamo Benzoni, Hist. Del Nuevo Mundo, lib. 1. fo. 12. In Venetia, 1572.

[2] Padre Joseph de Acosta, Hist Ind., lib. i. cap. 19.

[3] Juan de Mariana, Hist. España, lib xxvi. cap. 3.

[4] Herrera, Hist. Ind., decad ii lib. iii. cap. 1

[5] Commentarios de los Incas, lib. i. cap. 3.

[6] Names of historians who either adopted this story in detail or the charge against Columbus, drawn from it.

Bernardo Aldrete, Antiguedad de España, lib. iv. cap. 17, p. 567.

Roderigo Caro, Antiguedad, lib iii. cap. 76

Juan de Solorzano, Ind. Jure, tom. i. lib. i. cap 5.

Fernando Pizarro, Varones Illust. del Nuevo Mundo, cap. 2.

Agostino Torniel, Annal. Sacr., tom. i ann Mund., 1931, No. 48.

Pet. Damarez or De Mariz, Dial. iv de Var Hist., cap. 1.

Gregoria Garcia, Orig de los Indios. lib. i cap. 4, § 1.

Juan de Torquemanda Monarch Ind., lib xviii. cap. 1.

John Baptiste Riccioli Geograf Reform., lib. iii.

To this list of old authors may be added many others of more recent date.

have been echoed by others of more recent date; and thus a weighty charge of fraud and imposture has been accumulated against Columbus, apparently supported by a crowd of respectable accusers. The whole charge is to be traced to Gomara, who loosely repeated a vague rumor, without noticing the pointed contradiction given to it seventeen years before, by Oviedo, an ear-witness, from whose book he appears to have actually gathered the report.

It is to be remarked that Gomara bears the character, among historians, of inaccuracy, and of great credulity in adopting unfounded stories.[1]

It is unnecessary to give further refutation to this charge, especially as it is clear that Columbus communicated his idea of discovery to Paulo Toscanelli of Florence, in 1474, ten years previous to the date assigned by Garcilaso de la Vega for this occurrence.

No. XIII.

MARTIN BEHEM.

THIS able geographer was born in Nuremburg, in Germany, about the commencement of the year 1430. His ancestors were from the circle of Pilsner, in Bohemia, hence he is called by some writers Martin of Bohemia, and the resemblance of his own name to that of the country of his ancestors frequently occasions a confusion in the appellation.

It has been said by some that he studied under Philip Bervalde the elder, and by others under John Muller, otherwise called Regiomontanus, though De Murr, who has made diligent inquiry into his history, discredits both assertions. According to a correspondence between Behem and his uncle, discovered of late years by De Murr, it appears that the early part of his life was devoted to commerce. Some have given him the credit of discovering the island of Fayal, but this is an error, arising probably from the circumstance that Job de Huertar, father-in-law of Behem, colonized that island in 1466.

He is supposed to have arrived at Portugal in 1481, while Alphonso V was still on the throne; it is certain that shortly afterward he was in high repute for his science in the court of Lisbon, insomuch, that he was one of the council appointed by King John II. to improve the art of navigation, and by some he has received the whole credit of the memorable service rendered to commerce by that council, in the introduction of the astrolabe into nautical use.

In 1484 King John sent an expedition under Diego Cam, as Barros calls him, Cano according to others, to prosecute discoveries along the coast of Africa. In this expedition Behem sailed as cosmographer. They crossed the equinoctial line discovered the coast of Congo, advanced to twenty-two degrees forty-five minutes of south latitude,[2] and erected two

---

[1] "Francisco Lopez de Gomara, Presbitero, Sevillano, escribio con elegante estilo acerca de la cosas de las Indias, pero dexandose llevar de falsas narraciones." Hijos de Sevilla, Numero ii. p. 42, Let. F. The same is stated in Bibliotheca Hispana Nova, lib. i. p. 437.

"El Francisco Lopez de Gomara escrivio tantos borrones e cosas que no son verdaderas, de que ha hecho mucho daña a muchos escritores é coronistas que despues del Gomara han escrito en las cosas de la Nueva España   es porque les ha hecho errar el Gomara." Bernal Diaz del Castillo, Hist. de la Conquest de la Nueva España, Fin. de cap. 18.

"Tenia Gomara doctrina y estilo . . pero empleose en ordinar sin discernimiento lo que halló escrito por sus antecesores, y dió credito á petrañas no solo falsas sino inverisimiles." Juan Battista Muñoz, Hist. N Mundo, Prologo, p. 18.

[2] Vasconcelos, lib. 4

columns. on which were engraved the arms of Portugal, in the mouth of the River Zagra, in Africa, which thence, for some time, took the name of the River of Columns.[1]

For the services rendered on this and on previous occasions, it is said that Behem was knighted by King John in 1485, though no mention is made of such a circumstance in any of the contemporary historians. The principal proof of his having received this mark of distinction, is his having given himself the title on his own globe of *Eques Lusitanus.*

In 1486 he married at Fayal the daughter of Job de Huertar, and is supposed to have remained there for some few years, where he had a son named Martin, born in 1489. During his residence at Lisbon and Fayal, it is probable the acquaintance took place between him and Columbus, to which Herrera and others allude; and the admiral may have heard from him some of the rumors circulating in the islands, of indications of western lands floating to their shores.

In 1491 he returned to Nuremburg to see his family, and while there, in 1492, he finished a terrestrial globe, considered a masterpiece in those days, which he had undertaken at the request of the principal magistrates of his native city.

In 1493 he returned to Portugal, and from thence proceeded to Fayal.

In 1494 King John II., who had a high opinion of him, sent him to Flanders to his natural son Prince George, the intended heir of his crown. In the course of his voyage Behem was captured and carried to England, where he remained for three months detained by illness. Having recovered, he again put to sea, but was captured by a corsair and carried to France. Having ransomed himself, he proceeded to Antwerp and Bruges, but returned almost immediately to Portugal. Nothing more is known of him for several years, during which time it is supposed he remained with his family in Fayal, too old to make further voyages. In 1506 he went from Fayal to Lisbon, where he died.

The assertion that Behem had discovered the western world previous to Columbus, in the course of the voyage with Cam, was founded on a misinterpretation of a passage interpolated in the chronicle of Hartmann Schedel, a contemporary writer. This passage mentions, that when the voyagers were in the Southern Ocean not far from the coast, and had passed the line, they came into another hemisphere, where, when they looked toward the east, their shadows fell toward the south, on their right hand; that here they discovered a new world, unknown until then, and which for many years had never been sought except by the Genoese, and by them unsuccessfully.

" Hii duo, bono deorum auspicio, mare meridionale sulcantes, a littore non longe evagantes, superato circulo equinoctiali, in alterum orbem excepti sunt. Ubi ipsis stantibus orientem versus, umbra ad meridiem et lextram projiciebatur. Aperuêre igitur sua industria, alium orbem hactenus nobis incognitum et multis annis, a nullis quam Januensibus, licet frustra temptatum."

These lines are part of a passage which it is said is interpolated by a different hand, in the original manuscript of the chronicle of Schedel De Murr assures us that they are not to be found in the German translation of the book by George Alt, which was finished the 5th October, 1493. But even if they were, they relate merely to the discovery which Diego Cam made of the southern hemisphere, previously unknown, and of the coast of Africa beyond the equator, all which appeared like a new world, and as such was talked of at the time

---

[1] Murr, Notice sur M. Behaim.

The Genoese alluded to, who had made an unsuccessful attempt, were Antonio de Nolle with Bartholomeo his brother, and Raphael de Nolle his nephew. Antonio was of a noble family, and, for some disgust, left his country and went to Lisbon with his before-mentioned relatives in two caravels, sailing whence in the employ of Portugal, they discovered the island of St. Jago.[1]

This interpolated passage of Schedel was likewise inserted into the work De Europâ sub Frederico III. of Æneas Silvius, afterward Pope Pius II., who died in 1464, long before the voyage in question. The misinterpretation of the passage first gave rise to the incorrect assertion that Behem had discovered the New World prior to Columbus; as if it were possible such a circumstance could have happened without Behem's laying claim to the glory of the discovery, and without the world immediately resounding with so important an event. This error had been adopted by various authors without due examination; some of whom had likewise taken from Magellan the credit of having discovered the strait which goes by his name, and had given it to Behem. The error was too palpable to be generally prevalent, but was suddenly revived in the year 1786 by a French gentleman of highly respectable character of the name of Otto, then resident in New York, who addressed a letter to Dr. Franklin to be submitted to the Philosophical Society of Philadelphia, in which he undertook to establish the title of Behem to the discovery of the New World. His memoir was published in the Transactions of the American Philosophical Society, vol ii., for 1786, article No 35, and has been copied into the journals of most of the nations of Europe.

The authorities cited by M Otto in support of his assertion are generally fallacious, and for the most part given without particular specification. His assertion has been diligently and satisfactorily refuted by Don Christoval Cladera.[2]

The grand proof of M. Otto is a globe which Behem made during his residence in Nuremburg, in 1492, the very year that Columbus set out on his first voyage of discovery. This globe, according to M Otto, is still preserved in the library of Nuremburg, and on it are painted all the discoveries of Behem which are so situated that they can be no other than the coast of Brazil and the straits of Magellan. This authority staggered many, and if supported would demolish the claims of Columbus.

Unluckily for M Otto, in his description of the globe, he depended on the inspection of a correspondent. The globe in the library of Nuremburg was made in 1520 by John Schoener, professor of mathematics,[3] long after the discoveries and death of Columbus and Behem. The real globe of Behem, made in 1492, does not contain any of the islands or shores of the New World, and thus proves that he was totally unacquainted with them. A copy, or planisphere, of Behem's globe is given by Clauera in his Investigations.

---

[1] Barros, decad. i. lib. ii. cap 1. Lisbon, 1552.
[2] Investigaciones Historicas Madrid, 1794.
[3] Cladera, Investig Hist., p. 115.

No. XIV.

VOYAGES OF THE SCANDINAVIANS.

MANY elaborate dissertations have been written to prove that discoveries were made by the Scandinavians on the northern coast of America long before the era of Columbus; but the subject appears still to be wrapped in much doubt and obscurity.

It has been asserted that the Norwegians, as early as the ninth century, discovered a great tract of land to the west of Iceland, which they called Grand Iceland; but this has been pronounced a fabulous tradition. The most plausible account is one given by Snorro Sturleson, in his Saga or Chronicle of King Olaus. According to this writer, one Biorn of Iceland, sailing to Greenland in search of his father, from whom he had been separated by a storm, was driven by tempestuous weather far to the south-west, until he came in sight of a low country, covered with wood, with an island in its vicinity. The weather becoming favorable, he turned to the north-east without landing, and arrived safe at Greenland. His account of the country he had beheld, it is said, excited the enterprise of Leif, son of Eric Rauda (or Redhead), the first settler of Greenland. A vessel was fitted out, and Leif and Biorn departed alone in quest of this unknown land. They found a rocky and sterile island, to which they gave the name of Helleland; also a low sandy country covered with wood, to which they gave the name of Markland; and, two days afterward, they observed a continuance of the coast, with an island to the north of it. This last they described as fertile, well wooded, producing agreeable fruits, and particularly grapes, a fruit with which they were unacquainted. On being informed by one of their companions, a German, of its qualities and name, they called the country, from it, Vinland. They ascended a river, well stored with fish, particularly salmon, and came to a lake from which the river took its origin, where they passed the winter. The climate appeared to them mild and pleasant; being accustomed to the rigorous climates of the north. On the shortest day the sun was eight hours above the horizon. Hence it has been concluded that the country was about the 49th degree of north latitude, and was either Newfoundland, or some part of the coast of North America about the Gulf of St. Lawrence.[1] It is added that the relatives of Leif made several voyages to Vinland, that they traded with the natives for furs; and that, in 1121, a bishop named Eric went from Greenland to Vinland to convert the inhabitants to Christianity. From this time, says Forster, we know nothing of Vinland, and there is every appearance that the tribe which still exists in the interior of Newfoundland, and which is so different from the other savages of North America, both in their appearance and mode of living, and always in a state of warfare with the Esquimaux of the northern coast, are descendants of the ancient Normans.

The author of the present work has not had the means of tracing this story to its original sources. He gives it on the authority of M. Malte Brun, and Mr. Forster. The latter extracts it from the Saga or Chronicle of Snorro, who was born in 1179, and wrote in 1215; so that his account was formed long after the event is said to have taken place. Forster says "The facts which we report have been collected from a great number of Icelandic manuscripts, and transmitted to us by Torfæus in his two works entitled Veteris Grœnlandiæ Descriptio, Hafnia, 1706, and

---

[1] Forster's Northern Voyages, book ii. chap. 2.

Historia Winlandiæ Antiquæ, Hafnia, 1705." Forster appears to have no doubt of the authenticity of the facts. As far as the author of the present work has had experience in tracing these stories of early discoveries of portions of the New World, he has generally found them very confident deductions drawn from very vague and questionable facts Learned men are too prone to give substance to mere shadows, when they assist some preconceived theory. Most of these accounts, when divested of the erudite comments of their editors, have proved little better than the traditional fables, noticed in another part of this work, respecting the imaginary islands of St. Borondon, and of the Seven Cities

There is no great improbability, however, that such enterprising and roving voyagers as the Scandinavians may have wandered to the northern shores of America, about the coast of Labrador, or the shores of Newfoundland; and if the Icelandic manuscripts said to be of the thirteenth century can be relied upon as genuine, free from modern interpolation, and correctly quoted they would appear to prove the fact But granting the truth of the alleged discoveries, they led to no more result than would the interchange of communication between the natives of Greenland and the Esquimaux. The knowledge of them appears not to have extended beyond their own nation, and to have been soon neglected and forgotten by themselves.

Another pretension to an early discovery of the American continent has been set up, founded on an alleged map and narrative of two brothers of the name of Zeno, of Venice; but it seems more invalid than those just mentioned. The following is the substance of this claim.

Nicolo Zeno, a noble Venetian, is said to have made a voyage to the north in 1380, in a vessel fitted out at his own cost, intending to visit England and Flanders: but meeting with a terrible tempest was driven for many days he knew not whither, until he was cast away upon Friseland, an island much in dispute among geographers, but supposed to be the archipelago of the Ferroe islands. The shipwrecked voyagers were assailed by the natives: but rescued by Zichmni, a prince of the islands lying on the south side of Friseland, and duke of another district lying over against Scotland. Zeno entered into the service of this prince, and aided him in conquering Friseland, and other northern islands He was soon joined by his brother Antonio Zeno, who remained fourteen years in those countries.

During his residence in Friseland, Antonio Zeno wrote to his brother Carlo, in Venice, giving an account of a report brought by a certain fisherman, about a land to the westward. According to the tale of this mariner, he had been one of a party who sailed from Friseland about twenty-six years before, in four fishing-boats. Being overtaken by a mighty tempest, they were driven about the sea for many days, until the boat containing himself and six companions was cast upon an island called Estotiland, about one thousand miles from Friseland. They were taken by the inhabitants and carried to a fair and populous city, where the king sent for many interpreters to converse with them, but none that they could understand, until a man was found who had likewise been cast away upon the coast, and who spoke Latin They remained several days upon the island, which was rich and fruitful, abounding with all kinds of metals, and especially gold.[1] There was a high mountain in the centre, from which flowed four rivers which watered the whole country.

---

[1] This account is taken from Hackluyt, vol. iii. p. 123. The passage about gold and other metals is not to be found in the original Italian of Ramusio (tom. ii. p. 23) and is probably an interpolation

The inhabitants were intelligent and acquainted with the mechanical arts of Europe. They cultivated grain, made beer, and lived in houses built of stone. There were Latin books in the king's library, though the inhabitants had no knowledge of that language. They had many cities and castles, and carried on a trade with Greenland for pitch, sulphur, and peltry. Though much given to navigation, they were ignorant of the use of the compass, and finding the Frieslanders acquainted with it, held them in great esteem; and the king sent them with twelve barks to visit a country to the south, called Drogeo. They had nearly perished in a storm, but were cast away upon the coast of Drogeo. They found the people to be cannibals, and were on the point of being killed and devoured, but were spared on account of their great skill in fishing.

The fisherman described this Drogeo as being a country of vast extent, or rather a new world; that the inhabitants were naked and barbarous; but that far to the south-west there was a more civilized region, and temperate climate, where the inhabitants had a knowledge of gold and silver, lived in cities, erected splendid temples to idols, and sacrificed human victims to them, which they afterward devoured.

After the fisherman had resided many years on this continent, during which time he had passed from the service of one chieftain to another, and traversed various parts of it, certain boats of Estotiland arrived on the coast of Drogeo. The fisherman went on board of them, acted as interpreter, and followed the trade between the main-land and Estotiland for some time, until he became very rich; then he fitted out a bark of his own, and with the assistance of some of the people of the island, made his way back, across the thousand intervening miles of ocean, and arrived safe at Friesland. The account he gave of these countries, determined Zichmni, the prince of Friesland, to send an expedition thither, and Antonio Zeno was to command it. Just before sailing, the fisherman, who was to have acted as guide, died; but certain mariners, who had accompanied him from Estotiland, were taken in his place. The expedition sailed under command of Zichmni; the Venetian, Zeno, merely accompanied it. It was unsuccessful. After having discovered an island called Icaria, where they met with a rough reception from the inhabitants, and were obliged to withdraw, the ships were driven by a storm to Greenland. No record remains of any further prosecution of the enterprise.

The countries mentioned in the account of Zeno were laid down on a map originally engraved on wood. The island of Estotiland has been supposed by Malte-Brun to be Newfoundland; its partially civilized inhabitants the descendants of the Scandinavian colonists of Vinland; and the Latin books in the king's library to be the remains of the library of the Greenland bishop, who emigrated thither in 1121. Drogeo, according to the same conjecture, was Nova Scotia and New England. The civilized people to the south-west, who sacrificed human victims in rich temples, he surmises to have been the Mexicans, or some ancient nation of Florida or Louisiana.

The premises do not appear to warrant this deduction. The whole story abounds with improbabilities; not the least of which is the civilization prevalent among the inhabitants: their houses of stone, their European arts, the library of their king, no traces of which were to be found on their subsequent discovery. Not to mention the information about Mexico penetrating through the numerous savage tribes of a vast continent. It is proper to observe that this account was not published until 1558, long after the discovery of Mexico. It was given to the world by Francisco Marcolini, a descendant of the Zeni, from the fragments of letters said to have been written by Antonio Zeno to Carlo his brother.

' It grieves me,' says the editor, "that the book, and divers other writings concerning these matters, are miserably lost: for being but a child when they came to my hands, and not knowing what they were, I tore them and rent them in pieces, which now I cannot call to remembrance but to my exceeding great grief " [1]

This garbled statement by Marcolini, derived considerable authority by being introduced by Abraham Ortelius, an able geographer, in his Theatrum Orbis: but the whole story has been condemned by able commentators as a gross fabrication. Mr. Forster resents this, as an instance of obstinate incredulity, saying that it is impossible to doubt the existence of the country of which Carlo, Nicolo, and Antonio Zeno talk; as original acts in the archives of Venice prove that the chevalier undertook a voyage to the north; that his brother Antonio, followed him, that Antonio traced a map, which he brought back and hung up in his house, where it remained subject to public examination, until the time of Marcolini, as an incontestable proof of the truth of what he advanced. Granting all this, it merely proves that Antonio and his brother were at Friseland and Greenland. Their letters never assert that Zeno made the voyage to Estotiland. The fleet was carried by a tempest to Greenland, after which we hear no more of him; and his account of Estotiland and Drogeo rests simply on the tale of the fisherman, after whose descriptions his map must have been conjecturally projected. The whole story resembles much the fables circulated shortly after the discovery of Columbus, to arrogate to other nations and individuals the credit of the achievement.

M. Malte-Brun intimates that the alleged discovery of Vinland may have been known to Columbus when he made a voyage in the North Sea in 1477,[2] and that the map of Zeno, being in the national library at London, in a Danish work, at the time when Bartholomew Columbus was in that city, employed in making maps, he may have known something of it, and have communicated it to his brother.[3] Had M. Malte-Brun examined the history of Columbus with his usual accuracy, he would have perceived that, in his correspondence with Paulo Toscanelli in 1474, he had expressed his intention of seeking India by a route directly to the west. His voyage to the north did not take place until three years afterward. As to the residence of Bartholomew in London, it was not until after Columbus had made his propositions of discovery to Portugal, if not to the courts of other powers. Granting, therefore, that he had subsequently heard the dubious stories of Vinland, and of the fisherman's adventures, as related by Zeno, or at least by Marcolini, they evidently could not have influenced him in his great enterprise. His route had no reference to them, but was a direct western course, not toward Vinland, and Estotiland, and Drogeo, but in search of Cipango, and Cathay, and the other countries described by Marco Polo, as lying at the extremity of India.

No. XV.

CIRCUMNAVIGATION OF AFRICA BY THE ANCIENTS.

THE knowledge of the ancients with respect to the Atlantic coast of Africa is considered by modern investigators much less extensive than had been imagined; and it is doubted whether they had any practical

[1] Hackluyt, Collect. vol. iii. p. 127.
[2] Malte-Brun, Hist de Geog. tom i. lib. xvii.
[3] Idem, Geog Universelle, tom. iv Note su la découverte de l'Amérique

authority for the belief that Africa was circumnavigable. The alleged voyage of Eudoxus of Cyzicus, from the Red Sea to Gibraltar, though recorded by Pliny, Pomponius Mela, and others, is given entirely on the assertion of Cornelius Nepos, who does not tell from whence he derived his information. Posidonius (cited by Strabo) gives an entirely different account of this voyage, and rejects it with contempt.[1]

The famous voyage of Hanno the Carthaginian, is supposed to have taken place about a thousand years before the Christian era. The Periplus Hannonis remains, a brief and obscure record of this expedition, and a subject of great comment and controversy. By some it has been pronounced a fictitious work, fabricated among the Greeks, but its authenticity has been ably vindicated. It appears to be satisfactorily proved, however, that the voyage of this navigator has been greatly exaggerated, and that he never circumnavigated the extreme end of Africa. Mons. de Bougainville[2] traces his route to a promontory which he named the West Horn, supposed to be Cape Palmas, about five or six degrees north of the equinoctial line, whence he proceeded to another promontory, under the same parallel, which he called the South Horn, supposed to be Cape de Tres Puntas. Mons. Gosselin, however, in his Researches into the Geography of the Ancients (tome 1, p. 162, etc.), after a rigid examination of the Periplus of Hanno, determines that he had not sailed farther south than Cape Non. Pliny, who makes Hanno range the whole coast of Africa, from the straits to the confines of Arabia, had never seen his Periplus, but took his idea from the works of Xenophon of Lampsaco. The Greeks surcharged the narration of the voyager with all kinds of fables, and on their unfaithful copies, Strabo founded many of his assertions. According to M. Gosselin, the itineraries of Hanno, of Scylax, Polybius, Statius, Sebosus and Juba; the recitals of Plato, of Aristotle, of Pliny, of Plutarch, and the tables of Ptolemy, all bring us to the same results, and, notwithstanding their apparent contradictions, fix the limit of southern navigation about the neighborhood of Cape Non, or Cape Bojador.

The opinion that Africa was a peninsula, which existed among the Persians, the Egyptians, and perhaps the Greeks, several centuries prior to the Christian era, was not, in his opinion, founded upon any known facts; but merely on conjecture, from considering the immensity and unity of the ocean; or perhaps on more ancient traditions; or on ideas produced by the Carthaginian discoveries, beyond the Straits of Gibraltar, and those of the Egyptians beyond the Gulf of Arabia. He thinks that there was a very remote period, when geography was much more perfect than in the time of the Phenicians and the Greeks, whose knowledge was but confused traces of what had previously been better known.

The opinion that the Indian Sea joined the ocean was admitted among the Greeks, and in the school of Alexandria, until the time of Hipparchus. It seemed authorized by the direction which the coast of Africa took after Cape Aromata, always tending westward, as far as it had been explored by navigators.

It was supposed that the western coast of Africa rounded off to meet the eastern, and that the whole was bounded by the ocean, much to the northward of the equator. Such was the opinion of Crates, who lived in the time of Alexander; of Aratus, of Cleanthes, of Cleomedes, of Strabo, of Pomponius Mela, of Macrobius, and many others.

Hipparchus proposed a different system, and led the world into an

---

[1] Gosselin, Recherches sur la Géographie des Anciens, tom. 1 p 162, etc.
[2] Mémoirs de l'Acad. des Inscript., tom. xxvi.

error, which for a long time retarded the maritime communication of Europe and India. He supposed that the seas were separated into distinct basins, and that the eastern shores of Africa made a circuit round the Indian Sea, so as to join those of Asia beyond the mouth of the Ganges. Subsequent discoveries instead of refuting this error, only placed the junction of the continents at a greater distance. Marinus of Tyre, and Ptolemy, adopted this opinion in their works. and illustrated it in their maps. which for centuries controlled the general belief of mankind. and perpetuated the idea that Africa extended onward to the south pole. and that it was impossible to arrive by sea at the coasts of India. Still there were geographers who leaned to the more ancient idea of a communication between the Indian Sea and the Atlantic Ocean. It had its advocates in Spain, and was maintained by Pomponius Mela, and by Isidore of Seville. It was believed also by some of the learned in Italy, in the thirteenth, fourteenth, and fifteenth centuries; and thus was kept alive until it was acted upon so vigorously by Prince Henry of Portugal, and at length triumphantly demonstrated by Vasco de Gama, in his circumnavigation of the Cape of Good Hope.

No. XVI.

OF THE SHIPS OF COLUMBUS.

In remarking on the smallness of the vessels with which Columbus made his first voyage. Dr. Robertson observes that, "in the fifteenth century, the bulk and construction of vessels were accommodated to the short and easy voyages along the coast, which they were accustomed to perform." We have many proofs, however, that even anterior to the fifteenth century, there were large ships employed by the Spaniards, as well as by other nations. In an edict published in Barcelona, in 1354, by Pedro IV., enforcing various regulations for the security of commerce, mention is made of Catalonian merchant ships of two and three decks and from 8000 to 12,000 quintals burden.

In 1419, Alonzo of Aragon hired several merchant ships to transport artillery, horses, etc., from Barcelona to Italy, among which were two, each carrying one hundred and twenty horses, which it is computed would require a vessel of at least 600 tons.

In 1463, mention is made of a Venetian ship of 700 tons which arrived at Barcelona from England, laden with wheat.

In 1497, a Castilian vessel arrived there being of 12,000 quintals burden. These arrivals incidentally mentioned among others of similar size, as happening at one port, show that large ships were in use in those days.[1] Indeed, at the time of fitting out the second expedition of Columbus, there were prepared in the port of Bermeo, a Caracca of 1250 tons, and four ships of from 150 to 450 tons burden. Their destination, however, was altered, and they were sent to convoy Muley Boabdil, the last Moorish king of Granada, from the coast of his conquered territory to Africa.[2]

It was not for want of large vessels in the Spanish ports, therefore, that those of Columbus were of so small a size. He considered them best adapted to voyages of discovery, as they required but little depth of water, and therefore could more easily and safely coast unknown shores, and explore bays and rivers. He had some purposely constructed of a very small size for this service, such was the caravel, which in his third

---

Capmany, Questiones Criticas. Quest. 6.   [2] Archives de Ind. en Sevilla.

voyage he despatched to look out for an opening to the sea at the upper part of the Gulf of Paria, when the water grew too shallow for his vessel of one hundred tons burden.

The most singular circumstance with respect to the ships of Columbus is that they should be open vessels: for it seems difficult to believe that a voyage of such extent and peril should be attempted in barks of so frail a construction. This, however, is expressly mentioned by Peter Martyr, in his Decades written at the time; and mention is made occasionally, in the memoirs relative to the voyages written by Columbus and his son, of certain of his vessels being without decks. He sometimes speaks of the same vessel as a ship and a caravel. There has been some discussion of late as to the precise meaning of the term caravel. The Chevalier Bossi, in his dissertations on Columbus, observes that in the Mediterranean caravel designates the largest class of ships of war among the Mussulmans, and that in Portugal it means a small vessel of from 120 to 140 tons burden, but Columbus sometimes applies it to a vessel of forty tons.

Du Cange, in his glossary, considers it a word of Italian origin. Bossi thinks it either Turkish or Arabic, and probably introduced into the European languages by the Moors. Mr. Edward Everett, in a note to his Plymouth oration, considers that the true origin of the word is given in "Ferrarii Origines Linguæ Italicæ," as follows: "Caravela, navigii minoris genus. Lat. Carabus: Græce Karabron."

That the word caravel was intended to signify a vessel of a small size is evident from a naval classification made by King Alonzo in the middle of the thirteenth century. In the first class he enumerates *Naos*, or large ships which go only with sails, some of which have two masts, and others but one. In the second class smaller vessels as Carracas, Fustas, Ballenares, Pinazas, *Carabelas*, etc. In the third class vessels with sails and oars, as Galleys, Galeots, Tardantes, and Saetias.[1]

Bossi gives a copy of a letter written by Columbus to Don Raphael Xansis, treasurer of the King of Spain, an edition of which exists in the public library at Milan. With this letter he gives several wood-cuts of sketches made with a pen, which accompanied this letter, and which he supposes to have been from the hand of Columbus. In these are represented vessels which are probably caravels. They have high bows and sterns, with castles on the latter. They have short masts with large square sails. One of them, besides sails, has benches of oars, and is probably intended to represent a galley. They are all evidently vessels of small size, and light construction.

In a work called "Recherches sur le Commerce," published in Amsterdam, 1779, is a plate representing a vessel of the latter part of the fifteenth century. It is taken from a picture in the church of St. Giovanni e Paolo in Venice. The vessel bears much resemblance to those said to have been sketched by Columbus; it has two masts, one of which is extremely small with a lateen sail. The main-mast has a large square sail. The vessel has a high poop and prow, is decked at each end, and is open in the centre.

It appears to be the fact, therefore, that most of the vessels with which Columbus undertook his long and perilous voyages, were of this light and frail construction, and little superior to the small craft which ply on rivers and along coasts in modern days.

---

[1] Capmany, Quest. Crit.

No. XVII.

ROUTE OF COLUMBUS IN HIS FIRST VOYAGE.[1]

IT has hitherto been supposed that one of the Bahama Islands, at present bearing the name of San Salvador, and which is also known as Cat Island, was the first point where Columbus came in contact with the New World. Navarrete, however, in his introduction to the "Collection of Spanish Voyages and Discoveries," recently published at Madrid, has endeavored to show that it must have been Turk's Island, one of the same group, situated about 100 leagues (of 20 to the degree) S.E. of San Salvador. Great care has been taken to examine candidly the opinion of Navarrete, comparing it with the journal of Columbus, as published in the above-mentioned work, and with the personal observations of the writer of this article, who has been much among these islands.

Columbus describes Guanahani, on which he landed, and to which he gave the name of San Salvador, as being a beautiful island, and very large; as being level, and covered with forests, many of the trees of which bore fruit; as having abundance of fresh water, and a large lake in the centre; that it was inhabited by a numerous population; that he proceeded for a considerable distance in his boats along the shore, which trended to the N.N.E., and as he passed, was visited by the inhabitants of several villages. Turk's Island does not answer to this description.

Turk's Island is a low key composed of sand and rocks, and lying north and south, less than two leagues in extent. It is utterly destitute of wood, and has not a single tree of native growth. It has no fresh water, the inhabitants depending entirely on cisterns and casks in which they preserve the rain; neither has it any lake, but several salt-ponds, which furnish the sole production of the island. Turk's Island cannot be approached on the east or north-east side, in consequence of the reef that surrounds it. It has no harbor, but has an open road on the west side, which vessels at anchor there have to leave and put to sea whenever the wind comes from any other quarter than that of the usual trade breeze of N.E. which blows over the island; for the shore is so bold that there is no anchorage except close to it; and when the wind ceases to blow from the land, vessels remaining at their anchors would be swung against the rocks, or forced high upon the shore, by the terrible surf that then prevails. The unfrequented road of the Hawk's Nest, at the south end of the island, is even more dangerous. This island, which is not susceptible of the slightest cultivation, furnishes a scanty subsistence to a few sheep and horses. The inhabitants draw all their consumption from abroad, with the exception of fish and turtle, which are taken in abundance, and supply the principal food of the slaves employed in the salt-works. The whole wealth of the island consists in the produce of the salt-ponds, and in the salvage and plunder of the many wrecks which take place in the neighborhood. Turk's Island, therefore, would never be inhabited in a savage state of society, where commerce does not exist, and where men are obliged to draw their subsistence from the spot which they people.

Again: when about to leave Guanahani, Columbus was at a loss to

---

[1] The author of this work is indebted for this able examination of the route of Columbus to an officer of the navy of the United States, whose name he regrets the not being at liberty to mention. He has been greatly benefited, in various parts of this history, by nautical information from the same intelligent source

choose which to visit of a great number of islands in sight. Now there is no land visible from Turk's Island, excepting the two salt keys which lie south of it, and with it form the group known as Turk's Islands. The journal of Columbus does not tell us what course he steered in going from Guanahani to Concepcion, but he states that it was five leagues distant from the former, and that the current was against him in sailing to it: whereas the distance from Turk's Island to the Gran Caico, supposed by Navarrete to be the Concepcion of Columbus, is nearly double, and the current constantly to the W.N.W. among these islands, which would be favorable in going from Turk's Island to the Caicos.

From Concepcion, Columbus went next to an island which he saw nine leagues off in a westerly direction, to which he gave the name of Fernandina. This Navarrete takes to be Little Inagua, distant no less than twenty-two leagues from Gran Caico. Besides, in going to Little Inagua, it would be necessary to pass quite close to three islands, each larger than Turk's Island, none of which are mentioned in the journal. Columbus describes Fernandina as stretching twenty-eight leagues S.E. and N.W.: whereas Little Inagua has its greatest length of four leagues in a S.W. direction. In a word the description of Fernandina has nothing in common with Little Inagua. From Fernandina, Columbus sailed S.E. to Isabella, which Navarrete takes to be Great Inagua; whereas this latter bears S.W. from Little Inagua, a course differing 90° from the one followed by Columbus. Again Columbus, on the 20th of November, takes· occasion to say that Guanahani was distant eight leagues from Isabella; whereas Turk's Island is thirty-five leagues from Great Inagua.

Leaving Isabella, Columbus stood W.S.W. for the island of Cuba, and fell in with the Islas Arenas. This course drawn from Great Inagua would meet the coast of Cuba about Port Nipe: whereas Navarrete supposes that Columbus next fell in with the keys south of the Jumentos, and which bear W.N.W. from Inagua; a course differing 45° from the one steered by the ships. After sailing for some time in the neighborhood of Cuba, Columbus finds himself, on the 14th of November, in the sea of Nuestra Señora, surrounded by so many islands that it was impossible to count them: whereas, on the same day, Navarrete places him off Cape Moa, where there is but one small island, and more than fifty leagues distant from any group that can possibly answer the description.

Columbus informs us that San Salvador was distant from Port Principe forty-five leagues: whereas Turk's Island is distant from the point, supposed by Navarrete to be the same, eighty leagues.

On taking leave of Cuba, Columbus remarks that he had followed its coast for an extent of 120 leagues. Deducting twenty leagues for his having followed its windings, there still remain 100. Now, Navarrete only supposes him to have coasted this island an extent of seventy leagues.

Such are the most important difficulties which the theory of Navarrete offers, and which appear insurmountable. Let us now take up the route of Columbus as recorded in his journal, and, with the best charts before us, examine how it agrees with the popular and traditional opinion, that he first landed on the island of San Salvador.

We learn from the journal of Columbus that, on the 11th of October, 1492, he continued steering W.S.W. until sunset, when he returned to his old course of west, the vessels running at the rate of three leagues an hour. At ten o'clock he and several of his crew saw a light, which seemed like a torch carried about on land. He continued running on four hours longer, and had made a distance of twelve leagues farther west, when at two in the morning land was discovered ahead, distant two leagues. The twelve leagues which they ran since ten o'clock, with the two leagues distance from the land, form a total corresponding essentially with the distance and situation of Watling's Island from San Salvador; and it is thence presumed that the light seen at that hour was on Watling's Island, which they were then passing. Had the light been seen on land ahead, and they had kept running on four hours at the rate of three leagues an hour, they must have run high and dry on shore. As the admiral himself received the royal reward for having seen this light, as the first discovery of land, Watling's Island is believed to be the point for which this premium was granted.

On making land, the vessels were hove to until daylight of the same 12th of October; they then anchored off an island of great beauty, covered with forests, and extremely populous.

It was called Guanahani by the natives, but Columbus gave it the name of San Salvador. Exploring its coast, where it ran to the N.N.E., he found a harbor capable of sheltering any number of ships. This description corresponds minutely with the S.E part of the island known as San Salvador, or Cat Island, which lies east and west, bending at its eastern extremity to the N N.E., and has the same verdant and fertile appearance. The vessels had probably drifted into this bay at the S.E. side of San Salvador, on the morning of the 12th, while lying to for daylight; nor did Columbus, while remaining at the island, or when sailing from it, open the land so as to discover that what he had taken for its whole length was but a bend at one end of it, and that the main body of the island lay behind, stretching far to the N W From Guanahani, Columbus saw so many other islands that he was at a loss which next to visit. The Indians signified that they were innumerable, and mentioned the names of above a hundred He determined to go to the largest in sight, which appeared to be about five leagues distant; some of the others were nearer, and some farther off. The island thus selected, it is presumed, was the present island of Concepcion; and that the others were that singular belt of small islands, known as La Cadena (or the chain), stretching past the island of San Salvador in a S E. and N.W. direction, the nearest of the group being nearer than Concepcion, while the rest are more distant

Leaving San Salvador in the afternoon of the 14th for the island thus selected, the ships lay by during the night, and did not reach it until late in the following day, being retarded by adverse currents. Columbus gave this island the name of Santa Maria de la Concepcion; he does not mention either its bearings from San Salvador, or the course which he steered in going to it. We know that in all this neighborhood the current sets strongly and constantly to the W.N.W.; and since Columbus had the current against him, he must have been sailing in an opposite direction, or to the E.S.E. Besides, when near Concepcion, Columbus sees another island to the westward, the largest he had yet seen; but he tells us that he anchored off Concepcion, and did not stand for this larger island, because he could not have sailed to the west. Hence it is rendered certain that Columbus did not sail westward in going from San Salvador to Concepcion: for, from the opposition of the wind as there could be no other cause he could not sail toward that quarter. Now, on reference to the chart, we find the island at present known as Concepcion situated E.S.E. from San Salvador, and at a corresponding distance of five leagues.

Leaving Concepcion on the 16th of October, Columbus steered for a very large island seen to the westward nine leagues off, and which extended itself twenty-eight leagues in a S.E and N W direction. He was becalmed the whole day, and did not reach the island until the following morning, 17th of October. He named it Fernandina. At noon he made sail again, with a view to run round it, and reach another island called Samoet, but the wind being at S.E. by S., the course he wished to steer, the natives signified that it would be easier to sail round this island by running to the N.W. with a fair wind. He therefore bore up to the N W., and having run two leagues found a marvellous port, with a narrow entrance, or rather with two entrances, for there was an island which shut it in completely, forming a noble basin within. Sailing out of this harbor by the opposite entrance at the N.W., he discovered that part of the island which runs east and west. The natives signified to him that this island was smaller than Samoet, and that it would be better to return toward the latter. It had now become calm, but shortly after there sprung up a breeze from W.N.W., which was ahead for the course they had been steering; so they bore up and stood to the E.S.E. in order to get an offing; for the weather threatened a storm, which however dissipated itself in rain. The next day, being the 18th of October, they anchored opposite the extremity of Fernandina.

The whole of this description answers most accurately to the island of Exuma, which lies south from San Salvador, and S.W. by S. from Concepcion The only inconsistency is that Columbus states that Fernandina bore nearly west from Concepcion, and was twenty-eight leagues in extent. This mistake must have proceeded from his having taken the long chain of keys called La Cadena for part of the same Exuma; which continuous appearance they naturally assume when seen from Concepcion, for they run in the same S.E. and N.W. direction. Their bearings, when seen from the same point, are likewise westerly as well as south-westerly. As a proof that such was the case, it may be observed that, after having approached these islands, instead of the extent of Fernandina being increased to his eye, he now remarks that it was twenty leagues long, whereas before it was estimated by him at twenty-eight; he now discovers that instead of one island there were many, and alters his course southerly to reach the one that was most conspicuous.

The identity of the island here described with Exuma is irresistibly forced upon the mind. The distance from Concepcion, the remarkable port with an island in front of it, and farther on its coast turning off to the westward, are all so accurately delineated, that it would seem as though the chart had been drawn from the description of Columbus.

On the 19th of October, the ships left Fernandina, steering S.E. with the wind at north. Sailing three hours on this course, they discovered Samoet to the east, and steered for it, arriving at its north point before noon. Here they found a little island surrounded by rocks, with another reef of rocks lying between it and Samoet. To Samoet, Columbus gave the name of Isabella, and to the point of it opposite the little island, that of Cabo del Isleo, the cape at the S.W. point of Samoet, Columbus called Cabo de Laguna, and off this last his ships were brought to anchor. The little island lay in the direction from Fernandina to Isabella, east and west. The coast from the small island lay westerly twelve leagues to a cape, which Columbus called Hermosa from its beauty; this he believed to be an island apart from Samoet or Isabella, with another one between them Leaving Cabo Laguna, where he remained until the 20th of October, Columbus steered to the N E. toward Cabo del Isleo, but meeting with shoals inside the small island, he did not come to anchor until the day following. Near this extremity of Isabella they found a lake, from which the ships were supplied with water

This island of Isabella, or Samoet, agrees so accurately in its description with Isla Larga, which lies east of Exuma, that it is only necessary to read it with the chart unfolded to be convinced of the identity

Having resolved to visit the island which the natives called Cuba, and described as bearing W.S.W. from Isabella, Columbus left Cabo del Isleo at midnight, the commencement of the 24th of October, and shaped his course accordingly to the W.S.W. The wind continued light, with rain, until noon, when it freshened up, and in the evening Cape Verde, the S.W point of Fernandina, bore N.W. distant seven leagues. As the night became tempestuous, he lay to until morning, drifting according to the reckoning two leagues.

On the morning of the 25th he made sail again to W.S.W., until nine o'clock, when he had run five leagues; he then steered west until three, when he had run eleven leagues at which hour land was discovered, consisting of seven or eight keys lying north and south, and distant five leagues from the ships. Here he anchored the next day, south of these islands, which he called Islas de Arena; they were low, and five or six leagues in extent.

The distances run by Columbus, added to the departure taken from Fernandina and the distance from these islands of Arena at the time of discovering, give a sum of thirty leagues. This sum of thirty leagues is about three less than the distance from the S.W. point of Fernandina or Exuma, whence Columbus took his departure, to the group of Mucaras, which lie east of Cayo Lobo on the grand bank of Bahama, and which correspond to the description of Columbus. If it were necessary to account for the difference of three leagues in a reckoning, where so much is given on conjecture, it would readily occur to a seaman, that an allowance of two leagues for drift, during a long night of blowy weather, is but a small one. The course from Exuma to the Mucaras is about S.W. by W. The course followed by Columbus differs a little from this, but as it was his intention, on setting sail from Isabella, to steer W.S.W., and since he afterward altered it to west, we may conclude that he did so in consequence of having been run out of his course to the southward, while lying to the night previous.

Oct. 27. — At sunrise Columbus set sail from the isles Arenas or Mucaras, for an island called Cuba, steering S.S.W. At dark, having made seventeen leagues on that course, he saw the land, and hove his ships to until morning. On the 28th he made sail again at S.S.W., and entered a beautiful river with a fine harbor, which he named San Salvador. The journal in this part does not describe the localities with the minuteness with which every thing has hitherto been noted; the text also is in several places obscure.

This port of San Salvador we take to be the one now known as Caravelas Grandes, situated eight leagues west of Neuvitas del Principe. Its bearings and distance from the Mucaras coincide exactly with those run by Columbus; and its description agrees, as far as can be ascertained by charts, with the port which he visited.

Oct. 29. — Leaving this port, Columbus stood to the west, and having sailed six leagues, he came to a point of the island running N.W., which we take to be the Punta Gorda; and, ten leagues farther, another stretching easterly, which will be Punta Curiana. One league farther he discovered a small river, and beyond this another very large one, to which he gave the name of Rio de Mares. This river emptied into a fine basin resembling a lake, and having a bold entrance. it had for landmarks two round moutains at the S.W., and to the W.N.W. a bold promontory, suitable for a fortification, which projected far into the sea. This we take to be the fine harbor and river situated west of Point Curiana; its distance corresponds with that run by Columbus from Caravelas Grandes, which we have supposed identical with Port San Salvador. Leaving Rio de **Mares** the 30th of October, Columbus stood to the N.W. for fifteen leagues, when he saw a cape, to which he gave the name of Cabo de Palmas. This, we believe, is the one which forms the eastern entrance to Laguna de Moron. Beyond this cape was a river, distant, according to the natives, four days' journey from the town of Cuba; Columbus determined therefore to make for it.

Having lain to all night, he reached the river on the 31st of October, but found that it was too shallow to admit his ships. This is supposed to be what is now known as Laguna de Moron. Beyond this was a cape surrounded by shoals, and another projected still farther out. Between these two capes was a bay capable of receiving small vessels. The identity here of the description with the coast near Laguna de Moron seems very clear. The cape east of Laguna de Moron coincides with Cape Palmas, the Laguna de Moron with the shoal river described by Columbus ; and in the western point of entrance, with the island of Cabrion opposite it, we recognize the two projecting capes he speaks of, with what appeared to be a bay between them. This all is a remarkable combination, difficult to be found anywhere but in the same spot which Columbus visited and described. Further, the coast from the port of San Salvador had run west to Rio de Mares, a distance of seventeen leagues, and from Rio de Mares it had extended N.W. fifteen leagues to Cabo de Palmos; all of which agrees fully with what has been here supposed. The wind having shifted to north, which was contrary to the course they had been steering, the vessels bore up and returned to Rio de Mares.

On the 12th of November the ships sailed out of Rio de Mares to go in quest of Babeque, an island believed to abound in gold, and to lie E. by S. from that port. Having sailed eight leagues with a fair wind, they came to a river, in which may be recognized the one which lies just west of Punta Gorda. Four leagues farther they saw another, which they called Rio del Sol. It appeared very large, but they did not stop to examine it, as the wind was fair to advance. This we take to be the river now known as Sabana. Columbus was now retracing his steps, and had made twelve leagues from Rio de Mares, but in going west from Port San Salvador to Rio de Mares, he had run seventeen leagues. San Salvador, therefore, remains five leagues east of Rio del Sol; and, accordingly, on reference to the chart, we find Caravelas Grandes situated a corresponding distance from Sabana.

Having run six leagues from Rio del Sol, which makes in all eighteen leagues from Rio de Mares, Columbus came to a cape which he called Cabo de Cuba, probably from supposing it to be the extremity of that island. This corresponds precisely in distance from Punta Curiana with the lesser islands of Guajava, situated near Cuba, and between which and the greater Guajava Columbus must have passed in running in for Port San Salvador. Either he did not notice it, from his attention being engrossed by the magnificent island before him, or, as is also possible, his vessels may have been drifted through the passage, which is two leagues wide, while lying to the night previous to their arrival at Port San Salvador.

On the 13th of November, having hove to all night, in the morning the ships passed a point two leagues in extent, and then entered into a gulf that made into the S.S.W., and which Columbus thought separated Cuba from Bohio. At the bottom of the gulf was a large basin between two mountains. He could not determine whether or not this was an arm of the sea; for not finding shelter from the north wind, he put to sea again. Hence it would appear that Columbus must have partly sailed round the smaller Guajava, which he took to be the extremity of Cuba, without being aware that a few hours' sail would have taken him, by this channel, to Port San Salvador, his first discovery in Cuba, and so back to the same Rio del Sol which he had passed the day previous. Of the two mountains seen on both sides of this entrance, the principal one corresponds with the peak called Alto de Juan Daune, which lies seven leagues west of Punta de Maternillos. The wind continuing north, he stood east fourteen leagues from Cape Cuba, which we have supposed the lesser island of Guajava. It is here rendered sure that the point of little Guajava was believed by him to be the extremity of Cuba: for he speaks of the land mentioned as lying to leeward of the above-mentioned gulf as being the island of Bohio, and says that he discovered twenty leagues of it running E.S.E. and W.N.W.

On the 14th November, having lain to all night with a N.E. wind, he determined to seek a port, and if he found none to return to those which he had left in the island of Cuba: for it will be remembered that all east of little Guajava he supposed to be Bohio. He steered E. by S. therefore six leagues, and then stood in for the land. Here he saw many ports and islands: but as it blew fresh, with a heavy sea, he dared not enter, but ran the coast down N.W. by W. for a distance of eighteen leagues, where he saw a clear entrance and a port, in which he stood S.S.W. and afterward S.E., the navigation being all clear and open. Here Columbus beheld so many islands that it was impossible to count them. They were very lofty, and covered with trees. Columbus called the neighboring sea Mar de Nuestra Señora, and to the harbor near the entrance to these islands he gave the name of Puerto del Principe. This harbor he says he did not enter until the Sunday following, which was four days after. This part of the text of Columbus's journal is confused, and there are also anticipations, as if it had been written subsequently, or mixed together in copying. It appears evident that while lying to the night previous, with the wind at N.E., the ships had drifted to the N.W., and been carried by the powerful current of the Bahama channel far in the same direction. When they bore up, therefore, to return to the ports which they had left in the island of Cuba, they fell in to leeward of them, and now first discovered the numerous group of islands of which Cayo Romano is the principal. The current of this channel is of itself sufficient to have carried the vessels to the westward a distance of 20 leagues, which is what they had run easterly since leaving Cape Cuba, or Guajava, for it had acted upon them during a period of thirty hours. There can be no doubt as to the identity of these keys with those about Cayo Romano; for they are the only ones in the neighborhood of Cuba that are not of a low and swampy nature, but large and lofty. They enclose a free, open navigation, and abundance of fine harbors, in late years the resort of pirates, who found security and concealment for themselves and their prizes in the recesses of these lofty keys. From the description of Columbus, the vessels must have entered between the islands of Baril and Pacedon, and sailing along Cayo Romano on a S.E course, have reached in another day their old cruising ground in the neighborhood of lesser Guajava. Not only Columbus does not tell us here of his having changed his anchorage among these keys, but his journal does not even mention his having anchored at all, until the return from the ineffectual search after Babeque. It is clear, from what has been said, that it was not in Port Principe that the vessels anchored on this occasion, but it could not have been very distant, since Columbus went from the ships in his boats on the 18th November, to place a cross at its entrance. He had probably seen the entrance from without, when sailing east from Guajava on the 13th of November. The identity of this port with the one now known as Neuvitas el Principe seems certain, from the description of its entrance. Columbus, it appears, did not visit its interior.

On the 19th November the ships sailed again, in quest of Babeque. At sunset Port Principe bore S.S W, distant seven leagues, and having sailed all night at N.E. by N. and until ten o'clock of the next day (20th November), they had run a distance of fifteen leagues on that course. The wind blowing from E.S.E., which was the direction in which Babeque was supposed to lie, and the weather being foul, Columbus determined to return to Port Principe, which was then distant twenty-five leagues. He did not wish to go to Isabella, distant only twelve leagues, lest the Indians whom he had brought from San Salvador, which lay eight leagues from Isabella, should make their escape. Thus, in sailing N.E by N from near Port Principe, Columbus had approached within a short distance of Isabella. That island was then, according to his calculations, thirty-seven leagues from Port Principe, and San Salvador was forty-five leagues from the same point. The first differs but eight leagues from the truth, the latter nine; or from the actual distance of Neuvitas el Principe from Isla Larga and San Salvador. Again, let us now call to mind the course made by Columbus in going from Isabella to Cuba; it was first W.S.W , then W., and afterward S.S.W Having consideration for the different distances run on each, these yield a medium course not materially different from S.W Sailing then S W from Isabella, Columbus had reached Port San Salvador, on the coast of Cuba. Making afterward a course of N.E. by N from off Port Principe, he was going in the direction of Isabella Hence we deduce that Port San Salvador, on the coast of Cuba, lay west of Port Principe, and the whole combination is thus bound together and established The two islands seen by Columbus at ten o'clock of the same 20th November, must have been some of the keys which lie west of the Jumentos. Running back toward Port Principe, Columbus made it at dark, but found that he had been carried to the westward by the currents This furnishes a sufficient proof of the strength of the current in the Bahama channel; for it will be remembered that he ran over to Cuba with a fair wind After contending for four days, until the 24th November, with light winds against the force of these currents, he arrived at length opposite the level island whence he had set out the week before when going to Babeque.

We are thus accidentally informed that the point from which Columbus started in search of Babeque was the same island of Guajava the lesser, which lies west of Neuvitas el Principe. Further: at first he dared not enter into the opening between the two mountains, for it seemed as though the sea broke upon them; but having sent the boat ahead, the vessels followed in at S.W and then W. into a fine harbor. The level island lay north of it, and with another island formed a secure basin capable of sheltering all the navy of Spain. This level island resolves itself then into our late Cape Cuba, which we have supposed to be little Guajava, and the entrance east of it becomes identical with the gulf above mentioned which lay between two mountains, one of which we have supposed the Alto de Juan Daune, and which gulf appeared to divide Cuba from Bohio. Our course now becomes a plain one. On the 26th of November, Columbus sailed from Santa Catalina (the name given by him to the port last described) at sunrise. and stood for the cape at the S.E. which he called Cabo de Pico. In this it is easy to recognize the high peak already spoken of as the Alto de Juan Daune. Arrived off this he saw another cape, distant fifteen leagues, and still farther another five

leagues beyond it, which he called Cabo de Campana   The first must be
that now known as Point Padre, the second Point Mulas   their distances
from Alto de Juan Daune are underrated; but it requires no little experience to estimate correctly the distances of the bold headlands of Cuba, as
seen through the pure atmosphere that surrounds the island.

Having passed Point Mulas in the night, on the 27th Columbus looked
into the deep bay that lies S.E. of it, and seeing the bold projecting headland that makes out between Port Nipe and Port Banes, with those deep
bays on each side of it, he supposed it to be an arm of the sea dividing
one land from another with an island between them

Having landed at Taco for a short time, Columbus arrived in the evening of the 27th at Baracoa, to which he gave the name of Puerto Santo.
From Cabro del Pico to Puerto Santo, a distance of sixty leagues, he had
passed no fewer than nine good ports and five rivers to Cape Campana,
and thence to Puerto Santo eight more rivers, each with a good port; all
of which may be found on the chart between Alto de Juan Daune and
Baracoa.   By keeping near the coast he had been assisted to the S.E. by
the eddy current of the Bahama channel.   Sailing from Puerto Santo or
Baracoa on the 4th of December, he reached the extremity of Cuba the
following day, and striking off upon a wind to the S.E. in search of Babeque, which lay to the N E., he came in sight of Bohio, to which he gave
the name of Hispaniola.

On taking leave of Cuba, Columbus tells us that he had coasted it a
distance of 120 leagues.   Allowing twenty leagues of this distance for his
having followed the undulations of the coast the remaining 100 measured
from Point Maysi fall exactly upon Cabrion Key, which we have supposed the western boundary of his discoveries

The astronomical observations of Columbus form no objection to what
has been here advanced; for he tells us that the instrument which he
made use of to measure the meridian altitudes of the heavenly bodies was
out of order and not to be depended upon.   He places his first discovery,
Guanahani, in the latitude of Ferro, which is about 27° 30′ north   San
Salvador we find in 24° 30′ and Turk's Island in 21° 30′: both are very
wide of the truth, but it is certainly easier to conceive an error of three
than one of six degrees.

Laying aside geographical demonstration, let us now examine how historical records agree with the opinion here supported, that the island of
San Salvador was the first point where Columbus came in contact with
the New World.   Herrera, who is considered the most faithful and authen-
tic of Spanish historians, wrote his History of the Indies toward the
year 1600.   In describing the voyage of Juan Ponce de Leon, made to
Florida in 1512, he makes the following remarks:[1] "Leaving Aguada in
Porto Rico, they steered to the N.W. by N., and in five days arrived at an
island called El Viejo, in latitude 22° 30′.   The next day they arrived at a small island of the Lucayos, called Caycos.   On the eighth
day they anchored at another island called Yaguna in 24°, on the eighth day
out from Porto Rico.   Thence they passed to the island of Manuega, in
24° 30′, and on the eleventh day they reached Guanahani, which is in 25°
40′ north.   This island of Guanahani was the first discovered by Columbus on his first voyage, and which he called San Salvador."   This is the
substance of the remarks of Herrera, and is entirely conclusive as to the
location of San Salvador.   The latitudes, it is true, are all placed higher
than we now know them to be; that of San Salvador being such as to
correspond with no other land than that now known as the Berry Islands,

which are seventy leagues distant from the nearest coast of Cuba: whereas Columbus tells us that San Salvador was only forty-five leagues from Port Principe. But in those infant days of navigation, the instruments for measuring the altitudes of the heavenly bodies, and the tables of declinations for deducing the latitude, must have been so imperfect as to place the most scientific navigator of the time below the most mechanical one of the present.

The second island arrived at by Ponce de Leon, in his north-western course, was one of the Caycos; the first one, then called El Viejo, must have been Turk's Island, which lies S.E. of the Caycos. The third island they came to was probably Mariguana; the fourth, Crooked Island; and the fifth, Isla Larga. Lastly they came to Guanahani, the San Salvador of Columbus. If this be supposed identical with Turk's Island, where do we find the succession of islands touched at by Ponce de Leon on his way from Porto Rico to San Salvador?[1] No stress has been laid, in these remarks, on the identity of name which has been preserved to San Salvador, Concepcion, and Port Principe, with those given by Columbus, though traditional usage is of vast weight in such matters. Geographical proof, of a conclusive kind it is thought, has been advanced, to enable the world to remain in its old hereditary belief that the present island of San Salvador is the spot where Columbus first set foot upon the New World. Established opinions of the kind should not be lightly molested. It is a good old rule, that ought to be kept in mind in curious research as well as territorial dealings, "Do not disturb the ancient landmarks."

Note to the Revised Edition of 1848. — The Baron de Humboldt, in his "Examen Critique de l'histoire de la géographie du nouveau continent," published in 1837, speaks repeatedly in high terms of the ability displayed in the above examination of the route of Columbus, and argues at great length and quite conclusively in support of the opinion contained in it. Above all, he produces a document hitherto unknown, and the great importance of which had been discovered by M. Valeknaer and himself in 1832. This is a map made in 1500 by that able mariner Juan de la Cosa, who accompanied Columbus in his second voyage and sailed with other of the discoverers. In this map, of which the Baron de Humboldt gives an engraving, the islands as laid down agree completely with the bearings and distances given in the journal of Columbus, and establishes the identity of San Salvador, or Cat Island and Guanahani.

"I feel happy," says M. de Humboldt, "to be enabled to destroy the incertitudes (which rested on this subject) by a document as ancient as it is unknown; a document which confirms irrevocably the arguments which Mr Washington Irving has given in his work against the hypotheses of the Turk's Island."

In the present revised edition the author feels at liberty to give the merit of the very masterly paper on the route of Columbus where it is justly due. It was furnished him at Madrid by the late commander Alexander Slidel Mackenzie, of the United States navy, whose modesty shrunk from affixing his name to an article so calculated to do him credit, and which has since challenged the high eulogiums of men of nautical science.

No. XVIII.

PRINCIPLES UPON WHICH THE SUMS MENTIONED IN THIS WORK HAVE BEEN REDUCED INTO MODERN CURRENCY.

IN the reign of Ferdinand and Isabella the mark of silver, which was equal to 8 ounces or to 50 castillanos was divided into 65 reals, and each real into 34 maravedies; so that there were 2210 maravedies in the mark of silver. Among other silver coins there was the real of 8, which, consist-

---

[1] In the first chapter of Herrera's description of the Indies, appended to his history, is another scale of the Bahama Islands, which corroborates the above. It begins at the opposite end, at the N.W., and runs down to the S.E. It is thought unnecessary to cite it particularly.

ing of 8 reals. was. within a small fraction. the eighth part of a mark of silver, or one ounce. Of the gold-coins then in circulation the castillano or *dobla ae la vanda* was worth 490 maravedies. and the ducado 383 maravedies.

If the value of the maravedi had remained unchanged in Spain down to the present day. it would be easy to reduce a sum of the time of Ferdinand and Isabella into a correspondent sum of current money: but by the successive depreciations of the coin of Vellon, or mixed metals. issued since that period, the *real* and maravedi of Vellon, which had replaced the ancient currency, were reduced toward the year 1700. to about a third of the old *real* and maravedi, now known as the *real* and maravedi of silver. As, however, the ancient piece of 8 reals was equal approximately to the ounce of silver. and the duro, or dollar of the present day, is likewise equal to an ounce, they may be considered identical. Indeed, in Spanish America, the dollar, instead of being divided into 20 reals, as in Spain, is divided into only 8 parts called reals, which evidently represent the real of the time of Ferdinand and Isabella, as the dollar does the real of 8. But the ounce of silver was anciently worth 276¼ maravedies; the dollar, therefore, is likewise equal to 276¼ maravedies By converting then the sums mentioned in this work into maravedies they have been afterward reduced into dollars by dividing by 276¼.

There is still, however, another calculation to be made, before we can arrive at the actual value of any sum of gold and silver mentioned in former times. It is necessary to notice the variation which has taken place in the value of the metals themselves. In Europe, previous to the discovery of the New World, an ounce of gold commanded an amount of food or labor which would cost three ounces at the present day; hence an ounce of gold was then estimated at three times its present value. At the same time an ounce of silver commanded an amount which at present costs 4 ounces of silver. It appears from this, that the value of gold and silver varied with respect to each other, as well as with respect to all other commodities This is owing to there having been much more silver brought from the New World, with respect to the quantity previously in circulation, than there has been of gold. In the fifteenth century one ounce of gold was equal to about 12 of silver, and now, in the year 1827, it is exchanged against 16.

Hence giving an idea of the relative value of the sums mentioned in this work, it has been found necessary to multiply them by three when in gold, and by four when expressed in silver.[1]

It is expedient to add that the dollar is reckoned in this work at 100 cents of the United States of North America, and four shillings and sixpence of England.

No. XIX.

PRESTER JOHN:

SAID to be derived from the Persian *Prestegani* or *Perestigani*, which signifies apostolique; or *Preschtak Geham*, angel of the world. It is the name of a potent Christian monarch of shadowy renown, whose dominions were placed by writers of the middle ages sometimes in the remote parts of Asia and sometimes in Africa, and of whom such contradictory accounts were given by the travellers of those days that the very existence either of him or his kingdom came to be considered doubtful. It now

---

[1] See Caballero Pesos y Medidas. J. B. Say, Économie Politique.

appears to be admitted that there really was such a potentate in a remote part of Asia   He was of the Nestorian Christians, a sect spread throughout Asia, and taking its name and origin from Nestorius, a Christian patriarch of Constantinople.

The first vague reports of a Christian potentate in the interior of Asia, or as it was then called, India, were brought to Europe by the Crusaders, who it is supposed gathered them from the Syrian merchants who traded to the very confines of China.

In subsequent ages, when the Portuguese in their travels and voyages discovered a Christian king among the Abyssinians, called Baleel-Gian, they confounded him with the potentate already spoken of   Nor was the blunder extraordinary, since the original Prester John was said to reign over a remote part of India; and the ancients included in that name Ethiopia and all the regions of Africa and Asia bordering on the Red Sea and on the commercial route from Egypt to India

Of the Prester John of India we have reports furnished by William Ruysbrook, commonly called Rubruquis, a Franciscan friar sent by Louis IX., about the middle of the thirteenth century, to convert the Grand Khan   According to him, Prester John was originally a Nestorian priest, who on the death of the sovereign made himself King of the Naymans, all Nestorian Christians. Carpini. a Franciscan friar, sent by Pope Innocent in 1245 to convert the Mongols of Persia, says that Ocoday, one of the sons of Ghengis Khan of Tartary, marched with an army against the Christians of Grand India. The king of that country, who was called Prester John. came to their succor. Having had figures of men made of bronze, he had them fastened on the saddles of horses. and put fire within. with a man behind with a bellows. When they came to battle these horses were put in the advance, and the men who were seated behind the figures threw something into the fire, and blowing with their bellows. made such a smoke that the Tartars were quite covered with it.

They then fell on them. despatched many with their arrows. and put the rest to flight.

Marco Polo (1271) places Prester John near the great wall of China, to the north of Chan-si. in Teudich, a populous region full of cities and castles.

Mandeville (1332) makes Prester sovereign of Upper India (Asia). with four thousand islands tributary to him.

When John II. of Portugal was pushing his discoveries along the African coast, he was informed that 350 leagues to the east of the kingdom of Benin in the profound depths of Africa, there was a puissant monarch, called Ogave. who had spiritual and temporal jurisdiction over all the surrounding kings.

An African prince assured him, also. that to the east of Timbuctoo there was a sovereign who professed a religion similar to that of the Christians and was king of a Mosaic people.

King John now supposed he had found traces of the real Prester John. with whom he was eager to form an alliance religious as well as commercial. In 1487 he sent envoys by land in quest of him. One was a gentleman of his household, Pedro de Covilham; the other, Alphonso de Paiva. They went by Naples to Rhodes, thence to Cairo, thence to Aden on the Arabian Gulf above the mouth of the Red Sea.

Here they separated with an agreement to rendezvous at Cairo. Alphonso de Paiva sailed direct for Ethiopia: Pedro de Covilham for the Indies. The latter passed to Calicut and Goa, where he embarked for Sofala on the eastern coast of Africa, thence returned to Aden, and made his way back to Cairo. Here he learned that his coadjutor, Alphonso de

Paiva, had died in that city. He found two Portuguese Jews waiting for him with fresh orders from King John not to give up his researches after Prester John until he found him. One of the Jews he sent back with a journal and verbal accounts of his travels. With the other he set off again for Aden; thence to Ormuz, at the entrance of the gulf of Persia, where all the rich merchandise of the East was brought to be transported thence by Syria and Egypt into Europe.

Having taken note of every thing here, he embarked on the Red Sea, and arrived at the court of an Abyssinian prince named Escander (the Arabic version of Alexander), whom he considered the real Prester John. The prince received him graciously, and manifested a disposition to favor the object of his embassy, but died suddenly, and his successor Naut refused to let Covilham depart, but kept him for many years about his person, as his prime councillor, lavishing on him wealth and honors. After all, this was not the real Prester John, who as has been observed, was an Asiatic potentate.

No. XX.

MARCO POLO.[1]

THE travels of Marco Polo, or Paolo, furnish a key to many parts of the voyages and speculations of Columbus, which without it would hardly be comprehensible.

Marco Polo was a native of Venice, who, in the thirteenth century, made a journey into the remote, and, at that time, unknown regions of the East, and filled all Christendom with curiosity by his account of the countries he had visited. He was preceded in his travels by his father Nicholas and his uncle Maffeo Polo. These two brothers were of an illustrious family in Venice, and embarked about the year 1255 on a commercial voyage to the East. Having traversed the Mediterranean and through the Bosphorus, they stopped for a short time at Constantinople, which city had recently been wrested from the Greeks by the joint arms of France and Venice. Here they disposed of their Italian merchandise, and, having purchased a stock of jewellery, departed on an adventurous expedition to trade with the western Tartars, who, having overrun many parts of Asia and Europe, were settling and forming cities in the vicinity of the Wolga. After traversing the Euxine to Soldaia (at present Sudak), a port in the Crimea, they continued on, by land and water, until they reached the military court, or rather camp, of a Tartar prince, named Barkah, a descendant of Ghengis Khan, into whose hands they confided all their merchandise. The barbaric chieftain, while he was dazzled by their precious commodities, was flattered by the entire confidence in his justice manifested by these strangers. He repaid them with princely munificence, and loaded them with favors during a year that they remained at his court. A war breaking out between their patron and his cousin Hulagu, chief of the eastern Tartars, and Barkah being defeated, the Polos were embarrassed how to extricate themselves from the country and return home in safety. The road to Constantinople being cut off by

---

[1] In preparing the first edition of this work for the press the author had not the benefit of the English translation of Marco Polo, published a few years since, with admirable commentaries, by William Marsden, F.R.S. He availed himself, principally, of an Italian version in the Venetian edition of Ramusio (1606), the French translation by Bergeron, and an old and very incorrect Spanish translation. Having since procured the work of Mr. Marsden he has made considerable alterations in these notices of Marco Polo.

the enemy, they took a circuitous route, round the head of the Caspian Sea, and through the deserts of Transoxiana, until they arrived in the city of Bokhara, where they resided for three years.

While here there arrived a Tartar nobleman who was on an embassy from the victorious Hulagu to his brother the Grand Khan. The ambassador became acquainted with the Venetians, and finding them to be versed in the Tartar tongue, and possessed of curious and valuable knowledge, he prevailed upon them to accompany him to the court of the emperor, situated, as they supposed, at the very extremity of the East.

After a march of several months, being delayed by snow-storms and inundations, they arrived at the court of Cublai, otherwise called the Great Khan, which signifies King of Kings, being the sovereign potentate of the Tartars. This magnificent prince received them with great distinction; he made inquiries about the countries and princes of the West, their civil and military government, and the manners and customs of the Latin nation. Above all, he was curious on the subject of the Christian religion. He was so much struck by their replies, that, after holding a council with the chief persons of his kingdom, he entreated the two brothers to go on his part as ambassadors to the pope, to entreat him to send a hundred learned men well instructed in the Christian faith, to impart a knowledge of it to the sages of his empire. He also entreated them to bring him a little oil from the lamp of our Saviour, in Jerusalem, which he concluded must have marvellous virtues. It has been supposed, and with great reason, that under this covert of religion, the shrewd Tartar sovereign veiled motives of a political nature. The influence of the pope in promoting the crusades had caused his power to be known and respected throughout the East; it was of some moment, therefore, to conciliate his good-will. Cublai Khan had no bigotry nor devotion to any particular faith, and probably hoped, by adopting Christianity, to make it a common cause between himself and the warlike princes of Christendom, against his and their inveterate enemies, the soldan of Egypt and the Saracens.

Having written letters to the pope in the Tartar language, he delivered them to the Polos, and appointed one of the principal noblemen of his court to accompany them in their mission. On their taking leave he furnished them with a tablet of gold on which was engraved the royal arms; this was to serve as a passport, at sight of which the governors of the various provinces were to entertain them, to furnish them with escorts through dangerous places, and render them all other necessary services at the expense of the Great Khan.

They had scarce proceeded twenty miles, when the nobleman who accompanied them fell ill and they were obliged to leave him, and continue on their route. Their golden passport procured them every attention and facility throughout the dominions of the Great Khan. They arrived safely at Acre, in April, 1269. Here they received news of the recent death of Pope Clement IV., at which they were much grieved, fearing it would cause delay in their mission. There was at that time in Acre a legate of the holy chair, Tebaldo di Vesconti, of Placentia, to whom they gave an account of their embassy. He heard them with great attention and interest, and advised them to await the election of a new pope, which must soon take place, before they proceeded to Rome on their mission. They determined in the interim to make a visit to their families, and accordingly departed for Negropont, and thence to Venice, where great changes had taken place in their domestic concerns, during their long absence. The wife of Nicholas, whom he had left pregnant had died, in giving birth to a son, who had been named Marco.

As the contested election for the new pontiff remained pending for two years, they were uneasy, lest the Emperor of Tartary should grow impatient at so long a postponement of the conversion of himself and his people: they determined, therefore, not to wait the election of a pope, but to proceed to Acre, and get such despatches and such ghostly ministry for the Grand Khan as the legate could furnish. On the second journey, Nicholas Polo took with him his son Marco, who afterward wrote an account of these travels.

They were again received with great favor by the legate Tebaldo, who, anxious for the success of their mission, furnished them with letters to the Grand Khan, in which the doctrines of the Christian faith were fully expounded. With these, and with a supply of the holy oil from the sepulchre, they once more set out, in September, 1271, for the remote parts of Tartary. They had not long departed, when missives arrived from Rome, informing the legate of his own election to the holy chair. He took the name of Gregory X., and decreed that in future, on the death of a pope, the cardinals should be shut up in conclave until they elected a successor; a wise regulation, which has since continued, enforcing a prompt decision, and preventing intrigue.

Immediately on receiving intelligence of his election, he despatched a courier to the King of Armenia, requesting that the two Venetians might be sent back to him, if they had not departed. They joyfully returned, and were furnished with new letters to the Khan. Two elegant friars, also, Nicholas Vincenti and Gilbert de Tripoli, were sent with them, with powers to ordain priests and bishops and to grant absolution. They had presents of crystal vases, and other costly articles to deliver to the Grand Khan; and thus well provided, they once more set forth on their journey.[1]

Arriving in Armenia, they ran great risk of their lives from the war which was raging, the soldan of Babylon having invaded the country. They took refuge for some time with the superior of a monastery. Here the two reverend fathers, losing all courage to prosecute so perilous an enterprise, determined to remain, and the Venetians continued their journey. They were a long time on the way, and exposed to great hardships and sufferings from floods and snow-storms, it being the winter season. At length they reached a town in the dominions of the Khan. That potentate sent officers to meet them at forty days' distance from the court, and to provide quarters for them during their journey.[2] He received them with great kindness, was highly gratified with the result of their mission and with the letters of the pope, and having received from them some oil from the lamp of the holy sepulchre, he had it locked up, and guarded it as a precious treasure.

The three Venetians, father, brother, and son, were treated with such distinction by the Khan, that the courtiers were filled with jealousy. Marco soon, however, made himself popular, and was particularly esteemed by the emperor. He acquired the four principal languages of the country, and was of such remarkable capacity that, notwithstanding his youth, the Khan employed him in missions and services of importance, in various parts of his dominions, some to the distance of even six months' journey. On these expeditions he was industrious in gathering all kinds of information respecting that vast empire, and from notes and minutes made for the satisfaction of the Grand Khan, he afterward composed the history of his travels.

---

[1] Ramusio, tom. ii

[2] Bergeron, by blunder in the translation from the original Latin, has stated that the Khan sent 40,000 men to escort them. This has drawn the ire of the critics upon Marco Polo, who have cited it as one of his monstrous exaggerations

After about seventeen years residence in the Tartar court the Venetians felt a longing to return to their native country. Their patron was advanced in age and could not survive much longer, and after his death, their return might be difficult if not impossible. They applied to the Grand Khan for permission to depart, but for a time met with a refusal, accompanied by friendly upbraidings. At length a singular train of events operated in their favor: an embassy arrived from a Mogul Tartar prince, who ruled in Persia, and who was grand-nephew to the emperor. The object was to entreat, as a spouse, a princess of the imperial lineage. A grand-daughter of Cublai Khan, seventeen years of age, and of great beauty and accomplishments, was granted to the prayer of the prince, and departed for Persia with the ambassadors, and with a splendid retinue, but after travelling for some months, was obliged to return on account of the distracted state of the country.

The ambassadors despaired of conveying the beautiful bride to the arms of her expecting bridegroom, when Marco Polo returned from a voyage to certain of the Indian islands. His representations of the safety of a voyage in those seas, and his private instigations, induced the ambassadors to urge the Grand Khan for permission to convey the princess by sea to the Gulf of Persia, and that the Christians might accompany them, as being best experienced in maritime affairs. Cublai Khan consented with great reluctance, and a splendid fleet was fitted out and victualled for two years, consisting of fourteen ships of four masts, some of which had crews of two hundred and fifty men.

On parting with the Venetians the munificent Khan gave them rich presents of jewels, and made them promise to return to him after they had visited their families. He authorized them to act as his ambassadors to the principal courts of Europe, and, as on a former occasion, furnished them with tablets of gold, to serve, not merely as passports, but as orders upon all commanders in his territories for accommodations and supplies.

They set sail therefore in the fleet with the Oriental princess and her attendants and the Persian ambassadors. The ships swept along the coast of Cochin China, stopped for three months at a port of the island of Sumatra near the western entrance of the Straits of Malacca, waiting for the change of the monsoon to pass the Bay of Bengal. Traversing this vast expanse they touched at the island of Ceylon and then crossed the strait to the southern part of the great peninsula of India. Thence sailing up the Pirate coast, as it is called, the fleet entered the Persian Gulf and arrived at the famous port of Olmuz, where it is presumed the voyage terminated, after eighteen months spent in traversing the Indian seas.

Unfortunately for the royal bride who was the object of this splendid naval expedition, her bridegroom, the Mogul king, had died some time before her arrival, leaving a son named Ghazan, during whose minority the government was administered by his uncle, Kai-Khatu. According to the directions of the regent, the princess was delivered to the youthful prince, son of her intended spouse. He was at that time at the head of an army on the borders of Persia. He was of a diminutive stature but of a great soul, and, on afterwards ascending the throne, acquired renown for his talents and virtues What became of the Eastern bride, who had travelled so far in quest of a husband, is not known; but every thing favorable is to be inferred from the character of Ghazan.

The Polos remained some time in the court of the regent, and then departed, with fresh tablets of gold given by that prince, to carry them in safety and honor through his dominions. As they had to traverse many countries where the traveller is exposed to extreme peril, they appeared on their journeys as Tartars of low condition, having converted all their wealth into precious stones and sewn them up in the folds and linings of their coarse garments. They had a long, difficult, and perilous journey to Trebizond, whence they proceeded to Constantinople, thence to Negropont, and, finally to Venice, where they arrived in 1295, in good health, and literally laden with riches. Having heard during their journey of the death of their old benefactor, Cublai Khan, they considered their diplomatic functions at an end, and also that they were absolved from their promise to return to his dominions.

Ramusio, in his preface to the narrative of Marco Polo, gives a variety of particulars concerning their arrival, which he compares to that of Ulysses. When they arrived at Venice, they were known by nobody. So many years had elapsed since their departure without any tidings of them, that they were either forgotten or considered dead. Besides, their foreign garb, the influence of southern suns, and the similitude which men acquire to those among whom they reside for any length of time, had given them the look of Tartars rather than Italians.

They repaired to their own house, which was a noble palace, situated in the street of St. Giovanne Chrisostomo, and was afterward known by the name of la Corte de la Milione. They found several of their relatives still inhabiting it; but they were slow in recollecting the travellers, not knowing of their wealth, and probably considering them, from their coarse and foreign attire, poor adventurers returned to be a charge upon their families. The Polos, however, took an effectual mode of quickening the memories of their friends, and insuring themselves a loving reception. They invited them all to a grand banquet. When their guests arrived, they received them richly dressed in garments of crimson satin of Oriental fashion. When water had been served for the washing of hands, and the company were summoned to table, the travellers, who had retired, appeared again in still richer robes of crimson damask. The first dresses were cut up and distributed among the servants, being of such length that they swept the ground, which, says Ramusio, was the mode in those days with dresses worn within doors. After the first course, they again retired and came in dressed in crimson velvet, the damask dresses being likewise given to the domestics, and the same was done at the end of the feast with their velvet robes, when they appeared in the Venetian dress of the day. The guests were lost in astonishment, and could not comprehend the meaning of this masquerade. Having dismissed all the attendants, Marco Polo brought forth the coarse Tartar dresses in which they had arrived. Slashing them in several places with a knife, and ripping open the seams and lining, there tumbled forth rubies, sapphires, emeralds, diamonds, and other precious stones, until the whole table glittered with inestimable wealth, acquired from the munificence of the Grand Khan, and conveyed in this portable form through the perils of their long journey.

The company, observes Ramusio, were out of their wits with amazement, and now clearly perceived what they had at first doubted, that these in very truth were those honored and valiant gentlemen the Polos, and, accordingly, paid them great respect and reverence.

The account of this curious feast is given by Ramusio, on traditional authority, having heard it many times related by the illustrious Gasparo Malipiero, a very ancient gentleman, and a senator, of unquestionable veracity, who had it from his father, who had it from his grandfather, and so on up to the fountain-head.

When the fame of this banquet and of the wealth of the travellers came to be divulged throughout Venice, all the city, noble and simple, crowded to do honor to the extraordinary merit of the Polos. Maffeo, who was the eldest, was admitted to the dignity of the magistracy. The youth of the city came every day to visit and converse with Marco Polo, who was extremely amiable and communicative. They were insatiable in their inquiries about Cathay and the Grand Khan, which he answered with great courtesy, giving details with which they were vastly delighted, and, as he always spoke of the wealth of the Grand Khan in round numbers, they gave him the name of Messer Marco Milioni.

Some months after their return, Lampa Doria, commander of the Genoese navy, appeared in the vicinity of the island of Curzola with seventy galleys. Andrea Dandolo, the Venetian admiral, was sent against him. Marco Polo commanded a galley of the fleet. His usual good fortune deserted him. Advancing the first in the line with his galley, and not being properly seconded, he was taken prisoner, thrown in irons, and carried to Genoa. Here he was detained for a long time in prison, and all offers of ransom rejected. His imprisonment gave great uneasiness to his father and uncle, fearing that he might never return. Seeing themselves in this unhappy state, with so much treasure and no heirs, they consulted together. They were both very old men; but Nicola, observes Ramusio, was of a galliard complexion: it was determined he should take a wife. He did so; and to the wonder of his friends, in four years had three children.

In the mean while the fame of Marco Polo's travels had circulated in Genoa. His prison was daily crowded with nobility, and he was supplied with every thing that could cheer him in his confinement. A Genoese gentleman, who visited him every day, at length prevailed upon him to write an account of what he had seen. He had his papers and journals sent to him from Venice, and with the assistance of his friend, or, as some will have it, his fellow-prisoner, produced the work which afterward made such noise throughout the world

The merit of Marco Polo at length procured him his liberty. He returned to Venice, where he found his father with a house full of children. He took it in good part, followed the old man's example, married, and had two daughters, Moretta and Fantina. The date of the death of Marco Polo is unknown; he is supposed to have been, at the time, about seventy years of age On his death-bed he is said to have been exhorted by his friends to retract what he had published, or, at least, to disavow those parts commonly regarded as fictions. He replied indignantly that so far from having exaggerated, he had not told one half of the extraordinary things of which he had been an eye-witness.

Marco Polo died without male issue. Of the three sons of his father by the second marriage, one only had children — viz., five sons and one daughter. The sons died without leaving issue; the daughter inherited all her father's wealth and married into the noble and distinguished house of Trevesino. Thus the male line of the Polos ceased in 1417, and the family name was extinguished

Such are the principal particulars known of Marco Polo, a man whose travels for a long time made a great noise in Europe, and will be found to have had a great effect on modern discovery. His splendid account of the extent, wealth, and population of the Tartar territories filled every one with admiration The possibility of bringing all those regions under the dominion of the Church, and rendering the Grand Khan an obedient vassal to the holy chair was for a long time a favorite topic among the enthusiastic missionaries of Christendom, and there were many saints-errant who undertook to effect the conversion of this magnificent infidel.

Even at the distance of two centuries, when the enterprises for the discovery of the new route to India had set all the warm heads of Europe madding about these remote regions of the East, the conversion of the Grand Khan became again a popular theme, and it was too speculative and romantic an enterprise not to catch the vivid imagination of Columbus. In all his voyages, he will be found continually to be seeking after the territories of the Grand Khan, and even after his last expedition, when nearly worn out by age, hardships, and infirmities, he offered, in a letter to the Spanish monarchs, written from a bed of sickness, to conduct any missionary to the territories of the Tartar emperor, who would undertake his conversion.

No. XXI.

THE WORK OF MARCO POLO.

THE work of Marco Polo is stated by some to have been originally written in Latin,[1] though the most probable opinion is that it was written in the Venetian dialect of the Italian. Copies of it in manuscript were multiplied and rapidly circulated, translations were made into various languages, until the invention of printing enabled it to be widely diffused throughout Europe. In the course of these translations and successive editions, the original text, according to Purchas, has been much vitiated, and it is probable many extravagances in numbers and measurements with which Marco Polo is charged may be the errors of translators and printers.

When the work first appeared, it was considered by some as made up of fictions and extravagances, and Vossius assures us that even after the death of Marco Polo he continued to be a subject of ridicule among the light and unthinking, insomuch that he was frequently personated at masquerades by some wit or droll, who, in his feigned character, related all kinds of extravagant fables and adventures. His work, however, excited great attention among thinking men, containing evidently a fund of information concerning vast and splendid countries, before unknown to the European world. Vossius assures us that it was at one time highly esteemed by the learned. Francis Pepin, author of the Brandenburgh version, styles Polo a man commendable for his piety, prudence, and fidelity. Athanasius Kircher, in his account of China, says that none of the ancients have described the kingdoms of the remote East with more exactness. Various other learned men of past times have borne testimony to his character, and most of the substantial parts of his work have been authenticated by subsequent travellers. The most able and ample vindication of Marco Polo, however, is to be found in the English translation of his work, with copious notes and commentaries, by William Marsden, F.R.S. He has diligently discriminated between what Marco Polo relates from his own observation, and what he relates as gathered from others; he points out the errors that have arisen from misinterpretations, omissions, or interpretations of translators, and he claims all proper allowance for the superstitious coloring of parts of the narrative from the belief, prevalent among the most wise and learned of his day in miracles and magic. After perusing the work of Mr. Marsden, the character of Marco Polo rises in the estimation of the reader. It is evident that his narration, as far as related from his own observations, is correct, and that he had really traversed a great part of Tartary and China, and

---

[1] Hist. des Voyages. tom. xxvii. lib. iv. cap. 3. Paris, 1549.

navigated in the Indian seas. Some of the countries and many of the islands, however, are evidently described from accounts given by others, and in these accounts are generally found the fables which have excited incredulity and ridicule. As he composed his work after his return home, partly from memory and partly from memorandums, he was liable to confuse what he had heard with what he had seen, and thus to give undue weight to many fables and exaggerations which he had received from others.

Much has been said of a map brought from Cathay by Marco Polo, which was conserved in the convent of San Michale de Murano in the vicinity of Venice, and in which the Cape of Good Hope and the island of Madagascar were indicated, countries which the Portuguese claim the merit of having discovered two centuries afterward. It has been suggested also that Columbus had visited the convent and examined this map, whence he derived some of his ideas concerning the coast of India. According to Ramusio, however, who had been at the convent, and was well acquainted with the prior, the map preserved there was one copied by a friar from the original one of Marco Polo, and many alterations and additions had since been made by other hands, so that for a long time it lost all credit with judicious people, until on comparing it with the work of Marco Polo it was found in the main to agree with his descriptions.[1] The Cape of Good Hope was doubtless among the additions made subsequent to the discoveries of the Portuguese.[2] Columbus makes no mention of this map, which he most probably would have done had he seen it. He seems to have been entirely guided by the one furnished by Paulo Toscanelli, and which was apparently projected after the original map, or after the descriptions of Marco Polo and the maps of Ptolemy.

When the attention of the world was turned toward the remote parts of Asia in the fifteenth century, and the Portuguese were making their attempts to circumnavigate Africa, the narration of Marco Polo again rose to notice. This, with the travels of Nicolo de Comte, the Venetian, and of Hieronimo da San Stefano, a Genoese, are said to have been the principal lights by which the Portuguese guided themselves in their voyages.[3]

Above all, the influence which the work of Marco Polo had over the mind of Columbus gives it particular interest and importance It was evidently an oracular work with him. He frequently quotes it, and on his voyages supposing himself to be on the Asiatic coast, he is continually endeavoring to discover the islands and main-lands described in it, and to find the famous Cipango.

It is proper, therefore, to specify some of those places, and the manner in which they are described by a Venetian traveller that the reader may more fully understand the anticipations which were haunting the mind of Columbus in his voyages among the West Indian islands, and along the coast of Terra Firma.

The winter residence of the Great Khan, according to Marco Polo, was in the city of Cambalu, or Kanbalu (since ascertained to be Pekin), in the province of Cathay. This city, he says, was twenty-four miles square, and admirably built. It was impossible, according to Marco Polo, to de-

---

[1] Ramusio, vol ii p. 17.

[2] Mr. Marsden, who has inspected a splendid fac-simile of this map preserved in the British Museum, objects even to the fundamental part of it "where," he observes, "situations are given to places that seem quite inconsistent with the descriptions in the travels, and cannot be attributed to their author, although inserted on the supposed authority of his writings." Marsden's M. Polo. Introd. p. clii.

Hist. des Voyages tom xl. lib. xi chap. l.

scribe the vast amount and variety of merchandise and manufactures brought there; it would seem they were enough to furnish the universe. " Here are to be seen in wonderful abundance the precious stones, the pearls, the silks, and the diverse perfumes of the East: scarce a day passes that there does not arrive nearly a thousand cars laden with silk, of which they make admirable stuffs in this city."

The palace of the Great Khan is magnificently built, and four miles in circuit. It is rather a group of palaces. In the interior it is resplendent with gold and silver; and in it are guarded the precious vases and jewels of the sovereign. All the appointments of the Khan for war, for the chase, for various festivities, are described in gorgeous terms. But though Marco Polo is magnificent in his description of the provinces of Cathay, and its imperial city of Cambalu, he outdoes himself when he comes to describe the province of Mangi. This province is supposed to be the southern part of China. It contains, he says, twelve hundred cities. The capital Quinsai (supposed to be the city of Hang-cheu) was twenty-five miles from the sea, but communicated by a river with a port situated on the seacoast, and had great trade with India.

The name Quinsai, according to Marco Polo, signifies the city of heaven; he says he has been in it and examined it diligently, and affirms it to be the largest in the world; and so undoubtedly it is if the measurement of the traveller is to be taken literally, for he declares that it is one hundred miles in circuit. This seeming exaggeration has been explained by supposing him to mean Chinese miles or *li*, which are to the Italian miles in the proportion of three to eight; and Mr Marsden observes that the walls even of the modern city, the limits of which have been considerably contracted, are estimated by travellers at sixty *li*. The ancient city has evidently been of immense extent, and as Marco Polo could not be supposed to have measured the walls himself, he has probably taken the loose and incorrect estimates of the inhabitants He describes it also as built upon little islands like Venice, and has twelve thousand stone bridges,[1] the arches of which are so high that the largest vessels can pass under them without lowering their masts It has, he affirms, three thousand baths, and six hundred thousand families, including domestics. It abounds with magnificent houses, and has a lake thirty miles in circuit within its walls, on the banks of which are superb palaces of people of rank.[2] The inhabitants of Quinsai are very voluptuous, and indulge in all kinds of luxuries and delights, particularly the women, who are extremely beautiful. There are many merchants and artisans, but the masters do not work, they employ servants to do all their labor The province of Mangi was conquered by the Great Khan, who divided it into nine kingdoms, appointing to each a tributary king. He drew from it an immense revenue, for the country abounded in gold, silver, silks, sugar, spices, and perfumes.

---

[1] Another blunder in translation has drawn upon Marco Polo the indignation of George Hornius, who (in his Origin of America, iv. 3) exclaims, " Who can believe all that he says of the city of Quinsai? as for example, that it has stone bridges twelve thousand miles high'" etc. It is probable that many of the exaggerations in the accounts of Marco Polo are in fact the errors of his translators.

Mandeville, speaking of the same city, which he calls Causai, says it is built on the sea like Venice, and has twelve hundred bridges.

[2] Sir George Staunton mentions this lake as being a beautiful sheet of water, about three or four miles in diameter, its margin ornamented with houses and gardens of mandarins together with temples, monasteries for the priests of Fo, and an imperial palace.

ZIPANGU, ZIPANGRI, OR CIPANGO.

Fifteen hundred miles from the shores of Mangi, according to Marco Polo, lay the great island of Zipangu, by some written Zipangri, and by Columbus Cipango.[1] Marco Polo describes it as abounding in gold, which, however, the king seldom permits to be transported out of the island. The king has a magnificent palace covered with plates of gold, as in other countries the palaces are covered with sheets of lead or copper. The halls and chambers are likewise covered with gold, the windows adorned with it, sometimes in plates of the thickness of two fingers. The island also produces vast quantities of the largest and finest pearls, together with a variety of precious stones; so that, in fact, it abounds in riches. The Great Khan made several attempts to conquer this island, but in vain; which is not to be wondered at, if it be true what Marco Polo relates, that the inhabitants had certain stones of a charmed virtue inserted between the skin and the flesh of their right arms, which, through the power of diabolical enchantments, rendered them invulnerable. This island was an object of diligent search to Columbus.

About the island of Zipangu or Cipango, and between it and the coast of Mangi, the sea, according to Marco Polo, is studded with small islands to the number of seven thousand four hundred and forty, of which the greater part are inhabited There is not one which does not produce odoriferous trees and perfumes in abundance. Columbus thought himself at one time in the midst of these islands.

These are the principal places described by Marco Polo, which occur in the letters and journals of Columbus. The island of Cipango was the first land he expected to make, and he intended to visit afterward the province of Mangi, and to seek the Great Khan in his city of Cambalu, in the province of Cathay. Unless the reader can bear in mind these sumptuous descriptions of Marco Polo, of countries teeming with wealth, and cities where the very domes and palaces flamed with gold, he will have but a faint idea of the splendid anticipations which filled the imagination of Columbus when he discovered, as he supposed, the extremity of Asia It was his confident expectation of soon arriving at these countries, and realizing the accounts of the Venetian, that induced him to hold forth those promises of immediate wealth to the sovereigns, which caused so much disappointment, and brought upon him the frequent reproach of exciting false hopes and indulging in wilful exaggeration.

No. XXII.

SIR JOHN MANDEVILLE.

Next to Marco Polo the travels of Sir John Mandeville, and his account of the territories of the Great Khan along the coast of Asia, seem to have been treasured up in the mind of Columbus.

Mandeville was born in the city of St. Albans. He was devoted to

---

[1] Supposed to be those islands collectively called Japan. They are named by the Chinese, Ge-pen, the terminating syllable *gu* added by Marco Polo, is supposed to be the Chinese word *kue*, signifying kingdom, which is commonly annexed to the names of foreign countries. As the distance of the nearest part of the southern island from the coast of China, near Ning-po, is not more than five hundred Italian miles, Mr. Marsden supposes Marco Polo in stating it to be 1500, means Chinese miles, or li, which are in the proportion of somewhat more than one-third of the former.

study from his earliest childhood, and after finishing his general education applied himself to medicine. Having a great desire to see the remotest parts of the earth, then known, that is to say, Asia and Africa, and above all, to visit the Holy Land, he left England in 1332, and passing through France embarked at Marseilles. According to his own account he visited Turkey, Armenia, Egypt, Upper and Lower Lybia, Syria, Persia, Chaldea, Ethiopia, Tartary, Amazonia and the Indies, residing in their principal cities. But most he says he delighted in the Holy Land, where he remained for a long time, examining it with the greatest minuteness, and endeavoring to follow all the traces of our Saviour. After an absence of thirty-four years he returned to England, but found himself forgotten and unknown by the greater part of his countrymen, and a stranger in his native place. He wrote a history of his travels in three languages — English, French, and Latin — for he was master of many tongues. He addressed his work to Edward III. His wanderings do not seem to have made him either pleased with the world at large or contented with his home. He railed at the age saying that there was no more virtue extant, that the Church was ruined: error prevalent among the clergy: simony upon the throne: and, in a word, that the devil reigned triumphant. He soon returned to the continent, and died at Liege in 1372. He was buried in the abbey of the Guliemites, in the suburbs of that city, where Ortelius, in his Itinerarium Belgiæ, says that he saw his monument, on which was the effigy, in stone, of a man with a forked beard and his hands raised toward his head (probably folded as in prayer, according to the manner of old tombs) and a lion at his feet. There was an inscription stating his name, quality and calling (viz., professor of medicine), that he was very pious, very learned, and very charitable to the poor, and that after having travelled over the whole world he had died at Liege. The people of the convent showed also his spurs, and the housings of the horses which he had ridden in his travels.

The descriptions given by Mandeville of the Grand Khan, of the province of Cathay, and the city of Cambalu, are no less splendid than those of Marco Polo. The royal palace was more than two leagues in circumference. The grand hall had twenty-four columns of copper and gold. There were more than three hundred thousand men occupied and living in and about the palace, of which more than one hundred thousand were employed in taking care of ten thousand elephants and of a vast variety of other animals, birds of prey, falcons, parrots, and paroquets. On days of festival there were even twice the number of men employed. The title of this potentate in his letters was "Khan, the son of God, exalted possessor of all the earth, master of those who are masters of others." On his seal was engraved, "God reigns in heaven, Khan upon earth."

Mandeville has become proverbial for indulging in a traveller's exaggerations yet his accounts of the countries which he visited have been found far more veracious than had been imagined. His descriptions of Cathay and the wealthy province of Mangi, agreeing with those of Marco Polo, had great authority with Columbus.

No. XXIII.

THE ZONES.

THE zones were imaginary bands or circles in the heavens producing an effect of climate on corresponding belts on the globe of the earth. The polar circles and the tropics mark these divisions.

The central region, lying beneath the track of the sun, was termed the torrid zone; the two regions between the tropics and the polar circles were termed the temperate zones, and the remaining parts, between the polar circles and the poles, the frigid zones

The frozen regions near the poles were considered uninhabitable and unnavigable on account of the extreme cold. The burning zone, or rather the central part of it, immediately about the equator, was considered uninhabitable, unproductive and impassable in consequence of the excessive heat The temperate zones, lying between them, were supposed to be fertile and salubrious, and suited to the purposes of life

The globe was divided into two hemispheres by the equator, an imaginary line encircling it at equal distance from the poles The whole of the world known to the ancients was contained in the temperate zone of the northern hemisphere.

It was imagined that if there should be inhabitants in the temperate zone of the southern hemisphere. there could still be no communication with them on account of the burning zone which intervened.

Parmenides, according to Strabo. was the inventor of this theory of the five zones. but he made the torrid zone extend on each side of the equator beyond the tropics Aristotle supported this doctrine of the zones. In his time nothing was known of the extreme northern parts of Europe and Asia, nor of interior Ethiopia and the southern part of Africa. extending beyond the tropic of Capricorn to the Cape of Good Hope. Aristotle believed that there was habitable earth in the southern hemisphere. but that it was forever divided from the part of the world already known by the impassable zone of scorching heat at the equator.[1]

Pliny supported the opinion of Aristotle concerning the burning zones. "The temperature of the central region of the earth," he observes, "where the sun runs its course. is burnt up as with fire. The temperate zones which lie on either side can have no communication with each other in consequence of the fervent heat of this region." [2]

Strabo (lib. xi.). in mentioning this theory. gives it likewise his support; and others of the ancient philosophers, as well as the poets, might be cited to show the general prevalence of the belief.

It must be observed that. at the time when Columbus defended his proposition before the learned board at Salamanca. the ancient theory of the burning zone had not yet been totally disproved by modern discovery. The Portuguese. it is true, had penetrated within the tropics; but, though the whole of the space between the tropic of Cancer and that of Capricorn, in common parlance, was termed the torrid zone, the uninhabitable and impassable part, strictly speaking, according to the doctrine of the ancients, only extended a limited number of degrees on each side of the equator, forming about a third, or at most, the half of the zone. The proofs which Columbus endeavored to draw therefore from the voyages made to St. George la Mina, were not conclusive with those who were bigoted to the ancient theory, and who placed this scorching region still farther southward, and immediately about the equator.

---

[1] Aristot.. 2 Met. cap. 5.   [2] Pliny. lib 1. cap 61.

No. XXIV

OF THE ATALANTIS OF PLATO.

THE island Atalantis is mentioned by Plato in his dialogue of Timæus. Solon the Athenian lawgiver, is supposed to have travelled into Egypt. He is in an ancient city on the Delta, the fertile island formed by the Nile. and is holding converse with certain learned priests on the antiquities of remote ages. when one of them gives him a description of the island of Atalantis, and of its destruction. which he describes as having taken place before the conflagration of the world by Phaeton.

This island. he was told, had been situated in the Western Ocean. opposite to the Straits of Gibraltar There was an easy passage from it to other islands. which lay adjacent to a large continent. exceeding in size all Europe and Asia. Neptune settled in this island, from whose son Atlas its name was derived. and he divided it among his ten sons. His descendants reigned here in regular succcession for many ages. They made irruptions into Europe and Africa. subduing all Lybia as far as Egypt, and Europe to Asia Minor. They were resisted, however, by the Athenians, and driven back to their Atlantic territories. Shortly after this there was a tremendous earthquake and an overflowing of the sea. which continued for a day and a night. In the course of this the vast island of Atalantis. and all its splendid cities and warlike nations. were swallowed up, and sunk to the bottom of the sea. which, spreading its waters over the chasm, formed the Atlantic Ocean. For a long time, however, the sea was not navigable, on account of rocks and shelves, of mud and slime, and of the ruins of that drowned country.

Many, in modern times, have considered this a mere fable: others suppose that Plato, while in Egypt, had received some vague accounts of the Canary Islands, and, on his return to Greece, finding those islands so entirely unknown to his countrymen, had made them the seat of his political and moral speculations. Some, however, have been disposed to give greater weight to this story of Plato. They imagine that such an island may really have existed, filling up a great part of the Atlantic, and that the continent beyond it was America, which, in such case, was not unknown to the ancients. Kircher supposes it to have been an island extending from the Canaries to the Azores; that it was really ingulfed in one of the convulsions of the globe, and that those small islands are mere shattered fragments of it.

As a further proof that the New World was not unknown to the ancients, many have cited the singular passage in the Medea of Seneca, which is wonderfully apposite, and shows, at least, how nearly the warm imagination of a poet may approach to prophecy. The predictions of the ancient oracles were rarely so unequivocal.

> Venient annis
> Sæcula seris, quibus Oceanus
> Vincula rerum laxet, et ingens
> Pateat tellus, Typhisque novos
> Detegat orbes, nec sit terris
> Ultima Thule.

Gosselin, in his able research into the voyages of the ancients, supposes the Atalantis of Plato to have been nothing more nor less than one of the nearest of the Canaries, viz., Fortaventura or Lancerote.

No. XXV.

THE IMAGINARY ISLAND OF ST. BRANDAN.

ONE of the most singular geographical illusions on record is that which for a long while haunted the imaginations of the inhabitants of the Canaries. They fancied they beheld a mountainous island, about ninety leagues in length, lying far to the westward. It was only seen at intervals, but in perfectly clear and serene weather. To some it seemed one hundred leagues distant, to others forty, to others only fifteen or eighteen.[1] On attempting to reach it, however, it somehow or other eluded the search, and was nowhere to be found. Still there were so many eyewitnesses of credibility who concurred in testifying to their having seen it, and the testimony of the inhabitants of different islands agreed so well as to its form and position, that its existence was generally believed, and geographers inserted it in their maps. It is laid down on the globe of Martin Behem, projected in 1492, as delineated by M. de Murr, and it will be found in most of the maps, of the time of Columbus, placed commonly about two hundred leagues west of the Canaries. During the time that Columbus was making his proposition to the court of Portugal, an inhabitant of the Canaries applied to King John II. for a vessel to go in search of this island. In the archives of the Torre do Tombo[2] also, there is a record of a contract made by the crown of Portugal with Fernando de Ulmo, cavalier of the royal household, and captain of the island of Tercera, wherein he undertakes to go, at his own expense, in quest of an island or islands, or Terra Firma, supposed to be the island of the Seven Cities, on condition of having jurisdiction over the same for himself and his heirs, allowing one-tenth of the revenues to the king. This Ulmo, finding the expedition above his capacity, associated one Juan Alfonso del Estreito in the enterprise. They were bound to be ready to sail with two caravels in the month of March, 1487.[3] The fate of their enterprise is unknown.

The name of St. Brandan, or Borondon, given to this imaginary island from time immemorial, is said to be derived from a Scotch abbot, who flourished in the sixth century, and who is called sometimes by the foregoing appellations, sometimes St. Blandano, or St. Blandanus. In the Martyrology of the order of St. Augustine, he is said to have been the patriarch of three thousand monks. About the middle of the sixth century he accompanied his disciple, St. Maclovio, or St. Malo, in search of certain islands possessing the delights of paradise, which they were told existed in the midst of the ocean, and were inhabited by infidels. These most adventurous saints-errant wandered for a long time upon the ocean, and at length landed upon an island called Ima. Here St. Malo found the body of a giant lying in a sepulchre. He resuscitated him, and had much interesting conversation with him, the giant informing him that the inhabitants of that island had some notions of the Trinity, and, moreover, giving him a gratifying account of the torments which Jews and Pagans suffered in the infernal regions. Finding the giant so docile and reasonable, St. Malo expounded to him the doctrines of the Christian religion, converted him, and baptized him by the name of Mildum. The giant, however, either through weariness of life or eagerness to enjoy the

---

[1] Feyjoo, Theatro Critico, tom. iv d. 10, § 29.
[2] Lib iv. de la Chancelaria del Rey Dn. Juan II., fol 101.
[3] Torre do Tombo Lib. das Ylhas, f. 119.

benefits of his conversion, begged permission, at the end of fifteen days, to die again, which was granted him

According to another account, the giant told them he knew of an island in the ocean, defended by walls of burnished gold, so resplendent that they shone like crystal, but to which there was no entrance. At their request he undertook to guide them to it, and taking the cable of their ship, threw himself into the sea. He had not proceeded far, however, when a tempest rose, and obliged them all to return, and shortly after the giant died.[1] A third legend makes the saint pray to heaven on Easter day, that they may be permitted to find land where they may celebrate the offices of religion with becoming state. An island immediately appears, on which they land, perform a solemn mass and the sacrament of the Eucharist; after which, re-embarking and making sail, they behold to their astonishment the supposed island suddenly plunge to the bottom of the sea, being nothing else than a monstrous whale[2] When the rumor circulated of an island seen from the Canaries, which always eluded the search, the legends of St. Brandan were revived, and applied to this unapproachable land. We are told, also, that there was an ancient Latin manuscript in the archives of the cathedral church of the Grand Canary, in which the adventures of these saints were recorded. Through carelessness, however, this manuscript has disappeared.[3] Some have maintained that this island was known to the ancients, and was the same mentioned by Ptolemy among the Fortunate or Canary Islands, by the names of Aprositus,[4] or the Inaccessible; and which, according to friar Diego Philipo in his book on the Incarnation of Christ, shows that it possessed the same quality in ancient times of deluding the eye and being unattainable to the feet of mortals.[5] But whatever belief the ancients may have had on this subject, it is certain that it took a strong hold on the faith of the moderns during the prevalent rage for discovery; nor did it lack abundant testimonials. Don Joseph de Viera y Clavijo says, there never was a more difficult paradox nor problem in the science of geography; since to affirm the existence of this island is to trample upon sound criticism, judgment, and reason, and to deny it one must abandon tradition and experience, and suppose that many persons of credit had not the proper use of their senses.[6]

The belief in this island has continued long since the time of Columbus. It was repeatedly seen, and by various persons at a time, always in the same place and of the same form. In 1526 an expedition set off for the Canaries in quest of it, commanded by Fernando de Troya and Fernando Alvarez. They cruised in the wonted direction, but in vain, and their failure ought to have undeceived the public. "The phantasm of the island, however," says Viera, "had such a secret enchantment for all who beheld it, that the public preferred doubting the good conduct of the explorers, than their own senses." In 1570 the appearances were so repeated and clear that there was a universal fever of curiosity awakened among the people of the Canaries, and it was determined to send forth another expedition.

That they might not appear to act upon light grounds, an exact investigation was previously made of all the persons of talent and credibility who had seen these apparitions of land, or who had other proofs of its existence.

[1] Fr. Gregorio Garcia, Origen de los Indios, lib. i. cap. 9.
[2] Sigeberto. Epist ad Tietmar. Abbat.
[3] Nuñez de la Pena. Conquist de la Gran Canaria.
[4] Ptolemy, lib. iv. tom. iv.
[5] Fr. D. Philipo, lib viii. fol. 25.
[6] Hist Isl Can., lib. i. cap 28.

Alonzo de Espinosa, governor of the island of Ferro, accordingly made a report, in which more than one hundred witnesses, several of them persons of the highest respectability, deposed that they had beheld the unknown island about forty leagues to the north-west of Ferro; that they had contemplated it with calmness and certainty, and had seen the sun set behind one of its points.

Testimonials of still greater force came from the islands of Palma and Teneriffe. There were certain Portuguese who affirmed that, being driven about by a tempest, they had come upon the island of St. Borondon. Pedro Vello, who was the pilot of the vessel, affirmed that, having anchored in a bay, he landed with several of the crew. They drank fresh water in a brook, and beheld in the sand the print of footsteps, double the size of those of an ordinary man, and the distance between them was in proportion. They found a cross nailed to a neighboring tree; near to which were three stones placed in form of a triangle, with signs of fire having been made among them, probably to cook shell-fish. Having seen much cattle and sheep grazing in the neighborhood, two of their party armed with lances went into the woods in pursuit of them. The night was approaching, the heavens began to lower, and a harsh wind arose. The people on board the ship cried out that she was dragging her anchor, whereupon Vello entered the boat and hurried on board. In an instant they lost sight of land, being as it were swept away in the hurricane. When the storm had passed away, and the sea and sky were again serene, they searched in vain for the island; not a trace of it was to be seen, and they had to pursue their voyage, lamenting the loss of their two companions who had been abandoned in the wood.[1]

A learned licentiate, Pedro Ortiz de Funez, inquisitor of the Grand Canary, while on a visit at Teneriffe, summoned several persons before him, who testified having seen the island. Among them was one Marcos Verde, a man well known in those parts. He stated that in returning from Barbary and arriving in the neighborhood of the Canaries, he beheld land, which, according to his maps and calculations, could not be any of the known islands. He concluded it to be the far-famed St. Borondon. Overjoyed at having discovered this land of mystery, he coasted along its spell-bound shores until he anchored in a beautiful harbor formed by the mouth of a mountain ravine. Here he landed with several of his crew. It was now, he said, the hour of the Ave Maria, or of vespers. The sun being set, the shadows began to spread over the land. The voyagers having separated, wandered about in different directions, until out of hearing of each other's shouts. Those on board, seeing the night approaching, made signal to summon back the wanderers to the ship. They re-embarked, intending to resume their investigations on the following day. Scarcely were they on board, however, when a whirlwind came rushing down the ravine with such violence as to drag the vessel from her anchor and hurry her out to sea, and they never saw any thing more of this hidden and inhospitable island.

Another testimony remains on record in manuscript of one Abreu Galindo; but whether taken at this time does not appear. It was that of a French adventurer, who, many years before, making a voyage among the Canaries, was overtaken by a violent storm which carried away his masts. At length the furious winds drove him to the shores of an unknown island covered with stately trees. Here he landed with part of his crew, and choosing a tree proper for a mast, cut it down, and began to shape it for his purpose. The guardian power of the island, however,

<hr>

[1] Nuñez de la Pena, lib. i. cap. 1.   Viera Hist. Isl Cau., tom. i cap. 28.

resented as usual this invasion of his forbidden shores. The heavens assumed a dark and threatening aspect, the night was approaching, and the mariners, fearing some impending evil, abandoned their labor and returned on board. They were borne away as usual from the coast, and the next day arrived at the island of Palma.[1]

The mass of testimony collected by official authority in 1570 seemed so satisfactory that another expedition was fitted out in the same year in the island of Palma. It was commanded by Fernando de Villabolos, regidor of the island, but was equally fruitless with the preceding. St. Borondon seemed disposed only to tantalize the world with distant and serene glimpses of his ideal paradise, or to reveal it amid storms to tempest-tossed mariners, but to hide it completely from the view of all who diligently sought it. Still the people of Palma adhered to their favorite chimera. Thirty-four years afterward, in 1605, they sent another ship on the quest, commanded by Gaspar Perez de Acosta, an accomplished pilot, accompanied by the padre Lorenzo Pinedo, a holy Franciscan friar, skilled in natural science. St. Borondon, however, refused to reveal his island to either monk or mariner. After cruising about in every direction, sounding, observing the skies, the clouds, the winds, every thing that could furnish indications, they returned without having seen any thing to authorize a hope.

Upward of a century now elapsed without any new attempt to seek this fairy island. Every now and then, it is true, the public mind was agitated by fresh reports of its having been seen. Lemons and other fruits, and the green branches of trees which floated to the shores of Gomera and Ferro, were pronounced to be from the enchanted groves of St. Borondon. At length, in 1721, the public infatuation again rose to such a height that a fourth expedition was sent, commanded by Don Gaspar Dominguez, a man of probity and talent. As this was an expedition of solemn and mysterious import, he had two holy friars as apostolical chaplains. They made sail from the island of Teneriffe toward the end of October, leaving the populace in an indescribable state of anxious curiosity mingled with superstition. The ship, however, returned from its cruise as unsuccessful as all its predecessors.

We have no account of any expedition being since undertaken, though the island still continued to be a subject of speculation, and occasionally to reveal its shadowy mountains to the eyes of favored individuals. In a letter written from the island of Gomera, 1759, by a Franciscan monk, to one of his friends, he relates having seen it from the village of Alaxero at six in the morning of the third of May. It appeared to consist of two lofty mountains, with a deep valley between; and on contemplating it with a telescope, the valley or ravine appeared to be filled with trees. He summoned the curate Antonio Joseph Manrique, and upwards of forty other persons all of whom beheld it plainly.[2]

Nor is this island delineated merely in ancient maps of the time of Columbus. It is laid down as one of the Canary Islands, in a French map published in 1704; and Mons. Gautier, in a geographical chart, annexed to his Observations on Natural History, published in 1755, places it five degrees to the west of the island of Ferro, in the 29th deg. of N. latitude.[3]

Such are the principal facts existing relative to the island of St. Brandan. Its reality was for a long time a matter of firm belief. It was in vain that repeated voyages and investigations proved its non-existence: the

[1] Nuñez, Conquista le Gran Canaria. Viera, Hist., etc.
[2] Viera, Hist. Isl. Can. tom. i cap. 28.   [3] Ibid

public, after trying all kinds of sophistry, took refuge in the supernatural, to defend their favorite chimera. They maintained that it was rendered inaccessible to mortals by Divine Providence, or by diabolical magic. Most inclined to the former. All kinds of extravagant fancies were indulged concerning it,[1] some confounded it with the fabled island of the Seven Cities situated somewhere in the bosom of the ocean, where in old times seven bishops and their followers had taken refuge from the Moors. Some of the Portuguese imagined it to be the abode of their lost King Sebastian. The Spaniards pretended that Roderick, the last of their Gothic kings, had fled thither from the Moors after the disastrous battle of the Guadalete. Others suggested that it might be the seat of the terrestrial paradise, the place where Enoch and Elijah remained in a state of blessedness until the final day; and that it was made at times apparent to the eyes, but invisible to the search of mortals. Poetry, it is said, has owed to this popular belief one of its beautiful fictions, and the garden of Armida, where Rinaldo was detained enchanted, and which Tasso places in one of the Canary Islands, has been identified with the imaginary St. Borondon.[2]

The learned father Feyjoo[3] has given a philosophical solution to this geographical problem. He attributes all these appearances, which have been so numerous, and so well authenticated as not to admit of doubt, to certain atmospherical deceptions, like that of the Fata Morgana, seen at times in the Straits of Messina, where the city of Reggio and its surrounding country is reflected in the air above the neighboring sea: a phenomenon which has likewise been witnessed in front of the city of Marseilles. As to the tales of the mariners who had landed on these forbidden shores, and been hurried thence in whirlwinds and tempests, he considers them as mere fabrications.

As the populace, however, reluctantly give up any thing that partakes of the marvellous and mysterious, and as the same atmospherical phenomena, which first gave birth to the illusion, may still continue, it is not improbable that a belief in the island of St Brandan may still exist among the ignorant and credulous of the Canaries, and that they at times behold its fairy mountains rising above the distant horizon of the Atlantic.

No. XXVI.

THE ISLAND OF THE SEVEN CITIES

ONE of the popular traditions concerning the ocean, which were current during the time of Columbus, was that of the Island of the Seven Cities. It was recorded in an ancient legend, that at the time of the conquest of Spain and Portugal by the Moors, when the inhabitants fled in every direction to escape from slavery, seven bishops, followed by a great number of their people, took shipping and abandoned themselves to their fate, on the high seas. After tossing about for some time they landed on an unknown island in the midst of the ocean. Here the bishops burned the ships, to prevent the desertion of their followers, and founded seven cities. Various pilots of Portugal, it was said, had reached that island at different times, but had never returned to give any information concerning it, having been detained, according to subsequent accounts, by the successors of the bishops to prevent pursuit. At length,

---

[1] Viera, Hist. Isl. Can. tom. i. cap. 28.   [2] Viera, ubi sup.
[3] Theatro Critico. tom. iv. d. x.

according to common report, at the time that Prince Henry of Portugal was prosecuting his discoveries, several seafaring men presented themselves one day before him, and stated that they had just returned from a voyage, in the course of which they had landed upon this island. The inhabitants, they said, spoke their language, and carried them immediately to church, to ascertain whether they were Catholics, and were rejoiced at finding them of the true faith. They then made earnest inquiries, to know whether the Moors still retained possession of Spain and Portugal. While part of the crew were at church, the rest gathered sand on the shore for the use of the kitchen, and found to their surprise that one third of it was gold. The islanders were anxious that the crew should remain with them a few days, until the return of their governor, who was absent; but the mariners, afraid of being detained, embarked and made sail. Such was the story they told to Prince Henry, hoping to receive reward for their intelligence. The prince expressed displeasure at their hasty departure from the island, and ordered them to return and procure further information, but the men, apprehensive, no doubt, of having the falsehood of their tale discovered, made their escape, and nothing more was heard of them.[1]

This story had much currency. The Island of the Seven Cities was identified with the island mentioned by Aristotle as having been discovered by the Carthaginians, and was put down in the early maps, about the time of Columbus, under the name of Antilla.

At the time of the discovery of New Spain, reports were brought to Hispaniola of the civilization of the country: that the people wore clothing: that their houses and temples were solid, spacious, and often magnificent; and that crosses were occasionally found among them. Juan de Grivalja, being despatched to explore the coast of Yucatan, reported that in sailing along it he beheld, with great wonder, stately and beautiful edifices of lime and stone, and many high towers that shone at a distance.[2] For a time the old tradition of the Seven Cities was revived, and many thought that they were to be found in the same part of New Spain.

No. XXVII

DISCOVERY OF THE ISLAND OF MADEIRA.

THE discovery of Madeira by Macham rests principally upon the authority of Francisco Alcaforado, an esquire of Prince Henry of Portugal, who composed an account of it for that prince. It does not appear to have obtained much faith among Portuguese historians. No mention is made of it in Barros; he attributes the first discovery of the island to Juan Gonzales and Tristram Vaz, who he said descried it from Porto Santo, resembling a cloud on the horizon.[3]

The abbé Provost, however, in his general history of voyages, vol. 6, seems inclined to give credit to the account of Alcaforado. "It was composed," he observes, "at a time when the attention of the public would have exposed the least falsities; and no one was more capable than Alcaforado of giving an exact detail of this event, since he was of the number of those who assisted at the second discovery." The narrative,

<hr/>

[1] Hist. del Almirante, cap. 10.
[2] Torquemada Monarquia Indiana. lib. iv. cap. 4. Origen de los Indios por Fr. Gregorio Garcia, lib. iv. cap. 20.
[3] Barros, Asia, decad. i lib i. cap. 3

as originally written, was overcharged with ornaments and digressions. It was translated into French and published in Paris in 1671. The French translator had retrenched the ornaments. but scrupulously retained the facts. The story, however. is cherished in the island of Madeira, where a painting in illustration of it is still to be seen. The following is the purport of the French translation: I have not been able to procure the original of Alcaforado.

During the reign of Edward the Third of England, a young man of great courage and talent, named Robert Macham, fell in love with a young lady of rare beauty. of the name of Anne Dorset. She was his superior in birth, and of a proud and aristocratic family: but the merit of Macham gained him the preference over all his rivals. The family of the young lady, to prevent her making an inferior alliance. obtained an order from the king to have Macham arrested and confined. until by arbitrary means they married his mistress to a man of quality. As soon as the nuptials were celebrated, the nobleman conducted his beautiful and afflicted bride to his seat near Bristol. Macham was now restored to liberty. Indignant at the wrongs he had suffered, and certain of the affections of his mistress, he prevailed upon several friends to assist him in a project for the gratification of his love and his revenge. They followed hard on the traces of the new-married couple to Bristol. One of the friends obtained an introduction into the family of the nobleman in quality of a groom. He found the young bride full of tender recollections of her lover, and of dislike to the husband thus forced upon her. Through the means of this friend, Macham had several communications with her, and concerted means for their escape to France. where they might enjoy their mutual love unmolested.

When all things were prepared, the young lady rode out one day. accompanied only by the fictitious groom, under pretence of taking the air. No sooner were they out of sight of the house than they galloped to an appointed place on the shore of the channel, where a boat awaited them. They were conveyed on board a vessel, which lay with anchor a-trip and sails unfurled, ready to put to sea. Here the lovers were once more united. Fearful of pursuit, the ship immediately weighed anchor; they made their way rapidly along the coast of Cornwall, and Macham anticipated the triumph of soon landing with his beautiful prize on the shores of gay and gallant France. Unfortunately an adverse and stormy wind arose in the night; at daybreak they found themselves out of sight of land. The mariners were ignorant and inexperienced; they knew nothing of the compass, and it was a time when men were unaccustomed to traverse the high seas. For thirteen days the lovers were driven about on a tempestuous ocean, at the mercy of wind and wave. The fugitive bride was filled with terror and remorse, and looked upon this uproar of the elements as the anger of Heaven directed against her. All the efforts of her lover could not remove from her mind a dismal presage of some approaching catastrophe.

At length the tempest subsided. On the fourteenth day, at dawn, the mariners perceived what appeared to be a tuft of wood rising out of the sea. They joyfully steered for it, supposing it to be an island. They were not mistaken. As they drew near, the rising sun shone upon noble forests, the trees of which were of a kind unknown to them. Flights of birds also came hovering about the ship, and perched upon the yards and rigging, without any signs of fear. The boat was sent on shore to reconnoitre, and soon returned with such accounts of the beauty of the country, that Macham determined to take his drooping companion to the land, in hopes her health and spirits might be restored by refreshment and repose.

They were accompanied on shore by the faithful friends who had assisted in their flight. The mariners remained on board to guard the ship.

The country was indeed delightful. The forests were stately and magnificent; there were trees laden with excellent fruits, others with aromatic flowers; the waters were cool and limpid, the sky was serene, and there was a balmy sweetness in the air. The animals they met with showed no signs of alarm or ferocity, from which they concluded that the island was uninhabited. On penetrating a little distance they found a sheltered meadow, the green bosom of which was bordered by laurels and refreshed by a mountain brook which ran sparkling over pebbles. In the centre was a majestic tree, the wide branches of which afforded shade from the rays of the sun. Here Macham had bowers constructed and determined to pass a few days, hoping that the sweetness of the country and the serene tranquillity of this delightful solitude would recruit the drooping health and spirits of his companion. Three days, however, had scarcely passed when a violent storm arose from the north-east, and raged all night over the island. On the succeeding morning Macham repaired to the sea-side, but nothing of his ship was to be seen, and he concluded that it had foundered in the tempest.

Consternation fell upon the little band, thus left in an uninhabited island in the midst of the ocean. The blow fell most severely on the timid and repentant bride. She reproached herself with being the cause of all their misfortunes, and from the first, had been haunted by dismal forebodings. She now considered them about to be accomplished, and her horror was so great as to deprive her of speech; she expired in three days without uttering a word.

Macham was struck with despair at beholding the tragical end of this tender and beautiful being. He upbraided himself, in the transports of his grief, with tearing her from her home, her country, and her friends, to perish upon a savage coast. All the efforts of his companions to console him were in vain. He died within five days, broken-hearted; begging, as a last request, that his body might be interred beside that of his mistress, at the foot of a rustic altar which they had erected under the great tree. They set up a large wooden cross on the spot, on which was placed an inscription written by Macham himself, relating in a few words his piteous adventure, and praying any Christians who might arrive there to build a chapel in the place dedicated to Jesus the Saviour.

After the death of their commander, his followers consulted about means to escape from the island. The ship's boat remained on the shore. They repaired it and put it in a state to bear a voyage, and then made sail, intending to return to England. Ignorant of their situation, and carried about by the winds, they were cast upon the coast of Morocco, where, their boat being shattered upon the rocks, they were captured by the Moors and thrown into prison. Here they understood that their ship had shared the same fate, having been driven from her anchorage in the tempest, and carried to the same inhospitable coast, where all her crew were made prisoners.

The prisons of Morocco were in those days filled with captives of all nations, taken by their cruisers. Here the English prisoners met with an experienced pilot, a Spaniard of Seville, named Juan de Morales. He listened to their story with great interest; inquired into the situation and description of the island they had discovered; and, subsequently, on his redemption from prison, communicated the circumstances, it is said, to Prince Henry of Portugal.

There is a difficulty in the above narrative of Alcaforado in reconciling dates. The voyage is said to have taken place during the reign of Edward III., which commenced in 1327 and ended in 1378. Morales, to whom the English communicated their voyage, is said to have been in the service of the Portuguese, in the second discovery of Madeira, in 1418 and 1420. Even if the voyage and imprisonment had taken place in the last year of King Edward's reign, this leaves a space of forty years.

Hakluyt gives an account of the same voyage, taken from Antonio Galvano. He varies in certain particulars. It happened, he says, in the year 1344, in the time of Peter IV. of Aragon. Macham cast anchor in a bay since called after him Machio.

The lady being ill, he took her on shore, accompanied by some of his friends, and the ships sailed without them. After the death of the lady, Macham made a canoe out of a tree, and ventured to sea in it with his companions. They were cast upon the coast of Africa, where the Moors, considering it a kind of miracle, carried him to the king of their country, who sent him to the King of Castile. In consequence of the traditional accounts remaining of this voyage, Henry II. of Castile sent people, in 1395, to rediscover the island.

No. XXVIII.

LAS CASAS.

BARTHOLOMEW LAS CASAS, Bishop of Chiapa, so often cited in all histories of the New World, was born at Seville in 1474, and was of French extraction. The family name was Casaus. The first of the name who appeared in Spain served under the standard of Ferdinand III., surnamed the Saint, in his wars with the Moors of Andalusia. He was at the taking of Seville from the Moors, when he was rewarded by the king, and received permission to establish himself there. His descendants enjoyed the prerogatives of nobility, and suppressed the letter u in their name, to accommodate it to the Spanish tongue.

Antonio, the father of Bartholomew, went to Hispaniola with Columbus in 1493, and returned rich to Seville in 1498.[1] It has been stated by one of the biographers of Bartholomew Las Casas, that he accompanied Columbus in his third voyage in 1498, and returned with him in 1500.[2] This, however, is incorrect. He was, during that time, completing his education at Salamanca, where he was instructed in Latin, dialectics, logic, metaphysics, ethics, and physics, after the supposed method and system of Aristotle. While at the university, he had, as a servant, an Indian slave, given him by his father, who had received him from Columbus. When Isabella, in her transport of virtuous indignation, ordered the Indian slaves to be sent back to their country, this one was taken from Las Casas. The young man was aroused by the circumstance, and, on considering the nature of the case, became inflamed with a zeal in favor of the unhappy Indians, which never cooled throughout a long and active life. It was excited to tenfold fervor, when, at about the age of twenty-eight years, he accompanied the commander Ovando to Hispaniola in 1502, and was an eye-witness to many of the cruel scenes which took place under his administration. The whole of his future life, a space exceeding sixty years, was devoted to vindicating the cause, and endeavoring to meliorate the sufferings of the natives.

---

[1] Navarrete, Colec. Viag., tom. 1. Introd p lxx.
[2] T. A. Llorente, Œuvres de Las Casas, p. xi; Paris, 1822.

As a missionary, he traversed the wilderness of the New World in various directions, seeking to convert and civilize them: as a protector and champion, he made several voyages to Spain, vindicated their wrongs before courts and monarchs, wrote volumes in their behalf, and exhibited a zeal and constancy and intrepidity worthy of an apostle. He died at the advanced age of ninety-two years, and was buried at Madrid, in the church of the Dominican convent of Atocha, of which fraternity he was a member.

Attempts have been made to decry the consistency, and question the real philanthropy of Las Casas, in consequence of one of the expedients to which he resorted to relieve the Indians from the cruel bondage imposed upon them. This occurred in 1517, when he arrived in Spain, on one of his missions, to obtain measures in their favor from the government. On his arrival in Spain, he found Cardinal Ximenes, who had been left regent on the death of King Ferdinand, too ill to attend to his affairs He repaired, therefore, to Valladolid, where he awaited the coming of the new monarch Charles, Archduke of Austria, afterward the Emperor Charles V He had strong opponents to encounter in various persons high in authority, who, holding estates and repartimientos in the colonies, were interested in the slavery of the Indians Among these, and not the least animated, was the Bishop Fonseca, President of the Council of the Indies.

At length the youthful sovereign arrived, accompanied by various Flemings of his court, particularly his grand chancellor, Doctor Juan de Selvagio, a learned and upright man, whom he consulted on all affairs of administration and justice. Las Casas soon became intimate with the chancellor, and stood high in his esteem; but so much opposition arose on every side that he found his various propositions for the relief of the natives but little attended to. In his doubt and anxiety he had now recourse to an expedient which he considered as justified by the circumstances of the case.[1] The chancellor Selvagio and other Flemings who had accompanied the youthful sovereign, had obtained from him before quitting Flanders, licenses to import slaves from Africa to the colonies: a measure which had recently in 1516 been prohibited by a decree of Cardinal Ximenes while acting as regent. The chancellor, who was a humane man, reconciled it to his conscience by a popular opinion that one negro could perform, without detriment to his health, the labor of several Indians, and that therefore it was a great saving of human suffering. So easy is it for interest to wrap itself up in plausible argument! He might, moreover, have thought the welfare of the Africans but little affected by the change. They were accustomed to slavery in their own country, and they were said to thrive in the New World. "The Africans," observes Herrera, "prospered so much in the island of Hispaniola, that it was the opinion unless a negro should happen to be hanged, he would never die: for as yet none had been known to perish from infirmity. Like oranges, they found their proper soil in Hispaniola, and it seemed even more natural to them than their native Guinea."[2]

Las Casas finding all other means ineffectual, endeavored to turn these interested views of the grand chancellor to the benefit of the Indians. He proposed that the Spaniards, resident in the colonies, might

---

[1] Herrera clearly states this as an expedient adopted when others failed "Bartolomé de las Casas, viendo que sus conceptos hallaban en todas partes dificultad, i que las opiniones que tenia, por mucha familiaridad que havia seguido i gran credito con el gran Canciller, no podian haber efecto, *se volvió a otros expedientes. &c.*"—Decad. ii. lib. ii. cap. 2.

[2] Herrera, Hist. Ind., lib. ii. decad. iii. cap.

be permitted to procure negroes for the labor of the farms and the mines, and other severe toils, which were above the strength and destructive of the lives of the natives.[1] He evidently considered the poor Africans as little better than mere animals; and he acted like others, on an arithmetical calculation of diminishing human misery, by substituting one strong man for three or four of feebler nature. He, moreover, esteemed the Indians as a nobler and more intellectual race of beings, and their preservation and welfare of higher importance to the general interests of humanity.

It is this expedient of Las Casas which has drawn down severe censure upon his memory. He has been charged with gross inconsistency, and even with having originated this inhuman traffic in the New World. This last is a grievous charge; but historical facts and dates remove the original sin from his door, and prove that the practice existed in the colonies, and was authorized by royal decree, long before he took a part in the question.

Las Casas did not go to the New World until 1502. By a royal ordinance passed in 1501, negro slaves were permitted to be taken there, provided they had been born among Christians.[2] By a letter written by Ovando, dated 1503, it appears that there were numbers in the island of Hispaniola at that time, and he entreats that none more might be permitted to be brought.

In 1506 the Spanish government forbade the introduction of negro slaves from the Levant, or those brought up with the Moors; and stipulated that none should be taken to the colonies but those from Seville, who had been instructed in the Christian faith, that they might contribute to the conversion of the Indians.[3] In 1510 King Ferdinand, being informed of the physical weakness of the Indians, ordered fifty Africans to be sent from Seville to labor in the mines.[4] In 1511 he ordered that a great number should be procured from Guinea, and transported to Hispaniola, understanding that one negro could perform the work of four Indians.[5] In 1512 and '13 he signed further orders relative to the same subject. In 1516 Charles V. granted licenses to the Flemings to import negroes to the colonies. It was not until the year 1517 that Las Casas gave his sanction of the traffic. It already existed, and he countenanced it solely with a view to having the hardy Africans substituted for the feeble Indians. It was advocated at the same time, and for the same reasons, by the Jeronimite friars, who were missionaries in the colonies. The motives of Las Casas were purely benevolent, though founded on erroneous notions of justice. He thought to permit evil that good might spring out of it; to choose between two existing abuses, and to eradicate the greater by resorting to the lesser. His reasoning, however fallacious it may be, was considered satisfactory and humane by some of the most learned and benevolent men of the age, among whom was the Cardinal Adrian, afterward elevated to the papal chair, and characterized by gentleness and humanity. The traffic was permitted; inquiries were made as to the number of slaves required, which was limited to four thousand, and the Flemings obtained a monopoly of the trade, which they afterward farmed out to the Genoese.

Dr Robertson, in noticing this affair, draws a contrast between the conduct of the Cardinal Ximenes and that of Las Casas, strongly to the disadvantage of the latter. "The cardinal," he observes, "when solicited

---

[1] Herrera, Hist. Ind., decad. ii. lib. ii. cap. 20. [3] Ibid., d. ii. lib. iii. cap. 8.
[2] Ibid., d. i. lib. vi. cap. 20.   [4] Ibid., d. i. lib. viii. cap. 9.
[5] Ibid., d. i. lib. ix. cap. 6.

to encourage this commerce, peremptorily rejected the proposition, because he perceived the iniquity of reducing one race of men to slavery, when he was consulting about the means of restoring liberty to another; but Las Casas, from the inconsistency natural to men who hurry with head-long impetuosity toward a favorite point, was incapable of making this distinction. In the warmth of his zeal to save the Americans from the yoke, he pronounced it to be lawful and expedient to impose one still heavier on the Africans.[1]

This distribution of praise and censure is not perfectly correct. Las Casas had no idea that he was imposing a heavier, nor so heavy, a yoke upon the Africans. The latter were considered more capable of labor, and less impatient of slavery. While the Indians sunk under their tasks, and perished by thousands in Hispaniola, the negroes, on the contrary, thrived there. Herrera, to whom Dr Robertson refers as his authority, assigns a different motive, and one of mere finance, for the measures of Cardinal Ximenes. He says that he ordered that no one should take negroes to the Indies, because, as the natives were decreasing, and it was known that one negro did more work than four of them, there would probably be a great demand for African slaves, and a tribute might be imposed upon the trade, from which would result profit to the royal treasury.[2] This measure was presently after carried into effect, though subsequent to the death of the cardinal, and licenses were granted by the sovereign for pecuniary considerations. Flechier, in his Life of Ximenes, assigns another but a mere political motive for this prohibition. The cardinal, he says, objected to the importation of negroes into the colonies, as he feared they would corrupt the natives, and by confederacies with them render them formidable to government. De Marsolier, another biographer of Ximenes, gives equally politic reasons for this prohibition. He cites a letter written by the cardinal on the subject, in which he observed that he knew the nature of the negroes, they were a people capable, it was true, of great fatigue, but extremely prolific and enterprising; and that if they had time to multiply in America, they would infallibly revolt, and impose on the Spaniards the same chains which they had compelled them to wear.[3]

These facts, while they take from the measure of the cardinal that credit for exclusive philanthropy which has been bestowed upon it, manifest the clear foresight of that able politician; whose predictions with respect to negro revolt have been so strikingly fulfilled in the island of Hispaniola.

Cardinal Ximenes, in fact, though a wise and upright statesman, was not troubled with scruples of conscience on these questions of natural right; nor did he possess more toleration than his contemporaries toward savage and infidel nations. He was grand inquisitor of Spain, and was very efficient during the latter years of Ferdinand in making slaves of the refractory Moors of Granada. He authorized, by express instructions, expeditions to seize and enslave the Indians of the Caribbee islands, whom he termed only suited to labor, enemies of the Christians, and cannibals. Nor will it be considered a proof of gentle or tolerant policy, that he introduced the tribunal of the inquisition into the New World. These circumstances are cited not to cast reproach upon the character of Cardinal Ximenes, but to show how incorrectly he has been extolled at the expense of Las Casas. Both of them must be judged in connection with the customs and opinions of the age in which they lived.

[1] Robertson, Hist. America, p. 3.
[2] Porque como iban faltando los Indios se conocia que un negro trabajaba, mas que quatro, por lo qual habia gran demanda de ellos, parecia que se podia poner algun tributo en la saca, de que resultaria provecho á la Rl Hacienda Herrera, decad. ii. lib. ii. cap. 8.
[3] De Marsolier, Hist du Ministere Cardinal Ximenes, lib vi. Toulouse, 1694.

Las Casas was the author of many works, but few of which have been printed The most important is a general history of the Indies, from the discovery to the year 1520, in three volumes. It exists only in manuscript, but is the fountain from which Herrera, and most of the other historians of the New World, have drawn large supplies. The work though prolix, is valuable, as the author was an eye-witness of many of the facts, had others from persons who were concerned in the transactions recorded, and possessed copious documents. It displays great erudition, though somewhat crudely and diffusely introduced. His history was commenced in 1527, at fifty-three years of age, and was finished in 1559, when eighty-five. As many things are set down from memory, there is occasional inaccuracy, but the whole bears the stamp of sincerity and truth. The author of the present work, having had access to this valuable manuscript, has made great use of it, drawing forth many curious facts hitherto neglected; but he has endeavored to consult it with caution and discrimination, collating it with other authorities, and omitting whatever appeared to be dictated by prejudice or over-heated zeal.

Las Casas has been accused of high coloring and extravagant declamation in those passages which relate to the barbarities practised on the natives; nor is the charge entirely without foundation. The same zeal in the cause of the Indians is expressed in his writings that shone forth in his actions, always pure, often vehement, and occasionally unseasonable. Still, however, where he errs it is on a generous and righteous side. If one-tenth part of what he says he "witnessed with his own eyes" be true, and his veracity is above all doubt, he would have been wanting in the natural feelings of humanity had he not expressed himself in terms of indignation and abhorrence.

In the course of his work, when Las Casas mentions the original papers lying before him. from which he drew many of his facts, it makes one lament that they should be lost to the world Besides the journals and letters of Columbus. he says he had numbers of the letters of the Adelantado, Don Bartholomew. who wrote better than his brother, and whose writings must have been full of energy. Above all, he had the map, formed from study and conjecture. by which Columbus sailed on his first voyage. What a precious document would this be for the world! These writings may still exist. neglected and forgotten among the rubbish of some convent in Spain Little hope can be entertained of discovering them in the present state of degeneracy of the cloister. The monks of Atocha, in a recent conversation with one of the royal princes, betrayed an ignorance that this illustrious man was buried in their convent. nor can any of the fraternity point out his place of sepulture to the stranger.[1]

The publication of this work of Las Casas has not been permitted in Spain, where every book must have the sanction of a censor before it is committed to the press. The horrible picture it exhibits of the cruelties inflicted on the Indians would, it was imagined, excite an odium against their conquerors. Las Casas himself seems to have doubted the expediency of publishing it; for in 1560 he made a note with his own hand, which is preserved in the two first volumes of the original, mentioning that he left them in confidence to the college of the order of Predicators of St. Gregorio, in Valladolid, begging of its prelates that no secular person, nor even the collegians, should be permitted to read his history for

---

[1] In this notice the author has occasionally availed himself of the interesting memoir of Mon. J. A. Llorente, prefixed to his collection of the works of Las Casas collating it with the history of Herrera, from which its facts are principally derived.

the space of forty years; and that after that term it might be printed if consistent with the good of the Indies and of Spain.[1]

For the foregoing reason the work has been cautiously used by Spanish historians, passing over in silence, or with brief notice, many passages of disgraceful import. This feeling is natural, if not commendable, for the world is not prompt to discriminate between individuals and the nation of whom they are but a part. The laws and regulations for the government of the newly-discovered countries, and the decisions of the Council of the Indies on all contested points, though tinctured in some degree with the bigotry of the age, were distinguished for wisdom, justice, and humanity, and do honor to the Spanish nation. It was only in the abuse of them by individuals to whom the execution of the laws was intrusted, that these atrocities were committed. It should be remembered, also, that the same nation which gave birth to the sanguinary and rapacious adventurers who perpetrated these cruelties, gave birth likewise to the early missionaries, like Las Casas, who followed the sanguinary course of discovery, binding up the wounds inflicted by their countrymen, men who in a truly evangelical spirit braved all kinds of perils and hardships, and even death itself, not through a prospect of temporal gain or glory, but through a desire to meliorate the condition and save the souls of barbarous and suffering nations. The dauntless enterprises and fearful peregrinations of many of these virtuous men, if properly appreciated, would be found to vie in romantic daring with the heroic achievements of chivalry, with motives of a purer and far more exalted nature.

No. XXIX.

PETER MARTYR.

PETER MARTIR, or Martyr, of whose writings much use has been made in this history, was born at Anghierra, in the territory of Milan, in Italy, on the second of February, 1455. He is commonly termed Peter Martyr of *Angleria*, from the Latin name of his native place. He is one of the earliest historians that treat of Columbus, and was his contemporary and intimate acquaintance. Being at Rome in 1487, and having acquired a distinguished reputation for learning, he was invited by the Spanish ambassador, the Count de Tendilla, to accompany him to Spain. He willingly accepted the invitation, and was presented to the sovereigns at Saragossa. Isabella, amid the cares of the war with Granada, was anxious for the intellectual advancement of her kingdom, and wished to employ Martyr to instruct the young nobility of the royal household. With her peculiar delicacy, however, she first made her confessor, Hernando de Talavera, inquire of Martyr in what capacity he desired to serve her. Contrary to her expectation, Martyr replied, "In the profession of arms." The queen complied, and he followed her in her campaigns, as one of her household and military suite, but without distinguishing himself, and perhaps without having any particular employ in a capacity so foreign to his talents. After the surrender of Granada, when the war was ended, the queen, through the medium of the grand cardinal of Spain, prevailed upon him to undertake the instruction of the young nobles of her court.

Martyr was acquainted with Columbus while making his application to the sovereigns, and was present at his triumphant reception by Ferdinand and Isabella in Barcelona, on his return from his first voyage. He was continually in the royal camp during the war with the Moors, of

---

[1] Navarrete, Colec. de Viag., tom. i. p. lxxv.

which his letters contain many interesting particulars. He was sent ambassador extraordinary by Ferdinand and Isabella, in 1501, to Venice, and thence to the grand soldan of Egypt. The soldan, in 1490 or 1491, had sent an embassy to the Spanish sovereigns, threatening that, unless they desisted from the war against Granada, he would put all the Christians in Egypt and Syria to death, overturn all their temples, and destroy the holy sepulchre at Jerusalem. Ferdinand and Isabella pressed the war with tenfold energy, and brought it to a triumphant conclusion in the next campaign, while the soldan was still carrying on a similar negotiation with the pope. They afterward sent Peter Martyr ambassador to the soldan to explain and justify their measure. Martyr discharged the duties of his embassy with great ability; obtained permission from the soldan to repair the holy places at Jerusalem, and an abolition of various extortions to which Christian pilgrims had been subjected. While on this embassy, he wrote his work De Legatione Babylonica, which includes a history of Egypt in those times.

On his return to Spain he was rewarded with places and pensions, and in 1524 was appointed a minister of the Council of the Indies. His principal work is an account of the discoveries of the New World, in eight decades, each containing ten chapters They are styled Decades of the New World, or Decades of the Ocean, and, like all his other works, were originally written in Latin, though since translated into various languages. He had familiar access to letters, papers, journals, and narratives of the early discoverers, and was personally acquainted with many of them, gathering particulars from their conversation. In writing his Decades, he took great pains to obtain information from Columbus himself, and from others, his companions.

In one of his epistles (No. 153, January, 1494, to Pomponius Lætus), he mentions having just received a letter from Columbus, by which it appears he was in correspondence with him. Las Casas says that great credit is to be given to him in regard to those voyages of Columbus, although his Decades contain some inaccuracies relative to subsequent events in the Indies. Muñoz allows him great credit, as an author contemporary with his subject, grave, well cultivated, instructed in the facts of which he treats, and of entire probity. He observes, however, that his writings being composed on the spur or excitement of the moment, often related circumstances which subsequently proved to be erroneous; that they were written without method or care, often confusing dates and events, so that they must be read with some caution.

Martyr was in the daily habit of writing letters to distinguished persons, relating the passing occurrences of the busy court and age in which he lived. In several of these Columbus is mentioned, and also some of the chief events of his voyages, as promulgated at the very moment of his return. These letters not being generally known or circulated, or frequently cited, it may be satisfactory to the reader to have a few of the main passages which relate to Columbus. They have a striking effect in carrying us back to the very time of the discoveries.

In one of his epistles, dated Barcelona, May 1st, 1493, and addressed to C. Borromeo, he says: "Within these few days a certain Christopher Columbus has arrived from the western antipodes; a man of Liguria, whom my sovereigns reluctantly intrusted with three ships, to seek that region for they thought that what he said was fabulous. He has returned and brought specimens of many precious things, but particularly gold. which those countries naturally produce." [1]

---

[1] Opus Epist. P Martyris Anglerii, Epist. 131.

In another letter. dated likewise from Barcelona, in September following, he gives a more particular account. It is addressed to Count Tendilla, Governor of Granada. and also to Hernando Talavera, Archbishop of that diocese, and the same to whom the propositions of Columbus had been referred by the Spanish sovereigns. Arouse your attention. ancient sages," says Peter Martyr in his epistle: ' listen to a new discovery. You remember Columbus the Ligurian. appointed in the camp by our sovereigns to search for a new hemisphere of land at the western antipodes. You ought to recollect, for you had some agency in the transaction: nor would the enterprise, as I think, have been undertaken. without your counsel. He has returned in safety, and relates the wonders he has discovered. He exhibits gold as proofs of the mines in those regions: Gossampine cotton, also. and aromatics, and pepper more pungent than that from Caucasus. All these things, together with scarlet dye-woods. the earth produces spontaneously. Pursuing the western sun from Gades five thousand miles. of each a thousand paces, as he relates, he fell in with sundry islands, and took possession of one of them, of greater circuit, he asserts, than the whole of Spain. Here he found a race of men living contented, in a state of nature, subsisting on fruits and vegetables, and bread formed from roots. . . . These people have kings, some greater than others, and they war occasionally among themselves, with bows and arrows, or lances sharpened and hardened in the fire. The desire of command prevails among them, though they are naked. They have wives also. What they worship except the divinity of heaven, is not ascertained." [1]

In another letter, dated likewise in September, 1493, and addressed to the cardinal and vice-chancellor Ascanius Sforza, he says:

"So great is my desire to give you satisfaction, illustrious prince, that I consider it a gratifying occurrence in the great fluctuations of events, when any thing takes place among us, in which you may take an interest. The wonders of this terrestrial globe, round which the sun makes a circuit in the space of four and twenty hours, have, until our time, as you are well aware, been known only in regard to one hemisphere, merely from the golden Chersonesus to our Spanish Gades. The rest has been given up as unknown by cosmographers, and if any mention of it has been made, it has been slight and dubious. But now, O blessed enterprise! under the auspices of our sovereigns, what has hitherto lain hidden since the first origin of things, has at length begun to be developed. The thing has thus occurred — attend, illustrious prince! A certain Christopher Columbus, a Ligurian, despatched to those regions with three vessels by my sovereigns, pursuing the western sun above five thousand miles from Gades, achieved his way to the antipodes. Three and thirty successive days they navigated with nought but sky and water. At length from the mast-head of the largest vessel, in which Columbus himself sailed, those on the look-out proclaimed the sight of land. He coasted along six islands, one of them, as all his followers declare, beguiled perchance by the novelty of the scene, is larger than Spain."

Martyr proceeds to give the usual account of the productions of the islands, and the manners and customs of the natives, particularly the wars which occurred among them; " as if *meum* and *tuum* had been introduced among them as among us, and expensive luxuries, and the desire of accumulating wealth; for what, you will think, can be the wants of naked men ? " " What further may succeed," he adds, " I will hereafter signify. Farewell." [2]

---

[1] Opus Epist P. Martyris Anglerii, Epist. 134.   [2] Ibid., Epist. 135.

In another letter, dated Valladolid, February 1st, 1494, to Hernando de Talavera, Archbishop of Granada, he observes, "The king and queen, on the return of Columbus to Barcelona, from his honorable enterprise, appointed him admiral of the ocean sea, and caused him, on account of his illustrious deeds, to be seated in their presence, an honor and a favor, as you know, the highest with our sovereigns. They have despatched him again to those regions, furnished with a fleet of eighteen ships. There is prospect of great discoveries at the western antarctic antipodes. . . . "[1]

In a subsequent letter to Pomponius Lætus, dated from Alcala de Henares, December 9th, 1494, he gives the first news of the success of this expedition.

"Spain," says he, "is spreading her wings, augmenting her empire, and extending her name and glory to the antipodes. . . . Of eighteen vessels despatched by my sovereigns with the Admiral Columbus in his second voyage to the western hemisphere, twelve have returned and have brought Gossampine cotton, huge trees of dye-wood, and many other articles held with us as precious, the natural productions of that hitherto hidden world; and beside all other things, no small quantity of gold. O wonderful, Pomponius! Upon the surface of that earth are found rude masses of native gold, of a weight that one is afraid to mention. Some weigh two hundred and fifty ounces, and they hope to discover others of a much larger size, from what the naked natives intimate, when they extol their gold to our people. Nor are the Lestrigonians nor Polyphemi, who feed on human flesh, any longer doubtful. Attend — but beware! lest they rise in horror before thee! When he proceeded from the Fortunate Islands, now termed the Canaries, to Hispaniola, the island on which he first set foot, turning his prow a little toward the south, he arrived at innumerable islands of savage men, whom they called cannibals, or Caribbees: and these, though naked, are courageous warriors. They fight skilfully with bows and clubs, and have boats hollowed from a single tree, yet very capacious, in which they make fierce descents on neighboring islands, inhabited by milder people. They attack their villages, from which they carry off the men and devour them," etc.[2]

Another letter to Pomponius Lætus, on the same subject, has been cited at large in the body of this work. It is true these extracts give nothing that has not been stated more at large in the Decades of the same author, but they are curious, as the very first announcements of the discoveries of Columbus, and as showing the first stamp of these extraordinary events upon the mind of one of the most learned and liberal men of the age.

A collection of the letters of Peter Martyr was published in 1530, under the title of Opus Epistolarum, Petri Martyris Anglerii: it is divided into thirty-eight books, each containing the letters of one year. The same objections have been made to his letters as to his Decades, but they bear the same stamp of candor, probity, and great information. They possess peculiar value from being written at the moment, before the facts they record were distorted or discolored by prejudice or misrepresentation. His works abound in interesting particulars not to be found in any contemporary historian. They are rich in thought, but still richer in fact, and are full of urbanity, and of the liberal feeling of a scholar who has mingled with the world. He is a fountain from which others draw, and from which, with a little precaution, they may draw securely. He died in Valladolid, in 1526.

---

[1] Opus Epist. P. Martyris Anglerii, Epist. 141.   [2] Ibid., Epist. 147.

No. XXX.

OVIEDO.

GONZALO FERNANDEZ DE OVIEDO Y VALDES, commonly known as Oviedo, was born in Madrid in 1478, and died in Valladolid in 1557, aged seventy-nine years. He was of a noble Austrian family, and in his boyhood (in 1490) was appointed one of the pages to Prince Juan, heir apparent of Spain, the only son of Ferdinand and Isabella. He was in this situation at the time of the siege and surrender of Granada, was consequently at court at the time that Columbus made his agreement with the Catholic sovereigns, and was in the same capacity at Barcelona, and witnessed the triumphant entrance of the discoverer, attended by a number of the natives of the newly-found countries.

In 1513, he was sent out to the New World by Ferdinand to superintend the gold-foundries. For many years he served there in various offices of trust and dignity, both under Ferdinand, and his grandson and successor Charles V. In 1535, he was made alcayde of the fortress of St. Domingo in Hispaniola, and afterward was appointed historiographer of the Indies. At the time of his death, he had served the crown upward of forty years, thirty-four of which were passed in the colonies, and he had crossed the ocean eight times, as he mentions in various parts of his writings. He wrote several works, the most important is the chronicle of the Indies in fifty books, divided into three parts. The first part containing nineteen books was printed at Seville in 1535, and reprinted in 1547 at Salamanca, augmented by a twentieth book containing shipwrecks. The remainder of the work exists in manuscript. The printing of it was commenced at Valladolid in 1557, but was discontinued in consequence of his death. It is one of the unpublished treasures of Spanish colonial history.

He was an indefatigable writer, laborious in collecting and recording facts, and composed a multitude of volumes which are scattered through the Spanish libraries. His writings are full of events which happened under his own eye, or were communicated to him by eye-witnesses, but he was deficient in judgment and discrimination. He took his facts without caution, and often from sources unworthy of credit. In his account of the first voyage of Columbus, he falls into several egregious errors, in consequence of taking the verbal information of a pilot named Hernan Perez Matteo, who was in the interest of the Pinzons, and adverse to the admiral. His work is not much to be depended upon in matters relative to Columbus. When he treats of a more advanced period of the New World, from his own actual observation, he is much more satisfactory, though he is accused of listening too readily to popular fables and misrepresentations. His account of the natural productions of the New World, and of the customs of its inhabitants, is full of curious particulars; and the best narratives of some of the minor voyages which succeeded those of Columbus, are to be found in the unpublished part of his work.

No. XXXI.

CURA DE LOS PALACIOS.

ANDRES BERNALDES, or Bernal, generally known by the title of the curate of *Los Palacios*, from having been curate of the town of Los Palacios from about 1488 to 1513, was born in the town of Fuentes, and was for some time chaplain to Diego Deza, Archbishop of Seville, one of the greatest friends to the application of Columbus. Bernaldes was well acquainted with the admiral, who was occasionally his guest, and in 1496, left many of his manuscripts and journals with him, which the curate made use of in a history of the reign of Ferdinand and Isabella, in which he introduced an account of the voyages of Columbus. In his narrative of the admiral's coasting along the southern side of Cuba, the curate is more minute and accurate than any other historian. His work exists only in manuscript, but is well known to historians, who have made frequent use of it. Nothing can be more simple and artless than the account which the honest curate gives of his being first moved to undertake his chronicle. "I who wrote these chapters of memoirs," he says, "being for twelve years in the habit of reading a register of my deceased grandfather, who was notary public of the town of Fuentes, where I was born, I found therein several chapters recording certain events and achievements which had taken place in his time; and my grandmother his widow, who was very old, hearing me read them said to me, 'And thou, my son, since thou art not slothful in writing, why dost thou not write, in this manner, the good things which are happening at present in thy own day, that those who come hereafter may know them, and marvelling at what they read may render thanks to God.'

"From that time," continues he, "I proposed to do so, and as I considered the matter, I said often to myself, 'if God gives me life and health I will continue to write until I behold the kingdom of Granada gained by the Christians;' and I always entertained a hope of seeing it and did see it: great thanks and praises be given to our Saviour Jesus Christ! And because it was impossible to write a complete and connected account of all things that happened in Spain, during the matrimonial union of the king Don Ferdinand, and the queen Doña Isabella, I wrote only about certain of the most striking and remarkable events, of which I had correct information, and of those which I saw or which were public and notorious to all men."[1]

The work of the worthy curate, as may be inferred from the foregoing statement, is deficient in regularity of plan; the style is artless and often inelegant, but it abounds in facts not to be met with elsewhere, often given in a very graphical manner, and strongly characteristic of the times. As he was contemporary with the events and familiar with many of the persons of his history, and as he was a man of probity and void of all pretension, his manuscript is a document of high authenticity. He was much respected in the limited sphere in which he moved, "yet," says one of his admirers, who wrote a short preface to his chronicle, "he had no other reward than that of the curacy of Los Palacios, and the place of chaplain to the archbishop Don Diego Deza."

In the possession of O. Rich, Esq., of Madrid, is a very curious manuscript chronicle of the reign of Ferdinand and Isabella already quoted in this work, made up from this history of the curate of Los Palacios, and from various other historians of the times, by some contemporary writer. In his account of the voyage of Columbus, he differs in some trivial particulars from the regular copy of the manuscript of the curate. These variations have been carefully examined by the author of this work, and wherever they appear to be for the better, have been adopted.

---

[1] Cura de los Palacios. cap. 7.

No. XXXII.

**"NAVIGATIONE DEL RE DE CASTIGLIA DELLE ISOLE E PAESE NUO-
VAMENTE RITROVATE." "NAVIGATIO CHRISTOPHORI COLOMBI."**

THE above are the titles, in Italian and in Latin, of the earliest narratives of the first and second voyages of Columbus that appeared in print.
It was anonymous; and there are some curious particulars in regard to
it. It was originally written in Italian by Montalbodo Fracanzo, or
Fracanzano, or by Francapano de Montabaldo (for writers differ in regard to the name), and was published in Vicenza, in 1507, in a collection
of voyages, entitled Mondo Novo, e Paese Nuovamente Ritrovate. The
collection was republished at Milan, in 1508, both in Italian, and in a
Latin translation made by Archangelo Madrignano, under the title of
Itinerarium Portugallensium; this title being given, because the work
related chiefly to the voyages of Luigi Cadamosto, a Venetian in the
service of Portugal.

The collection was afterward augmented by Simon Grinæus with other
travels, and printed in Latin at Basle, in 1533,[1] by Hervagio, entitled
Novus Orbis Regionum, etc. The edition of Basle, 1555, and the Italian
edition of Milan, in 1508, have been consulted in the course of this work.

Peter Martyr (Decad. 2, Cap. 7) alludes to this publication, under the
first Latin title of the book, Itinerarium Portugallensium, and accuses
the author, whom by mistake he terms Cadamosto, of having stolen the
materials of his book from the three first chapters of his first Decade of
the Ocean, of which, he says, he granted copies in manuscript to several
persons, and in particular to certain Venetian ambassadors. Martyr's
Decades were not published until 1516, excepting the first three, which
were published in 1511, at Seville.

This narrative of the voyages of Columbus is referred to by Gio. Batista
Spotorno, in his historical memoir of Columbus, as having been written
by a companion of Columbus

It is manifest, from a perusal of the narrative, that though the author
may have helped himself freely from the manuscript of Martyr, he must
have had other sources of information. His description of the person of
Columbus as a man tall of stature and large of frame, of a ruddy complexion and oblong visage, is not copied from Martyr, nor from any
other writer. No historian had, indeed, preceded him, except Sabellicus,
in 1504; and the portrait agrees with that subsequently given of Columbus in the biography written by his son.

It is probable that this narrative, which appeared only a year after the
death of Columbus, was a piece of literary job-work, written for the collection of voyages published at Vicenza; and that the materials were
taken from oral communication, from the account given by Sabellicus,
and particularly from the manuscript copy of Martyr's first decade

No. XXXIII.

ANTONIO DE HERRERA

ANTONIO HERRERA DE TORDESILLAS, one of the authors most frequently cited in this work, was born in 1565, of Roderick Tordesillas,

---

[1] Bibliotheca Pinello.

and Agnes de Herrera, his wife. He received an excellent education, and entered into the employ of Vespasian Gonzago,, brother to the Duke of Mantua, who was Viceroy of Naples for Philip the Second of Spain. He was for some time secretary to this statesman, and intrusted with all his secrets. He was afterward grand historiographer of the Indies to Philip II., who added to that title a large pension. He wrote various books, but the most celebrated is a General History of the Indies, or American Colonies, in four volumes, containing eight decades. When he undertook this work all the public archives were thrown open to him, and he had access to documents of all kinds. He has been charged with great precipitation in the production of his two first volumes, and with negligence in not making sufficient use of the indisputable sources of information thus placed within his reach. The fact was, that he met with historical tracts lying in manuscript, which embraced a great part of the first discoveries, and he contented himself with stating events as he found them therein recorded. It is certain that a great part of his work is little more than a transcript of the manuscript history of the Indies by Las Casas, sometimes reducing and improving the language when tumid; omitting the impassioned sallies of the zealous father, when the wrongs of the Indians were in question; and suppressing various circumstances degrading to the character of the Spanish discoverers. The author of the present work, has, therefore, frequently put aside the history of Herrera, and consulted the source of his information, the manuscript history of Las Casas.

Muñoz observes that "in general Herrera did little more than join together morsels and extracts, taken from various parts, in the way that a writer arranges chronologically the materials from which he intends to compose a history;" he adds, that "had not Herrera been a learned and judicious man, the precipitation with which he put together these materials would have led to innumerable errors." The remark is just; yet it is to be considered, that to select and arrange such materials judiciously, and treat them learnedly, was no trifling merit in the historian.

Herrera has been accused also of flattering his nation; exalting the deeds of his countrymen, and softening and concealing their excesses. There is nothing very serious in this accusation. To illustrate the glory of his nation is one of the noblest offices of the historian; and it is difficult to speak too highly of the extraordinary enterprises and splendid actions of the Spaniards in those days. In softening their excesses he fell into an amiable and pardonable error, if it were indeed an error for a Spanish writer to endeavor to sink them in oblivion.

Vossius passes a high eulogium on Herrera. "No one," he says, "has described with greater industry and fidelity the magnitude and boundaries of provinces, the tracts of sea, positions of capes and islands, of ports and harbors, the windings of rivers and dimensions of lakes; the situation and peculiarities of regions, with the appearance of the heavens, and the designation of places suitable for the establishment of cities." He has been called among the Spaniards the prince of the historians of America, and it is added that none have risen since his time capable of disputing with him that title. Much of this praise will appear exaggerated by such as examine the manuscript histories from which he transferred chapters and entire books, with very little alteration, to his volumes; and a great part of the eulogiums passed on him for his work on the Indies, will be found really due to Las Casas, who has too long been eclipsed by his copyist. Still Herrera has left voluminous proofs of industrious research, extensive information, and great literary talent. His works bear the mark of candor, integrity, and a sincere desire to record the truth.

He died in 1625, at sixty years of age, after having obtained from Philip IV. the promise of the first charge of secretary of state that should become vacant.

No. XXXIV.

BISHOP FONSECA.

THE singular malevolence displayed by Bishop Juan Rodriguez de Fonseca toward Columbus and his family, and which was one of the secret and principal causes of their misfortunes, has been frequently noticed in the course of this work. It originated, as has been shown, in some dispute between the admiral and Fonseca at Seville in 1493, on account of the delay in fitting out the armament for the second voyage, and in regard to the number of domestics to form the household of the admiral. Fonseca received a letter from the sovereigns, tacitly reproving him, and ordering him to show all possible attention to the wishes of Columbus, and to see that he was treated with honor and deference. Fonseca never forgot this affront, and, what with him was the same thing, never forgave it. His spirit appears to have been of that unhealthy kind which has none of the balm of forgiveness; and in which, a wound once made, forever rankles. The hostility thus produced continued with increasing virulence throughout the life of Columbus, and at his death was transferred to his son and successor. This persevering animosity has been illustrated in the course of this work by facts and observations, cited from authors, some of them contemporary with Fonseca, but who were apparently restrained by motives of prudence from giving full vent to the indignation which they evidently felt. Even at the present day, a Spanish historian would be cautious of expressing his feelings freely on the subject, lest they should prejudice his work in the eyes of the ecclesiastical censors of the press. In this way Bishop Fonseca has in a great measure escaped the general odium his conduct merited.

This prelate had the chief superintendence of Spanish colonial affairs, both under Ferdinand and Isabella, and the Emperor Charles V. He was an active and intrepid, but selfish, overbearing, and perfidious man. His administration bears no marks of enlarged and liberal policy; but is full of traits of arrogance and meanness. He opposed the benevolent attempts of Las Casas to ameliorate the condition of the Indians, and to obtain the abolition of repartimientos; treating him with personal haughtiness and asperity.[1] The reason assigned is that Fonseca was enriching himself by those very abuses, retaining large numbers of the miserable Indians in slavery, to work on his possessions in the colonies.

To show that his character has not been judged with undue severity, it is expedient to point out his invidious and persecuting conduct toward Hernando Cortez. The bishop, while ready to foster rambling adventurers who came forward under his patronage, had never the head or the heart to appreciate the merits of illustrious commanders like Columbus and Cortez.

At a time when disputes arose between Cortez and Diego Velazquez, governor of Cuba, and the latter sought to arrest the conqueror of Mexico in the midst of his brilliant career, Fonseca, with entire disregard of the merits of the case, took a decided part in favor of Velazquez. Personal

---

[1] Herrera, Hist. Ind., decad. ii lib. ii. cap. 3.

interest was at the bottom of this favor; for a marriage was negotiating between Velazquez and a sister of the bishop.[1] Complaints and misrepresentations had been sent to Spain by Velazquez of the conduct of Cortez. who was represented as a lawless and unprincipled adventurer attempting to usurp absolute authority in New Spain. The true services of Cortez had already excited admiration at court. but such was the influence of Fonseca, that, as in the case of Columbus, he succeeded in prejudicing the mind of the sovereign against one of the most meritorious of his subjects. One Christoval de Tapia, a man destitute of talent or character, but whose greatest recommendation was his having been in the employ of the bishop,[2] was invested with powers similar to those once given to Bobadilla to the prejudice of Columbus. He was to inquire into the conduct of Cortez, and in case he thought fit. to seize him, sequestrate his property, and supersede him in command. Not content with the regular official letters furnished to Tapia, the bishop, shortly after his departure, sent out Juan Bono de Quexo with blank letters signed by his own hand, and with others directed to various persons, charging them to admit Tapia for governor, and assuring them that the king considered the conduct of Cortez as disloyal. Nothing but the sagacity and firmness of Cortez prevented this measure from completely interrupting, if not defeating his enterprises; and he afterward declared, that he had experienced more trouble and difficulty from the menaces and affronts of the ministers of the king than it cost him to conquer Mexico.[3]

When the dispute between Cortez and Velazquez came to be decided upon in Spain, in 1522. the father of Cortez, and those who had come from New Spain as his procurators, obtained permission from Cardinal Adrian. at that time governor of the realm, to prosecute a public accusation of the bishop. A regular investigation took place before the Council of the Indies of their allegations against its president. They charged him with having publicly declared Cortez a traitor and a rebel; with having intercepted and suppressed his letters addressed to the king, keeping his Majesty in ignorance of their contents and of the important services he had performed. while he diligently forwarded all letters calculated to promote the interest of Velazquez; with having prevented the representations of Cortez from being heard in the Council of the Indies, declaring that they should never be heard there while he lived; with having interdicted the forwarding of arms, merchandise, and re-enforcements to New Spain; and with having issued orders to the office of the India House at Seville to arrest the procurators of Cortez and all persons arriving from him, and to seize and detain all gold that they should bring. These and various other charges of similar nature were dispassionately investigated. Enough were substantiated to convict Fonseca of the most partial, oppressive and perfidious conduct, and the cardinal consequently forbade him to interfere in the cause between Cortez and Velazquez, and revoked all the orders which the bishop had issued, in the matter, to the India House of Seville. Indeed Salazar, a Spanish historian, says that Fonseca was totally divested of his authority as president of the council, and of all control of the affairs of New Spain, and adds that he was so mortified at the blow, that it brought on a fit of illness, which well-nigh cost him his life.[4]

The suit between Cortez and Velazquez was referred to a special tri-

---

[1] Herrera, Hist Ind., decad. iii lib. iv. cap. 3.
[2] Ibid., decad. iii. lib. i cap. 15.
[3] Ibid., decad. iii. lib. iv. cap. 3.
[4] Salazar, Conq. de Mexico, lib. i. cap. 2.

bunal, composed of the grand chancellor and other persons of note, and was decided in 1522. The influence and intrigues of Fonseca being no longer of avail, a triumphant verdict was given in favor of Cortez, which was afterward confirmed by the Emperor Charles V., and additional honors awarded him This was another blow to the malignant Fonseca, who retained his enmity against Cortez until his last moment, rendered still more rancorous by mortification and disappointment.

A charge against Fonseca, of a still darker nature than any of the preceding, may be found lurking in the pages of Herrera, though so obscure as to have escaped the notice of succeeding historians. He points to the bishop as the instigator of a desperate and perfidious man, who conspired against the life of Hernando Cortez. This was one Antonio de Villafaña, who fomented a conspiracy to assassinate Cortez, and elect Francisco Verdujo, brother-in-law of Velazquez, in his place. While the conspirators were waiting for an opportunity to poniard Cortez, one of them, relenting, apprised him of his danger. Villafaña was arrested. He attempted to swallow a paper containing a list of the conspirators, but being seized by the throat, a part of it was forced from his mouth containing fourteen names of persons of importance. Villafaña confessed his guilt, but tortures could not make him inculpate the persons whose names were on the list, whom he declared were ignorant of the plot. He was hanged by order of Cortez.[1]

In the investigation of the disputes between Cortez and Velazquez, this execution of Villafaña was magnified into a cruel and wanton act of power; and in their eagerness to criminate Cortez the witnesses on the part of Alvarez declared that Villafaña had been instigated to what he had done by letters from Bishop Fonseca! (Que se movió a lo que hizo con cartas del obispo de Burgos.[2]) It is not probable that Fonseca had recommended assassination, but it shows the character of his agents, and what must have been the malignant nature of his instructions, when these men thought that such an act would accomplish his wishes. Fonseca died at Burgos on the 4th of November, 1554, and was interred at Coca.

No. XXXV.

OF THE SITUATION OF THE TERRESTRIAL PARADISE.

THE speculations of Columbus on the situation of the terrestrial paradise, extravagant as they may appear, were such as have occupied many grave and learned men. A slight notice of their opinions on this curious subject may be acceptable to the general reader, and may take from the apparent wildness of the ideas expressed by Columbus.

The abode of our first parents was anciently the subject of anxious inquiry; and indeed mankind have always been prone to picture some place of perfect felicity, where the imagination, disappointed in the coarse realities of life, might revel in an Elysium of its own creation. It is an idea not confined to our religion, but is found in the rude creeds of the most savage nations, and it prevailed generally among the ancients. The speculations concerning the situation of the garden of Eden resemble those of the Greeks concerning the garden of the Hesperides; that region of delight, which they forever placed at the most remote verge of the known world; which their poets embellished with all the charms of fiction; after which they were continually longing, and which they could never

---

[1] Herrera, Hist. Ind., decad. iii. lib. i. cap. 1.   [2] Ibid., decad. iii. lib. i. cap. 3.

find. At one time it was in the Grand Oasis of Arabia. The exhausted travellers, after traversing the parched and sultry desert, hailed this verdant spot with rapture; they refreshed themselves under its shady bowers, and beside its cooling streams, as the crew of a tempest-tossed vessel repose on the shores of some green island in the deep, and from its being thus isolated in the midst of an ocean of sand, they gave it the name of the Island of the Blessed. As geographical knowledge increased, the situation of the Hesperian gardens was continually removed to a greater distance. It was transferred to the borders of the great Syrtis, in the neighborhood of Mount Atlas. Here, after traversing the frightful deserts of Barca, the traveller found himself in a fair and fertile country, watered by rivulets and gushing fountains. The oranges and citrons transported hence to Greece, where they were as yet unknown, delighted the Athenians by their golden beauty and delicious flavor, and they thought that none but the garden of the Hesperides could produce such glorious fruits. In this way the happy region of the ancients was transported from place to place, still in the remote and obscure extremity of the world, until it was fabled to exist in the Canaries, thence called the Fortunate, or the Hesperian Islands. Here it remained, because discovery advanced no farther, and because these islands were so distant, and so little known, as to allow full latitude to the fictions of the poet.[1]

In like manner the situation of the terrestrial paradise, or garden of Eden, was long a subject of earnest inquiry and curious disputation, and occupied the laborious attention of the most learned theologians. Some placed it in Palestine or the Holy Land; others in Mesopotamia, in that rich and beautiful tract of country embraced by the wanderings of the Tigris and the Euphrates; others in Armenia, in a valley surrounded by precipitous and inaccessible mountains, and imagined that Enoch and Elijah were transported thither, out of the sight of mortals, to live in a state of terrestrial bliss until the second coming of our Saviour. There were others who gave it situations widely remote, such as in the Trapoban of the ancients, at present known as the island of Ceylon; or in the island of Sumatra; or in the Fortunate or Canary Islands; or in one of the islands of Sunda; or in some favored spot under the equinoctial line.

Great difficulty was encountered by these speculators to reconcile the allotted place with the description given in Genesis of the garden of Eden; particularly of the great fountain which watered it, and which afterward divided itself into four rivers, the Pison or Phison, the Gihon, the Euphrates, and the Hiddekel. Those who were in favor of the Holy Land supposed that the Jordan was the great river which afterward divided itself into the Phison, Gihon, Tigris, and Euphrates, but that the sands have choked up the ancient beds by which these streams were supplied; that originally the Phison traversed Arabia Deserta and Arabia Felix, whence it pursued its course to the Gulf of Persia; that the Gihon bathed Northern or Stony Arabia and fell into the Arabian Gulf or the Red Sea; that the Euphrates and the Tigris passed by Eden to Assyria and Chaldea, whence they discharged themselves into the Persian Gulf.

By most of the early commentators the River Gihon is supposed to be the Nile. The source of this river was unknown, but was evidently far distant from the spots whence the Tigris and the Euphrates arose. This difficulty, however, was ingeniously overcome, by giving it a subterranean course of some hundreds of leagues from the common fountain, until it issued forth to daylight in Abyssinia.[2] In like manner, subterranean

[1] Gosselin, Recherches sur la Géog des Anciens, tom. i.
[2] Feyjoo, Theatro Critico, lib. vii. § 2.

courses were given to the Tigris and the Euphrates, passing under the Red Sea, until they sprang forth in Armenia, as if just issuing from one common source. So also those who placed the terrestrial paradise in islands, supposed that the rivers which issued from it, and formed those heretofore named, either traversed the surface of the sea, as fresh water, by its greater lightness, may float above the salt, or that they flowed through deep veins and channels of the earth, as the fountain of Arethusa was said to sink into the ground in Greece, and rise in the island of Sicily, while the River Alpheus pursuing it, but with less perseverance, rose somewhat short of it in the sea.

Some contended that the deluge had destroyed the garden of Eden, and altered the whole face of the earth; so that the rivers had changed their beds, and had taken different directions from those mentioned in Genesis; others, however, among whom was St. Augustine, in his commentary upon the Book of Genesis, maintained that the terrestrial paradise still existed, with its original beauty and delights, but that it was inaccessible to mortals, being on the summit of a mountain of stupendous height, reaching into the third region of the air, and approaching the moon; being thus protected by its elevation from the ravages of the deluge.

By some this mountain was placed under the equinoctial line; or under that band of the heavens metaphorically called by the ancients "the table of the sun,"[1] comprising the space between the tropics of Cancer and Capricorn, beyond which the sun never passed in his annual course. Here would reign a uniformity of nights and days and seasons, and the elevation of the mountain would raise it above the heats and storms of the lower regions. Others transported the garden beyond the equinoctial line, and placed it in the southern hemisphere; supposing that the torrid zone might be the flaming sword appointed to defend its entrance against mortals. They had a fanciful train of argument to support their theory. They observed that the terrestrial paradise must be in the noblest and happiest part of the globe; that part must be under the noblest part of the heavens, as the merits of a place do not so much depend upon the virtues of the earth as upon the happy influences of the stars and the favorable and benign aspect of the heavens. Now, according to philosophers, the world was divided into two hemispheres. The southern they considered the head, and the northern the feet, or under part; the right hand the east, whence commenced the movement of the primum mobile, and the left the west, toward which it moved. This supposed, they observed that as it was manifest that the head of all things, natural and artificial, is always the best and noblest part, governing the other parts of the body, so the south being the head of the earth, ought to be superior and nobler than either east, or west, or north: and in accordance with this, they cited the opinion of various philosophers among the ancients, and more especially that of Ptolemy, that the stars of the southern hemisphere were larger, more resplendent, more perfect, and of course of greater virtue and efficacy than those of the northern: an error universally prevalent until disproved by modern discovery. Hence they concluded that in this southern hemisphere, in this head of the earth, under this purer and brighter sky, and these more potent and benignant stars, was placed the terrestrial paradise.

Various ideas were entertained as to the magnitude of this blissful region. As Adam and all his progeny were to have lived there, had he not sinned, and as there would have been no such thing as death to

---

[1] Herodot., lib. iii. Virg., Georg. i. Pomp. Mela, lib. iii. cap. 10.

thin the number of mankind, it was inferred that the terrestrial paradise must be of great extent to contain them. Some gave it a size equal to Europe or Africa others gave it the whole southern hemisphere. St. Augustine supposed that as mankind multiplied, numbers would be translated without death to heaven; the parents, perhaps, when their children had arrived at mature age; or portions of the human race at the end of certain periods, and when the population of the terrestrial paradise had attained a certain amount.[1]

Others supposed that mankind, remaining in a state of primitive innocence, would not have required so much space as at present. Having no need of rearing animals for subsistence, no land would have been required for pasturage; and the earth not being cursed with sterility, there would have been no need of extensive tracts of country to permit of fallow land and the alternation of crops required in husbandry. The spontaneous and never-failing fruits of the garden would have been abundant for the simple wants of man. Still, that the human race might not be crowded, but might have ample space for recreation and enjoyment, and the charms of variety and change, some allowed at least a hundred leagues of circumference to the garden.

St. Basilius in his eloquent discourse on paradise[2] expatiates with rapture on the joys of this sacred abode, elevated to the third region of the air, and under the happiest skies. There a pure and never-failing pleasure is furnished to every sense. The eye delights in the admirable clearness of the atmosphere, in the verdure and beauty of the trees, and the never-withering bloom of the flowers The ear is regaled with the singing of the birds, the smell with the aromatic odors of the land. In like manner the other senses have each their peculiar enjoyments. There the vicissitudes of the season are unknown, and the climate unites the fruitfulness of summer, the joyful abundance of autumn, and the sweet freshness and quietude of spring. There the earth is always green, the flowers are ever blooming, the waters limpid and delicate, not rushing in rude and turbid torrents, but swelling up in crystal fountains, and winding in peaceful and silver streams. There no harsh and boisterous winds are permitted to shake and disturb the air, and ravage the beauty of the groves, there prevails no melancholy, nor darksome weather, no drowning rain, nor pelting hail, no forked lightning, nor rending and resounding thunder; no wintry pinching cold, nor withering and panting summer heat; nor any thing else that can give pain or sorrow or annoyance, but all is bland and gentle and serene; a perpetual youth and joy reign throughout all nature, and nothing decays and dies.

The same idea is given by St. Ambrosius, in his book on Paradise,[3] an author likewise consulted and cited by Columbus He wrote in the fourth century, and his touching eloquence and graceful yet vigorous style, insured great popularity to his writings. Many of these opinions are cited by Glanville, usually called Bartholomeus Anglicus in his work De Proprietatibus Rerum: a work with which Columbus was evidently acquainted. It was a species of encyclopædia of the general knowledge current at the time, and was likely to recommend itself to a curious and inquiring voyager. This author cites an assertion as made by St. Basilius and St. Ambrosius, that the water of the fountain which proceeds from the garden of Eden falls into a great lake with such a tremendous noise

---

[1] St. August., lib. ix. cap 6. Sup. Genesis.
[2] St. Basilius was called the great. His works were read and admired by all the world, even by Pagans. They are written in an elevated and majestic style, with great splendor of idea, and vast erudition.
[3] St. Ambrosius, Opera. Edit Coignard Parisiis MDCXC.

that the inhabitants of the neighborhood are born deaf: and that from this lake proceed the four chief rivers mentioned in Genesis.[1]

This passage, however, is not to be found in the Hexameron of either Basilius or Ambrosius, from which it is quoted; neither is it in the oration on Paradise by the former, nor in the letter on the same subject written by Ambrosius to Ambrosius Savinus. It must be a misquotation by Glanville. Columbus, however, appears to have been struck with it, and Las Casas is of opinion that he derived thence his idea that the vast body of fresh water which filled the Gulf of La Ballena or Paria, flowed from the fountain of Paradise, though from a remote distance; and that in this gulf, which he supposed in the extreme part of Asia, originated the Nile, the Tigris, the Euphrates, and the Ganges, which might be conducted under the land and sea by subterranean channels, to the places where they spring forth on the earth and assume their proper names.

I forbear to enter into various other of the voluminous speculations which have been formed relative to the terrestrial paradise, and perhaps it may be thought that I have already said too much on so fanciful a subject; but to illustrate clearly the character of Columbus, it is necessary to elucidate those veins of thought passing through his mind while considering the singular phenomena of the unknown regions he was exploring, and which are often but slightly and vaguely developed in his journals and letters. These speculations, likewise, like those concerning fancied islands in the ocean, carry us back to the time, and make us feel the mystery and conjectural charm which reigned over the greatest part of the world, and have since been completely dispelled by modern discovery. Enough has been cited to show that in his observations concerning the terrestrial paradise, Columbus was not indulging in any fanciful and presumptuous chimeras, the offspring of a heated and disordered brain. However visionary his conjectures may seem, they were all grounded on written opinions held little less than oracular in his day; and they will be found on examination to be far exceeded by the speculations and theories of sages held illustrious for their wisdom and erudition in the school and cloister.

No. XXXVI.

WILL OF COLUMBUS.

IN the name of the Most Holy Trinity, who inspired me with the idea, and afterward made it perfectly clear to me, that I could navigate and go to the Indies from Spain, by traversing the ocean westwardly; which I communicated to the King, Don Ferdinand, and to the queen, Doña Isabella, our sovereigns; and they were pleased to furnish me the necessary equipment of men and ships, and to make me their admiral over the said ocean, in all parts lying to the west of an imaginary line, drawn from pole to pole, a hundred leagues west of the Cape de Verde and Azore Islands; also appointing me their viceroy and governor over all continents and islands that I might discover beyond the said line west-

---

[1] Paradisus autem in Oriente, in altissimo monte, de cujus cacumine cadentes aquæ, maximum faciunt lacum, que in suo casu tantum faciunt strepitum et fragorem, quod omnes incolæ, juxta prædictum lacum, nascuntur surdi, ex immoderato sonitu seu fragore sensum auditus in parvulis corrumpente. *Ut dicit Basilius in Hexameron, similiter et Ambros.* Ex illo, lacu, velut ex uno fonte, procedunt illa flumina quatuor, Phison, qui et Ganges, Gyon, qui et Nilus dicitur, et Tigris ac Euphrates. Bart. Angl. de Proprietatibus rerum, lib 15, cap. 112. Francofurti, 1540.

wardly; with the right of being succeeded in the said offices by my eldest son and his heirs forever; and a grant of the tenth part of all things found in the said jurisdiction; and of all rents and revenues arising from it; and the eighth of all the lands and every thing else, together with the salary corresponding to my rank of admiral, viceroy, and governor, and all other emoluments accruing thereto, as is more fully expressed in the title and agreement sanctioned by their highnesses.

And it pleased the Lord Almighty, that in the year one thousand four hundred and ninety-two, I should discover the continent of the Indies and many islands, among them Hispaniola, which the Indians call Ayte, and the Monicongos, Cipango. I then returned to Castile, to their highnesses, who approved of my undertaking a second enterprise for further discoveries and settlements; and the Lord gave me victory over the island of Hispaniola, which extends six hundred leagues, and I conquered it and made it tributary; and I discovered many islands inhabited by cannibals, and seven hundred to the west of Hispaniola, among which is Jamaica, which we call Santiago; and three hundred and thirty-three leagues of continent from south to west, besides a hundred and seven to the north, which I discovered in my first voyage, together with many islands, as may more clearly be seen by my letters, memorials, and maritime charts. And as we hope in God that before long a good and great revenue will be derived from the above islands and continent, of which, for the reasons aforesaid, belong to me the tenth and the eighth, with the salaries and emoluments specified above; and considering that we are mortal, and that it is proper for every one to settle his affairs, and to leave declared to his heirs and successors the property he possesses or may have a right to: Wherefore I have concluded to create an entailed estate (mayorazgo) out of the said eighth of the lands, places, and revenues, in the manner which I now proceed to state.

In the first place, I am to be succeeded by Don Diego, my son, who in case of death without children is to be succeeded by my other son Ferdinand; and should God dispose of him also without leaving children and without my having any other son, then my brother Don Bartholomew is to succeed; and after him his eldest son; and if God should dispose of him without heirs, he shall be succeeded by his sons from one to another forever; or, in the failure of a son, to be succeeded by Don Ferdinand, after the same manner, from son to son successively; or in their place by my brothers Bartholomew and Diego. And should it please the Lord that the estate, after having continued for some time in the line of any of the above successors, should stand in need of an immediate and lawful male heir, the succession shall then devolve to the nearest relation, being a man of legitimate birth, and bearing the name of Columbus derived from his father and his ancestors. This entailed estate shall in nowise be inherited by a woman, except in case that no male is to be found, either in this or any other quarter of the world, of my real lineage, whose name, as well as that of his ancestors, shall have always been Columbus. In such an event (which may God forefend), then the female of legitimate birth, most nearly related to the preceding possessor of the estate, shall succeed to it; and this is to be under the conditions herein stipulated at foot, which must be understood to extend as well to Don Diego, my son, as to the aforesaid and their heirs, every one of them, to be fulfilled by them; and failing to do so they are to be deprived of the succession, for not having complied with what shall herein be expressed; and the estate to pass to the person most nearly related to the one who held the right; and the person thus succeeding shall in like manner forfeit the estate, should he also fail to comply with said conditions; and another person, the nearest of my lineage, shall succeed, provided he abide by them, so that they may be observed forever in the form prescribed. This forfeiture is not to be incurred for trifling matters, originating in lawsuits, but in important cases, when the glory of God, or my own, or that of my family, may be concerned, which supposes a perfect fulfilment of all the things hereby ordained; all which I recommend to the courts of justice. And I supplicate his Holiness, who now is, and those that may succeed in the Holy Church, that if it should happen that this my will and testament has need of his holy order and command for its fulfilment, that such order be issued in virtue of obedience, and under penalty of excommunication, and that it shall not be in any wise disfigured. And I also pray the king and queen, our sovereigns, and their eldest-born, Prince Don Juan, our lord, and their successors, for the sake of the services I have done them, and because it is just, that it may please them not to permit this my will and constitution of my entailed estate to be any way altered, but to leave it in the form and manner which I have ordained, forever, for the greater glory of the Almighty, and that it may be the root and basis of my lineage, and a memento of the services I have rendered their highnesses; that, being born in Genoa, I came over to serve them in Castile, and discovered to the west of Terra Firma the Indies and islands before mentioned. I accordingly pray their highnesses to order that this my privilege and testament be held valid, and be executed summarily and without any opposition or demur, according to the letter. I also pray the grandees of the realm and the lords of the council, and all others having administration of justice, to be pleased not to suffer this my will and testament to be of no avail, but to cause it to be fulfilled as by me ordained; it being just that a noble, who has served the king and queen, and the kingdom, should be respected in the disposition of his estate by will, testament, institution of entail or inheritance, and that the same be not infringed either in whole or in part.

In the first place, my son Don Diego, and all my successors and descendants, as well as my brothers Bartholomew and Diego, shall bear my arms, such as I shall leave them after my days, without inserting any thing else in them; and they shall be their seal to seal withal. Don Diego my son, or any other who may inherit this estate, on coming into possession of the inheritance, shall sign with the signature which I now make use of, which is an X with an S over it, and an M with a Roman A over it, and over that an S, and then a Greek Y, with an S over it, with its lines and points as is my custom, as may be seen by my signatures, of which there are many, and it will be seen by the present one.

He shall only write "the Admiral," whatever other titles the king may have conferred on him. This is to be understood as respects his signature, but not the enumeration of his titles, which he can make at full length if agreeable, only the signature is to be "the Admiral."

The said Don Diego, or any other inheritor of this estate, shall possess the offices of admiral of the ocean, which is to the west of an imaginary line, which his highness ordered to be drawn, running from pole to pole a hundred leagues beyond the Azores, and as many more beyond the Cape de Verde Islands, over all which I was made by their order. their admiral of the sea, with all the pre-eminences held by Don Henrique in the admiralty of Castile, and they made me their governor and viceroy perpetually and forever, over all the islands and main-land discovered, or to be discovered, for myself and heirs, as is more fully shown by my treaty and privileges as above mentioned.

Item: The said Don Diego, or any other inheritor of this estate, shall distribute the revenue which it may please our Lord to grant him, in the following manner, under the above penalty.

First — Of the whole income of this estate, now and at all times, and of whatever may be had or collected from it, he shall give the fourth part annually to my brother Don Bartholomew Columbus, Adelantado of the Indies; and this is to continue till he shall have acquired an income of a million of maravadises, for his support, and for the services he has rendered and will continue to render to this entailed estate, which million he is to receive, as stated, every year, if the said fourth amount to so much, and that he have nothing else; but if he possess a part or the whole of that amount in rents, that henceforth he shall not enjoy the said million, nor any part of it, except that he shall have in the said fourth part unto the said quantity of a million, if it should amount to so much: and as much as he shall have of revenue beside this fourth part, whatever sum of maravadises of known rent from property or perpetual offices, the said quantity of rent or revenue from property or offices shall be discounted; and from the said million shall be reserved whatever marriage portion he may receive with any female he may espouse; so that whatever he may receive in marriage with his wife, no deduction shall be made on that account from said million, but only for whatever he may acquire, or may have, over and above his wife's dowry, and when it shall please God that he or his heirs and descendants shall derive from their property and offices a revenue of a million arising from rents, neither he nor his heirs shall enjoy any longer any thing from the said fourth part of the entailed estate, which shall remain with Don Diego, or whoever may inherit it.

Item: From the revenues of the said estate, or from any fourth part of it (should its amount be adequate to it), shall be paid every year to my son Ferdinand two millions, till such a time as his revenue shall amount to two millions, in the same form and manner as in the case of Bartholomew, who, as well as his heirs, are to have the million or the part that may be wanting.

Item: The said Don Diego or Don Bartholomew shall make, out of the said estate, for my brother Diego, such provision as may enable him to live decently, as he is my brother, to whom I assign no particular sum, as he has attached himself to the church, and that will be given him which is right: and this to be given him in a mass, and before any thing shall have been received by Ferdinand my son, or Bartholomew my brother, or their heirs, and also according to the amount of the income of the estate. And in case of discord, the case is to be referred to two of our relations, or other men of honor; and should they disagree among themselves, they will choose a third person as arbitrator, being virtuous and not distrusted by either party.

Item: All this revenue which I bequeath to Bartholomew, to Ferdinand, and to Diego, shall be delivered to and received by them as prescribed under the obligation of being faithful and loyal to Diego my son, or his heirs, they as well as their children; and should it appear that they, or any of them, had proceeded against him in any thing touching his honor, or the prosperity of the family, or of the estate, either in word or deed, whereby might come a scandal and debasement to my family, and a detriment to my estate; in that case, nothing further shall be given to them or him, from that time forward, inasmuch as they are always to be faithful to Diego and to his successors.

Item: As it was my intention, when I first instituted this entailed estate, to dispose, or that my son Diego should dispose for me, of the tenth part of the income in favor of necessitous persons, as a tithe, and in commemoration of the Almighty and Eternal God; and persisting still in this opinion, and hoping that his High Majesty will assist me, and those who may inherit it, in this or the New World, I have resolved that the said tithe shall be paid in the manner following:

First — It is to be understood that the fourth part of the revenue of the estate which I have ordained and directed to be given to Don Bartholomew, till he have an income of one million, includes the tenth of the whole revenue of the estate; and that as in proportion as the income of my brother Don Bartholomew shall increase, as it has to be discounted from the revenue of the fourth part of the entailed estate, that the said revenue shall be calculated, to know how much the tenth part amounts to; and the part which exceeds what is necessary to make up the million for Don Bartholomew shall be received by such of my family as may most stand in need of it, discounting it from said tenth, if their income do not amount to fifty thousand maravadises; and should any of these come to have an income to this amount, such a part shall be awarded them as two persons, chosen for the purpose, may determine along with Don Diego, or his heirs. Thus, it is to be understood that the million which I leave to Don Bartholomew comprehends the tenth of the whole revenue of the estate; which revenue is to be distributed among my nearest and most needy relations in the manner I have directed; and when Don Bartholomew have an income of one million, and that nothing more shall be due to him on account of said fourth part, then, Don Diego my son, or the person who may be in possession of the estate, along with the two other persons which I shall herein point out, shall inspect the accounts, and so direct that the tenth of the revenue shall still continue to be paid to the most necessitous members of my family that may be found in this or any other quarter of the world, who shall be diligently sought out; and they are to be paid out of the fourth part from which Don Bartholomew is to derive his million; which sums are to be taken into account, and deducted from the said tenth, which, should it amount to more, the overplus, as it arises from the fourth part, shall be given to the most necessitous persons as aforesaid; and should it not be sufficient that Don Bartholomew shall have it until his own estate goes on increasing, leaving the said million in part or in the whole.

Item: The said Don Diego my son, or whoever may be the inheritor, shall appoint two persons of conscience and authority, and most nearly related to the family, who are to examine the revenue and its amount carefully, and to cause the said tenth to be paid out of the fourth from which Don Bartholomew is to receive his million, to the most necessitated members of my family that may be found here or elsewhere, whom they shall look for diligently upon their consciences; and as it might happen that said Don Diego, or others after him, for reasons which may concern their own welfare, or the credit and support of the estate, may be unwilling to make known the full amount of the income; nevertheless I charge him on his conscience to pay the sum aforesaid; and I charge them, on their souls and consciences, not to denounce or make it known, except with the consent of Don Diego, or the person that may succeed him; but let the above tithe be paid in the manner I have directed.

Item: In order to avoid all disputes in the choice of the two nearest relations who are to act with Don Diego or his heirs, I hereby elect Don Bartholomew my brother for one, and Don Fernando my son for the other; and when these two shall enter upon the business, they shall choose two other persons among the most trusty, and most nearly related, and these again shall elect two others when it shall be question of commencing the examination; and thus it shall be managed with diligence from one to the other, as well in this as in the other of government, for the service and glory of God, and the benefit of the said entailed estate.

Item: I also enjoin Diego, or any one that may inherit the estate, to have and maintain in the city of Genoa, one person of our lineage to reside there with his wife, and appoint him a sufficient revenue to enable him to live decently, as a person closely connected with the family, of which he is to be the root and basis in that city; from which great good may accrue to him, inasmuch as I was born there, and came from thence.

Item: The said Don Diego, or whoever shall inherit the estate, must remit in bills, or in any other way, all such sums as he may be able to save out of the revenue of the estate, and direct purchases to be made in his name, or that of his heirs, in a stock in the Bank of St. George, which gives an interest of six per cent and in secure money; and this shall be devoted to the purpose I am about to explain.

Item: As it becomes every man of property to serve God, either personally or by means of his wealth, and as all moneys deposited with St. George are quite safe, and Genoa is a noble city, and powerful by sea, and as at the time that I undertook to set out upon the discovery of the Indies, it was with the intention of supplicating the king and queen, our lords, that whatever moneys should be derived from the said Indies, should be invested in the conquest of Jerusalem: and as I did so supplicate them; if they do this, it will be well; if not, at all events, the said Diego, or such person as may succeed him in this trust, to collect together all the money he can, and accompany the king our lord, should he go to the conquest of Jerusalem, or else go there himself with all the force he can command; and in pursuing this intention, it will please the Lord to assist toward the accomplishment of the plan; and should he not be able to effect the conquest of the whole, no doubt he will achieve it in part. Let him therefore collect and make a fund of all his wealth in St. George of Genoa, and let it multiply there till such time as it may appear to him that something of consequence may be effected as respects the project on Jerusalem; for I believe that when their highnesses shall see that this is contemplated, they will wish to realize it themselves, or will afford him, as their servant and vassal, the means of doing it for them.

Item: I charge my son Diego and my descendants, especially whoever may inherit this estate, which consists, as aforesaid, of the tenth of whatsoever may be had or found in the Indies, and the eighth part of the lands and rents, all which, together with my rights and emoluments as admiral, viceroy, and governor, amount to more than twenty-five per cent; I say that I require of him to employ all this revenue, as well as his person and all the means in his power, in well and faithfully serving and supporting their highnesses, or their successors, even to the loss of life and property; since it was their highnesses, next to God, who first gave me the means of getting and achieving this property, although, it is true, I came over to these realms to invite them to the enterprise, and that a long time elapsed before any provision was made for carrying it into execution; which, however, is not surprising, as this was an undertaking of which all the world was ignorant, and no one had any faith in it; wherefore I am by so much the more indebted to them, as well as because they have since also much favored and promoted me.

Item: I also require of Diego, or whomsoever may be in possession of the estate, that in the case of any schism taking place in the Church of God, or that any person of whatever class or condition should attempt to despoil it of its property and honors, they hasten to offer at the feet of his holiness, that is, if they are not heretics (which God forbid!) their persons, power, and wealth, for the purpose of suppressing such schism, and preventing any spoliation of the honor and property of the church.

Item: I command the said Diego, or whoever may possess the said estate, to labor and strive for the honor, welfare. and aggrandizement of the city of Genoa. and to make use of all his power and means in defending and enhancing the good and credit of that republic, in all things not contrary to the service of the church of God. or the high dignity of our king and queen, our lords, and their successors.

Item: The said Diego, or whoever may possess or succeed to the estate. out of the fourth part of the whole revenue, from which, as aforesaid. is to be taken the tenth, when Don Bartholomew or his heirs shall have saved the two millions, or part of them, and when the time shall come of making a distribution among our relations, shall apply and invest the said tenth in providing marriages for such daughters of our lineage as may require it, and in doing all the good in their power.

Item: When a suitable time shall arrive, he shall order a church to be built in the island of Hispaniola, and in the most convenient spot, to be called Santa Maria de la Concepcion; to which is to be annexed an hospital, upon the best possible plan, like those of Italy and Castile, and a chapel erected to say mass in for the good of my soul, and those of my ancestors and successors with great devotion, since no doubt it will please the Lord to give us a sufficient revenue for this and the aforementioned purposes.

Item: I also order Diego my son, or whomsoever may inherit after him, to spare no pains in having and maintaining in the island of Hispaniola, four good professors of theology, to the end and aim of their studying and laboring to convert to our holy faith the inhabitants of the Indies; and in proportion as, by God's will, the revenue of the estate shall increase, in the same degree shall the number of teachers and devout increase, who are to strive to make Christians of the natives; in attaining which no expense should be thought too great. And in commemoration of all that I hereby ordain, and of the foregoing, a monument of marble shall be erected in the said church of la Concepcion, in the most conspicuous place, to serve as a record of what I here enjoin on the said Diego, as well as to other persons who may look upon it; which marble shall contain an inscription to the same effect.

Item: I also require of Diego my son, and whomsoever may succeed him in the estate, that every time, and as often as he confesses, he first show this obligation, or a copy of it, to the confessor, praying him to read it through, that he may be enabled to inquire respecting its fulfilment; from which will redound great good and happiness to his soul.

S.

S A S.

X. M. Y.

EL ALMIRANTE.

No. XXXVII.

SIGNATURE OF COLUMBUS.

As every thing respecting Columbus is full of interest, his signature has been a matter of some discussion. It partook of the pedantic and bigoted character of the age, and perhaps of the peculiar character of the man, who considering himself mysteriously elected and set apart from among men for certain great purposes, adopted a correspondent formality and solemnity in all his concerns. His signature was as follows:

S.

S. A. S.

X M Y.

XPO FERENS.

The first half of the signature, XPO (for CHRISTO). is in Greek letters; the second, FERENS. is in Latin. Such was the usage of those days: and even at present both Greek and Roman letters are used in signatures and inscriptions in Spain.

The ciphers or initials above the signature are supposed to represent a pious ejaculation. To read them one must begin with the lower letters, and connect them with those above. Signor Gio. Batista Spotorno conjectures them to mean either Xristus (Christus) Sancta Maria Yosephus, or, Salve me, Xristus, Maria, Yosephus.

The *North American Review*, for April, 1827, suggests the substitution of Jesus for Josephus, but the suggestion of Spotorno is most probably correct, as a common Spanish ejaculation is "Jesus Maria y José."

It was an ancient usage in Spain, and it has not entirely gone by, to accompany the signature with some words of religious purport. One object of this practice was to show the writer to be a Christian. This was of some importance in a country in which Jews and Mohammedans were proscribed and persecuted.

Don Fernando. son to Columbus, says that his father. when he took his pen in hand, usually commenced by writing "Jesus cum Maria sit nobis in via;" and the book which the admiral prepared and sent to the sovereigns, containing the prophecies which he considered as referring to his discoveries, and to the rescue of the holy sepulchre, begins with the same words. This practice is akin to that of placing the initials of pious words above his signature, and gives great probability to the mode in which they have been deciphered.

INDEX.

Printed in the United Kingdom
by Lightning Source UK Ltd.
124389UK00001B/294/A